ACCLAIM FOR H. L. M E N C K E N ' S

MY LIFE AS
AUTHOR AND EDITOR

"Incomparable . . . a literary event of some moment. . . . Here is something new from the cynic laureate of the American century. . . . What reader could ask for more?" —*Wall Street Journal*

"It crackles with his inimitable, often furious, always witty and laser-precise prose. . . . Mencken, typically American, narrow-minded but big-visioned and energetic, is a craggy . . . mountain on the landscape of American letters." —*Mirabella*

"[A] vivid memoir. . . . [Mencken] was a dissenter, bellicose, unafraid, self-confident, irreverent, independent, and irascible. . . . His recitals of various rowdy episodes enliven the memoir. He seldom used a dull word where . . . a sardonic jibe will do. . . . Few journalists . . . are now as outspoken and fearless as Mencken was, nor do they command the language as he did, nor yet have his disdain for substantial reputations." —*Washington Monthly*

"All the susceptibilities of booboisie and intelligentsia are once more on display here. A reader watches, nostalgically, as Mencken shoots them down . . . like carnival ducks. . . . A matchless guide to American literary life in the years just before and after World War I." —*New Criterion*

"Mencken wrote the liveliest prose of almost any American who ever lived." —*Chicago Tribune*

"Here is quintessential Mencken, a harshly realistic opinion, expressed in terms deliberately offensive to conventional literary views of the time. A merciless assault on mushy optimism." —*San Francisco Chronicle*

MY LIFE AS
AUTHOR AND EDITOR

MY LIFE AS AUTHOR AND EDITOR

H. L. MENCKEN

*Edited and
with an Introduction by
Jonathan Yardley*

VINTAGE BOOKS
A DIVISION OF RANDOM HOUSE, INC.
NEW YORK

FIRST VINTAGE BOOKS EDITION, JANUARY 1995

Library of Congress has cataloged the Knopf edition as follows:

Mencken, H. L. (Henry Louis), 1880–1956.
My life as author and editor / by H. L. Mencken:
edited and with an introduction by Jonathan Yardley.
p.   cm.
Includes index.
ISBN 0-679-41315-4
1. Mencken, H. L. (Henry Louis), 1880–1956—Biography.
2. Authors, American—20th century—Biography.
3. Editors—United States—Biography.
I. Yardley, Jonathan.   II. Title.
PS3525.E43Z468   1992
818'.5209—dc20
[B]   92-4496
CIP
Vintage ISBN: 0-679-74102-X

BOOK DESIGN BY PETER A. ANDERSEN

Manufactured in the United States of America
10   9   8   7   6   5   4   3   2   1

EDITOR'S INTRODUCTION

IN FEBRUARY OF 1941 Henry Louis Mencken severed all but the slenderest of ties with the *Sunpapers* of Baltimore, which he had joined in 1906 and to which he had brought a considerable measure of national and international renown. It was a decision eerily reminiscent of one made a quarter century earlier, when in circumstances almost exactly the same he had taken almost exactly the same step.

In the winter of 1941 as in the fall of 1915, the United States was on the verge of joining those nations allied in world war against an imperial Germany. It was a venture Mencken opposed with as much vehemence as he had ever mustered against any of the innumerable nuisances that stirred his bile; in this opposition—in 1941 as in 1915— he was in direct disagreement with the editorial policies of the *Sunpapers*. Although the editors continued to publish his antiinterventionist, pro-German commentaries, the newspaper's hierarchy regarded them—and thus him—as deeply embarrassing; Mencken in turn was no less confounded by what he considered the imbecilic policies of the *Sunpapers*, which he saw as both blindly Anglophiliac and inexcusably subservient to his personal bête noire, Franklin Delano Roosevelt.

In 1915 the *Sunpapers* had squashed Mencken; his column in the *Evening Sun*, "The Free Lance," was terminated and he was reduced to behind-the-scenes labors. In 1941 matters proceeded at a more gentlemanly level, no doubt in acknowledgment of the immense prestige Mencken had accumulated in the interim. Indeed, this time it was Mencken himself who took the initiative and volunteered to cease writing for the *Sunpapers*, an offer that was accepted with transparent relief. But, whether by his own choice or that of his editors, the effect was the same: Mencken no longer had a public forum in Baltimore, the center of his universe.

Yet however strong his feelings about the war may have been,

Mencken accepted his second exile with considerably more aplomb than he had his first. In part, no doubt, this is explained by the differences between the two Germanys; the Kaiser may have been defensible but Hitler was not, and even Mencken found it difficult to make a case on his behalf. In larger part, though, the explanation lies in Mencken's age. He was sixty years old, not thirty-five; his beloved wife, Sara, had died six years earlier; and, although the major work of his life was done, he had found a new and comforting occupation.

Mencken had become a memoirist. Bits and pieces of reminiscence that he had originally published in Harold Ross's *New Yorker* had been put into a book called *Happy Days* in 1940 and had been a great success; readers who remembered Mencken only vaguely as a disagreeable controversialist, or had forgotten him altogether, were surprised and delighted by these sunny, uproarious tales of life in old Baltimore. They wanted more, and so too did Alfred A. Knopf, Mencken's publisher. Thus, even as he left the *Sunpapers*, Mencken was hard at work on *Newspaper Days*, to be published later that year, and the concluding volume of the *Days* trilogy, *Heathen Days*, would soon be under way.

The satisfactions these books brought to Mencken evidently were considerable, but in reaching back into his immense storehouse of memory he had more in mind than mere nostalgia. Constitutionally incapable of throwing anything away, he had accumulated over four decades at the center of American cultural life "a great deal . . . that belonged, not only to my personal *curriculum vitae*, but also to the literary history of the United States in my time." He meant to make an orderly record of it, "for the use of resurrection men in the years to come," but also, I think, to keep alive in those distant years the memory of H. L. Mencken himself.

Work on this project began on November 28, 1942, halted in July of 1943 "to make way for *The American Language, Supplement I*," resumed in July of 1945, "halted again at the end of 1945 to make way for *Supplement II*," resumed sometime in 1948 but halted for good in November of that year as a consequence of the severe stroke that rendered Mencken unable to write for the remaining seven years of his life. The manuscript's title was *My Life As Author and Editor 1896——*; at some point after Mencken's stroke it was packed into heavy wooden boxes, sealed with steel bands, and deposited at the

Enoch Pratt Free Library in Baltimore "on the explicit and irrevocable understanding that it is not to be open to anyone, under any circumstances whatever, until either January 1, 1980, or thirty-five years after the death of the author, whichever may be the later."

The thirty-five-year provision took effect upon Mencken's death in 1956; the boxes were opened at the Pratt on January 29, 1991. The volume now before you is a distillation of what was found therein. Unlike the material in other boxes opened at the same time, which contained a memoir called *Thirty-Five Years of Newspaper Work, 1906–41*, the manuscript of *My Life As Editor and Author* proved to be unfinished; in his determination to enter every bit of detail into the record Mencken too often had bogged down in minutiae and had managed to reach only 1923 in a chronicle that, if complete, would have covered a quarter century more.

At first glance this seems a great disappointment. Although this professional memoir does cover much of importance—Mencken's apprenticeship, his coeditorship with George Jean Nathan of *The Smart Set*, his early books, his alliance with Knopf, his immensely complicated relationship with Theodore Dreiser—it leaves much more untouched: his departure, with Nathan, from *The Smart Set* at the end of 1923; his inauguration the next year with Nathan and Knopf of the incalculably influential *American Mercury*; his breaks with Nathan and Dreiser; his resignation from *The American Mercury* in 1933; and, most grievously, that entire period beginning in the mid-1920s and ending a decade later when, as editor, newspaperman, and author, he towered over the American scene as has no literary or journalistic figure before or since.

That is the memoir he didn't write, and it is a pity we do not have it. But as it turns out, the memoir he did write is quite enough; at its end the reader feels far more satisfied than disappointed. The explanation is that in the first third of his career Mencken met virtually all the people who were important to it; in writing his memoir he set down his impressions of these people as each appeared on the scene, and thus we have almost all of them substantially whole. Dreiser, Nathan, Knopf, Sinclair Lewis, Anita Loos, Scott Fitzgerald: the portrait of each is amply fleshed. Among those with whom Mencken was intimate, only Joseph Hergesheimer is significantly absent from this narrative; and, with all due regard to Hergesheimer, the decline in his reputation renders this an entirely bearable loss.

Others, more neglected now even than Hergesheimer, are rescued by Mencken from the distant past. James Huneker, James Branch Cabell, Hendrik Willem Van Loon, Zoë Akins, Willard H. Wright (a.k.a. S. S. Van Dine), Paul de Kruif, Fielding H. Garrison: all are brought back to life in Mencken's blunt prose. As for Robert Rives La Monte, Harry Kemp, Lilith Benda, Thyra Samter Winslow, Eltinge F. Warner, John Adams Thayer, Ruth Suckow, Abraham Cahan, Julia Peterkin, Isaac Goldberg: only within the bosoms of their families do they live on, but Mencken makes us glad to have met them.

His gifts as portraitist, we learn, were as great as his gifts for ridicule and invective. He was fiercely candid—his accounts of Dreiser, Lewis, and Fitzgerald are, when the evidence calls for it, entirely ruthless—yet he could be unexpectedly kind. He suffered the stupendous shortcomings of all three of these men not merely because his regard for their work was so high but because in each instance he saw through to the human being within and liked much of what he saw. His capacity for compassion was considerable, as suggested by his sympathy for young Scotty Fitzgerald: "I often think of this poor girl's unhappy youth with an insane mother and a dipsomaniac father, and of her baleful heritage."

Here is another surprise: he loved women. To be sure, it has long been understood that he was an occasional visitor to Baltimore's cathouses and that he conducted various amours with women of more respectable standing, but the assumption has been that at heart he was a man's man, or, in today's enlightened coinage, a male chauvinist pig. Even his Septembral marriage to Sara Haardt has been interpreted by some as an aberrant act—a kindness to a young admirer who, he knew at the hour of their nuptials, was fatally tubercular—though passages in *The Diary of H. L. Mencken* (1989) have forced a reconsideration of that ill-informed and condescending judgment.

But *My Life As Editor and Author* changes the picture entirely. Certainly it is true that in this as in other matters Mencken was a man of his time and class, with his own full measure of the prejudices to which both were inclined. Yes, he did write (tongue surely in cheek) of Sarah Dreiser that "she had failed dismally in the prime duty of every wife, which is to be charming to her lord," but over and over he demonstrated a willingness to accept women as intellectual equals that was, for someone so inherently conservative as he, a considerable departure from the norm. He admired Willa Cather, Anita Loos, and Zoë Akins; he had the highest esteem for the writing of Lilith Benda and Thyra Samter Winslow and liked the writers as well; he took self-evident delight in G. Vere Tyler, "a very amiable fat woman, skillful at doing saucy novelettes."

He liked a good time, and was drawn to women who shared that inclination. For evidence of this, see his riotous account of a boozy night with Zoë Akins, Ethel Barrymore, and one Jobyna Howland, these last two being "the champion lady boozers of Broadway, and Zoë herself was no dilettante at the bottle." It is Jobyna Howland, by the way, who inspired one of this volume's most delicious asides: "The love agonies of a woman six feet in height are always extra poignant." See as well his account of a visit, with Nathan, to the apartment of a semipro poetess named Jean Allen. The guests came armed with gin, vermouth, and absinthe, the result of which being that "our hostess passed out, both Nathan and I fell down the stairway of her elegant duplex apartment, and Nathan lost his watch in a snowdrift outside the house." As these brief quotations suggest, women inspired Mencken to especially lively, carefree, and vivid prose.

Here we have Mencken the bon vivant, a figure only dimly glimpsed in most previous writing by or about him. His playful evenings in Baltimore with the Saturday Night Club and the Sunday Dinner Club have been amply documented, but this is another Mencken altogether, one who took no offense on those occasions when "the proceedings sometimes became very gay." Although he was contemptuous of those who could not hold their liquor, he was capable of taking it to excess at times and was not too proud to admit its effects upon his slumbers, his memory, and his digestion. Anyone who thinks that his life was spent alone at the typewriter will quickly be disabused of that by the numerous tales herein of misspent hours, most of them amusingly told and all of them agreeably humanizing.

"I was born, " he tells us, "with an extraordinary amount of reserve energy." That, if anything, is understatement. The self-portrait he paints is of a man forever on the go, whether in the social ramble or in a professional life so busy and diverse as to stagger the imagination. He was a prominent newspaperman who not merely wrote prodigiously but also played an active role in the editorial development, and at times the management, of the *Sunpapers;* his correspondence came in by the avalanche, and he answered each letter the day it was received; he read most manuscripts submitted to *The Smart Set,* journeyed regularly to New York for consultations with Nathan and others, and helped decide even the most minor questions of layout and design; he wrote books—a total of more than two dozen during his lifetime—some of them collections of journalism but others, most notably *The American Language,* the result of laborious, painstaking toil; and he functioned—by correspondence, by telephone, in person— as counselor, patron, "fugleman," and hand-holder to a generation of American writers. He was also, it should be added, a full-time hypochondriac.

He tells us about all of this not boastfully but in the matter-of-fact style that seems to have been his actual manner. He didn't need to brag because he was so implacably, unalterably convinced of the soundness of his convictions and actions that, he assumed, no sane person need be persuaded to agree. Such supreme self-confidence is by no means an entirely attractive quality, but it was essential Mencken and he cannot be viewed apart from it.

He was also, during the time covered by this memoir, "a sassy fellow" and "an ambitious young man." This is a Mencken whom we do not know well, so it is both a pleasure and an education to see so much of him in this volume. The Mencken of legend is a familiar figure: the mature Sage of Baltimore, portly and self-assured, gazing dourly out at the world through owlish spectacles, a rancid "Uncle Willie" cigar clamped in his teeth. But this Mencken is thicker in the hair and (sometimes) thinner in the paunch, his eyes firmly fixed on the main chance. Eagerly and coolly, he watches the lights around his name grow ever brighter: newspapers at home and abroad report his opinions, his words are quoted in publishers' advertisements, a professor of journalism asks to include one of his articles in a text-book—and at last, on June 11, 1921, in a crowning glory, "the New York *Evening Mail* listed Nathan and me among persons 'who need no press agents,' along with Margot Asquith, Lloyd George, William J. Bryan, Andrew Volstead and Babe Ruth"!

He had a flair for self-promotion and wasn't in the least ashamed to employ it. His "plan of goading enemies into spreading my name was one that I often practiced," it being "to my interest to be de-nounced more than to be praised, and I sometimes went to great efforts, not always ingenuous, to bring that about." If the occasion called for it, he could be positively devious, as in the stratagem he conjured up in order to weasel out of the hands of a publisher with whom he was unhappy, the John Lane Company, and into those of Alfred A. Knopf—a mean piece of deceit upon which he reports with unmistakable delight.

Nor was he any literary or journalistic purist. When *The Smart Set* needed an infusion of cash, as more often than not it did, he leaped gleefully at the chance to make a disreputable dollar. Over the years he and Nathan invented, manufactured, and merchandised three pulp magazines—*Parisienne Monthly Magazine, Saucy Stories,* and *Black Mask*—as cash cows, and at one point they were eager to do another called *Pretty Girls,* the "whole contents" of which "were to consist of full-page photographs of sightly wenches, reproduced in rotogravure, which had been only lately perfected in Germany." The publisher of *The Smart Set,* Eltinge Warner, "reported that the cost would be prohibitive, " but Mencken says, with a straight face, that "I believed, and still believe, that he was wrong."

The plain and invigorating fact is that in these years while he was yet a prodigy, his days as eminence still well before him, Mencken was having himself one hell of a ball. Not even a setback so severe as his wartime separation from the *Evening Sun* held him back for long; he merely used the period to bolster *The Smart Set,* work on his books, and otherwise increase the public's awareness of himself and his works. After a long morning's labors of the mind he thought nothing of retreating to the small backyard of his house on Hollins Street to work in the garden or build an elegant brick fence; after bathing, he put in a full evening's work at the typewriter and then downed a few gallons of pilsner to wash away such cares as the day had brought.

He was a force of nature, brushing aside all objects animal and mineral in his headlong rush to the éclat that surely awaited him. He seized each day, shook it to within an inch of its life, then gaily went on to the next. In the vast galley of portraits he constructs, none is more vivid or memorable than that of the author himself; indeed, nowhere else in his writing, *The Diary* and the *Days* books included, do we see Mencken more sharply than we do in these pages, usually if not always to his advantage.

Mencken's impregnable self-confidence is, to my taste, the least appealing of his traits, suggesting as it does an incapacity for self-doubt or real self-scrutiny. But in the wake of *The Diary*, it surely need not be said that in the minds of many others the largest of Mencken's warts is what they perceive as his anti-Semitism. Those inclined to this view will find more support for it here, for I have made certain not to excise any material that might be unfavorable to Mencken in that regard: Stelle Golde, editorial secretary at *The Smart Set*, was "a grotesque Brooklyn Jewess"; Otto H. Kahn, the financier, was "an extremely offensive Jew"; Ben Hecht, "Jew-like . . . had a touch of the world-savior in him"; Edgar Selwyn had "but little suggestion of the Jewish in his appearance and manner, and I got on with him very well"; George Nathan had "a typically Jewish inferiority complex"; members of a firm of "Jewish music-publishers" were "prehensile kikes." Etcetera. There is more, none of it is pretty, and to the best of my knowledge every word of it is included in this volume; no whitewash is intended or desired.

Yet there is evidence to the contrary as well. The first and in some ways most important is the aforementioned matter of time and class. Racial and ethnic slurs were commonplace among even educated Americans of the day, as was the habit of identifying people by their racial or ethnic origins. Wops, micks, bohunks, kikes, spades, krauts, spics, frogs, limeys: the vocabulary of offhand denigration was rich and employed liberally. Mencken, whose sense of his own Teutonic blood grew ever stronger over the years, not merely was predisposed to such utterances but was doubly so because he so clearly believed in the superior gifts and character of his own people.

Beyond that, there is the old some-of-his-best-friends argument, which in Mencken's case carries considerable force. Apart from Baltimore, where his social circle tended to be *Sunpapers*-WASPish or drinking-club-Teutonic, many of the people to whom Mencken was closest were Jewish. Alfred Knopf, George Nathan, Philip Goodman: he had intense affection and admiration for these three men, all Jews, and they felt the same way about him. Readers looking for evidence of this will find much in these pages, especially in regard to Mencken's friendship with Goodman. In later years Knopf, should the issue of Menckenian anti-Semitism be raised in his presence, bristled in angry denial. Ruth Goodman Goetz, Goodman's daughter, described Mencken in a speech presented at the Enoch Pratt Library in 1988 as "one of the most free and unbigoted of men."

Mrs. Goetz also said, in that same speech, that Mencken's failure to distrust or denounce Hitler was damning—who could say otherwise?—and that a letter in which he expressed his ambivalent feelings about Jews is "the letter of an anti-semite, and we cannot dodge it or ignore it." Yet she then noted his "extraordinary legacy" of what she called "truthifying American literature" and closed by saying: "Is such a man a bigot? Yes, I think he is—and I treasure his memory."

My own view, similar if slightly different, is that if by the standards of our day Mencken was anti-Semitic, by those of his own he was not. Inasmuch as he lived in his time and not in ours, it is by this we should judge and, I believe, acquit him. This conclusion has not been reached lightly, easily, or frivolously, and legitimate objections to it certainly do exist. But in my judgment it is both appropriate and fair.

As to the other questions raised by this narrative and self-portrait, most of them have been dealt with before. Although *My Life As Author and Editor* is, as Mencken intended it to be, a contribution to American literary and journalistic history, little of that contribution lies in its disclosures about what Mencken did and why he did it. His history of the *Smart Set* years adds nothing of substance to what we already know from earlier histories and biographies; on the basis of this, it seems reasonable to doubt that much would have been added to our knowledge of the *American Mercury* period had Mencken's health permitted him to finish the story. The long account of his dealings with Dreiser, though interesting on its face, goes over ground already thoroughly explored by Dreiser's biographers, and the correspondence between the two men has been published in two massive volumes.

Rather than new detail or unexpected insights, what we are given in *My Life As Author and Editor* is the period and its people in Mencken's own words, heard now for the first time. Thus, for example, when Mencken describes Dreiser as "essentially a German peasant, oafish, dour and distrustful of all mankind"; when he says that Dreiser had "a vast confidence in ghosts, banshees and hobgoblins, and there were whole areas in which his thinking was hard to distinguish from hallucination"; when he then adds that "I had a considerable fondness for him, mainly, I suppose, because of my awareness of his intense unhappiness"—when he says all of this we realize that we are hearing a voice from the grave, one no biographer could hope to approximate.

This sense of immediacy is, to my taste, above all else what gives *My Life As Author and Editor* its place in the literature of its time. In the best sense, it is a period piece: it takes the reader into its world and brings that world alive. If its prose does not rank with Mencken's most original or arresting, bear in mind the quite astonishing fact that it was not written on Mencken's trusty old Corona typewriter but dictated to his faithful secretary, Mrs. Rosalind Lohrfinck. Thus, it is, in all its great length, not merely an invaluable memoir, but a tour de force.

THE MANUSCRIPT OF *My Life As Author and Editor* consists of 1,025 pages of double-spaced typescript, interspersed with innumerable single-spaced footnotes and extracts; 34 appendices running to a total of 717 pages, also both double- and single-spaced; and 56 pages of a single-spaced "progressive index." By conservative estimate, the total word count is somewhere between 300,000 and 400,000 words—all this to cover barely two-fifths of Mencken's professional life.

Given that Mencken's prose was impeccable and his sense of structure was at worst competent, the editorial challenge the manuscript presents is therefore primarily one of sheer length. In trimming the manuscript by approximately 60 percent I was guided by these considerations: an impatience with Mencken's penchant for trivial and unilluminating detail; a conviction that much of his dutiful record-keeping merely got in the way of the story he had to tell; a belief that what is not merely most interesting and entertaining about this memoir, but also most important, is its portraiture.

With those assumptions in mind, I made certain basic decisions:

(1) Mencken's account of his apprenticeship—which in the original runs to a breathtaking 107 pages and contains interminable excerpts from his juvenilia—I reduced to its barest minimum; this will be found in Chapter I, with blank spaces separating discrete portions of the narrative.

(2) In satisfying his appetite for the encyclopedic, Mencken filled paragraph upon paragraph with the names of those who had contributed to *The Smart Set*'s various departments in each year of his coeditorship; virtually all such lists have been eliminated, save a handful that have been retained in order to convey some flavor of the original.

(3) Mencken's account of his financial affairs cites not merely chapter and verse but line and syllable as well. Though other people's

money is always of compelling interest, it seemed to me that Mencken carried the subject beyond the pale, and I trimmed accordingly; even so, there remains quite enough about his exchequer to satisfy all save the Internal Revenue Service. Incidentally, multiplying Mencken's figures by ten will give the reader of the 1990s a rough notion of the current value of the dollars and cents that flowed through his hands.

(4) All of Mencken's footnotes have been eliminated. A very few have been incorporated into the text in order to identify figures who might otherwise remain mysterious. Those footnotes that do appear are my own, and I have kept them to the absolute minimum. Unlike the *Diary*, which demanded extensive annotation, the memoirs are almost entirely self-explanatory; if Mencken does not identify a character at first mention he does so immediately thereafter, and to intrude with footnoted minibiographies struck me as wholly unnecessary and gratuitous.

(5) Mencken chose to tell his story chronologically rather than thematically, a decision that I in turn chose to respect. This means that his ongoing affairs, most particularly his dealings with Dreiser, come and go as chronology dictates. However tempting it may have been to move masses of text hither and yon, giving the narrative a structural clarity that Mencken himself eschewed, in this case the intentions of the author were clear and honoring them seemed a matter of good faith.

(6) Mencken quoted extensively from his book reviews and reviews others wrote of his own work. I have been merciless in expunging all but the most pertinent of these from the text. Mencken's literary opinions are well known and widely available through books still in print, as are others' opinions of him and his work. *My Life As Author and Editor* is a work of recollection rather than literary criticism, and I have edited it as such, keeping firmly in mind that nothing on earth is staler than a stale book review.

(7) Of the thirty-four appendices with which Mencken burdened his text, I have included only three in their proper position at the end; these are documents relating to editorial policy at *The Smart Set* and to the whimsical office management of its editors. All the rest have been eliminated except five, which have been incorporated into the text where it seemed most suitable. These are reminiscences of James Huneker, Ezra Pound, Frank Harris, Sinclair Lewis, and James Branch Cabell.

Within the limits set by these decisions I have let Mencken be

Mencken; to do otherwise would be an act of presumption beyond my imagination. Though I have not used ellipses to indicate cuts within the text, I have retained Mencken's own words in all instances save a couple in which unmistakable errors of fact or syntax were committed; these I have silently corrected. Persons having legitimate scholarly or journalistic reasons for examining the original, uncut manuscript may apply to the Enoch Pratt Free Library for permission to do so.

I have no doubt that Mencken expected this manuscript to be published, as is strongly suggested by the language of his preface. I like to think that, however much he might complain about the shrinkage to which his efforts have been subjected, he would acknowledge that their essence has been honored and preserved.

I AM GRATEFUL to Dawn Converse, of Word Processing Unlimited, who once again has done me invaluable service in transferring untidy material to the tidy universe of WordPerfect; Averil Kadis, of the Enoch Pratt Free Library, firm and faithful guardian of all things Menckenian; and, most particularly, Ashbel Green, of Alfred A. Knopf, an old and treasured friend with whom I have at last been given, in this project, the opportunity to collaborate.

JONATHAN YARDLEY
Baltimore, December 11, 1991

PREFACE

THIS RECORD was suggested by my experience while making the first sketches for my *Days* books. Their writing was often interrupted by halts to verify a name or a date, or to reinforce otherwise a not too accurate memory, so the thought inevitably occurred to me that the going would be much easier if I had my memorabilia better arranged and documented. It was more or less my intention, at that time, to do a *Days* volume on my adventures as a magazine editor and a writer and reviewer of books, but in the end I had to abandon it for several reasons, not the least of which was that many of the men and women who would have had to be discussed in such a book were still alive and seemed likely to outlive me, and it would have been impossible to write of some of them with any frankness without offending them beyond endurance. But when I contemplated my almost interminable files—for I have always been one to keep records, and have an instinctive reluctance to destroy a document—it became manifest that there was a great deal in them that belonged, not only to my personal *curriculum vitae*, but also to the literary history of the United States in my time, and so it seemed worth while to get them into something approaching good order, for the use of resurrection men in the years to come.

As in the case of my *Thirty-Five Years of Newspaper Work, July 30, 1906 to the End of 1941*, I have tried here to maintain a reasonable objectivity, but without, I fear, any great success. After all, the story I have to tell is *my* story, though it deals mainly with other persons, and it would be an affectation for me to say that I have made it entirely impartial. With many of those persons, as the narrative shows, my relations were very intimate. I was not only privy to their professional plans and aspirations; in many cases I also had close contact with their private lives, and helped them to rejoice when they were happy as I tried to console them when they were not. I had a considerable influence upon some of them, both as critic and as friend. It has thus seemed best to deal with them freely, depicting them precisely as I saw them, and without any vain effort to distinguish sharply between what was significant about them and what was merely amusing, which is to say, essentially human.

It is not possible, at this time, to say what their literary heirs and assigns will be interested in, if, indeed, there is any interest in them at all. But if there is, then it will plainly be an advantage to have their stories in some detail, and that detail I have tried to set down. Inevitably there must come a time when confidences no longer run. Nearly all the persons here discussed, male or female, were writers, editors or publishers, and hence offered themselves for public inspection and invited public approval. I believe that, as in the case of candidates for office, that act materially conditions the ordinary right to privacy. The goods that a writer produces can never be impersonal; his character gets into them as certainly as it gets into the work of any other creative artist, and he must be prepared to endure investigation of it, and speculation upon it, and even gossip about it.

It has been my own fixed habit, ever since I began to get any notice, to suffer without protest anything that was printed about me, however inaccurate and unfair. In that department I have surely experienced as much enmity as any other American writer of my class and generation, but I have departed from my rule of silent endurance only in a few cases, and for extraordinary reasons, and every such departure is recounted at length in this memorandum. My belief in free speech is so profound that I am seldom tempted to deny it to the other fellow. Nor do I make any effort to differentiate between that other fellow right and that other fellow wrong, for I am convinced that free speech is worth nothing unless it includes a full franchise to be foolish and even to be malicious. My own stock of malice is rather under than above the average, for I am almost devoid of any capacity for either envy or moral indignation, but nevertheless I have some strong likes and dislikes, and in this narrative I have made no attempt to conceal them. If, when and as what I have here written ever comes to judgment I assume that its judges will be able to estimate its honesty or lack of honesty with sufficient acumen.

My own generation has insisted on seeing me as a sort of reformer, bent furiously upon bringing about changes in the course of American letters, and, as it must naturally follow, upon the general pattern of

American life. In so far as I have been discussed at all, it has nearly always been in that character. One faction has praised me on the ground that my influence was good, and another (and much larger one) on the ground that it was bad. And against the two has stood a third that has denied that I had any influence at all, and gloated over the fact as if it were the answer to a just God to saucy and preposterous pretensions.

All I can say, as the end of my life approaches, reviewing my professional career with some attempt at and approach to objectivity, is that I was never conscious of any such aims. I wrote what I wrote because it was in my nature to do so, and for no other reason. As I have often observed, my fundamental satisfaction was indistinguished from the satisfaction that a hen enjoys in laying an egg. When, as a result of my writing, customers and followers appeared, and imitation gave evidences of approval, my delight was always moderate and not infrequently minus, for I have always had a great dislike for converts and disciples. They are, by my definition, second- and third-rate men, and I much prefer the company of their betters.

It would, however, be mere foppery for me to allege that I was indifferent to the reactions of readers who were also friends, or that I never made any conscious effort to influence them. I did so without question in certain cases—for example, those of Dreiser and Hergesheimer—but I think I may add without pretense that I failed completely every time. Those who actually followed me were for the most part strangers, and with very few exceptions they were men in whom I had no interest whatsoever.

The existence of this lengthy record alongside the half-million words record of my adventures on newspapers indicates how widely, in my writing days, I have dispersed my energies. I have carried on, in fact, three distinct trades—that of an active daily journalist, that of a magazine editor, and that of a critic of books and ideas—and for years on end I have been busy at all three simultaneously. There were times when the amount of work that this involved was almost appalling, and I marvel today, looking back on such years as 1924, how I ever managed to do it. I suppose that the reason was that I was born with an extraordinary amount of reserve energy. As this narrative shows, I have been in indifferent health, or, at all events, full of minor discomforts, nearly all my life, but it was seldom that I was ever actually floored, and so long as I could sit up I usually contrived to do a hard day's work. In all this there was never the slightest consciousness of hortatory or pedagogical purpose. I wrote on and on, not because I desired to teach anyone anything, or to save anyone from sin, but simply and solely because I enjoyed it. The purely physical effort, to be sure, was sometimes fatiguing, but I got constant stimulation out of the flow of my own ideas, and no other enterprise ever gave me the same pleasure, or ever the half of it. My leisure for writing was always limited, for I invariably had other jobs on my hands, and sometimes they were onerous, but like any other true journalist I worked well under pressure, and enjoyed doing it. My letters show how often I was on the verge of being swamped, and sometimes a project that interested me greatly had to be postponed indefinitely, or even abandoned, but on the whole I got through what I attempted to do, which is perhaps as much as any man can ask for in this world.

Down to a few years ago I cherished plans for several books that must now be chalked off to advancing age and the general account of profit and loss, but I do not waste any time regretting them, for it was not idleness that wrecked them but other work. In this area I am a complete fatalist, and, as the following story shows, some of my most laborious, and, to me, important enterprises were undertaken almost fortuitously. No writer, in truth, is ever really a free agent. What he does in his trade is determined not only by his immediate environment and the ideational currents of his time, but also and more especially by the play of inherited forces and predispositions within him.

My records, as I have said, have been kept in good order, and I am in hopes that some literary historian or other will find them useful in the years to come. My surviving incoming letters are arranged in folders, and all save those from Maryland worthies (which have gone or are to go to the Pratt Library, Baltimore) are to be given to the New York Public Library at my death. Perhaps half of these letters are from authors, and many of them discuss the work of those authors. Unhappily, the collection is far from complete, for most of the correspondence I received as editor of the *Smart Set* went into the files of that magazine, and was lost when I left it. The same thing happened to many of the letters I received as editor of the *American Mercury*. Moreover, I have always destroyed purely personal letters, especially when they came from women, and have never made any effort to preserve those received from persons of no significance, *i.e.*, the great bulk of readers—tens of thousands of them. But such as it is, the collection contains some long runs of very interesting correspondence—for example, from Dreiser, Hergesheimer, Cabell, Huneker, Ezra Pound, E. L. Masters, Sinclair Lewis, E. W. Howe, Fielding H. Garrison and other such contemporaries.

My own letters are widely dispersed, and most of them, I suppose, are lost. In 1942 Dr. Julian P. Boyd, librarian of Princeton University, undertook a somewhat madcap plan to bring out a volume of them, while I was still alive, and to that end made diligent efforts to round them up. Nothing came of his projected book, but he was successful in getting together a great many letters, and has very politely sent me copies of those he has recovered, though in many more cases he could report only dry hauls. I was considerably shocked when my niece, Virginia Mencken Morrison, told me that, on her marriage in 1941, she had destroyed all the letters received from me since her childhood. They would have been useful to Boyd, for there was a time when Virginia showed an inclination toward writing and I made diligent efforts to help her, but now they are gone, and that is the end of it.

Most of my manuscripts, notebooks and souvenirs of one sort or another were bound in a long series of volumes after my wife's death in 1935, and a hundred or more of these volumes are in the Enoch Pratt Free Library, Baltimore. I deposited them there on the condition that no one should have access to them during my lifetime without my permission. Many more are waiting to follow them at my death, and the Pratt Library also has or will have all my copies of my own books, my clipping-books, a collection of books discussing me, and all the books and pamphlets by other Menckens that I have been able to assemble. I have been a user of the Pratt Library since boyhood, and it gave me whatever education I may be said to have, so it seemed appropriate for it to receive my private records. But my incoming letters, as I have said, are to go to the New York Public Library, for it specializes in literary memorabilia as the Library of Congress specializes in politicians. Like my own papers, my autographed presentation books and other association items have gone or are to go to the Pratt Library.

H. L. MENCKEN

MY LIFE AS
AUTHOR AND EDITOR

CHAPTER I

M Y FIRST APPEARANCE in print was in the Baltimore *American* some time during the summer of 1896, but despite a diligent search of the *American's* files I have been unable to establish the exact date. My debut was made with a set of satirical verses, and they had to do with the National League pennant that the once-famous Baltimore Orioles baseball team had won in 1894 and 1895 and was to win again in 1896. All Baltimore, in those days, was baseball crazy, and I was a violent fan myself. The pennant of 1894, hoisted proudly upon a tall pole in the centerfield of the Baltimore grounds, had begun to yield to the weather by the summer of 1896, and it was to its sadly dilapidated appearance that I tuned my maiden lay. That lay survives in typescript and the typescript is plainly marked "Summer of 1896," and though, as I have said, I have been unable to find the piece in the files of the *American*, I remember very clearly that it was printed there. It was as follows:

Ode to the Pennant on the Centerfield Pole

> O wilted rag!
> Neglected, lone, forlorn;
> Washed by the storms and by the breezes torn,
> Thou art the emblem of great victories won
> In ninety-four and -five. The blazing sun
> Now fades thy bright complexion
> O sea-sick flag!
> O aged rag!
> Though high thy drooping head may raise
> We know thou hast seen better days.

> Thy wasted form
> And hungry, homeless air
> Seems sad in one who erstwhile was so fair;
> Thy ragged edges and each tattered strand
> Show that thou'lt soon be in a better land—
> A happier, fairer section.
> Prey of the storm!
> Take chloroform!
> For though thy head full high may raise
> We know thou hast seen better days!

The appearance of these lines in print naturally gave me a great thrill, and I set to work at once to write more. No copies of its successors have been preserved and I do not recall their themes, but I remember clearly that they were of the same satirical tendency. The *American* failed to print any of them. It was not until November 19, 1897, that I appeared in its columns again, and then it was in the role of a much more serious poet. My contribution was entitled "The Gordon Highlanders," and, like "Ode to the Pennant," was printed unsigned. It was inspired by the storming of the Dargai heights by the British Army on October 20, a gallant incident of the typically English and incompetent Tirah campaign. I had by that time become so fanatical an admirer of Rudyard Kipling that I swallowed his imperialist politics along with his poetry.

My father had subscribed to *Once-a-Week*, the predecessor of *Collier's*, in 1888. With it, at intervals of two weeks, came a long succession of paper-bound books—not the cheap trash so popular at the time, but reprints of really good stuff. Among them was a set of Tennyson's poems in five or six volumes, and new books by a number of living English and American authors of some contemporary importance, for example, Justin McCarthy and Edgar Fawcett. On November 15, 1890, there appeared *Plain Tales from the Hills*, by a new author named Rudyard Kipling. I was, at that time, still too young to appreciate it, but a few years later I grew up to it and was tremendously impressed by it, and thereafter I read the whole of Kipling's existing canon, including especially *Barrack-Room Ballads*. As a result I became a Kipling fanatic of the first chop, and when I began to write myself I naturally tried to imitate my idol. His influence upon me continued strong until the end of my teens and was still visible in some of the doggerel in my first book, *Ventures into Verse*, published in 1903. The chief decoration of my bedroom in Hollins Street was a group of four or five portraits of him, brought together in one frame. Worse, I not only tried to write like him, using always his very worst models; I also took over a large part of his ideology, and its effects appeared in "The Gordon Highlanders" even before I had achieved any grip on his tricks of phrase and versification.

But this influence, though it was powerful, was by no means unchallenged. The literary movement of the 90's, now pretty well forgotten, was powerful while it lasted, and on no one did it operate more effectively than on young Harry Mencken. To be sure, I could never make out precisely what it was about, but neither could most of its principal proponents. Like them, I was content to accept it without too careful scrutiny as a salubrious revolt against the trite and time-worn, a breaking-out of new and glorious paths, an exploration of hitherto untrod realms of the psyche. It was carried on largely by means of *Tendenz* magazines, and I read all of them. There was in Baltimore Street east of Carey a small newsdealer named George Plitt who stocked them, and I was his prize customer. They were, fortunately enough, predominantly inexpensive: many sold for five or ten cents, and there was even one that sold for two. I bought an armful every month, and read them all assiduously, though their contents often puzzled me and not infrequently seemed to me to be insane.

What I got out of them, in the end, had two halves. The first was a conviction that the orthodox writing of the time was largely bilge, and deserved to be put down. The second was a taste for preciosity, especially as it was manifested in verse forms. If the time had been the teens of the Twentieth Century instead of the last decade of the Nineteenth I'd have taken to free verse inevitably; as it was I tried my hand at the old French forms that so many of the révoltés affected. The green sickness took me pretty far from the simple brass-band rhythms of Kipling, and the harsh disharmony between the two addled me, and so probably ruined me as a versifier—a consummation that I see no reason to regret today. But I do not regret the time wasted upon my painful efforts to drive both horses, for I am convinced that writing verse is the best of all preparations for writing prose. It makes the neophyte look sharply to his words, and improves that sense of rhythm and tone-color—in brief, that sense of music—which is at the bottom of all sound prose, just as it is at the bottom of all sound verse.

AT ONE DELIRIOUS PERIOD —it must have been in 1897—I resolved solemnly to write at least one poem every day, and for weeks on end I actually did so. Many of these compositions were submitted to the magazines of the time, but their editors were coy, and it was not until 1899, after I had become a reporter on the Baltimore *Morning Herald*, that I made any sales. My first of any importance was of an apostrophe to my hero Kipling, done during the early autumn of 1899. About a year later, on October 28, 1900, I began a weekly column of prose and verse for the editorial page of the *Morning Herald*—at no increase, of course, in my salary—and into that column I poured my rejected MSS. The verse part of it did not last very long, for I was still hopeful of making sales in that department and too busy to write anything new. I did actually sell a poem now and then, for example, to *Leslie's Weekly*, the *New England Magazine*, the *National Magazine* of Boston, and *Life*. These, and the pieces printed in the *Herald*, made up the contents of my first book, *Ventures into Verse*. I am astonished, thumbing through that embarrassing volume, to observe how little critical sense I had in 1902, when it was put together. It includes some imitations of Kipling that must hold a world's record for banality, and some essays in old French forms that are almost as bad, but it also shows a few things that are markedly better.

Moreover, I had in hand, by the time the book came out, a number of pieces that were superior to anything in it; no doubt I held them out because I hoped to sell them to magazines. This last possibility had been impressed upon me by an unhappy experience while I was still contributing verse to the *Morning Herald:* I sold a triolet called "A Few Lines" to the *Smart Set* on June 28, 1901, and then had to recall it because it had slipped into my column on October 28, 1900. But allowing everything for such considerations, I am amazed that I should have been idiot enough to burden the little book with such trash as "The Orf'cer Boy," "Faith" and "A Ballad of Looking." The better pieces that were unsold, and some that I wrote during the year or two following *Ventures into Verse*, knocked about my desk for years, and some of them did not see print until George Jean Nathan and I took over the *Smart Set* in 1914, and found ourselves so short of copy (and money) that I had to throw in large wads of my own rejected MSS., both in prose and verse.

BEFORE 1900 was half gone I was hard at work on short stories. The first that I sold was "The Cook's Victory," a tale of the Chesapeake Bay oyster fleet, born of my investigation as a reporter of the shanghaiing of men that went on along the Baltimore waterfront. It went to *Short Stories* and was published in the issue for August, 1900. In February, 1901, I followed it with "The Woman and the Girl," in August of the same year with "Like a Thief in the Night," in January, 1903, with "A Double Rebellion," in August, 1902, with "Firing and Watering," and in January, 1903, with "The Passing of a Profit." *Short Stories* paid me $15 for each of these stories, and though the price was very low, even for those times, I was content, for their publication greatly increased my credit in the *Herald* office, just as it was increased by the publication of my dithyrambs to Kipling in the *Bookman* for December, 1899. I learned thereby a very useful fact, too little noted by young journalists, to wit, that the prestige of a reporter is even more nourished by what he does outside the office than by what he does inside and for it. A few other members of the *Herald* staff were also trying to write—mainly comic opera libretti, but also short stories—but I was the only one that could show anything even remotely describable as success. Thus I began to stand out sharply from the herd, and enjoyed an advantage whenever the time came to choose men for promotion.

I GOT MY FIRST real leg up when Ellery Sedgwick, then editor of *Frank Leslie's Popular Monthly*, bought a story that was at first entitled "The Sword of the Vanquished," and there began a friendly association that, though it was never exactly intimate, was very stimulating and useful to me, and still continues. Sedgwick was then but twenty-nine years old and I was not yet twenty-one. A Brahmin of the Brahmins, he had taken his A.B. at Harvard in 1894, and spent a year teaching at Groton, and was to marry a Cabot three years later. In 1899 he had published a life of Thomas Paine, but he had no talent for writing and well knew it, so his energies were given over to editing, for which he had a marked aptitude. He put in four years on the *Youth's Companion* and then went to New York as editor of *Frank Leslie's Popular Monthly*, at that time a magazine of respectable position and not to be confused with *Leslie's Weekly*. I wrote "The Sword of the Vanquished" early in 1901, and submitted it to the *Saturday Evening Post* and *Short Stories* before sending it to Sedgwick. He accepted it under date of April 20.

Here was encouragement indeed. My other editors had been polite, but that was all. Sedgwick went further, and I began to glow with the feeling, so pleasant to a young author and so stimulating, that an editor was really interested in me. I replied gratefully, and at my suggestion the name of the story was changed to "The Flight of the Victor." Sedgwick wrote to me on April 29 that he proposed to print the story in his August, 1901, issue, but it was delayed for some reason unknown, and did not come out until September. He informed me that it was the custom of *Leslie's* to pay for MSS. three months in advance of publication, but here there was an even longer delay, and I did not get my pay for "The Flight of the Victor" until October 19. The amount was $50—the largest that I had received up to that time for a short story, or, in fact, for anything else.

ON SEDGWICK'S PUBLICATION of "The Flight of the Victor," I had received a letter from Richard G. Badger, a Boston book publisher, asking if I had "enough other stories, as good as this, to form a volume" and saying that if so he had a proposition to make that he believed would interest me. Badger was what is known in the trade as a lemon-squeezer—that is, he devoted himself to printing books at the expense of their authors. His chief customers, of course, were ninth-rate poets, but he occasionally snared a more considerable fish—for example, Edgar Lee Masters, whose *Maximilian*, a drama in blank verse, he was to bring out in 1902. Unhappily, I was innocent of publishing ways in 1901, and knew nothing of Badger's ill repute, so I replied politely and even eagerly, and a few days later he asked me to send him all the stories I had published to date, and suggested that it might be a good idea to let him handle the magazine sales of those I might write thereafter. I answered that I had too few published stories to make a book, but that I was hopeful of amassing enough by March, 1902. Also, I sent him such stories as I had, and he wrote to me at length on September 21, explaining his scheme.

I must have been sorely tempted, but fortunately enough, my total cash assets, in 1902, were somewhat short of the $300 that he demanded "toward the expense of publication," and the hatred of debt that had been talked into me by my father made it impossible for me to ask my mother for a loan. Thus the negotiations languished, and soon broke off. But they had filled me with a hot desire to bring out a book, and in November, 1902, having accumulated enough stories to make one, I put eleven of them together and submitted them to the New York publishing firm of F. A. Stokes & Company, a reputable house. They were rejected so promptly that I was left crushed, and hence ready for another approach by the insidious Badger. He made it toward the end of the year, and in January, 1903, I sent him twenty stories, apparently on the understanding that, if we came to terms, he was to select twelve.

But I still lacked the $300, and moreover, I was beginning to be suspicious of Badger, so I refused to trade. On January 21 he began a follow-up with a letter proposing to reduce my proposed contribution to $200, with a 33⅓ share of "the gross proceeds." Hoping to fetch me quickly, he enclosed a contract embodying these revised terms, but by this time I had begun to hear something about him, and declined to sign it. No doubt he kept on with his follow-up, but I was not to be had, and in the end I stopped answering his letters. The unsigned contract is still among my papers. It is possible that I approached other publishers during 1903 and 1904, but if so I have forgotten it, and I am inclined to believe that I didn't, for by this time I was beginning to realize sadly that fiction was hardly my trade.

CHAPTER II

I T IS PROBABLE that my Nietzsche,[1] with maybe some help from my Shaw,[2] got me the job of literary reviewer of the *Smart Set* in 1908, and so began a connection with that magazine which ran on until the end of 1923. When the post was offered to me by Fredric Weldin Splint, then the editor, it was as a bolt from the blue, for I had never heard of Splint, and the one thing that I had ever sold to the *Smart Set*—a triolet—had had to be recalled. For some reason or other I did not ask him how he had come to think of me, probably because I assumed as a matter of course that I had been suggested by Channing Pollock, who was doing a monthly dramatic review for the magazine at the time, and with whom I had been on friendly terms since 1902. Later on, I was told by someone now forgotten that I had been nominated by Dreiser, then editor of the *Delineator*, with whom I had been in contact since 1907. It was not until 1939 that I asked Splint himself about these varying reports, and was informed by him that I was actually brought to his attention by Norman Boyer, a former Baltimore *Herald* reporter who was then his assistant on the *Smart Set*. When I learned this so long afterward I was greatly surprised, for Boyer, though he was a Baltimorean, had worked in Baltimore for only a short time, and I hardly knew him. He had been attracted, I suppose, by my Shaw and my Nietzsche, and maybe also by my contributions to the *Herald* before 1906 and to the *Sun* afterward.

Splint's proposal was that I should fill eight pages of his space every

1. *Philosophy of Friedrich Nietzsche* (Boston: Luce, 1908).
2. *George Bernard Shaw: His Plays* (Boston: Luce, 1905).

month, and should have $50 for my pains, with the review books thrown in as my perquisite. I did not look this gift horse in the mouth, but fell to gratefully and with great energy. My Nietzsche was off my hands, and I had no other major works on the stocks, so there was plenty of time for the new job. But I found it, at the start, somewhat onerous, for I developed a certain amount of stage-fright, and I still recall with what uneasy painstaking I labored at my first article, which came out in the issue for November, 1908.

Splint, a very amiable fellow, professed to be pleased by my first article, and my relations with him were cordial until he left the magazine in 1911. It was still owned in those days by the celebrated Colonel William d'Alton Mann of *Town Topics*, and his chief agent in its management was his daughter, Mrs. Wray, the wife of a state senator in New Jersey. She was a woman to whom the gift of beauty had been denied, but she had a certain amount of intelligence and tried hard to keep the *Smart Set* above the level of the scandals that had engulfed her father. I saw her only seldom, but she was always very polite to me.

I never met her father in those days, but after becoming one of the editors of the *Smart Set* myself I saw him off and on, and was greatly attracted by his grand air and shameless roguery, for swindlers of all sorts have always interested me. He had started the magazine with the issue for March, 1900, and during its first years it was a great success, for its contributors included many of the best writers thrown up by the movement of the 90's in the United States, and it sometimes went near enough to the line of impropriety to pass as very piquant. Its boldest ventures in that direction, of course, would seem banal today, but during the first decade of the Twentieth Century the Comstocks were all-powerful in New York and moreover Mann was generally disreputable on account of *Town Topics* and his blackmailing schemes, so he had to step carefully.

Under Splint the magazine maintained its original format, with a novelette every month and a story in French, but its heyday had passed, and it was probably losing money. At all events, Mann wanted to sell it, and in 1911 he found a purchaser in John Adams Thayer, who had got a fortune out of *Everybody's* magazine. Characteristically, he rooked Thayer, and by the almost incredible device of selling him the magazine without letting him discover that it had an outstanding issue of bonds. Thayer did not learn about them until he had paid the purchase price and taken possession. He then sued Mann, and the case dragged on in the courts for several years. The end must have been a compromise, for in my time as editor, though some of the bonds were still outstanding, and in Mann's possession, the amount seems to have been reduced.

This effort to do in Thayer, though it was surely villainous enough, did not content the voracious old colonel, for in addition he made plans to set up a new magazine in competition with the *Smart Set*, and so recover as much as possible of what he had sold. That magazine appeared on the stands in August, 1912, and bore the name of *Snappy Stories*. The principal feature of its cover was the two long s's that were the trademark of the *Smart Set*, and in its contents it imitated most of the things that gave the *Smart Set* character—for example, the monthly novelette. Its fiction, like the *Smart Set's*, was advanced for the time—but always a little more advanced. Indeed, it quickly got a reputation for salacity, and that reputation back-flared against the *Smart Set* itself, which began to be confused with the newcomer. Mann stopped short of imitating the cadet gray of the *Smart Set's* covers, but, as I have said, he boldly borrowed the two long s's, and at a superficial glance the two magazines looked pretty much alike.

The man he put in charge of *Snappy Stories* was a scoundrel named W. M. Clayton, who had been the circulation manager of the *Smart Set*. This Clayton was commonly reputed in New York to be the colonel's illegitimate son, and there was certainly a good deal of resemblance between them, both physically and morally. He was a smart circulation manager, and quickly forced the sales of *Snappy Stories* above those of the *Smart Set*. Thayer raged and roared against this unfair competition, but his lawyers advised him that he could do nothing about it.

When Thayer became owner of the *Smart Set* I had heard of him only vaguely, and when I met him I was not greatly impressed. A native of Boston, and then just fifty years old, he had started out in life as a journeyman printer, but had moved into advertising and at thirty-one became the advertising manager of the *Ladies' Home Journal*. It was then entering upon an era of immense prosperity, and Thayer got the credit for its steady gains in linage. In 1899 he moved to the *Delineator*, and there he remained until 1903, when he and Erman J. Ridgway, backed by George Warren Wilder, the principal factor in the Butterick Company, which owned the *Delineator*, bought *Everybody's*, then owned by John Wanamaker, for $75,000, and quickly turned it into a great success.

That success was mainly, and perhaps even wholly, due to the publication of Thomas W. Lawson's "Frenzied Finance" series in 1904. Those were the palmy days of the muckraking magazines, and the Lawson articles put *Everybody's* at the head of the procession. After the great Baltimore fire of 1904, when all the banks and brokerage houses of Baltimore moved to the Mt. Vernon Place region, I once saw two or three hundred of their inmates rush out to storm a pushcart laden with the latest issue of the magazine. The circulation of *Everybody's*, which had been small under Wanamaker, rose to 600,000 under Thayer and Ridgway, and they wallowed in money. The editor of the magazine, John O'Hara Cosgrave, got the credit for the Lawson series, and for several years was hymned by the success writers of the time as a genius, but Thayer once told me that he (Thayer) had actually induced Lawson to become a contributor, and that Cosgrave had been against it. But after three years of partnership Thayer and Ridgway fell out, and Thayer withdrew. The cause of their disagreement was Ridgway's launching of a grandiose project to publish a weekly in fourteen cities simultaneously. Thayer thought that the scheme was insane, and he was right, for the weekly, launched by Ridgway alone, with the backing of Wilder, was done for after nineteen issues.

Thayer, with a small fortune in his hands, moved to Paris, set up as a boulevardier, and remained abroad until he bought the *Smart Set* in 1911. His New York apartment, when I first became acquainted with him, was full of souvenirs of his European sojourn. The carpet in the drawing-room, I recall, was snow-white, there were many objects of art in the worst French taste of the time, and among the bibelots was a manuscript of the Koran in Arabic, bought in Cairo at a high price and probably excessively modern.

Thayer, while he was in Paris, had visiting-cards made that followed the European style for persons of importance: that is, they gave only his surname. These he continued to use in New York. He and Mrs. Thayer (they were childless) had a French car (automobiles of any sort were then still rarities) and a French chauffeur whose name, as pronounced by Thayer, became O-jane. They had an elaborate country-place at Westport, Connecticut, and I was invited there a number of times for staff parties. I recall one that included a trip to a nearby beach, and a lunch which consisted, at Thayer's order, of clams—and champagne!

At that party he and I happened to resort to the *pissoir* together, and as we stood in adjoining stalls he boasted that, at the age of fifty, he was at the very height of his intellectual, physical and sexual powers, and a fair match, at affairs of business, for any man in America. He was essentially a comic character, and though I got on with him well enough, he was something of a nuisance to me. When he lost the *Smart Set* in 1914 he began going downhill very rapidly, and when he died in 1936, aged 75, he had lost his place at Westport and was almost broke.

Splint gave me a free hand in his book reviews, and so far as I can recall never made a suggestion about my treatment of this or that book. In my second article, that for December, 1908, I delivered a blast for Joseph Conrad, whose *The Point of Honor* had just come out, and in the same article I said a kind word for Joseph Medill Patterson's *A Little Brother of the Rich* and raised my beginning doubts about H. G. Wells. In my third article, for January, 1909, I pointed out some of the deficiencies of Edith Wharton, then accepted gravely by all the old-time reviewers as a genius beyond cavil. In my fourth I performed a barbaric war dance upon *The Shadow World*, by the old quack Hamlin Garland, and so ranged him among my implacable enemies—a company that gradually grew in numbers and virulence as article followed article.

In March, 1909, I made another violent enemy by reviling William Stanley Braithwaite, a learned blackamoor who made a good thing, in those innocent days, out of an annual anthology of bad poetry, and at the same time I paid my ironical respects to Richard G. Badger, the Boston lemon-squeezer, whose effort to induce me to pay for a volume of my short stories has been recorded. In June, 1909, I gave the lead in my article to James Huneker's *Egoists*, which I described as "an entertaining and illuminating book; a book of sound, workmanlike quality." I had been praising Huneker in newspaper articles since 1903 or thereabout, and had received a note of thanks from him in 1905, but he took no notice of my review of *Egoists* and I did not meet him until 1914. We then became instant friends, and remained on close terms until his death in 1921, when I was asked by T. R. Smith, then editor of the *Century*, to do a memoir on him for that magazine.

I HAD BEEN a very warm admirer of Huneker ever since the days of the old *Criterion* and had had my first contact with him back in 1905, when I whooped up his *Iconoclasts* in the Baltimore *Herald*, sent him a clipping, and got a letter from him, thanking me politely and adding, "When it comes to good fellowship you can't better a newspaper man's amiability to his fellow-sufferer." But I never met him until the early part of 1914, just before Willard H. Wright was fired as editor of the *Smart Set*. He was aware of me, of course, for, following my first blast in 1905, I had reviewed his *Egoists* with high praise in the *Smart Set* for June, 1909, and his *The Pathos of Distance* in October, 1913. Wright had picked up an acquaintance with him, and when he expressed a desire to meet me a lunch party was arranged at the old Grand Union Hotel opposite the Grand Central Station.

George Jean Nathan was with us, and we sat from one o'clock until after five, delighted by Huneker's gorgeous flow of talk. I recall that as we entered the dining-room he asked where the *pissoir* was, and chose a table quite close to it. "A beer-drinker," he explained, "should always keep near headquarters. It is silly to waste time walking to and from it." Huneker's drink was Pilsner, and we got down a large quantity of it in the course of the afternoon, and had to resort to headquarters frequently. His conversation was a really amazing compound of scandalous anecdotes, shrewd judgments and devastating witticisms, and Wright, Nathan and I simply wallowed in it. He and I became good friends at once, and I saw him often and heard from him pretty regularly. Our usual meeting place was Lüchow's in 14th Street. He and a group of his cronies had a *Stammtisch* there—in the room behind the bar, only ten steps from the *pissoir*. It was too large for a small party, but when we went there together he always chose a table near it. There he would get down five, six or eight *Seidel* of Pilsner at lunch: it was, he argued, the best drink ever invented, and one of the great and durable glories of the human race.

Of the strange things he told me at those beery sessions, I have forgotten 99%, but a few, at least, of the more instructive survive in memory. One was to the effect that Lillian Russell, on the day of her marriage to her third husband, John Chatterton (known professionally as Signor Perugini), gave a series of farewell parties to four of her other admirers. The wedding was to be in the evening, and she took on No. 1 at 10 a.m. Before noon he had had his fill of her favors, and his place in her bed was taken by No. 2, and so on until the whole squad had been served. Huneker hinted that he was himself one of the quartet.

I also recall a tale about the early days of Mary Garden. She was then studying singing in Paris, and was so poor that she often went hungry. Huneker was living there at the time with Sibyl Sanderson, the soprano for whom Massenet wrote *Thaïs*, and they had a very comfortable and even luxurious establishment, for Sibyl was a favorite at the Paris Grand-Opera. Also, she was a very kindly woman, so she fell into the habit of inviting La Garden to breakfast. The three, said Huneker, usually breakfasted together, in Sibyl's bedroom. This must have been in the middle 90's. In 1900 La Garden made her debut in *Louise* at the Opéra-Comique and was a great success, and in 1907 she was back in New York as one of the stars of Oscar Hammerstein's opera company at the Manhattan Opera House. Soon afterward Huneker encountered her at a musical party, and she pretended that she had never met him before. This upset him considerably, but he fell in with her masquerade, and in the end got mashed on her. When he published his *Bedouins* in 1920 it turned out to be largely devoted to her, and of its six illustrations four were portraits of her. Nathan and I joshed him about this, but he protested that his admiration was for the artist only.

Another of his tales was about Antonin Dvořák, the Czech composer, who came out to New York in 1892 to teach composition at the National Conservatory. Huneker, who was a member of the staff of the conservatory, was told off to show him New York on his arrival, and naturally took him to Lüchow's. The Pilsner there, of course, was an old story to Dvořák, and he expressed a desire to try some American drink. Huneker thereupon called for a Manhattan cocktail for him, and the master liked it so much that he asked for another at once. Before the food came on he had drunk five, and during the meal he drank five more.

Thereafter he spent a large part of his spare time at Lüchow's, and became so assiduous an addict to Manhattans that the bosses of the conservatory began to fear that he would drink himself to death. Later, when he moved on to one of the Czech colonies in the upper Middle East, it was not the low state of civilization there that made him unhappy, but the lack of decent Manhattans. Huneker said that Dvořák, in aspect, well bore out Brahms's description of him as *der*

Bauer in Frack.[3] He looked like a badly barbered farmer, but dressed very elegantly—according to his notions. His necktie was a satin Ascot and in it he wore no less than five scarf-pins.

Yet another of Huneker's tales was the death of Walt Whitman. He got it, he said, from Horace Traubel, who was Whitman's amanuensis and valet. Old Walt's last moments were at hand, with Horace in attendance upon him at the little house in Camden, N.J. Finally, the dying poet whispered: "Lift me up, Horace; I want to shit." These, according to Huneker, were his authentic last words.

Huneker's given names were James Gibbons, and he let it be understood that he was a nephew (sometimes a cousin) of Cardinal Gibbons, and had been named after him. Whether or not this was true I do not know: I always had some doubt of it. He described himself in *Who's Who in America* as "g.s. James Gibbons (Irish poet)," and it is much more likely that he was named after this grandfather. One of his favorite ideas, labored at length whenever he was in his cups, was to the effect that all persons of any distinction in the world, regardless of their apparent race, were Jews. I heard him, at different times, ascribe this Jewishness to men as diverse as Nietzsche, Goethe, Tschaikovsky, Emerson, Johann Strauss and Edgar Allan Poe.

Once, at Lüchow's I challenged his theory by pointing to himself. "What!" he exclaimed. "Can't you see my nose?" And he turned his head so that I caught his profile. His nose was, in fact, a somewhat formidable organ, but there was certainly nothing Jewish about it. Instead, it suggested a Roman emperor of the decadence, for there was an almost straight line from its tip to the top of his forehead. By the time I knew him it had been considerably damaged by the attrition of the elements and the effects of alcohol, and was a mauve shade and rather squashy in texture. Its capillaries stood out sharply, and no one could have mistaken it for the nose of an ascetic. On December 13, 1914, he was in a taxicab accident that broke it (besides blacking his eyes and wrecking his false teeth) and thereafter, for a year at least, it was a dreadful spectacle indeed.

But Huneker, though he drank large quantities of Pilsner as long as it was obtainable, was by no means a drunkard. When he had a free afternoon he liked to abandon himself to the malt and hops in a

3. "The peasant in a dress coat."

liberal and spacious manner, and he always complained that my work cut our luncheons too short, even though they commonly ran beyond four o'clock, but while he was at his desk he kept cold sober, and it was seldom, in the days when I knew him, that he showed any effects of drink. His usual garrulity was augmented a bit, but that was all. He once told me that his family, though Irish (he himself was born in Philadelphia) came originally from Hungary, and cited his surname in proof thereof. That proof, of course, was mere guessing, and without philological substance. As a matter of fact, the name Hunec appears in *Domesday Book*.

Huneker was not tall, but he was very sturdy in build, with a straight back and broad shoulders. It would be an exaggeration to call him distinguished in appearance, but nevertheless he was plainly no ordinary man. His eyes were blue, he was clean shaven, and in the days when I knew him his hair was thinning and almost white. He wore the wing collars that had been fashionable in his youth, and presented a somewhat dressy aspect. He was married, I think, three times, but he never mentioned his marriages in *Who's Who*. By his first wife, a sculptor, he had a son who, at the time of his own death in 1921, was a ticket-seller at the Metropolitan Opera House. This was his only child. His last wife was one Josephine, a woman plainly of Jewish blood. Ben De Casseres once told me that she had been a chambermaid in a small hotel in Irving Place, where Huneker once had a room. She survived him, and is still alive (1948).

Huneker (after a futile struggle with the law) had started out as a pianist, and his talk was full of references to piano music, but I never heard him play, and neither, so far as I know, did any of his other common associates. Maybe that was because he lived far out in the wilds of Brooklyn, and very few of those associates ever visited his home. It was in an apartment-house called the Westminster Court, in the Flatbush section. There he lived an almost hermit-like life with Josephine, broken by an occasional trip to Atlantic City or some other nearby resort. Twice, while I knew him, he went to Havana, mainly to get rid of hay-fever, which floored him every August. Before World War I he had gone to Europe every year, and in 1920 he made a final trip to London for the New York *World*.

He worked very hard during the last years of his life, coming in by subway every evening of the musical season to cover concerts or the opera for the *World*, *Sun* or *Times*, but he was never well paid, and very often he was hard pressed for cash. His books were highly esteemed but only by a relatively small circle, and his royalties were always meagre. Writing was never easy for him, and when he had a magazine article or story in hand he dug himself in Brooklyn and was not seen on Manhattan Island for days. There was a curious modesty about him, not unmingled with timorousness. My own florid praises of him always embarrassed him, and he was distressed whenever I coupled them with denunciations of other men, which was usually. When, in *A Book of Prefaces*, I sneered at his old colleague, Henry Edward Krehbiel, he protested that I had been unjust—that Krehbiel was really a very learned man, and worthy of respect. I refused to agree. I also refused to agree when Huneker gave me to understand that he was flattered by the fact that the Scribners published his books. This seemed to me to be preposterous. The truth was that the Scribners should have been flattered by the fact that Huneker let them publish him: he was one of the best Americans on their list. But old Jim would not have it so.

His low income made it necessary for him to be careful about money, and so he got the reputation in New York of being stingy. This was undeserved, at least in my experience: he was always eager to take his turn paying luncheon checks. But he practiced a number of petty economies that helped the legend. One was his refusal to lay in letter paper with his address printed on it. He used, instead, plain notepaper of the cheapest sort—and then went to the trouble to write his full address at the top of a letter. He was also accused, in New York, of selling books that had been given to him by authors, and this, I believe, was a fact. He did so in order to clean up his quarters and raise a few dollars against the expenses of his annual trip to Europe. Most of the books he so sold, of course, were not worth keeping, but their authors naturally objected to his selling them without tearing out their inscriptions. But in the practice he was certainly not solitary. Many and many's the time I have encountered presentation copies of my own books in second-hand catalogues.

When Nathan and I took over the *Smart Set* it was not difficult for us to recruit Huneker for it, for he was in sympathy with our program, his market was narrow, and he needed money. Unhappily, he worked very slowly and fetched up ideas for articles and stories only at longish intervals, so what we got from him at the start were mainly dogs-eared MSS. that he had been playing with, off and on, for a long while.

* * *

On November 7, 1918 he wrote to me that the MS. of his long-promised and long-delayed novel was completed at last, and that he would deliver it to Nathan in the near future, but I had become somewhat cynical about it by this time, and as a matter of fact I did not actually see it until a year later. I heard nothing from him after this for five months. In April, 1919, Nathan, John D. Williams—a theatrical manager and a friend of Nathan's—and I met him at Sherry's, at Fifth Avenue and 45th Street, and we put in a couple of hours palavering upon the horrors of the time, especially the complete disappearance of Pilsner and the threat that Prohibition would soon be upon us.

On September 30 he reported once more that his novel was finished, and described it as "a horror—but might run for three months in *S.S.* without interference"—and again it did not appear. I had been fooled so often about the novelette that I refused to believe that it was finished at last, but on the morning of November 15, 1919, as I was sitting in the *Smart Set* office with Nathan, old Jim marched in with the MS. under his arm. I was just about to leave for Baltimore, so I grabbed it from him and read it on the train. When I got home that night I wrote to Nathan:

> The Huneker novel is superb. It is an absolute riot of obscenity. He not only has them diddling all over the place, he makes jokes about constipation, menstruation, Lesbianism, etc. The girls are raped, back-scuttled and otherwise delighted. It is an amazing piece of work, and it contains the best stuff the old boy has ever done. Read the soliloquy beginning on page 108 when you get the MS. When I read it on the train I yelled aloud.

All this was quite sincere: I really enjoyed the thing immensely, but it was obvious that printing it in a magazine, in that golden age of comstockery, would be altogether impossible. Even bowdlerized, it would remain dangerous. I returned the MS. to Nathan at once, and he agreed with me in both particulars. Meanwhile, T. R. Smith, then the literary adviser of Horace Liveright, proposed to bring it out in a so-called private edition: printing such things was one of Liveright's specialties. Smith and Liveright issued a limited edition of 1,200 copies in 1920.[4]

4. The novel was *Painted Veils.*

Death, by now, was fast creeping up on Huneker, but his friends did not realize it, and neither, I suppose, did he. His discomforts increased all through 1920. Nathan and I saw him for the last time at lunch at Lüchow's in June 1920. He looked somewhat thin and pasty, but we ascribed his appearance, not to illness, but to the fact that he was drinking tea. Tea in Lüchow's, the citadel of Pilsner!— a comic spectacle, to be sure, but not without its elements of the tragic. He told us that he drank it, not because his doctor had alarmed him about his glycosuria, but because, since the Prohibition curse had descended upon the country, there was nothing else for him to drink. He had tried near-beer, but in those first days of the dry murrain it was dreadful stuff indeed, and he could not get it down. Later on, as the arts of the bootlegger developed, potable beverages, including even beer, began to appear in New York, and across the river in New Jersey the malt liquor improved so rapidly that by 1924 it was quite as good as the majority of American brews had ever been before the war.

But by that time poor Huneker was dead. He had been failing, in fact, ever since the last drop of Pilsner went down his throat. To be sure, he had kept on working; indeed, he had produced more during his last five years than in any lustrum preceding, but it was uphill effort, and there had been many interruptions by his gradually encroaching illness. He kept at it, however, with great courage, and was full of activity and enterprise until the very end.

He died at his home in Brooklyn on February 9, 1921. What fetched him in the end, I believe, was not diabetes, but heart failure. There was a funeral service for him at the Town Hall in New York, but I did not attend it. Nathan, who was present, told me that it was really impressive, with speeches much less offensive than mortuary oratory usually is.

Immediately after his death the Scribners began to make plans for a volume of his letters, and it was brought out in October, 1922, ostensibly edited by his widow. Seventeen of the letters in the collection were to me. They were, in the main, polite and feeble, and quite misrepresentative of his generally lively and often tart epistolary style. The flabbiness of the book, in fact, strongly suggested that it would be easy to put together a much better one, and this was done in 1924 by T. R. Smith, with Mrs. Huneker appearing again as the ostensible editor. The title of the new volume was *Intimate Letters of James*

Gibbons Huneker, and it was published by Smith's employer, Horace Liveright, in a limited edition of 2,050 numbered copies.

In 1928 the Scribners asked me to edit, with an introduction, a volume of selections from his essays, and I did so. The book came out in 1929 under the title of *Essays by James Huneker*, and there was an English reprint the next year. It had a very fair sale. Most of Huneker's original volumes are now out of print (1942), but that is not true, I believe, of his *Old Fogy*, first brought out by Theodore Presser, the Philadelphia music publisher, in 1913. *Old Fogy* was always my favorite among all his books, and more than once, in the 1914–1920 era, I tried to induce him to do some additional chapters for the *Smart Set*, but he pleaded that he had lost the mood and could not recover it. After his death I suggested to Alfred Knopf that a new edition of it might do well, and Knopf agreed, but when he asked the Presser firm for permission to reprint it he was told that a sentimental attachment to the book stood in the way of letting any other publisher have it.

Soon after Huneker's death the news went about that he had died penniless, and that his widow, Josephine, was in sore straits. The usual busybodies thereupon got together and launched a scheme for an auction sale of his library. It turned out, of course, that his library was small and consisted mainly of books of no value, for, as I have recorded, he was in the habit of periodically turning autographed presentation copies into cash. The busybodies then proposed that his friends, on the pretext of buying such books as were in hand, contribute to a fund for the widow, and I did so. That she was ever actually in want I doubt. In 1922 she got some income from the first collection of his letters, and in 1924 she got more from the second. I saw her in New York now and then, and she showed no sign of distress. She was living, in fact, in a hotel, and in 1929 she took a trip abroad.

In 1937 a nun named Sister Miriam, R.S.M., professor of English at Misericordia College, Dallas, Pa., wrote to me that she was working for a Ph.D. degree at the Catholic University in Washington, and proposed to make her thesis a study of Huneker. She had heard, she said, that he was reconciled to the Catholic Church on his death-bed, and died in the odor of sanctity. This seemed to me to be nonsense, but I was polite, and on August 8, 1937, Sister Miriam came to see me in Baltimore, accompanied by another member of her order. I tried to discourage her, for it was only too plain that old Jim was hardly a suitable subject for a nun's dissertation, but she persisted.

What professor it was at the Catholic University that encouraged Sister Miriam in her fantastic plan I never found out, but after a while I gathered that he had been overruled by others. The faculty finally got rid of her by plucking her on her examination, but she continued to cherish hopes of doing Huneker some day—and of proving that he had died anointed with holy oils —and accordingly kept the books that I had lent to her. In 1942 I asked her to send them back, and she did so.

My reviews in the *Smart Set* began to attract attention after they had been going on for a few months. The first favorable notice of them, I believe, was printed in the *Star of Hope*, the paper printed by the convicts at Sing Sing. In one of the 1909 issues Convict No. 57544 said that they were "about the best ever." When, in July, 1909, I undertook to set down a list of twelve new novels that were worth reading, it was noticed in the Boston *Transcript* by E. F. Edgett. Edgett spoke of the *Smart Set* as a "magazine not hitherto looked upon as a court of last literary resort, " but reprinted my list and treated it seriously enough. On it were the following books:

Tono-Bungay, by H. G. Wells
The Power of a Lie, by Johan Bojer
Lewis Rand, by Mary Johnston
Septimus, by W. J. Locke
9009, by James Hopper and Fred R. Bechdolt
Fraternity, by John Galsworthy
The Point of Honor, by Joseph Conrad
The Eternal Boy, by Owen Johnson
The Journal of a Neglected Wife, by Mabel Urner
Dragon's Blood, by Henry M. Rideout
Cherub Devine, by Sewell Ford
The Man in Lower Ten, by Mary Roberts Rinehart

This was not a bad list, and I am disposed to stand by it after a third of a century, though some of the authors whose names were on it afterward vanished into obscurity and nonentity. I kept banging away at Wells for his frequent descents to Marxian tub-thumping, but praised him every time he forgot the sorrows of the proletariat and wrote an honest novel. My first notice of James Branch Cabell, devoted to his *Cords of Vanity*, was printed in June, 1909. In it I said of him: "There is a distinction in his style—a quality as rare in American novels as Christian charity in a Christian bishop—and he has an artist's feeling for form and color, not to mention a musician's feeling for rhythm."

Theodore Dreiser's *Sister Carrie* had made a powerful impression on me, and I was eager to write about him, but the chance did not offer until he published his second novel, *Jennie Gerhardt*, in 1911. I had only six pages in November of that year, but I devoted three of them to him, and the title I put above my article was "A Novel of the First Rank." Of it I said:

> Nothing of the art of the literary lapidary is visible in this novel. Its form is the simple one of a panorama unrolled. Its style is unstudied to the verge of barrenness. There is no painful groping for the exquisite, inevitable word; Mr. Dreiser seems content to use the common, even the commonplace coin of speech. . . . The thing could have been done only in the way that it has been done. As it stands, it is a work of art from which I for one would not care to take anything away—not even its gross crudities, its incessant returns to C major. It is a novel that depicts the life we Americans are living with extreme accuracy and criticizes that life with extraordinary insight. It is a novel, I am convinced, of the very first consideration.

Thus I praised Cabell for the artfulness of his style, and apologized for Dreiser's lack of it. That dichotomy ran through all the reviews I was destined to do for the *Smart Set*, and for the *American Mercury* after it. My central theory was that an author was entitled to choose his own manner, his own weapons. If, having made his choice, he produced a work of genuine vitality, giving a plausible picture of human life as he had seen it, and devoid of fustian and brummagem, then I was for him; but if there was any sign of falseness or affectation in him, then I was against him.

Thus, in my first year as a critic, I praised such diverse authors as Joseph Conrad, Mary Roberts Rinehart, Leonid Andreiyeff, Zona Gale, John La Farge, Helen Green, Frank T. Bullen and Lizette Woodworth Reese, pointed out the deficiencies of a string of current favorites running from Edith Wharton to William Allen White, and tried to sort out the good from the bad in Wells, O. Henry, May Sinclair, W. Somerset Maugham, Ellen Glasgow and John Galsworthy. It was a hard year's work, involving a heavy burden of reading, but I enjoyed it very much, and looking back on it today I am not ashamed of it. Novels were my principal provender, for that was an era of novels, but I seized every chance to get out of the dream world into the real one. In a review of John Graham Brooks's *As Others See Us*, printed in February, 1909, I began what was to be a long exploration of the American character, and in reviews of *The Privileged Classes*, by Barrett Wendell, in March of the same year, and of *The People at Play*, by Rollin Lynde Hartt, in September, I returned to the subject and sought to illuminate it with observations that were certainly not those of a patriot.

Conrad, when I first began writing about him in 1908, was no more than a name in the United States: his first six books had six different publishers and his first eight had seven. Even in England, before the appearance of *'Twixt Land and Sea* in 1912, he had barely a *succès d'estime*, though Galsworthy and Wells were both whooping for him. But though the response at first was small, I kept on writing about him through the years of my service on the *Smart Set*, and after a while I began to make converts, as the correspondence that came in showed. Nor was my writing confined to the *Smart Set:* I also put in frequent licks for him in the Baltimore *Sun*, especially after the evening edition was set up. In the same way, after the publication of *Jennie Gerhardt* in 1911 gave me my chance, I kept on banging away for Dreiser, and not only in the *Smart Set* and the *Sun:* for example, I also reviewed *The Financier* for the New York *Times*, and in August, 1917, I contributed an article entitled "The Dreiser Bugaboo" to the *Seven Arts*.

These exertions not only got notice for Conrad and Dreiser; they also got notice for me, and though some of it was not friendly, it was all welcome to an ambitious young man. It was, of course, uphill work, slugging for such men in the prewar years, for the Hamilton Wright Mabies and Henry Van Dycks were still dominant in American criticism, and it was not until 1910 that any American critic of respectable standing—William Lyon Phelps—ventured to praise even Mark Twain without reservations. But time was on my side, and by the beginning of World War I, I had a very considerable following, and was beginning to be taken seriously, though usually also furiously. The intellectual chaos that followed the war made things easier for me, as it did for most of the men I admired, and by 1920 the Mabies and Van Dycks were almost forgotten.

In the days before I set up shop as a book reviewer my library in Hollins Street was very meagre, and I deliberately kept it so, for I had learned to depend upon a branch of the Pratt Library that was only two blocks away, and also made frequent use of the old central library in Mulberry Street. But as review books began to pour in I naturally kept some of them, and so my quarters in the third-floor hall-room in Hollins Street became outgrown, and I had to move to a larger room in the back third story. Part of it was used as a store-room, and that part was separated from the rest by a wooden partition. Along this partition I had bookcases built, with glass doors, and pretty soon they were full to overflowing.

I did not, of course, keep all the review books that came in: there were soon too many of them for that, and besides, most of them were trash. In 1909 I established a trading arrangement with H. E. Buchholz, assistant to Dr. Guy Carleton Lee, literary editor of the *Sun* from 1901 to 1908, whereby I traded him current novels for the better books that had accumulated in Lee's storehouse—usually, six novels for a good book. I thus acquired a number of books that I admired, chiefly scientific, and Buchholz simultaneously got a steady supply of bad novels for his wife, whose tastes were somewhat infantile. When Buchholz's stock began to run out, I established a similar trading arrangement with William V. Pippen, a second-hand bookseller in Eutaw Street, Baltimore, and after a while I transferred to another and more amusing bookseller, Samuel Cator, in Howard Street. At Cator's death I turned to the Leary, Stuart Company in Philadelphia, and my exchanges with it still go on.

I had been introduced to Dreiser's *Sister Carrie* by George Bronson Howard, and had a very high opinion of it, but down to August, 1907, I had no sort of contact with the author. Then, under date of August 23, he wrote to me as follows:

Mr. George Bronson Howard, of your city, has suggested to me that you were just the person to get out a popular edition of a German Philosopher or Dramatist which could be sold to schools and colleges and to the general reading public. He thought that a condense and popular edition of Schopenhauer would be very much in your line.

This letter was written on the stationery of the *Delineator*, of which Dreiser had lately become editor. What led Howard to make his suggestion I do not know, but probably it was something that he had heard from me about my book on Nietzsche, then in progress. I replied politely, and on September 16 Dreiser followed with a letter explaining that he was speaking for B. W. Dodge & Company, a new firm of book publishers of which I then knew nothing. I later found that the head of the house, Dodge, was an old-timer in the publishing business, and of very good reputation—save for the fact that he had taken to drink. Dreiser, I believe, had a stake in the venture, and continued to have faith in Dodge to the end.

But in 1907 I was too busy with my Nietzsche to undertake another treatise on a German philosopher, so I declined to do the book that Dreiser had in mind, and instead tried to sell him, in his capacity as a magazine editor, some of the medical articles that Hirshberg[5] and I were concocting. Dreiser, who assumed that Hirshberg was their sole author, liked the first that I sent in so well that he bought it for the *Delineator*. Its title was "The Slaughter of the Innocents." This was on September 24, 1907, and he said he would pay $100 for it. In the same letter he suggested two further articles, "If My Baby Had Pneumonia" and "If My Baby Had Diphtheria." "The Slaughter of the Innocents," as it stood, was too long for the *Delineator*, but after one of the women in the magazine's office had made a vain effort to cut it down, I did so myself and it went into type. Hirshberg and I did the proposed article on diphtheria at once, and soon followed with the one on pneumonia, and Dreiser suggested yet another on scarlet fever.

On November 8 he paid me, not $100, but $125 for "The Slaughter of the Innocents," and another $125 for the diphtheria article, and a little later he sent me an article by some other contributor, entitled "What Science Has Done for the Child," and asked me to give him Hirshberg's and my joint opinion of it. "There will be other things from time to time in this connection," he wrote on December 14, "and when it amounts to a half dozen I shall pay you something for

5. Leonard K. Hirshberg, a Baltimore physician.

editorial services." It must have been soon after this that I went to New York, called at the *Delineator* office, and saw him for the first time.

I remember over all these years how incongruous it seemed to me for the author of *Sister Carrie* to be the editor of a woman's magazine. He was then thirty-six years old, but seemed older, for he was a somewhat solemn fellow externally, and it was not until I knew him better that I discovered his loutish humor. I well recall how I was amused by his curious habit of folding his handkerchief as he talked. He would arrange it in an elaborate series of pleats, and then shake it out and begin all over again. He occupied a huge office in the new hexagonal building of the Butterick Company, and was attended by several secretaries. He told me after we became better acquainted that he was paid $10,000 a year as editor, a very large sum for those days, and much more than he had got in his previous editorial jobs—as editor of *Every Month* in 1895–96, of *Smith's Magazine* (one of the Street & Smith pulps) in 1905–06, and of *Broadway Magazine* in 1906–07.

On April 24, 1908, Dreiser wrote to me saying that he was setting up a literary supplement in the *Delineator*, and proposing that I let him use my name as "associate and contributor." The others invited, he said, were Ludwig Lewisohn, Joseph H. Coates, Charles Hanson Towne, Peter B. McCord, Arthur Henry and Gustavus Myers—all of them, as I found later, friends of his. My name, he explained, would be used "on the editorial writing paper only." I do not recall writing anything for this literary supplement, nor even whether I let him use my name.

On April 25, 1909, Dreiser offered me "an editorial position on the *Delineator* at $50 per," but I of course declined. On July 11, 1909, he wrote to me: "As a side line I have secured control of the *Bohemian* and am going to revise it vastly. You belong by nature and ability. Won't you come across with something real snappy?" My response must have been faint, for on August 3 he was writing to me again, urging me to "make a suggestion or two for the *Bohemian*." I sent in my first contribution while this letter was on its way to me. It was an editorial entitled "A Plea For Profanity." Dreiser accepted it at once, and it was printed in the *Bohemian* for November. He paid me $10 for it. On August 18 he accepted another on divorce and rejected one on the diamond-back terrapin of the Chesapeake, and enclosed five suggestions for others. On September 25 he accepted "The Artist," and on October 16 he telegraphed: "Need 3 funny editorials bad. Can I get them Monday?" The three were dispatched at once, and two days later he acknowledged receipt of them. I wrote various others during the weeks following, and they bulked large in the two or three issues that Dreiser edited. At Thanksgiving, 1909, he and his wife came down to Baltimore for dinner in Hollins Street. I recall nothing of the meeting save that he was then a teetotaler, and got pretty well jiggered by the rum in the pumpkin pie. No doubt we discussed future projects, both for the *Delineator* and for the *Bohemian*, but if so those relating to the latter were never carried out, for it failed to catch on, and on December 16 Dreiser wrote to me that it had been suspended. He owed me, at that time, $50 for "The Artist" and $10 each for five or six editorials, and he offered to assume personal responsibility of the debt. I refused, of course, to let him do so, but I proceeded on the assumption that title to "The Artist" had returned to me, and so felt free to reprint it in the *Smart Set* in August, 1916.

Meanwhile, the Mencken-Hirshberg series of medical articles went on in the *Delineator*, and I also contributed some short pieces to a Men's Page that Dreiser had set up. By the end of 1909 there were fifteen medical articles, and early in 1910 they were published as a book by the Butterick Company, under the title of *What You Ought to Know About Your Baby*. It was signed by Hirshberg, and my name did not appear on it, though I had written every word of text. It ran to 97 pages, and apparently had a large circulation among readers of the *Delineator*. Then it disappeared, and not until years afterward did book-collectors discover that I had a hand in it. When this discovery was made in 1928 or thereabout, at the height of the craze for American first editions, it came into heavy demand, and the price went high. For a while it was sold as "reputedly" by me, but I put an end to this mystification by admitting my authorship. It now appears in all bibliographies of my writings.

My excoriation of Upton Sinclair in my first article for the *Smart Set* in November, 1908, and my sneers at H. G. Wells in my second brought me a remonstrance from a queer fellow named Robert Rives La Monte, then serving as literary editor of the Baltimore *News* in succession to E. A. U. Valentine and Virginia Woodward Cloud.

This La Monte was not a Baltimorean, but a native of Brooklyn, nor was he a newspaper man, but a lawyer. What brought him to Baltimore I forget, if indeed I ever knew, nor do I recall how he got his job on the *News*. La Monte, who was then forty-two years old, professed to be a Socialist, and after leaving the *News*, where his service was short, became Sunday editor of the New York *Call*, then the chief Socialist organ in the United States. When he wrote to me to protest against my low view of the Marxian revelation and its prophets I replied politely, and soon afterward we met and had a friendly palaver.

The upshot was that he proposed that he and I exchange a series of letters on the subject, with a view to making a book. He had one book behind him—a poor thing called *Socialism, Positive and Negative*, published by Kerr, the official Socialist publisher, in 1907— and I had two, so it seemed likely that anything we did together would have a chance of getting into print. I therefore agreed, and La Monte at once had at me with his first letter, a somewhat long one, ending thus: "If you wish to see better manners, more worthy fiction, higher art, and nobler drama, as I know you do, your only course is to become a Socialist comrade, and give us your aid in hastening the advent of the Social Revolution. Will you do it?" I replied, of course, that I would not, and so our correspondence was under way. Before it had gone very far La Monte gave up his job on the *News* and moved to New Canaan, Connecticut, but we kept on as arranged, and our book was finished before the end of 1909.

I must have told Dreiser about this project soon after it was launched, and La Monte must have spread news of it among his Socialist friends, for I find a letter from Dreiser, dated January 30, 1909, which indicates that he hoped to get the book for B. W. Dodge & Company and that an order for a thousand copies had already come in from a wholesaler of Socialist books. But La Monte, to whom I left the business of placing it, was eager to have it bear the imprint of a more distinguished publisher than Dodge, and some time toward the middle of 1909 he landed *Men vs. the Man*—for that is what we decided to call it—with the old and rich firm of Henry Holt & Company. I had nothing to do with this, and my first letter from Henry Holt, dated December 21, 1909, shows that by that time all arrangements had been made. The book came out in March, 1910, and got, on the whole, a somewhat skeptical press.

The business brought me into contact with old Henry Holt, who was already close to seventy years old. Later on I got to know him pretty well, and saw him with some frequency, for one of his daughters was married to a Baltimore surgeon of my acquaintance, Joseph C. Bloodgood, and he often visited her. He was himself, in fact, a Baltimorean by birth, and one Sunday, when he and I were taking a walk, he showed me his childhood home at the northwest corner of Lombard and Penn Streets. In his youth that had been a fine neighborhood, but by 1910 it was much decayed, and we found the house occupied by Lithuanian immigrants. Holt was very tall and very slim, and with his large dark eyes showing curious dark pigmentation beneath he had an unusual appearance. He was a great talker, and loved to give advice to his authors.

He was an extraordinarily opinionated fellow, and most of his opinions, as I soon learned, were rubbish. His efforts to promote simplified spelling were ardent; in the later years of his long life he took to spiritualism, greatly to the horror of his surgeon son-in-law, Bloodgood. Bloodgood was himself an eccentric. He operated on me in the summer of 1910, and we became well acquainted. Learning about my collaboration with Hirshberg in medical articles, he asked me to give him some help in a campaign he was then launching—one of an almost interminable series. Its aim was to make women familiar with the early signs of cancer, and so bring them to operation the sooner, to the enhancement of their chances of surviving. This aim was a reasonable one, and Bloodgood probably did some good, but he also accomplished a great deal of mischief, for his proclamations to the laity spread wild and unnecessary alarms, and filled his anteroom with women suffering from nothing worse than cancerophobia.

He was one of the most earnest and humorless men I have ever known. His office was filled at all times with propaganda leaflets of a dozen different sorts, and he spent a large part of his time and energy circulating them. Those that appeared under his name were mainly my own, for he wrote so badly that he was almost illiterate. He would prepare the material and then I would write the text. This went on for five or six years, to my increasing discomfort; in the end I threw up the business as an unmitigated nuisance.

Bloodgood fitted into the Holt family admirably, for all of its members were uplifters of one sort or another. The son by the old man's first marriage, Roland, was a promoter of arty theatrical performances in New York; the eldest daughter, Winifred, devoted herself to succoring and harassing the blind; the younger daughter, Mrs. Bloodgood, was a do-gooder in general practice, and the old man himself whooped up not only simplified spelling and spiritualism, but also various other crazes. Only the young son of his second marriage, Eliot, showed any sign of normalcy—and Eliot was a drunkard.

Old Holt's publishing business was very profitable, and he had a large income from it. As he approached eighty his own share in its management grew less and less active, and he gave over most of his time to the various insane causes that he advocated. This left the conduct of affairs, at least in theory, to his son Roland, but Roland was virtually a half-wit, so the burden really fell on two employes, Alfred Harcourt and Donald C. Brace, both of them highly competent men. When, in 1919, the old man brought young Eliot into the office, Harcourt and Brace began to be uneasy, for it seemed to indicate that Eliot and Roland would share the business after their father's death. They accordingly tackled the old man on the subject, demanding immediate partnerships in the firm, and some insurance against the imbecilities of Roland and Eliot *post mortem*. But instead of giving them what they so plainly deserved Holt adopted a lofty attitude, and let them understand that they were still only employes and would remain so.

The upshot was that they withdrew, and, along with a pedagogue named Will D. Howe, organized the firm of Harcourt, Brace & Howe. Their principal backer, I believe, was Joel T. Spingarn, but they also had others, and could have had yet others, for they were very well regarded in the trade. Their new firm was an immediate success, and as it went up the old firm of Henry Holt & Company went down. By the time the old man died in 1926, at the age of eighty-six, Roland (who died himself in 1931) and Eliot had made a mess of the business, and the house is now (1942) only a minor factor in publishing.

Curiously enough, Harcourt, years later, was to make precisely the same mistake that old Holt had made. He had only one son, but that son, Hastings, was quite as bad as Roland and Eliot Holt, and when he was introduced into the business and began to take a more and more active hand in it the father's partner, Brace (Howe had meanwhile retired), and the principal employes were full of disquiet. In the end Hastings became so obnoxious that they joined in a demand on his father that he be sent away, and, when the father refused, set up what amounted to a revolt. Its consequence was that not only was the son forced out, but also the father, who retired on the pretense of illness. Thus history repeated itself almost literatim, and Alfred Harcourt, despite his intelligence, added one more stone to the massive pile of proof that human beings learn nothing by experience.

Men vs. the Man was a complete failure. Holt's royalty reports show that, down to July, 1911, he had sold but 326 copies, and down to October 25, 1917, but 552. Inasmuch as La Monte and I were to receive no royalties until 1,000 had been sold, our receipts from the book were precisely nothing. This was discouraging, certainly, and La Monte took it very badly, though the book at least got him into *Who's Who in America.* (I had got into the 1908–09 volume on the strength of my Shaw and Nietzsche books.) He continued his Socialist activities until the outbreak of World War I, when the decision of the German Socialists to support the Kaiser drove him out of the party. Ever thereafter, until he disappeared from *Who's Who* with the 1942–43 volume, he added to his autobiography: "Not identified with Socialist party since Aug., 1914." He withdrew into his ivory tower at New Canaan, and I heard nothing from him until 1923, when, under the date of August 22, he sent me a manuscript that had been rejected by the *Atlantic Monthly*, apparently hoping that I would take it for the *American Mercury*, the rumor of which had already got about. Or maybe he intended it for the *Smart Set:* his letter is not clear.

In any case I rejected it, and after that I did not hear from him again until 1925, when he tried me with another manuscript, which I likewise declined. Then another silence until January 22, 1928, when he sent me a long and surprising letter denouncing Marcel Proust and Wyndham Lewis for treating homosexuality as abnormal, and suggesting that I join in his denunciation. It was possible to interpret his letter as that of a normal man revolting against the current laboring of the subject, but it was also possible to see it as the protest of a homosexual, so I replied to it warily, and did not accept when, in May, 1928, he invited me to join him in entertaining Lewis in New York. Since then I have not heard from him. He became a town judge in New Canaan in 1933, but since 1937 has apparently been without occupation, and living on the means inherited from his rich father. He is now (1942) about seventy-five years old.

I took the failure of *Men vs. the Man* more philosophically than

La Monte, if only because my share in the writing of it helped me to sort out and organize my ideas, and so gave me a better command of my professional equipment. My basic point of view, of course, went back to my early teens, and has never changed in any essential during the half century since. Under the influence of my father, who was always the chief figure in his small world and hence inclined toward complacency, I emerged into sentience with an almost instinctive distrust of all schemes of revolution and reform. They were, to me, only signs and symptoms of a fundamental hallucination, to wit, the hallucination that human nature could be changed by passing statutes and preaching gospels—that natural law could be repealed by taking thought.

I do not recall a time when I ever departed from that conviction in the slightest, and it always amuses me when I am accused of being a fallen-away Liberal, for I was never anything even remotely resembling what passes for a Liberal in the United States, as the ensuing narrative will show. Even as a boy I never had any belief in religion, and even as a youth I never went through the Socialist green sickness that was then almost universal. I was against Bryan the moment I heard of him, and my interest in Roosevelt 1 was always born of delight in the mountebank, not of belief in the prophet. As I have recorded in *Newspaper Days*, my first adventures as a reporter convinced me that the uplift in all its branches was only buncombe. I was not, of course, a partisan of the economic royalists who then ran the Republic—on the contrary, I believed that most of them were thieves and that all of them were frauds—but it seemed to me that, at their worst, they were appreciably better than the Chaldeans and soothsayers who proposed to drive them out of power, if only because they were at least more or less competent at their nefarious business. Competence, indeed, was my chief admiration, then as now, and next to competence I put what is called being a good soldier— that is, not whining. For the rest, I inclined toward my father's Chinese doctrine that the first of positive duties was to keep one's engagements.

All these predispositions showed themselves in my first writings, and were visible in almost every line of my Shaw and Nietzsche books. But it took *Men vs. the Man* to set me to amassing logical support for them. La Monte, who knew all the Socialist clichés, was really a formidable opponent, and I had to do some hard digging in order to meet him effectively. That digging clarified and crystallized my ideas, and by the time our correspondence was at an end I was sure of myself, and ready to take on all comers. In fact, I was ready to take on something on the order of leadership in the long war against utopianism that was getting under way, for I was a sassy fellow, and thus willing to state brazenly doctrines that most other Americans of my general habits of thought held *in petto*, and were too timid to utter. This sassiness was noted by some of the reviewers of *Men vs. the Man*, and even though the book was a failure it got a lot of useful attention for me, and gave me the beginnings of an audience.

That audience was gradually widened by my *Smart Set* articles; in fact, it had begun to widen before *Men vs. the Man* was published. Though there was an occasional bitter caveat by proponents of the old order, my following among the younger critics of the time went on increasing, for I led them in a battle against false gods and false values that they knew to be salutary and necessary. Typical of them was Willard Huntington Wright, then the very youthful literary editor of the Los Angeles *Times*, and later to become, at my nomination, editor of the *Smart Set*. Wright's eager support was a useful acquisition, but he was, after all, a follower rather than a collaborator, and I think I was much more bucked up by the overtures of Percival Pollard. Pollard was the first man of the 90's, forgetting the depressing Charles Henry Meltzer, that I came into contact with, and I esteemed him not only because of his own competence as a critic, but also because of his close association with men that I admired even more—for example, James Huneker. We had our first exchanges in 1906, and remained on good terms until his death in Baltimore at the end of 1911. There were many things on which we did not see eye to eye, but in general our positions were substantially the same, and I was delighted to join him in his denunciation of the extraordinarily puerile official criticism of the time.

The differences between Pollard and myself were vastly less numerous and important than our agreements. He was one of a small group of violent enthusiasts for Ambrose Bierce, and made various efforts to recruit me for it, but without success, for though I had a relish for Bierce's epigrams, I thought his short stories rather artificial, and his critical writing—especially his insistence on what he chose to regard as "pure" English—as decidedly second-rate.

CHAPTER III

THE ADVENT OF John Adams Thayer as publisher of the *Smart Set* was destined to have profound effects upon my fortunes, but I did not, of course, know it at the time. Simultaneously the departure of F. W. Splint left him without an editor, but he made shift, during his first months, to get along with a jury rig manned by Norman Boyer, who had been Splint's assistant, and Mark Lee Luther. Luther had written a number of novels and was a very pleasant fellow, but he had had no editorial experience, and put in all his time in the office doggedly reading manuscripts—at least 99% of which were hopeless.

Boyer was almost as unproductive. So far as I can recall, the only idea he ever had in his life was the idea of making me book reviewer for the magazine. He seemed, indeed, to be in a sort of daze, and when, on my visits to New York, Thayer called an editorial council he never had anything to offer. He had a small automobile—still a novelty in those days—and spent most of his evenings, as I learned from his talk, roving the suburbs of New York on his way to and from dances. He was, I believe, a graduate of the Johns Hopkins, and he continued an ardent fraternity man. Nathan and I often drew him out on the subject of the dances he attended, for we could imagine no more dismal way of spending an evening, but he had no sense of humor, and never suspected that we were poking fun at him.

Boyer's lethargy, and the incompetence of Luther, soon made Thayer uneasy, and he began to take an active hand in the editorship of the magazine. His first device for bucking it up was to engage Herbert Kaufman to write a monthly article for it. This Kaufman, a Washingtonian born in 1878, was then in high repute among advertising men, and had also a large popular following, almost comparable to that of Dr. Frank Crane. He wrote sonorous platitudes in prose and verse, and was looked upon as a wizard by his customers. Unhappily, he was obviously out of place in a magazine supposed to be sophisticated, but poor Thayer admired him and so hung on to him. Even Luther and Boyer, as dull as they were, writhed under his balderdash, but they were too feeble in spirit to face the matter out with Thayer.

Thayer's second device in aid of the languishing *Smart Set* was to urge me to do more writing for it. He had seen specimens of my "Free Lance" column in the Baltimore *Evening Sun* and liked them, so he proposed that I undertake something of the sort for the magazine. This, of course, was an impossibility, for the virtue of the "Free Lance" was its immediate timeliness, and in a monthly that timeliness would be impossible. But Thayer kept on pressing me, and early in 1912 I succumbed.

My first extra-review contribution, however, was not the new department, but a two-page article on the New York horse-show, printed in January 1912 under the title of "Horsetales." Thayer insisted on me coming to New York to see the show, and I recall going up in the late afternoon, dressing on the train, and then returning to Baltimore by sleeper. He had taken a box at the show, and was himself arrayed in his best party clothes. I had lately bought a new silk hat, and I remember over all these years how vastly he admired it.

The first appearance of the new department was in April, 1912, and it bore the title of "Pertinent and Impertinent." It was signed Owen Hatteras—a *nom de plume* that was to appear in the *Smart Set* scores of times during the ensuing twelve years. Just how I came to hit on it I forget, but I recall vaguely that it was somehow suggested by the Captain Kettle stories of C. J. Cutcliffe Hyne. Thayer, who was always niggardly with money, promised me $50 for each installment of "Pertinent and Impertinent," which was what I was still getting for my book article, but when, in May, 1912, exigencies of make-up reduced my space to two pages the check that reached me was for but $12.50. This seemed unfair to me, and I responded by reducing the amount of material I sent in. After May, in fact, I ceased to send in any at all, and the department disappeared from the magazine until April, 1913, when it was revived as a collaboration, with Wright and George Jean Nathan also contributing to it.

Meanwhile, Thayer was making heavy weather of it with Luther and Boyer, and began proposing to me that I take over the editorship of the magazine. This, in its way, was flattering, but I was hardly tempted, for on the one hand I was firmly resolved to stay on living in Baltimore, and on the other hand I had no confidence in Thayer. I managed to put him off during the early part of 1912, but by the spring he was in a really desperate frame of mind, and I saw that the only way to get rid of him was to find him another editor. My thoughts naturally turned to Wright, whose book reviews for the Los Angeles *Times* followed my own line almost exactly, and who seemed to be an intelligent and up-and-coming fellow. I had met him a little while before on one of his trips east, for he was not only literary editor of the *Times* but also in charge of its book advertising. Sounding him out on the subject, I found that he was very eager to come to New York, so I suggested to Thayer that he be invited to make the trip for inspection. The result was that he was hired. This was in November of 1912 and he lasted hardly more than a year.

He was, in many ways, an excellent editor, and greatly improved the magazine. But he was extravagant in his expenditures and liked to flout the Comstocks, so he kept the niggardly, timorous and puritanical Thayer in a considerable sweat. Both of them belabored me with their grievances, and late in 1913 I advised them to part as soon as possible and call it a day. This was done early in 1914 and Thayer once more tried to induce me to become editor myself. When I refused again he went on with Luther and Boyer, and presently, when Luther threw in the sponge, with Boyer alone. This was his unhappy situation when World War I came down upon him, and he got into a panic and lost the magazine.

Before Wright became editor I had expounded to him my scheme for a series of character sketches of American cities, each to be done by someone on the ground, and he was greatly taken by it. It started off with my "Good Old Baltimore," in May, 1913, and Wright's contribution was "Los Angeles, the Chemically Pure." This was before the great days of the movies had begun, but Los Angeles was already attracting the retired farmers of the Cow States, and in consequence it swarmed with reformers and evangelists of all sorts. Wright had been brought up in the town and knew it well, and his description of its imbecilities was done with magnificent malice. The article was denounced furiously by the Los Angeles newspapers, and made a great sensation all along the Pacific coast.

Wright was eager, of course, to get me into the magazine as often as possible, and I was very willing to write for him, for his ideas and mine were much alike. A series of articles that I had long projected, on the character, notions, faiths, ideals and follies of the typical American, was begun in June, 1913, and continued in July, August, September and October, and in February, 1914, and my plan and hope was to go on with it until I had a book, but for some reason that I forget I abandoned it, and most of the material that I had accumulated for it went into other books—notably A Book of Prefaces, Notes on Democracy, and the six Prejudices. Wright liked my "Beeriad," published in April, 1913, so much that it suggested to him a cooperative book on the night life of the principal European cities, and at his suggestion I wrote "At Large in London" for it. This was published in the Smart Set for June, 1913, under the nom de plume of George Weems Peregoy. Meanwhile, Wright himself wrote a chapter on Vienna and the better part of one on London, and Nathan wrote chapters on Paris and Berlin.

The result was Europe After 8.15, which was brought out in 1914, just before the beginning of World War I. My contributions were "The Beeriad," with its title changed to "Munich," and the first and last parts of the London chapter. I also contributed "Seeing the World" (which appeared in the Smart Set for November, 1913) as the preface, with its title changed to "Preface in the Socratic Manner." The book, overtaken by the war, which destroyed the Europe it described, was a complete failure. So far as I can recall, Wright, Nathan and I never received a cent from it. Wright went abroad to gather material for it, and in some way or other induced the stingy Thayer to pay his expenses. I well remember Thayer's bitter complaint that Wright's two chapters for it, printed in the Smart Set, cost $400 apiece.

He was also upset by the cost of the dummy for the weekly that Wright, Nathan and I projected. The yearning to operate a weekly was common to all newspaper men of our generation and even Thayer, as a former printer, showed some sign of it. Thus it was easy for Wright, who led in the enterprise, to get a hearing from him for the idea that a brisk weekly in the Smart Set manner would have a better chance of success than the magazine itself. He went no further than showing a mild interest, but Wright, believing that the sight of an actual dummy might fetch him, proceeded at once to put one together. It had blue covers and the name of the newcomer was to be the *Blue Weekly*. Wright wrote a sort of salutatory announcing that it was to be violently against virtually everything that the right-thinking Americans of the time regarded as sacred, from Christianity to democracy, and Nathan and I threw in some notes and squibs to the same general effect.

All this alarmed the conventional Thayer, and he refused to proceed. Wright thereupon decided that he should be punished for his doubts, and accordingly sent him the bill for the dummy, which amounted, as I recall it, to about $65. Thayer paid the bill, but only under bitter protest, and his dudgeon unquestionably entered into his decision to get rid of Wright. Rather curiously, he did not lay any of the blame on Nathan and me: all his ire was heaped upon Wright. But what mainly moved him to change editors was Wright's frequent choice of fiction that was too high in flavor for the taste of the time. Only a small part of it was actually salacious, as salacity was then understood; most of it was simply shocking in other ways—for example, a gruesome story called "Bachelor Embalmerus," by one Barry Benefield, a young fictioneer in whom Wright had great hopes, but who soon blew up. Thayer, who was a prude even before he was a skinflint, objected to such stuff, so he and Wright were often at odds. In the autumn of 1913, largely through my intercession, they agreed to bury the hatchet, but less than two months later they were rowing again, and early in 1914 Wright cleared out.

After Wright departed Thayer was fool enough to let it be known that the magazine was to be sterilized, and the results were disastrous. The net sales in the heyday of Wright, in 1913, had sometimes gone about 50,000 a month, and even in January, 1914 there were 48,496. But in February they dropped to 46,571, in March to 40,333, and in May to 35,549, and when war began to threaten they went below 30,000.

Wright's editorship was profitable to me while it lasted, for he not only induced Thayer to raise my honorarium for the monthly book article from $50 to $65 and then to $100; he also bought a good deal of other stuff from me, so that my income from the magazine, which had been $962.50 in 1912, increased to $1747.65 in 1913. This lifted my total income for 1913, including an allowance of $100 for review books, to $4656.48, which was no mean revenue for a bachelor in those days.

In the days before the war my *Smart Set* reviews got steadily increasing notice, and it came to be a sort of common assumption that

I was the chief fugleman of a new criticism, principally aimed at overturning the old American idols. Already in December, 1912, *Current Literature*, the *Time* of the era, was speaking of me as "a distinguished Baltimore Nietzschean," and more often than not my ideas were assimilated with those of Nietzsche, and his with mine, sometimes to my considerable embarrassment. My reviews began to be quoted in publishers' advertising and on the slip-covers of books, and I was often besought to write blurbs (always in vain) or to sit on committees (usually so).

But in April, 1914, I succumbed to an invitation from Doubleday, Page & Company to join Booth Tarkington and Walter Prichard Eaton in a committee formed to whoop up Joseph Conrad. This scheme, I expect, was hatched by Alfred Knopf, who was then working for Doubleday, but I am not sure. Tarkington drew up a manifesto and I must have signed it, but I do not recall any of the other proceedings of the committee, save that when Tarkington asked Woodrow Wilson to say something good about Conrad, Wilson replied that he had never read him. He was certainly not alone in those days, for it was some years later before Conrad began to be accepted as an author really worth reading.

In 1913 and thereafter my miscellaneous articles got quite as much notice as my book reviews—for instance, the American series, which began in the *Smart Set* in June, 1913. Sometimes the reaction was friendly, but quite as often it was hostile. The two articles I did for the *Atlantic Monthly* in 1914—"Newspaper Morals" in March and "The Mailed Fist and Its Prophet" in November—were generally condemned. Ralph Pulitzer, who had succeeded his father as head of the New York *World* in 1911 and was to wreck it in the years to come, demanded that Sedgwick give him space in the *Atlantic* to answer me, and his six-page counterblast was printed in June, 1914. I took no notice of it, for I had already begun to believe that it was vain to engage in defensive operations. Anyone who felt aggrieved was free, so far as I was concerned, to revile me all he pleased; the one thing I asked was liberty to expose and expound my own ideas. When World War I started Nietzsche became one of the chief bugaboos of the English, and hence of all right-thinking Americans, and I was denounced sharply for spreading his wicked ideas. Rather curiously the intensely pro-English New York *Tribune*—of all papers!—went to my rescue after the appearance of my *Atlantic* article.

Sedgwick liked it himself and wrote to me on September 10 that it was "brilliantly phrased and as extravagantly immoral as I had hoped." On October 8 he wrote suggesting another article on newspapers, and I seem to have replied that I'd prefer to discuss the war, for on October 13 he said: "A paper from you on the war, and there would not be one stone of the *Atlantic* left upon another." But when in January, 1915, he stopped off in Baltimore to see me, he seems to have changed his mind, for I proceeded with it. It was delayed by my efforts to reduce my weight, which involved going on the water-wagon and following a strict diet, and so made work almost impossible. But when I finished the diet (with a net loss of 17 pounds) I fell to work, and by May the article was in his hands. On May 18 he wrote to me:

> I am writhing and twisting inside. Your reprehensible paper is damnably effective. No pro-German onslaught I have seen compares with it, and had it come to me before the *Lusitania* tragedy, I should have felt no scruple about it. Now, however, it is within the bounds of possibility that we shall have war with Germany before this paper can be printed, and, of course, I have no desire to foment treason. I am, therefore, going to ask you to let me keep the manuscript a few days longer to see what will come. If affairs quiet down, I should like to use the paper; but I should like to ask whether you will allow me to print it under some caption which will act as a literary shock-absorber. For instance, why not call it "A Disciple of Nietzsche," or—but you would not like that—"The German Speaks." What I want is to notify the reader what he is in for and not ambush him.

I had no objection, but Sedgwick's fears continued, and on June 24 he wrote to me that he had decided finally that the article was too dangerous for the *Atlantic*. "Let me say in my own defense," he said, "that it is not often that I am so irresolute. I really hated to lose your paper, which is as stinging a piece of journalism as I have seen in twelve months." He added that he had sent a copy of it to "Herr [Owen] Wister [a violent Anglophile], who had inwardly digested it with profit." What became of it I do not know; no copy of it survives in my files. I am even uncertain about its contents, but it must have been a loud and gaudy onslaught on Wilson for his bogus neutrality.

I had told Sedgwick about my project for a character study of the American, and he had read the chapters that had appeared in the

Smart Set. He now asked me to let him have the remaining ones for the *Atlantic*, but, as I have recorded, I soon dropped the book, and it was never resumed. What I had written, however, did not go to waste. One of the *Smart Set* articles, "The American: His Language" (August, 1913), afterward made the nucleus of *The American Language*; another, "The American: His New Puritanism" (February, 1914), paved the way for *A Book of Prefaces*, and others were to leave their marks on *Notes on Democracy* and *Treatise on Right and Wrong*.

THE NOSE-DIVE that the *Smart Set* had taken after the departure of Wright at the beginning of 1914 left Thayer in no condition, whether financial or psychological, to withstand the shock of World War I. How much he was losing, by the opening of the summer, I do not know, but it must have been a substantial sum every month, for he was behind in his payments for paper and other supplies, and showing rapidly increasing signs of nervousness. Every time I saw him he besought me to take the editorship, and when I declined he offered it to Nathan, but both of us, by this time, had become so firmly convinced that he was an incurable jackass that we wanted to have no truck with him. We were now getting $100 a month apiece for our regular articles, and the money they brought in was as welcome as the chances they provided for stirring up the animals, but we were both pretty sure that, if the *Smart Set* blew up, we could transfer them elsewhere, and probably at better pay.

MY OWN FINANCIAL SITUATION, for a couple of years past, had been very comfortable. I was getting $50 a week from the Baltimore *Evening Sun*, and knew that I could get more if I demanded it. I had entree to the *Atlantic Monthly* and other highly solvent magazines, and was beginning to cherish hope that, despite the failure of all my books, so far, to bring me in any revenue, I would be making money out of their successors soon or late. I had already, in fact, saved enough money to buy some bonds, and in 1913 they paid me $140 in interest.

As for Nathan, he was in general practice as a writer for the magazines, and doing very well. During one month in 1914 he had something on the order of twenty articles printed. Most of them were short and brought little, but the aggregate made him comfortable, and I recall him saying that he found it very easy to make $100 a week. His play reviews, like my book articles, had begun to attract some attention, and after 1915 he confined his writing pretty strictly to the theatre. One of his steady patrons, up to that time, was Pop Taylor, editor of the *Associated Sunday Magazines*, who once employed him to ghost a series of tall tales by William J. Burns, the detective. I had never met him before he joined the *Smart Set*, a month or two after my own advent, and at the start his articles rather repelled me, for they were written in an extremely labored and even tortured style. But in a little while, under the admonitions of Splint, he began to write more simply, and presently we were good friends, for his interests and mine, with respect to the magazine, were more or less identical. When I first knew him he was living in a small apartment at the Royalton, at 44 West 44th Street, with a young Austrian named Edward Wanner, who was engaged in the bentwood furniture business in New York. But Wanner soon disappeared, and after that Nathan moved to a large apartment in the Royalton and lived alone. He is still living there today (1945).

I went abroad in the spring of 1914 and so did Nathan, and we met in Paris, whither Wright had gone after Thayer had fired him. The three of us, along with two Baltimore friends of mine, had a gaudy time, but when we started homeward Nathan and I traveled in different ships. On the voyage he had a chance encounter with a stranger named Eltinge F. Warner, a graduate of Princeton who was in the magazine business, and out of that encounter flowed our joint operation of the *Smart Set* from the late summer of 1914 to the end of 1923. Warner and Nathan tell two stories of this meeting. Nathan says that while he was promenading the deck one morning he passed a man wearing an overcoat precisely like his own, and that the two stopped to compare the coats, and so became acquainted. Warner says that he recalls no similarity of overcoats; his recollection is that they met in the smokeroom. They had a few drinks together, shook hands at the pier, and neither expected to see the other again.

This must have been in July, 1914. Warner was then publisher of *Field & Stream*, a monthly devoted to outdoor sports, and his backer was Eugene F. Crowe, head of the Perkins-Goodwin Company, a rich firm of paper jobbers which supplied many magazines, including the *Smart Set*. Early in August he was summoned to Crowe's office and informed that an additional job was ready for him. The *Smart*

Set, it appeared, was in serious difficulties. It had been losing money for some time, and now the shock of the war, and especially the closing of the New York Stock Exchange on July 31, had reduced its owner, Thayer, to a state of panic bordering upon hysteria. Crowe, alarmed for the safety of his paper bill, proposed to take over the magazine, throw Thayer out, stall off the other creditors, and try to operate it. Thayer, he said, was willing to surrender it on those terms, but the question of operation presented difficulties. Warner had had some experience as circulation manager of *Pearson's* Magazine in his first days out of college, and had been managing *Field & Stream* successfully for a few years, but the *Smart Set*, which called itself "A Magazine of Cleverness" and had a reputation for extreme sophistication, was something else again. Crowe himself had nothing to offer about how it should be run: he was a business man pure and simple, and was chiefly concerned about recovering the debt due him and converting a bankrupt customer into a solvent one.

As for Warner, he was equally devoid of ideas: in fact, he had never so much as read an issue of the magazine, for he was a Philistine of the first chop and all his interests, private as well as business, were centered in *Field & Stream*. But he was disinclined to fail Crowe, who had backed him generously, so he agreed to take over the *Smart Set*—provided he could find a competent editor. But where? Who? Suddenly he recalled that the man he had met aboard ship was a member of the staff of the magazine, and after some difficulty, fetched up his name. Perhaps he would have someone to suggest. Approached, it turned out that he had no one, but in the course of the talk he made such an impression on Warner that Warner presently offered the editorship to *him*. Nathan had refused it under Thayer, as I had, but now he began to be tempted. He asked for a little while to think it over—and then called me up in Baltimore. He was willing, he told me, to give the venture a trial, but only on condition that I would agree to join him. I came to New York the next day and we discussed it at length. In the end I agreed to go along with him on two conditions. The first was that I should not be required to move to New York—that all my work should be done in Baltimore, and that Nathan himself should hold the fort at the New York office. The second was that he and I should have a third interest, between us, in the new company, and that we should pay nothing for that interest.

The first of these conditions Nathan agreed to readily enough, but when we tackled Warner he objected to the second. He and Crowe, he said, were willing to give Nathan and me a third of the magazine, but they thought we should make some sort of payment for our stock, if only a small token payment. These negotiations, beginning on Saturday, August 8, continued into Sunday. At first, as I recall it, Warner, obviously instructed by Crowe, wanted us to put up $750 apiece—ostensibly for only a part of our stock but actually to cover all of it. When we refused he began reducing the amount, and eventually came down to $150 cash. Nathan, by this time, was willing to agree, if only to get the parley over, but I took him outside and insisted that we must stand pat. It was not our business, I argued, to finance the magazine; we'd be doing quite enough for it if we lifted it out of its wallow and made it self-sustaining. Crowe should carry the whole financial burden.

In the end Nathan adopted that view also, and we presented our ultimatum to Warner. Unhappily, he could not give us a yes-or-no answer for he was, after all, only the agent of Crowe—and Crowe was somewhere in New England, on a honeymoon with his third wife. After long efforts, Warner found him by long-distance telephone, enjoying himself in some small-town hotel. Pulled away from the connubial couch, he protested that our proposal was an outrage upon every canon of sound business, but in the end he agreed to give it prayerful consideration, and a few days later came to terms. We were to pay nothing whatever for our allotment of 440 shares apiece, but we agreed severally, as a sop to Crowe's feelings, to take an option on 50 additional shares at $15, which worked out to $750 for each of us. For this option, which was to run for six months, we were to pay nothing, and we'd be under no obligation, of course, to take it up. When this arrangement was agreed to I returned to Baltimore. On Wednesday, August 12, Nathan telegraphed to me as follows:

Magazine ours. Assume control today. Important you come up soon. Papers to be signed. Need your decision. Eureka.

I made another trip to New York at the end of the week, and on Saturday, August 15, a contract was signed by Warner, by Nathan and me acting together, and by H. H. Stark as agent of the Perkins Goodwin Company, *i.e.*, Crowe. Crowe, as I was to learn later, never signed anything himself if he could help it. All his business, whether on behalf of the Perkins-Goodwin Company or on his own account, was carried on through lawyers and stooges. Stark, who was treasurer of the company, was one of these stooges. Thayer's control of the John Adams Thayer Corporation had been wrested from him by Crowe personally, acting by terror and hullabaloo, but in the contract the 2740 shares of Thayer stock were represented to be the property of Stark. Unhappily, there were some shares in other hands, beyond Thayer's reach, and there were also the bonds that the nefarious Colonel Mann had saddled on him, and both had to be taken into account in preparing the contract.

What the debt of the John Adams Thayer Corporation was at the time Crowe collared it I do not recall precisely, but my recollection is that it was about $24,000. The chief creditor was Crowe's own Perkins Goodwin Company, to which Thayer owed about $10,000 for paper. The other creditors were the printer, the ink man and various other such minor *Lieferanten*, and old Colonel Knox, the hat manufacturer, who was the owner of the Knox Building at 452 Fifth Avenue, on the southwest corner of 40th Street, in which the *Smart Set* had its offices. The building was small and the *Smart Set* offices occupied the whole of its fifth floor, with windows looking out upon the Public Library and up Fifth Avenue. The rent was $5,000 a year. Thayer was considerably in arrears, but to what extent I do not know.

Crowe proceeded against the other creditors with characteristic ruthlessness. On the threat of throwing the John Adams Thayer Corporation into bankruptcy, and so reducing the value of their claims to next to nothing (for it had no assets save its office furniture and its so-called good-will) he induced all of them either to give him receipts for the money due them or to sell him their claims at cut-throat discounts. How much they thus agreed to write off to profit and loss I do not know, but the total debt, including Crowe's own claim (which was not diminished a cent), but excluding the bond issue, was quickly brought down to about $12,000, which we gradually paid off in the course of the next few years. Thus Crowe, without losing a cent of his paper bill, got control of the magazine for nothing.

The John Adams Thayer Corporation survived only until December 15, 1914. Then its name was changed to the Smart Set Company, Inc., and the new name appeared on the flagstaff of the January,

1915, issue. The lease on the offices in the Knox Building had a couple of years to run, and we were very eager to get rid of it, for the rent was too high for us. Nathan and I were told off to tackle Colonel Knox on the subject, and he gave us a release at once, saying politely that he was eager to help two ambitious young men but actually glad to be rid of a tenant who had already rooked him. Warner then took very much smaller and cheaper quarters in a loft building at 456 Fourth Avenue, and the *Smart Set* and *Field & Stream* moved into them before the end of August. We stayed there until the early spring of 1915, when we moved to rather better offices at 221 Fourth Avenue. There we remained until a year later, when we moved into the new Printing Crafts Building at 8th Avenue and 34th Street.

Nathan and I put in the week-end of August 15 making a hurried but intensive investigation of the *Smart Set's* editorial affairs. We found that Luther and Boyer had accumulated a good many completely useless manuscripts, and that the editorial staff was heavy with minor functionaries. One girl, for example, devoted her whole time to keeping a record of manuscripts received. We abolished her office and her record instantly, for the only discernible function of the latter was to provide evidence for authors who wrote in to complain that their manuscripts had not been returned and to make claims for damages. Thereafter we kept no record whatsoever of manuscripts received from volunteers. We read them as expeditiously as possible, and returned those that were rejected, but when an author alleged that one he had sent in had not been accounted for we simply denied that it had ever been received.

We kept one editorial secretary, a grotesque Brooklyn Jewess named Stella Golde, but fired all the rest. Luther and Boyer, shocked by Thayer's desertion and knowing that they would have no place in the future conduct of the business, remained away from the office, and we had to explore it without their aid. They had already sent the October issue to press, but we were confronted by the need of putting November together before September 15, so we gave all their accumulated manuscripts a rapid and hopeful reading. What we found was mainly rubbish—the heaped up bad buys of years, some of them going back to Wright's days as editor and even before. We sent some of them to an agent for resale, set aside others for use later on, and threw away the rest.

Meanwhile, Warner was making a similar examination of the business office, which had been in charge, under Thayer, of an old fellow named Voorhees. Voorhees was on the job, and gave useful assistance, but there was no place for him in the new organization, and he was notified. A few days later he came rushing in with the appalling news that Boyer had committed suicide. Boyer had been getting $60 a week from Thayer, and had concluded, it appeared, that it would be impossible to find another job as good. This was probably not true, for he had had enough experience to make him more or less useful in any other magazine office, and plenty of jobs were offering at the time, but such was his belief, and so he made away with himself. Nathan and I were naturally upset, but we could see no reason for blaming ourselves for his death: we were simply trying to make the best of a bad situation, and if anyone was responsible for Boyer's loss of his post it was not us, but Thayer. In any case, he was a foolish fellow, and, as I have recorded, had always impressed us as only half alive. His suicide got only a few lines in the newspapers and was quickly forgotten.

Voorhees soon vanished, and Luther was already gone, and I never saw either of them again. Years later Luther wrote to me and we exchanged a few letters, but they have been lost, and I do not recall ever seeing him. He is now (1942) seventy-two years old and at last account was living in Los Angeles. He has published nothing since 1934. I also received occasional letters from Thayer, but we met only once or twice during the twenty-two years to his death in 1936, and then only casually. He gradually went downhill, and, as I have said, died broke. But he was full of schemes to the end.

Nathan and I reached a working arrangement in short order, and it remained unchanged so long as we edited the *Smart Set* together. By this arrangement he was in charge of the office, and was responsible for the copy-reading of manuscripts and the make-up of the magazine. My job was to obtain those manuscripts. This I did from Baltimore, though I came to New York every third or fourth week for what, at least in theory, was an editorial consultation. All manuscripts that were sent to the office were shipped to me in Baltimore, and there I read them. If I found one that I liked I marked it "Yes" and sent it to Nathan. If he, too, liked it, he had it set up at once, and the author's check went out at the end of the week. If, on the contrary, he dissented, the manuscript was returned to the author at once. We agreed that we should never waste any time on the discussion of manuscripts. The "No" of either of us was final.

This scheme worked perfectly for ten years. There was never any excuse for debates and quarrels, for the editor who had voted "Yes" was forbidden by our understanding to demand reasons from the editor who voted "No." When a manuscript reached Nathan before I had seen it (as sometimes happened when an author he knew sent it in), and he liked it, he marked it "Yes" and sent it to me, and the scheme worked in reverse order. If I liked it I added my "Yes" and returned it to him for copy-reading. If I dissented I mailed it back to the author at once. This plan was so simple and so practicable that we often wondered that no other editors had ever thought of it. In all the other magazine offices that we were acquainted with, save those operated as despotisms by solo editors, a vast amount of time and energy was wasted upon editorial debates.

We also wondered why none of our colleagues had hit on the device of staying away from their offices. Nathan came to the *Smart Set* office every morning, but remained, on the average day, no more than an hour, and I was present only at intervals of two or three weeks, and then only for a few days. Thus we escaped the burden of listening to the countless visitors who infest such places—mainly bad authors hoping to sell their manuscripts, not on the merits thereof but by selling talk. Virtually all our business was done by mail, and it was thus possible for us to do it at our own convenience, and with expedition. On my trips to and from New York I read more manuscripts than the average editor could get through in ten times the time in his office. It was not until long afterward that I discovered that a number of English magazine editors had practiced keeping clear of their offices before we thought of it. So far as I know, no American editor has ever done likewise to this day.

Nathan, at our first palaver on ways and means, made an excellent suggestion that I was glad to agree to. It was that we insist that all contributors to the magazine be paid promptly. We could not hope to pay them well—in fact, our standard rate was only two cents a word, and we went below it much oftener than we went above it—but there was no reason why current editorial vouchers should not be cleared off at the end of every week, and this was done throughout our ten years. It was Nathan's belief, born of his wide experience with magazines, that most authors would make no protest against meagre pay if they got their money without delay, and I agreed fully, and it turned out to be a fact. So far as I can recall, only one contributor ever gave us any trouble and he was Frank Harris. He demanded five cents a word and got it—for "How I Discovered Bernard Shaw," printed in July, 1915—but he got it only once.

As strange as it may seem, most of the other magazines of the time, even the rich ones, kept their authors waiting interminably. That was especially true of the Hearst magazines. They paid good prices, but sometimes a contributor had to wait months for his money. The only salient exception, at the time we took over the *Smart Set*, was the *Saturday Evening Post*. Its editor, George Horace Lorimer, not only paid much higher prices for manuscripts than had ever been paid before; he also paid off once a week, so that the average author had to wait but three days for his money. As a result Lorimer got first whack at virtually all the better fiction of the time, and I was soon to notice, reading manuscripts, that a large proportion of the short stories that reached me were of 7,000 or 8,000 words—the length he preferred with his small type, but one that was too long for all other magazines. The fictioneers all aimed at him, and what the rest of us got from them was only what he had rejected. After August, 1914, the *Smart Set* paid as promptly as the *Saturday Evening Post*, and so we had second choice, despite our low pay—and first choice of most of the stuff that was obviously outside the field of the *Post*.

We also made a great point of reporting promptly on all manuscripts. Those that were sent to the office were shipped to me by express twice a week, and I usually went through them on the day I received them. Those that were rejected were on their way back to their authors before midnight. When I marked a manuscript "Yes" and Nathan agreed an acceptance was sent out just as promptly. Whenever I was taken out of service by newspaper work or by a holiday, he managed the whole business in the same expeditious way, and vice versa. We thus got a good name in the trade, and received frequent manuscripts from authors who might have looked for much more money elsewhere.

DURING OUR FIRST FEW WEEKS, unhappily, very few likely manuscripts came into the office, for the flow of them is always low in summer; moreover, the news had got about that the *Smart Set* was in difficulties, and most writers of any experience had become wary of it. We sent out a hurry call to all the authors that we knew—not a very large company in those days—but their response was not too eager, nor, in most cases, very prompt. All these things, taken together, left a large gap, and as the dead-line approached Nathan and I became alarmed, and began throwing in compositions of our own, some of them done posthaste but most of them rescued from our files of unsold manuscripts.

My own contributions to that first number, in addition to my book article, included a sixteen-page short story, "The Barbarous Bradley," signed by my name; a page of buffoonery entitled "Ah, che la morte!," signed Raoul della Torre; a sheaf of epigrams signed W. L. D. Bell; two others without signature; a score more for the bottoms of the pages; some selections from the current platitudinarians; a skit called "The Rewards of Science," signed R. B. McLoughlin; "A Litany for Week-days," signed Owen Hatteras; a three-pager called "Thoughts on Mortality," signed William Fink; a poem, "The Old Trails," signed Harriet Morgan; another, "The Ballade of Cockaigne," signed Herbert Winslow Archer; a third, "Song," signed Janet Jefferson; a couple of squibs signed Marie de Verdi and George Weeks Peregoy; and another three-pager entitled "Epithalamium" and signed Francis Clegg Thompson. Altogether, I filled nearly forty of the one hundred and fifty-six pages of that first number—and all for the $100 that was my pay for my book articles: the rest was thrown in *ad majorem Dei gloriam*.

Nathan contributed only his article on the theatre and a ten-page burlesque headed D.S.W., but that was not because he was unwilling to do his share, but simply because his share consisted mainly in organizing and running the office. Our names did not appear on the flagstaff as editors, though Nathan's was there as secretary of the John Adams Thayer Corporation. But in our second issue, for December, 1914, the *Smart Set's* trade-mark, "A Magazine of Cleverness," was removed from between the two long s's on the contents page, and "Edited by George Jean Nathan and H. L. Mencken" was substituted. Along the top of the cover of our first issue ran the warning: "Beware of Cheap Imitations of the *Smart Set*"—a sort of first notice to Colonel Mann and his bastard son, Clayton. Under the cover drawing by James Montgomery Flagg, in black and red on the *Smart Set's* traditional cadet gray, was another legend: "No Stories of the Eternal Triangle! Nothing Less Than a Quadrangle!!" But though "A

Magazine of Cleverness" disappeared from the contents page it survived on the covers until November, 1919, mainly because we could never think of anything better.

Inside, we experimented with many other mottoes—among them, "The magazine that's read in the Pullman"; "A magazine of caviare for the general"; "No cheap nastiness; no cheap sentimentality; no cheap anything"; "A magazine for the modish"; "Something lively; something striking; something new"; "A polite magazine for polite people"; "We don't buy names; we make them"; "An amusing magazine for amusing people"; "The vintage magazine"; "The magazine of the drawing-room"; "Primus inter omnes"; "The magazine that other magazine editors read"; "A magazine with many imitators and no imitations"; "Angels could do no more"; "Belles lettres et comme humeur"; "Allegro con brio"; "Alla modern"; "The magazine for the civilized minority" and "The aristocrat among magazines"—but we did not like any of them, and only the last was ever used with any frequency. In 1918 we abandoned mottoes altogether. The cadet gray of the cover survived, but the formalized drawing showing an elegant gentleman bowing to a curtsying lady soon yielded to more conventional designs, and in 1915 we changed it from black and red to full color.

Our first issue was unquestionably a sorry one, but it was at least better than the other literary magazines of November, 1914, and so it got a hospitable reception, and the circulation that had been falling so ominously during Thayer's last year did not fall any further. Our next issue was measurably better, for its show-piece was a one-act play by Theodore Dreiser, "The Blue Sphere" by title, and there were excellent contributions by writers dead and forgotten today, but who had some skill, and, what was quite as important, who fitted neatly into the scheme of things that Nathan and I had in mind for the Smart Set—a scheme based principally on a civilized skepticism, but also demanding adroit and colorful writing. We had no room for quacks, but neither did we have any room for the solemn enemies of quacks: our aim was to have at the illusions and delusions of the time with good humor, and also with some show of good manners. Thus we were delighted when stuff meeting that prescription began to flow in, and our second number pleased us a great deal better than our first.

Nathan's contributions consisted only of his review of the new plays and a skit entitled "And a Little Child Shall Lead Them," signed Millicent Dobbs Kenny. But he had so much to do in the office during those first months that I did not expect him to supply much copy. There was not only the feverish business of writing to authors about the new plans of the magazine, and trying to induce the good ones to send in suitable manuscripts; there was also the need to listen to Warner, to his circulation manager, to his advertising manager, to his head bookkeeper (Arthur W. Sutton), and to various minor functionaries. Half the time of a magazine editor, like half the time of a newspaper editor, must be devoted to giving audience to such persons. They have, by journalistic custom, free access to him, and they make frequent use of it, to the damage of his proper work and the ruin of his temper.

Warner, a brisk and vain fellow, had a great many ideas, and though most of them were bad they had to be listened to. When I was in New York I took my share of the punishment, but Nathan had it day in and day out. To be sure, we had insisted from the start that Warner should have no actual voice in the editorial conduct of the magazine, but nevertheless he was free to say his say about anything that had a bearing on circulation, and he did constantly. More, he retailed suggestions that came in from Crowe, who never read anything but harbored a literary critic at his fireside in the person of the mother of his new third wife. In the course of time Nathan and I learned how to deal with Crowe, and even Warner was put (never, alas, permanently) in his place, but during the first few months we were hard beset, and especially Nathan.

My book article in our second issue not only sneered at the bestsellers; it also had some tart things to say about the first novel of a newcomer who was destined to do first-rate work. He was Joseph Hergesheimer and his book was *The Lay Anthony*. The idea in it, I said, was "magnificently ironical" and in the hands of a Joseph Conrad, a Hermann Sudermann or a Max Beerbohm it might have made a first-rate story, but "this Mr. Hergesheimer, alas, is not up to it. . . . In brief, the book is botched in the writing; the author's planning is far ahead of his execution. But let us at least remember him as one who made a creditable attempt. Novels with genuine ideas in them are not so common that we can afford to sniff at them."

Hergesheimer, at that time, was quite unknown, and until his novel reached me from its publisher, Mitchell Kennerley, I had not heard of him. My notice of his book naturally upset him somewhat, and on November 20, 1914, he sent me a long letter of protest in which there was some indignation, but there was also a civilized spirit, so I replied very politely. He and I continued in friendly correspondence, and after a while we met, took to each other instantly, and established an intimacy that has continued to this day.

CHAPTER IV

THE NEWS that Nathan and I had taken over the editorship of the *Smart Set* did not get much space in the newspapers, but such comment as there was was friendly. A notice in the Boston *Advertiser* of October 21, 1914, was perhaps typical: "They are not members of Anthony Comstock's League for the Emasculation of Literature, and the *Smart Set* under their management may be expected to divest itself of the fig leaf which it recently donned with so much éclat." This, of course, was a crack at Thayer's imbecile efforts, after he had fired Wright, to convince the nobility and gentry that the magazine had become respectable. On November 29, with our first two numbers out, the New Orleans *Picayune* said: "After a wobbly period, during which the *Smart Set* did not seem certain whether to remain naughtily clever, or to become prim, proper and dull, it has decided upon the former course. It has now, as editors, two very witty men, so the prevailing tone of humor in the December number is not surprising."

Such notices began to multiply after the beginning of 1915, and there was a gradual recovery of circulation. How many copies we sold of our first issue I can't find from my meagre records, but they show that our net sales for January, 1915, were 35,285, and in July were 45,637. This was a pleasant reversal of the process that had been going on during the last months of Thayer. His circulation in January, 1914, had been 48,496, but by July it was 30,636. These declines involved heavy losses, for the *Smart Set's* sales were almost wholly from news-stands, and the American News Company had the privilege of returning all unsold copies. There was a constant temptation to try to foster sales by increasing the print-order, which meant distribution on more stands, and to that temptation Thayer constantly succumbed. In order to sell 46,571 copies in February, 1914, he printed 74,000. The 27,429 that were returned not only had to be sold for next to nothing as waste paper; he also had to pay the News Company a couple of cents a copy for returning them.

Warner, who was usually prudent in business, cut down the print-order as soon as he took charge of the *Smart Set,* and in January, 1915, it was but 60,000. The next month he lifted it a thousand, but thereafter he proceeded very cautiously, urged on by Nathan and me, and by April, 1915, our returns were down to 22,514. In July they were actually down to 18,136. Unhappily, this record-breaking low inspired Warner to optimism, and despite my and Nathan's protests he lifted the print-order again. The result was that the returns leaped to 25,379 in September, and, after a recession in October and November, to the staggering total of 37,772 in December.

I received a report on the returns every week. I had no desire to see it, but Warner insisted on sending it to me. When they were high I was affected very unpleasantly—and when, for the week of December 16, 1915, an extraordinary accumulation lifted them to 11,044, I had something almost approaching a fit. The monthly reports on checks received from the News Company made more agreeable reading. That for January, 1915, was $5,155.55, but in February there was a drop to $4,240.32. After that, however, they increased slowly, and the check for August was for $6,777.43. This rise in revenues from circulation was encouraging, but it was not accompanied by any increase in receipts from advertising, and so the treasury continued to be pretty bare.

Inasmuch as Nathan and I were to get no salaries as editors until the floating debt of $12,000 had been paid off and a surplus of $6,000 had been accumulated, it began to be evident that we were in for a long wait. At the end of the year, however, as the expiration date of the option that we had acquired on August 15, 1914, approached, and Crowe began to hint that we ought to take it up, we saw a chance to agitate for salaries at once, and after some resistance Crowe succumbed. The first payment, of $250 apiece, was made on March 13, 1915, but it was entered as for January. This was at the rate of $50 a week, and simultaneously Warner began to be paid $100 a week. These salaries continued through 1915, though with certain arrearages, and as a result my receipts from the magazine for the year amounted to $3,690 and my total income was $6,218.46.

Nathan and I put a great deal of hard work into the magazine during our first year as its editors. Down to October 23, 1915, I continued to carry on my daily "Free Lance" column in the Baltimore *Evening Sun*, and it was thus impossible for me to make any considerable stays in New York, or to get there very often. But Nathan and I managed our collaboration well enough by mail, reinforced by an occasional palaver at the week-end. My newspaper work had made me known as pro-German, and as Wilson gradually carried the United States toward participation in the war there were frequent denunciations of me in the pro-English papers. Nathan was inclined the same way as I was, but his sentiments had attracted less notice. Warner, on the other hand, was a violent partisan of England. In view of this situation Nathan and I decided that the only way out was to avoid all discussion of the war in the *Smart Set*, and even all mention of it. As strange as it may seem, we actually carried out that resolution to the letter. All the other American magazines, after 1914, were full of war fustian, but not the *Smart Set*. We kept diligently to what we conceived to be our proper business, which was the printing of the best stuff in prose or verse that we could find—civilized in point of view, written with some sense of style, and devoid of all moral purpose.

During our first year we unearthed a large number of authors who could meet our specifications—some of them at home and the rest abroad. The majority, after we had got out of them all that was useful to our purposes, disappeared into the more conventional magazines, or were snared by the emerging movies, or vanished altogether—for example, Austin Adams, G. Vere Tyler (a very amiable fat woman, skillful at doing saucy novelettes), Maurice Joy, Gertrude Macaulay (a Canadian), Paul Hervey Fox, Scammon Lockwood, Phyllis Bottome, Viola Burhans, Lee Pape and Marshall Hugh Irish. But there were also some who showed sounder and more durable stuff—for example, Lord Dunsany, James Joyce, Ezra Pound, Edgar Lee Masters, and Zoë Akins, Sherwood Anderson and Ben Hecht. In this rounding up of new authors I naturally had more of a hand than Nathan, if only because my book reviews had made me known as a friend of young aspirants, and many of them, hearing that I was now an editor, wrote to me. I was polite to all of them, and though the overwhelming majority of the manuscripts that poured in on me were hopeless, there were more than occasional glints of better stuff.

Also, I received frequent tips from other authors, appreciative readers and literary friends. It was Schaff[1] who directed my attention to Lord Dunsany, and Ezra Pound who interested me in Joyce. I wrote to Dunsany immediately after Nathan and I took over in August, 1914, asking him for anything he had, whether plays, sketches or verse. He replied cordially from Dunsany Castle, County Meath, Ireland, under date of September 27, saying that he knew the *Smart Set* and would be delighted to contribute, and enclosing two short sketches and a play. After that Dunsany was in almost every number, and sometimes two or three times, for we had early decided that the old magazine rule against showing the same name in a given table of contents more than once was only rubbish. Early in 1915 Dunsany joined his regiment, the Inniskilling Fusiliers, and on April 25, 1916, was wounded. But while he was in the field I kept in communication with him through his wife, and by May 13 he was back in Ireland and sending me more manuscripts. We kept on printing him so long as he continued to write, and were always very glad to do so, for his stuff was full of strange fancy and often showed really magnificent writing. Nathan and I always believed that his "The Assignation," with which we opened our March, 1915, issue, was one of the best things we ever published. After the war Dunsany made a visit to the United States and we met him in New York. He was an immensely tall fellow of the guardsman type, wearing a moth-eaten fur overcoat and exhibiting a really remarkable appetite. I remember that he expressed a desire one day to try American oysters, and that when we took him to a chophouse he got down thirty-six large ones.

Pound wrote to me about Joyce from England on February 2, 1915, and gave me his address in Trieste, where he was making a miserable living as a teacher of languages. Pound hailed from Idaho and was the son of a minor functionary in the Philadelphia Mint, but he had been living in England for some years before this, and was a leading figure in a New Poetry Movement then under way there. I had reviewed his "Provença" at some length in the *Smart Set* for April, 1911, and his translations of Guido Cavalcanti in the issue for April, 1913, and had suggested to Boyer and then to Wright that he be invited to contribute to the magazine. He was a diligent propagandist for other authors of his general way of thinking, and the first letter from him

1. Harrison Hale Schaff, a partner in the Boston publishing firm of Luce & Company, which issued Mencken's books on Shaw and Nietzsche.

that I can recover is one to Boyer dated February 26, 1914, recommending Richard Aldington.

I got into direct communication with him during 1914, and when Nathan and I took over the *Smart Set* his suggestions became frequent. When he wrote to me about Joyce I asked him to send me some of Joyce's short stories, and this he did at once. They were "The Boarding-House" and "A Little Cloud." Nathan and I liked them so much that we decided to print both of them in the next number to be made up, which was that for May, 1915. They were the first things by Joyce ever to appear in an American magazine. Meanwhile, on March 3, I wrote to Joyce himself at the Trieste address given to me by Pound, and on April 20 received a reply from him. It was dated c/o Gioacchino Veneziani, Murano, Venice, Italy, March 23, 1915, and was as follows:

> I am in receipt of your kind letter of 3 instant. Although I am still living at the address to which your letter was sent and although it reached me quite safely I think it better to reply to you from the above address and beg you to send your reply also the same way. You will easily understand the reason of this rather complicated arrangement.
>
> I am pleased to hear that two of my stories appeared in your magazine. Could you perhaps send me a copy of the number in which they appeared? I thank you also for your good opinion of my book. I gather from your letter that an American edition of *Dubliners* has been published. Will you please tell me what is the name of the American publisher? I have been cut off from communication with my English publisher since the outbreak of the war and know nothing of this new edition.
>
> A novel of mine, *A Portrait of the Artist As a Young Man*, has been running in the *Egoist* (London). The last installment will be published, I think, next month. If you wish to consider it Mr. Pound or the editor of the *Egoist* will be able to give you what information you need. I hope it will come out in book form before the end of the year: but possibly its serial publication in the way you suggest might be arranged so as to be completed before the date of the English publication in book form.
>
> I thank you also for your kind offer to help me to an American audience and hope you will forgive me for asking you to send me

the information I desire as it is rather difficult for me for the moment to obtain it in the usual way.

Joyce lingered on at Zurich until the end of the war, working on *Ulysses*. Then he moved to Paris, where he lived until his death on January 13, 1941. I passed through Zurich myself early in 1917, on my way from Berlin to Paris and home, but I was so busy that I could not look him up. I received occasional letters and postcards from him, but he was in bad health and sent in no more manuscripts for the *Smart Set*. On March 16, 1917, he wrote to me about a story by one Geller, apparently a Zuricher of his acquaintance, who had mailed it to me some time before, but I never got it. After June, 1917, I heard no more from him, and I never met him.

When *Ulysses* was nearing completion, in 1920 or thereabout, Pound sent several chapters from it to the *Little Review* in New York, of which he was the London correspondent, and they were printed therein. It is unlikely that I'd have printed them if he had sent them to me, for *Ulysses* seemed to me to be deliberately mystifying and mainly puerile, and I have never been able to get over a suspicion that Joyce concocted it as a kind of vengeful hoax. Writing excellent stuff in conventional patterns, he had got very little attention and was so hard up that he had to go on teaching languages to keep alive, but from the moment he took to the literary bizarreries of Greenwich Village and began to push them further than Greenwich Village (or even the Left Bank) had ever dared, he was a made man. All the addicts to *Schwärmerie* began whooping him up as the St. John of a new and revolutionary gospel, and a rich woman in Paris staked him to $3,000 a year. The rest of his life, though it was badgered by frequent ill health and increasing blindness, was comfortable and even luxurious compared to the days of *Dubliners* and *A Portrait of the Artist*. His later work was hollow stuff, as was that of his imitators.

Pound made his own first appearance in the *Smart Set* under its new editors in the issue for July, 1915, with a seventeen-line poem called "Love Song to Eunoe." Nathan did not like his stuff, and so gave the piece a bad place in the make-up and omitted the author's name from the table of contents. We printed a second poem, "Albatre," in August, 1915, and a third, "Her Little Black Slippers," in October, but if he appeared at all afterward it was not often. From 1916 onward he had an American outlet in the *Little Review*. It not only printed his own fulminations in prose and verse in almost every issue; it also printed the other authors he favored. My correspondence with him continued until after the beginning of World War II, though I never met him save once, and that was in New York in May, 1939. He was then on one of his rare visits to the United States. Soon afterward he sailed for Italy, where he had been living off and on since 1921. There his headquarters were at Rapallo, on the Ligurian coast near Genoa, where one of his neighbors was Max Beerbohm.

I recall how amazed I was when he gave me a description of Beerbohm's house. I naturally supposed that the aloof and elegant Max lived in a secluded villa comparable to Horace's in the Sabine Hills, but Pound said no. It was actually, he told me, only an apartment above a garage on the main highway along the Mediterranean shore, and the noise of the motor-cars roaring along the road was so deafening that the front rooms were virtually uninhabitable. In this inferno Max and his wife, the former Florence Kahn, one of the early Ibsen actresses, lived and had their being. He wrote little, and that little was only a nostalgic reminiscence of the great days of *Zuleika Dobson*. Listening to Pound, I could not help recalling my immense delight when *Zuleika* came out in 1911. I read it one day on the train, bound for New York, and when I got back to Baltimore wrote a review of it that was really exultant. And now poor Max, at sixty-eight, was cooped in misery above the Italian garage. When news came, in 1941, that he had been knighted, I could only laugh again.

POUND WAS BORN in 1885. He looked older than his age, for he wore a somewhat unkempt beard, and suggested both a French artist of the days of "La Vie de Bohème" and a seedy German professor. His first letters to me, in 1914 and 1915, were mainly given over to trying to sell me, not his own stuff, but that of others. He was the center in London of a literary coterie that promoted a new and somewhat vague evangel called Vorticism and included some authors of talent, but also a great many quacks, and it was always difficult for him to distinguish between the one and the other. On February 3, 1915, he was writing to me in behalf of "the last intelligent man I've found, a young American, T. S. Eliot." But at other times he recommended newcomers of less capacity, though some of them fitted more or less neatly into the scheme of the *Smart Set*. His letters, as we became better acquainted, were increasingly frank and rowdy, and not only the state of literature was discussed in them, but also the state of the world in general, with particular reference to its insane politics.

Some of his letters were not dated, and others were dated inaccurately—for example, one dated February 21, 1914, which nevertheless began: "My researches lead me to conclude that nearly everybody stopped writing at the outbreak of the war." Obviously this was written in 1915. After he moved to Italy, in 1925 or thereabout, he took to dating his letters according to the Fascist chronology—so many years after the march on Rome. Nathan did not like his stuff, and so we printed much less of it than I'd have liked to. On April 18, 1915, he sent me the first part of a long satirical poem which I voted for, but which Nathan killed by his "No." I was out of sympathy with most of Pound's literary notions, and especially his Vorticism nonsense, but it was plain from the start that we had many ideas and prejudices in common—for example, our violent dissent from the orthodox American credo and from that moral order of the world on which it was so innocently based.

Our correspondence fell off in the late summer of 1915, but was revived a year later, when Pound wrote to me applauding my brutal flogging of one William T. Ellis, a Philadelphia moralist, in the *Smart Set* for August, 1916. "The man," he said, "lived in our village and was one of the plagues of my youth." In September I asked him to sign the protest against the suppression of Dreiser's The "*Genius*", and he not only did so, but made propaganda for Dreiser in London. "Still," he wrote on September 27, 1916, "the country, U.S.A. is hopeless and may as well go to hell its own way. . . . Seriously, I think what is wrong is simply that neither England nor America have had an Eighteenth Century deist. . . . Religion is the root of all evil, or damn near all." I must have been looking forward, even at that early date, to a better magazine than the *Smart Set*, for in the same letter Pound protested that "*better* is such a bloody ambiguous word." He added, however: "Perhaps the new magazine is intended to be a bit more 'weighty,' in which case you are on the right road."

On August 21, 1917, Pound wrote to me at length about the award of the Henry Howland Memorial Prize by Yale University to Rupert Brooke—a grotesque example of the Anglomania of the time. Brooke, in fact, was already dead, and moreover, the Howland Prize had been set up to encourage American poets. "My attitude," wrote

Pound, "is NOT personal, it is inconceivable that these things should come my way, even were all the poets of England dead, or living, or whatever is THE disqualification."

Pound must have been very hard up in those days, for his revenue from the *Little Review* was meagre (if indeed he got any revenue from it at all), his poetry had only a limited market, and his frequent ventures into magazine publishing in London—for example, with *Blast*, the organ of the Vorticist hallucination—were always financial failures. He was a man of great talent, but he could never throw off his American heritage, and so he wasted two-thirds of his time and energy upon various schemes of reform, some of them purely literary but the rest largely political. He could never understand my complete lack of messianic passion, and often had at me in a violent and even abusive fashion, seeking to awake in me a yearning to improve the world. This, of course, was quite impossible, for I was simply born without the capacity for it. But despite this sharp difference in our views, we remained on friendly terms, and he whooped up my books in London and looked to me to do the same for his in the United States.

On February 2, 1921, he wrote to me from St. Raphael on the Côte d'Azur, hinting that life in France was not as comfortable as he had expected, and saying, "I think I shall get naturalized in Luxembourg." After that our correspondence lagged until 1925, by which time he was established at Rapallo, where he has been ever since. When the *American Mercury* got under way I naturally asked him to contribute to it, but the few things he sent in were all wild propaganda for his increasingly extravagant ideas, and I never printed any of them. I urged him to come back to the United States, if only for the purpose of getting his bearings, but he refused. "As fer seein the rebooblik," he wrote from Rapallo on March 24, 1926, "gees, bo, do you think the rebooblik is contained in its geographic borders? Nah, the damn thing oozes out; some of its prime specimens, carrying all the aroma of the great open drifts, flop up almost on one's door step (fortunately this one is five flights up)." He could never understand my refusal to get into a lather about the imbecilities of the time.

Pound obviously resented his failure to get into the *American Mercury*, and showed it from time to time. Indeed, his letters after 1927 exhibited an increasing hostility. "I have long thought," he wrote to me idiotically on December 9, 1932—he made the year XI—"that you shd NOT confine yr reading to the mss submitted to yr somewhat elderly magazine: such confination ineluctably tending to convince you that ALL the intelligence of the western slice is confined to one head in Cathedral st. Read only such mss as arrive every second Thursday before eleven a.m. and look about you a bit more."

I heard no more from him until toward the end of 1936. He had meanwhile abandoned all creative writing, and was apparently devoting his time and energy to the brummagem crusades that I had refused to be interested in. Under date of November 3, Anno XIV (*i.e.*, 1936), he sent me a long and abusive letter, arguing that my refusal was wicked and deserved the condemnation of all forward-looking men. My first impulse, of course, was to make no reply to this outburst, for its springs lay only too plainly in Pound's own growing frustrations, but on reflection I decided that an old acquaintance deserved some sort of answer, and so I sent him the following November 28:

> You made your great mistake when you abandoned the poetry business, and set up shop as a wizard in general practice. You wrote, in your day, some very good verse, and I had the pleasure, along with other literary buzzards, of calling attention to it at the time. But when you fell into the hands of those London log-rollers, and began to wander through pink fogs with them, all your native common sense oozed out of you, and you set up a caterwauling for all sorts of brummagem Utopias, at first in the aesthetic region only but later in the regions of political and aesthetic baloney. Thus a competent poet was spoiled to make a tin-horn politician.

On February 10, 1941, the newspapers reported that Pound was making short-wave broadcasts in defense of Mussolini. I never listened in on them, but apparently they were extremely critical of Roosevelt's frantic efforts to horn into the war, for such notice as they got was hostile. In June, 1942, when the Swedish ship *Drottningholm* arrived in New York with Americans repatriated from Italy, one of them—name not given—told the reporters that Pound had tried to get passage in the ship, but had been refused an American visa. This, of course, seemed highly improbable. He was a very curious fellow— immensely talented but with an unmistakable flavor of the mountebank. Despite his rantings against academic and other orthodox rumble-bumble he accepted the *Dial* Prize in 1927 and permitted Hamilton College, his *alma mater*, to give him an honorary doctorate during his visit home in 1939. He was married in 1914 to Dorothy Shakespear, an English poetess, and by 1929 they had a three-year-old son laboring under the name of Omar Shakespear Pound. The newspapers reported at the time that Pound wanted to make the poor child's first name Homer, but that his wife objected to the combination of Homer and Shakespear, and they compromised on Omar.

MASTERS, in those days, was almost unknown as an author. He had printed four books—all of them, I believe, at his own expense—and written two unproduced plays, but none of these things had made any stir. In so far as he had been heard of at all, it was as a radical lawyer in Chicago—the partner of Clarence S. Darrow and an eager follower of Bryan in 1896, 1900 and 1908. But he had now withdrawn in disgust from the law firm of Darrow, Masters and Wilson, and was practicing in Chicago on his own, and his radical fires were beginning to cool. In his later years he was to be extremely critical of both Darrow and Bryan.

I heard no more from or of Masters until July 26, 1914, when Dreiser wrote to me that he was contributing some remarkable poems to the St. Louis *Mirror*, published by William Marion Reedy. I wrote to him at once, asking if there were any in the series that the *Smart Set* could make a bid for, and he replied by sending me some clippings from the *Mirror*, and seven poems in manuscripts. On the latter he wrote, "All of them have been published, but I haven't them in print, so send you these." One of the clippings was a metrical poem headed "The Spooniad"; the rest of the pieces were extracts from *The Spoon River Anthology*. I saw at once, of course, that the stuff was first-rate, and made an immediate effort to get the rest of it for the *Smart Set*, but I was too late, for Masters had promised it to Reedy. Thus Nathan and I, in our first year, missed a chance to offer a really distinguished contribution to American letters. Moreover, it was precisely the sort of thing we wanted to print, in point of view, in manner and even in form.

The Spoon River Anthology, of course, was an immense success, and I was eager to get some possible additions to it for the *Smart Set*. But Masters wrote no more in that mood until some years later; during 1915 he busied himself with poems of a far different sort. Some of these he sent to me—among them, a ballad called "The Death of Sir Launcelot." I wrote to Dreiser on April 22, 1915, that I had bought the latter "three months ago" and we printed it in our issue for September. I liked it very much, but Nathan was far from enthusiastic about it, and when another poem, "The City," came in in September, he seems to have voted against it. That was the end of Masters in the *Smart Set*. But I reviewed his successive books in my monthly book articles—*Songs and Satires* in February, 1917, *Toward the Gulf* in June, 1918, and *Starved Rock* in June, 1920. The first-named, it seemed to me, was decidedly inferior to *The Spoon River Anthology*, and I said so. But I added: "One thing, at least, may be said of Mr. Masters: he is never downright dull. An eager and agile intelligence is visible in everything he does; if he is not actually a first-rate poet he is at all events a sharp-witted and interesting man." I was also dubious about "Starved Rock," but repeated my compliments to the author. "What stands behind his verse and quasi-verse," I said, "is the charm of an unusual personality. The plain truth about him is that he is a better man than most of our poets—more intelligent, more thoughtful, more civilized. . . . In *The Spoon River Anthology* he introduced the truth into American poetry—a savoury and memorable novelty, but probably highly deleterious to the poetry." Of "Starved Rock" itself I said only that there was "enough good in the bad to give me pause." My correspondence with Masters fell off after 1915, and was not resumed until 1924, when he began contributing to the *American Mercury*. He had then moved to New York, and since then I have seen him very often, and exchanged letters with him almost constantly.

I FIRST HEARD of Zoë Akins when Mitchell Kennerley published her play, *Papa*, in the autumn of 1914. It made something of a sensation, and no wonder, for it was a piece of fantastic irony of a sort quite new to the American theatre, and indeed not common in any theatre. There was, to be sure, preciosity in it, but it was preciosity that was calculated, adroit and highly effective. Unhappily, the piece did not reach the stage until 1919, for, as I said in my review in the February, 1915, *Smart Set*, it was "almost as immoral, and hence almost as reprehensible," by the prissy standards still current in the war days, as *A Country Wife* or *The Old Bachelor*. "It is not realistic, and it is not intended to be realistic. It lies upon the border-line between reality and fantasy; it is half amazingly plausible and half deliciously impossible. Who else in America has done such work? I can recall no one. This Miss Akins blazes a new path among us, and does it with extraordinary assurance and success."

Zoë was then living in St. Louis, where her father, a Republican politician, was the postmaster. She was born in a small town called Humansville, Missouri, in 1886, and had got her start on Reedy's *Mirror*. Reedy never paid anything for contributions, and most of the things he printed in the *Mirror* (including his own articles) were trash, but now and then he flushed a newcomer of talent. His greatest discovery, of course, was Edgar Lee Masters, but Zoë Akins certainly deserves to be remembered among the few others of any size. After her removal to New York she let it be known that he had not only discovered her but also seduced her, and in the course of time she pushed this catastrophe back in time until in the end he was depicted as undoing her when she was but sixteen years old. This, if true, put it in 1902, when Reedy himself was forty.

Zoë, I believe, did not begin to contribute to the *Mirror* until some years afterward. She was in the *Century*, *Harper's*, the *Forum* and *Hampton's* by 1910, always with poems, and her first book, *Interpretations*, consisting of a gathering of them, was brought out in 1911. She informed me in her letter of June 2, 1915, that she was then writing a weekly article on American poetry for the *Mirror*, and had done fifteen to date. She also reported that she was managing a series of matinee theatrical performances in St. Louis (some of them in a restaurant), and that she had lately appropriated Dunsany's "The Tents of the Arabs" (*Smart Set*, March, 1915) without asking either Dunsany's permission or ours.

She was busy in those days with plays both long and short, and full of hopes of getting them to the stage, but she was doomed to a long series of disappointments, and there were times when she was very low in mind. "I'm afraid," she wrote to me on September 19, 1915, "I'm an early failure. The audiences repel me, and the work itself is never right. That's why I've published nothing and sent you nothing." A little while later she wrote: "Saint Louis is a terrible place for one who ought to work. And I'm a suburbanite and it takes me 8 times as long as it should to get any place or do anything. I want to get rich on plays! And go to live in the exact center of the world— N.Y., I suppose. . . . No, I don't think I care much where I live."

CHAPTER V

UNFORTUNATELY, the rise in circulation that had begun with our first number, that of November, 1914, did not continue uninterruptedly, and after we reached a peak of 45,637 in July, 1915, there began a disquieting bogging down. My incomplete records do not show the precise figures for the months after July, but I recall that we had got below 40,000 by the end of the year. This recession, of course, was mainly due to World War I, which had got us the magazine but also brought us a heap of troubles. During the first months the war seemed far away to most Americans, but after the sinking of the *Lusitania* it came closer and closer, and by the summer of 1915 all rational persons began to anticipate— and I so predicted in my "Free Lance" department in the Baltimore *Evening Sun*—that Wilson would take the United States into it soon or late. Thus interest in the sort of stuff we were printing in the *Smart Set* began to be a good deal less than eager, and by the end of 1915 we were thrown for support upon a relatively small group of antinomians, none of them actively interested in the salvation of humanity. They were, of course, the very persons we were aiming at, and we had a lot of fun catering to them, but there were not enough of them to make the *Smart Set* the big success that appeared to be ahead during our first months.

The effects of the war upon advertising were even more deleterious. Warner, when we took over the magazine, was hopeful of at least doubling its advertising revenue before the end of 1914, but that hope was not borne out, for instead of a rise in linage there was actually a fall. He was a very energetic fellow and put in a great deal of hard work on his job, but all in vain. Not only did the growing war paralysis baffle him; he also was brought up by various other obstacles. One of the worst was a rule set up by the principal advertising agencies to the effect that they would not put their clients' money into all-fiction magazines. The *Smart Set* was certainly not all-fiction, but they insisted upon so classifying it, and poor Warner was never able to dissuade them. He thereupon transferred his efforts to their clients, and not infrequently he called me in for help. Once, I remember, I tackled the Resinol Chemical Company in Baltimore, and another time the Pompeian Olive Oil Corporation, both times without result.

Such advertising as was offered early in 1915 was mainly of an undesirable sort—announcements of bust-developers, send-no-money ads, and so on. Warner's advertising manager on *Field & Stream*, Irving T. Myers, was supposed to help in canvassing for the *Smart Set*, but his services turned out to be worth nothing. Most of the advertising in *Field & Stream* was small stuff that was rounded up by mail solicitations, and in consequence Myers, who was a complete idiot, spent a large part of his time writing long letters to *Smart Set* prospects who never replied. Indeed, his imbecile efforts did much more harm than good, and I think he was largely responsible for the loss of some old *Smart Set* standbys—for example, the Gorham Company, Ridgway's Tea and Mme. Helena Rubinstein. He was a stupid prissy fellow who lived in a dull suburb and was a churchgoer, and the sort of stuff that Nathan and I put into the magazine shocked him painfully. He never made any editorial suggestions—I assume that, imbecile though he was, he was yet bright enough to figure out what would have happened if he had—but I recall that he told me one day that he was moving into a new house in his Lonesomehurst and asked me to contribute my review copies of books toward its furnishing. Such persons are hard to bear.

Thus our prospects were not too bright at the beginning of 1915, despite the good showing that we were making editorially, and it began to be evident that it would be a long while before we had paid off the floating debt of $12,000, accumulated a surplus of $6,000, and so become eligible for salaries under the agreement of August 15, 1914. This made Nathan and me unhappy, for we were putting a great deal of hard work into the magazine, and if we were not actually meeting the terms of the agreement we were nevertheless keeping it afloat, rehabilitating its good-will, and preparing the way for its possible restoration to solvency when times improved.

Our chance to cash in on this service ahead of time came in February, 1915, when the option that we had taken on additional *Smart Set* stock was about to expire. By the terms of that option, each of us acquired a right to buy fifty more shares from Crowe at $15 apiece, making a total of $750. Crowe was eager for us to take it up, but when he approached us we told him it was quite impossible for us to do so. Working for the *Smart Set* without salary, we were forced, we said, to resort to other writing in order to sustain ourselves, and our onerous *Smart Set* duties left us so little time for it that it barely supported us. It was therefore out of the question, we said, for us to put up the immense sum of $750 apiece for additional shares of stock in a magazine that was barely making a living, and would probably never get beyond that mark unless it was stimulated with fresh capital.

The inference was, of course, that Crowe himself ought to supply that new capital. He had, as a result of his seizure of the magazine from Thayer, converted a bankrupt paper customer into one that paid its bills promptly, and in addition he had acquired a large stock ownership in a property that promised, on some remote and hypothetical day, to be very profitable. That promise, we pointed out politely, was mainly if not wholly due to our own diligent labor and singular editorial skill. We were doing all the work, and he was simply taking what amounted to a free ride. If the magazine ever began to make money on a large scale he would get much more of it than we would, and meanwhile we were slaving away in his interest.

These considerations we laid before Crowe in tones not unmixed with moral indignation. We were, we said, willing and even eager to take up the additional stock, but our financial condition was so precarious that it would be impossible unless the terms of the agreement of August 15, 1914, were modified sufficiently to put us on salary at once. As strange as it may seem Crowe consented to this, though he must have been well aware that our account of our financial state was considerably exaggerated. It may be that we convinced him that it was unjust to ask us to go on working for nothing, and that he thus let down his usual truculent business guard, and it may be that the amount involved seemed so small to him—he was making enormous profits out of paper and wood-pulp as a result of the war shortages— that he did not care.

All I can record is that, to our considerable surprise, he agreed after a merely formal resistance to put us on the *Smart Set* payroll at $50 a week apiece if we would agree in our turn to take up our options, and that the deal was so made. It went into effect on March 13, when each of us received a check for $250 for his January salary. Our February salaries, $200 apiece, followed in April, our March and April salaries, $400, in May, and the rest in due course. By December 16, when our November salaries were paid, we had received $2,400 each, in addition to $100 a month for our review articles. On March 20, more than a month after the expiration of the option, which was for six months from August 15, 1914, we took it up. In payment for the fifty shares of stock I gave Crowe five notes for $150 each, and Nathan did the same. These notes were for two, four, six, eight and ten months. By the time the last of them was paid off, on January 20, 1916, each of us had received $2,600 in salary—$2,400 for 1915 and $200 on January 13, 1916. This was plainly a very good trade for the $750 which taking up the notes cost us. Also, we had the shares of additional stock, which made each of us the owner of four hundred ninety shares apiece.

Its value, unhappily, was uncertain, and in all probability it was less than the $15 a share that we had paid for the additional fifty. There was no assurance that the *Smart Set* would earn enough to continue paying our salaries, nor was it likely that Crowe would be willing to make good its probable deficits. As a matter of fact, it began to fall behind toward the end of 1916, and when the year closed it owed Nathan and me our salaries for October, November and December, and in 1917 it paid me but $1,400 on that account. Warner was uneasy from the time the payment of salaries began, fearing that Crowe would soon repent, and so were we. It was already plain that the *Smart Set*, barring some act of God, would never make us rich, but Nathan and I were eager to go on with it, for it gave us a free forum and got us a great deal of useful notice, and Warner was eager too, for having it along with *Field & Stream* enhanced his prestige as a publisher, and also tended to reduce his *Field & Stream* overhead.

We talked the situation over at length, and came to the conclusion that the way out lay in starting still another magazine—one that would be reasonably sure to bring in a substantial revenue. The pulp magazines were just then beginning to make money and we resolved to set up one. If the broken-down hacks who were operating some of the most successful of them could get away with it, then why not such smart fellows as Warner, Nathan and me? Crowe, consulted, agreed to go along with us. Even if our proposed pulp failed, the net loss would not be large, and if it made a hit with the morons it would not only pay well in itself, but also further reduce the overhead on the *Smart Set* and *Field & Stream*. The result was the *Parisienne Monthly Magazine*, the first issue of which was dated July, 1915.

Nathan and I had a grand time planning it. We did not, of course, take it seriously, but looked to it to give us some pleasant sport as well as some needful revenue. Its name was chosen in order to turn to advantage the Francophilia prevailing at the time, but we could not resist the temptation to make it a sort of burlesque of the French *Kultur*. We established the rule that all the stories in it should have a French, or at all events, a European setting, and when a likely one came in that was laid elsewhere we did not hesitate to change its scene. This revision Nathan usually undertook, for, as in the case of the *Smart Set*, he was charged with the copy-reading and the make-up. We sent out word to all the hacks of the time that manuscripts were needed, and they piled in at once, and in large quantity. Like the manuscripts addressed to the *Smart Set*, they were shipped to me in Baltimore for reading, and when I found one that I liked I marked it "Yes" and returned it to Nathan. Those that I disapproved were sent back to their authors from Baltimore, and at once. If Nathan agreed with my "Yes" he put the manuscripts bearing it into type at once; if he disagreed it was returned to the author without notifying me.

The milieu of every story had to be that of high society. All their heroes had to be wealthy and, if possible, titled, and all their heroines beautiful. Our favorite setting was the French Riviera, which, though it had been paralyzed by the war, still seemed to the American booboisie to be the world capital of opulence and intrigue. We decided to illustrate the magazine, and accordingly called in a gang of third-rate artists and put them to work. They produced not only full-page illustrations, but also a large number of small line drawings for use at the bottoms of pages, and the best of these little pictures we used over and over again. The magazine had a cover in full colors, and was printed on news-print with a slightly greenish cast—as we explained, because green was grateful to the eyes. We organized a separate corporation to publish it, and gave the corporation the name of Les Boulevards Publishing Company. Warner was its president and treasurer, and Arthur W. Sutton, his bookkeeper, its secretary. Nathan and I, of course, did not appear on the flagstaff, and relatively few persons, even among our contributors, knew that we were running the magazine. In corresponding with authors we did not hesitate to sign the names of imaginary editors—chiefly suggesting Frenchmen. Not infrequently the same hack contributed three or four stories to the same issue, and sometimes they were printed under as many different pseudonyms, usually invented by Nathan.

He, Warner, Crowe and I put up the money needed to launch the newcomer, in equal amounts. It was, in fact, only a small sum, for we got credit for the paper from Crowe and for the printing from the printers of the *Smart Set*. How many copies of the first issue were printed I forget, but I think it was about 60,000. That first issue was almost a clean sell-out, and when the American News Company reported on it at the end of July we found that we had made a net profit of more than $1,000. Our manufacturing expense had been $3,045 and our editorial costs $405, with $38 added as the *Parisienne*'s share of the rent for the small offices then occupied by the *Smart Set* and *Field & Stream* at Fourth Avenue. Warner was so vastly encouraged that he immediately jumped the print-order to 100,000 copies a month, and by the end of 1915 we were beset by cruelly heavy returns, but the margin of profit was so large—the magazine sold at 15 cents—that we made money every month.

The success of the magazine made something of a sensation in the publishing circles of New York, and convinced Crowe that we were editors of a high degree of acumen. Unhappily, it also aroused the baser passions of old Colonel Mann's bastard son, Clayton, whose nefarious imitation of the *Smart Set*, *Snappy Stories* by name, now had a new and apparently formidable competitor. Clayton, a scoundrel if there ever was one, sought revenge by a characteristic device. That is, he had one of his agents complain to the New York Society for the Prevention of Vice that the *Parisienne* was obscene. This was either late in August or early in September, 1915. There was, of course, no truth in the allegation, for the magazine was actually innocuous to the point of banality, but the society in those days had a new chief snouter, John S. Sumner by name, and he was eager to get into the papers, so he decided to make a raid. In order to do so it was first necessary to prove a sale by some competent person at the publishing office, and Sumner accordingly sent one of his goons to 331 Fourth Avenue.

As luck had it, this goon encountered Myers, the advertising manager. On the representation that he was thinking of taking some advertising he had no difficulty in inducing the stupid Myers to hand him a copy. An hour later a cop arrived with warrants for Myers and Warner, and they had to give bail for their appearance in Special Sessions to answer a charge of printing, publishing and circulating an indecent magazine. This business, of course, was upsetting to Nathan and me, for though we were not directly involved, we feared the effect on Warner, who had social ambitions and would be in a panic if the newspapers made a scandal of the proceedings. We were also uneasy about Crowe, who would undoubtedly run amuck if his connection with the *Parisienne* became known, no matter what the issue of the case.

Nathan called me up in Baltimore with the news as I was hard at work on a book article, and insisted that I come to New York at once. I arrived there on Saturday night, with the half-finished article in my pocket, and we put in the evening at our favorite drinking place, Rogers' chop-house at Sixth Avenue and 45th Street, discussing the situation. After we had decided on a plan of action Nathan suggested that I had better stay over until Monday, to take on Warner and Crowe.

The next day, Sunday, I decided to kill time by finishing my book article, but since I had brought no typewriter with me, I was forced to resort to dictation. To that end I telephoned to our office secretary, Miss Golde, at her home in Brooklyn, and she set out for the Webster Hotel in 45th Street, where I was staying. I had taken a parlor as well as a bedroom, and asked the clerk if there would be any objection to my working in it with Miss Golde. When he hemmed and hawed I assured him, which was a fact, that the lady was of such low pulchritude that he would be convinced, on seeing her, that I intended no malpractice with her. He was visibly shocked when she came in, not only by her squat figure and really startling lack of facial beauty, but also by her gaudy and preposterous Sunday clothes, but he insisted nevertheless that the door of the parlor must be kept open while I gave her my dictation, and during the process a bell-boy looked in several times. Poor Golde was in such a state of alarm that she could barely do her work. She had visions of Warner and Myers rotting among the scorpions and lizards on Blackwell's Island, for in those days the Comstocks were still very potent in New York, and usually won their cases.

But Nathan and I believed that they could be beaten, if not by hook then by crook, and when we sat down with Warner and Crowe on Monday morning we insisted that there be a vigorous defense. We could see nothing obscene in the passages that the Comstocks complained of, and we were convinced that no judge or jury would ever decide against the magazine. We knew, however, that the Comstocks, who were quite unscrupulous, would probably propose that the case be settled with a plea of guilty and a light fine, and we devoted ourselves to convincing Warner that any such plea would hang over his head for the rest of his life. He agreed without much argument, and it was decided to employ a good lawyer and make a vigorous fight.

Myers was not consulted, for we were all out of conceit with him for his stupidity in succumbing to the Comstocks' agent: he should have suspected something was afoot when so mysterious and unlikely an advertising prospect tackled him. Indeed, Nathan and I could not help cackling when we reflected that the prissy Myers, who was not responsible for the magazine and probably never read it, was one of the accused, whereas its two editors were not so much as mentioned in the case. Even Warner, who had little sense of humor, saw the comedy there. Nathan and I, returning to Rogers' that night, tried to figure out the public effect in Myers' Christian suburb when he went on trial. He was, we knew, in a condition of terror bordering on hysteria, and we frankly enjoyed it. Indeed, we were not far from hoping that he would be convicted, though it was plain that if he were the magazine would be seriously damaged. He annoyed us by his smug imbecility, and we resented his grotesque ineptitudes as advertising manager of the *Smart Set*.

Crowe had a large and complicated legal staff and on it were lawyers fit for all sorts of jobs, from the most dignified to the most dubious. One of them was a Jew whose name I forget: all I recall is that part of his business was to supervise Crowe's veneries and see that he was not blackmailed. This Jew advised that the defense be intrusted to some high-toned jurisconsult of his own race, and named Joseph M. Proskauer. Proskauer, he explained, was not only a smart lawyer of impeccable reputation, but also stood very high in Tammany Hall and had been frequently mentioned for a Supreme Court judgeship. He would make a powerful impression upon the lowly shysters who sat as judges in Special Sessions, and his prestige would also serve to influence the newspapers in their handling of the case.

So he was duly hired, and after a little delay the case was called for trial. I remember that Nathan and I went down to the court with Warner in his open car, and that the day was so cold that we were very uncomfortable. On the way he told us that word had come from Proskauer, at the last minute, that one of the three judges had let it be known, through a runner, that his mind was full of doubts, and he thought that $500 might help him to resolve them in favor of the defendant. Nathan and I advised, of course, that the money be paid, for it seemed a cheap way out, and Warner agreed. When we got to court we tried to figure out which of the judges was the doubtful one, but had to give it up.

The evidence consisted merely in proving the purchase of the magazine from Myers and in handing up a copy for the judge's inspection, and the defense was confined to a motion for a demurrer, on the ground that no case had been made out, and an eloquent speech in support of it by Proskauer. I recall that he depicted Warner and Myers as faithful husbands, sincere patriots and business men of unsurpassed rectitude, and that Nathan and I could hardly keep from laughing. At the end of his remarks the three judges put their heads together, and presently announced that they had sustained the demurrer by a vote of two to one. The dissentient was a bellicose Irishman, but though he glared at the two culprits he did not say anything. We never found out which of the other judges got the $500, but I always suspected an Italian named John J. Freschi. Proskauer charged $1,000 for his services, and we considered the money well spent. He was really very high-toned, and, as Crowe's lawyer predicted, the newspapers treated him and the magazine politely.

Clayton's sinister scheme to undo us thus failed, but it left a sting behind, and for some time thereafter Warner was busy with schemes of revenge. They took, chiefly, the form of a plan to put the Comstocks on *Snappy Stories*, which actually printed a great deal of blue stuff, and was doing some damage to the *Smart Set*, which was sometimes confused with it. In it Clayton followed our make-up closely, with the addition of six pages of half-tone portraits of beauties of the time. He also made efforts to rope our authors, and now and then he succeeded. But most of all he imitated the *Smart Set* on his own covers, which brazenly showed the two long S's that were our trademark. Nathan and I were naturally against Warner's plan to have him raided, for we feared that if it were executed it might only bring down the Comstocks upon the *Smart Set*. But it was plain that something would have to be done to teach him a lesson, and during the spring of 1916 we hit upon a plan. It was to bring out a new pulp magazine that should do to *Snappy Stories* what *Snappy Stories* was doing to the *Smart Set*.

The result was *Saucy Stories*, the first issue of which was dated August, 1916. We had learned all the tricks of pulp magazine editing by this time, and the magazine we produced was really very nifty, considering its lowly aims. The two long S's were on the cover, and inside was a mass of much better stuff than Clayton had been printing in *Snappy Stories*. I included, before the year was out, work by all the best hack writers of the time, and also some by authors of a considerably better sort.

Both the *Parisienne* and *Saucy Stories*, in their first months, were such successes that it seemed to Nathan and me to be a rational idea to try to sell our shares in them to Warner and Crowe while the going was still good. It was, of course, some fun putting them together, at least at the start, but that fun quickly picked up the character of chore, and we began to be eager to get rid of it and devote our time to more pleasant if less profitable enterprises. I had quit my job on the Baltimore *Evening Sun* on September 1, 1915, mainly because I was convinced that it would soon be impossible for me to say my say with complete freedom, for Wilson was plainly trying to take the United States into war, and when he did so the howling of Anglomaniacs would be supplanted by that of professional patriots. I had resolved when I first began to merchant opinion in newspapers and magazines that I'd write precisely what I believed or nothing at all, and it was now manifest that it would be increasingly difficult to write what I believed. I could do it in my book reviews by ignoring the war as much as possible, and I could also do it, at all events to a reasonable extent, in the books that I had in mind, but it was already becoming impracticable in hotly controversial newspaper articles. After I abandoned my "Free Lance" column in the *Evening Sun* I continued to supply it with signed editorial page articles, but I gave but little attention to them, and knew that I would have to abandon them when Wilson got into the war. Thus I wrote less and less as 1916 wore on, and with less and less satisfaction.

During the summer I began to itch to see something of the war itself, and discussed plans to that end with Paul Patterson.[1] The *Sun-papers* were still making heavy weather of it, but he was willing to stake me to a moderate amount, and we soon came to a tentative agreement. Inasmuch as it was my plan to have a look from the German side, it was manifest that haste was necessary, for the Germans would naturally bar Americans after Wilson had horned in, and might do it at any moment on the score of his bitter partisanship for England. Unhappily, it was impossible to ask Nathan to take on the whole burden of running the *Smart Set*, the *Parisienne* and *Saucy Stories*, even for the few months that I proposed to be abroad, and so there was another and pressing reason for desiring to sell out the two latter. He offered to look after the *Smart Set* indefinitely, for it was uncertain just when I would return, and in case the United States entered the war while I was in Germany I might be detained there for the duration, but he bucked, and quite properly, at being saddled with the two pulps also. So we resolved to tackle Warner and Crowe, and I was told off for the job, for Nathan had conceived a favorable opinion of my bargaining capacity.

Warner, at the start, refused flatly to trade, for he believed that Nathan and I were necessary to both magazines, but I kept at him persistently, and by the middle of October, 1916, I had got him into a buying mood, and with him Crowe. I recall that our last palaver was held in a luxurious suite that he was occupying in the Ritz Hotel. He had taken it in order to work out an advertising bill that the Ritz owed to the *Smart Set*, but that fact did not diminish his voluptuous enjoyment of its luxuries. I spent the night with him and we carried on our negotiations while lying in elegant twin beds. He was still uneasy about the raid of the Comstocks on the *Parisienne*, and feared that it might be repeated, for the Comstocks were notoriously bad losers and well knew that there had been something dubious about the prompt acquittal of Warner and Myers. But I managed to reassure him, and he finally agreed to pay Nathan and me $20,000 for our two quarter-shares in the magazine.

The question of *Saucy Stories* presented even greater difficulties,

1. Paul Patterson, president and publisher of the *Sunpapers* of Baltimore.

for it was but a few months old, and though it was selling very well there was no telling what it would be doing a year hence, with new editors. In the end I offered to throw it in as an unknown quantity, and so the business was accomplished. The contract of sale was signed on October 24, 1916, and the money was paid a few days afterward. I was now free to proceed with my projected trip to the war, and began at once to make arrangements.

CHAPTER VI

O N MY RETURN from the war in the early part of 1917 I began to lose interest in the *Smart Set*, though I continued to edit it with Nathan, in a state of gradually augmenting reluctancy until the end of 1923. There were a number of reasons for my dissatisfaction. One was that it had begun to be evident that the magazine would never be much of a success, financially speaking, despite the fact that it got a good deal of notice, and had a distinct place in the national scene, and a following of very faithful, not to say fanatical readers. Another was that, though it gave me a chance to say my say with a very large degree of freedom, it offered me a rather narrow field, and I was eager to bulge into larger ones.

By the end of 1916 I had been writing its book reviews for more than eight years, and had pretty well expounded all the ideas I had to present regarding the nature of *belles lettres*, and the faults and virtues of the principal authors of the time. In my newspaper work I had written about life itself far more than about books, and though I managed to do so also to some extent in my reviews, they nevertheless kept me more or less hobbled. In the jottings signed William Drayham ("A Few Pages of Notes," January 15; "Four Notes," August, 1915), I revealed the way my mind was inclining, and in April, 1919, I was to open a forum for a wider range of ideas under the title of "Repetition Generale," but in 1917 I had not yet solved my problem, and so felt cribbed, cabined and confined.

Moreover, I was oppressed by the title of the *Smart Set*, which was plainly silly, and set up assumptions that it was difficult to overcome. More than once Nathan and I played with plans to change it, but when at last we resolved to execute one of them we were hauled up by the discovery that, under the terms of the mortgage behind the bonds held by Colonel Mann, it could not be done without his permission. We knew enough of him by that time to be sure that he would not agree without undertaking some sort of compensatory blackmail, so we resigned ourselves to the discomforts and embarrassments of editing what to many persons seemed to be a society journal, with touches of the scandalous inherited from its old alliance with *Town Topics*. We tried to console ourselves by reflecting that Dreiser had once edited the *Delineator* and Arnold Bennett a magazine called *Woman*, but out of that reflection we got only cold comfort.

There were yet other grounds for my discontent, chiefly revolving around Crowe and Warner. Both were competent business men, and in all their transactions with Nathan and me were not only extremely punctilious but also most polite, but they were Philistines of the crassest sort, and it was certainly no pleasure to have to listen to them. We liked Crowe better than Warner, if only because we saw him seldomer. We early made the discovery that he was a somewhat gay dog under his stiff exterior, and so, when the chance offered, provided him with the kind of entertainment he seemed to like. This usually took the form of dinner with a group of not too squeamish women, easily recruited by Nathan from his friends in the theatre. I should add that we also enjoyed these occasional parties ourselves, especially when Kay Laurell was present.

This Kay Laurell was a slim, not too young and far from beautiful woman, but she had all the arts of the really first-rate harlot, and was, in fact, the most successful practitioner of that trade of her generation in New York. Nathan had a friend, Edgar Selwyn (*geb.* Solomon), then an actor and later a moving-picture producer, who was violently in love with her and wanted to marry her, and it was through him that we met her. She was a walking encyclopedia of the town scandal, and once she had become convinced that we had no designs on her professional stock in trade she gave us her confidence and was very amusing. As a matter of fact, her cadaverous frame, colorless hair and large hands and feet damped all our natural fires, and more than once I have lain in a bed with her at her apartment without having the slightest impulse to use her carnally. She often dropped in at the *Smart Set* office while we were at 331 Fourth Avenue, and we saw her not infrequently outside—chiefly at Selwyn's apartment, or at the parties we arranged for Crowe and Warner.

She was a daughter of a letter-carrier in Buffalo, and her actual surname, which she once confided to me, had a German smack. She started out in life as a telephone operator, and became a long distance operator in the first days of the long distance telephones. One night, when she did some slight favor for a New York theatrical manager calling from there, he promised, in the custom of his craft, to do her a favor in return, and she asked him to get her a job as a chorus girl. He invited her to New York, and she was presently hoofing for Flo Ziegfeld. She made up very well, and though she couldn't act and was an indifferent dancer, Ziegfeld finally found her useful as a statuesque lay figure. She was the girl who, in the grand finale, waved the American flag. She became popular in theatrical society, and eventually married Winfield R. Sheehan, later a leading figure in the movies. After their separation she took up with Selwyn. She was, however, much too smart to marry him, though she lived with him off and on for some years. Instead, she resorted to piracy on the high seas of the town, and became an enormous success.

She had all the equipment needed in her profession. On the one hand she was an extremely shrewd judge of men, and on the other hand she was completely devoid of either sentimentality or libido. She once told me that any woman of decent appearance could get money out of men by sleeping with them, but that she thought it took real skill to get the money and evade the sleeping. This was her invariable custom whenever possible—not that she objected to the sleeping, but simply that she wanted to demonstrate her virtuosity, even if only to herself. Once a rich American, in the palmy days of the Cuban sugar boom, came to town and got mashed on her. He proposed to take her back to Cuba and keep her and offered her all sorts of gorgeous inducements. She was, of course, not inclined to anything of the sort, but she managed to get a ruby ring worth $30,000 out of him. She had a regular arrangement with Tiffany, whereby she could sell back such presents. Tiffany paid her a reasonable price for them, and in addition supplied her with imitations which always fooled the donors. She had a large collection of such simulacra of presents that she had got from men.

Crowe met her at a party that Nathan and I gave at the Beaux-Arts restaurant at Sixth Avenue and 40th Street, then one of our favorite hang-outs. He became enamoured of her at first sight, and a little while later she came in with the news that he had made her a formal proposition. If she would go with him on a brief business trip to Philadelphia she could expect to get an honorarium of $1,000. She asked us if his promise was to be relied on, and we assured her that it was. The next week the journey was duly made, and on her return she reported that Crowe had sent her a check for $1,000. Characteristically, he did not sign it himself, but had it signed by the Jewish lawyer mentioned a little while back. He had heard of the Mann Act, and wanted to avoid being blackmailed.

Kay, of course, would not have blackmailed a friend of Nathan's and mine, but she had no compunction about rooking other rich admirers. One of her victims was Otto H. Kahn, an extremely offensive Jew who had a great deal of money and was one of the leading figures of New York in his day. He was little more than five feet in height, but he was a very vain fellow and fancied himself as a lady's man. His taste ran to extremely young girls, and it became a kind of custom for the New York harpies to tempt him with specimens below legal age, and then hold him up. One night Kay came to the *Smart Set* office while Nathan and I were working overtime there and told us that she had snared Otto with a girl a few months under the legal age. She said she couldn't make up her mind whether to let him off for, say, $25,000 or $30,000, and so gain his gratitude, or take him for a considerable amount, say, $100,000. We told her that in our judicial opinion it was a folly to compromise in such delicate cases. If she was going to blackmail him at all, she had better rook him for the maximum amount that he would pay. Later on she told us that she actually got something on the order of $50,000 from him. When she demanded $100,000 he brought up a whole battalion of lawyers, and Kay said she compromised in order to get rid of them.

Kay disappeared from New York after the war, and I heard presently that she was living in England. Then came news that she had fallen virtuously in love with a young and penniless Englishman, then that she had married him, and a little while later that she died in childbirth. It seemed a grotesque ending for such a woman. So far as I know, Crowe's trip to Philadelphia with her was his first and last professional transaction with her. He was unaware, of course, that Nathan and I knew about it, and would sometimes inquire about her politely. She told me once that going to bed with men did not disgust her—that is, if they were reasonably sober and well-mannered—but that she got next to no pleasure out of their operations below the girdle. What her customers saw in her as a boudoir companion I could never make out. I liked to listen to her chatter, but as I have said, she did not fill me with amorous ambition. Once she told me that she was often pursued by homosexual women, and I began to suspect that she was herself a member of the fraternity, which was then attracting a good deal of notice in New York, but she assured me that she was not.

She pretended, like many of the superior ornaments of her trade, to a certain intellectuality, and her apartment was full of bookcases, but the books in them were mainly trash, and I doubt that she ever read them. But whether intellectual or not, she was certainly a very smart gal, and she contributed not a little to my education. Much of what I got from her, in fact, went into *In Defense of Women*, especially the revision published in 1922. She was not, however, the woman whose charming and instructive talk is described in Section 46 of that revision. The model for my portrait there was a half-Jewish lady who had been a successful actress and was later to have a brief time of glory as a movie star. She was theoretically virtuous and afterward married very well, so her name is neither here nor there.

Crowe was dead when Nathan and I quit the *Smart Set* at the end of 1923 and we had seen little of him in our later years on the magazine. He died on August 27, 1921, and probably left a large estate, for he had made a great deal of money during the war. Once, in 1915 or thereabout, he took me down to the Brooklyn waterfront and showed me a pile of Swedish wood-pulp that he owned—not as the head of the Perkins-Goodwin Company, but personally. He had got it in just before the war, and he told me that his profit at the time I saw it was already beyond $1,000,000. It was at least one hundred and fifty feet long, forty feet wide and twenty feet high, and in fact looked like a young pyramid.

Crowe was always very polite to me, and as my books began to appear showed a certain kind of respect for me. He also professed to believe that I was a competent business man. I can't say I ever really liked him, for he was too cold and remote for that, but I nevertheless had friendly feelings toward him. When the United States entered the war he got into a panic, and laid in rifles to defend the Perkins-Goodwin offices, in the Aeolian Building in 42nd Street, overlooking the New York Public Library and Bryant Park. What he feared I don't know: probably an attack by Zeppelins. This vastly amused Nathan and me.

We were also amused by Warner, but he irritated us too, for he was a good deal of what came, after 1922, to be called a Babbitt, and we could never make him understand what the *Smart Set* was about. He was extraordinarily ignorant of everything save sports, and once astounded us by asking us the meaning of *psychology*. He had found the word in the *Smart Set*, and said that it had puzzled him: he pronounced it *pissicology*. He was competent enough as a publisher, and very honorable in his business dealings, but he affected the manner of a high-powered business executive of the time, and we found it very hard to listen to him. He called a conference of the heads of departments every time I was in New York, and not infrequently, after a wet night with Nathan, Wright and other friends, I sat through one of those conferences with only the vaguest notion of what was going on.

Whenever Nathan and I had lunch with him, which was unhappily often, he always fished out a large gold leadpencil, and proceeded to cover the table-cloth with optimistic calculations. He had many plans for new magazines, but the only ones we ever set up with him—the *Parisienne, Saucy Stories* and *Black Mask*—were our ideas, not his. In the course of our endless palavers we discussed and debated many others. One, I recall, was to be entitled *Pretty Girls*, and its whole contents were to consist of full-page photographs of sightly wenches, reproduced in rotogravure, which had been only lately perfected in Germany. Nathan and I went to a great deal of trouble to round up photographs, but Warner, after a really dizzy scurrying about, reported that the cost would be prohibitive. I believed, and still believe, that he was wrong.

He had few ideas about the editorial conduct of the *Smart Set*, for its contents, in the main, were over his head, but when he ventured to suggest one we always slapped him down roughly, for it was bad enough to listen to the suggestions of Crowe's mother-in-law, relayed to us through Crowe and Warner, as I have recorded. In the field of circulation, however, he was very fertile and we had to listen to him. In 1917 or thereabout he got into a row with the American News Company, and set up his own wholesale organization, but it was a costly failure, and in the end he had to go back to the News Company.

Warner was a small fellow but sturdy, and moved briskly. In order to increase his height he wore shoes with very high heels. He had, in those days, a small black moustache and kept it waxed. He was extremely vain of his appearance, and fancied himself a good hand with women. Once he invited Nathan and me to meet his latest conquest. She turned out to be a bleached blond radiating whore from every pore, and the next day at the office we warned him to beware of her. When he insisted that she was actually a Southern girl of good family we resolved to give him a scare. To that end we got from Philip Goodman some copies of a bogus letter-head that he had had printed: it purported to be that of a Jewish law firm called Fishbein, Goldfarb, Spritzwasser and Fishbein, or something of the sort. On this letter-head we wrote Warner a letter saying that Miss——(the name of the whore) was pregnant by him, and demanding a settlement. He was so scared that he came rushing to us with the letter, asking for advice. We let him writhe a while, and then let him know that it was bogus and that we had written it. He thereupon had several hundred copies of the letter-head printed, and spent most of his time during the week following writing similar letters to his friends.

Warner had social ambitions, and for a long while tried to horn into Long Island society. To that end he took a house on the dunes at Easthampton, and proceeded to give a series of expensive parties, but his climbing came to nothing and he never managed to get into any really swagger club. He was a diligent and even slavish follower of what he called vogue, and could no more imagine buying a golf stick, a necktie or a hat from a store not in fashion than he could imagine arraying himself in the garments of a Trappist. He spent a great deal of time inquiring into such matters. I often asked him, just to test him, where the best collar buttons or penknives or inkwells were to be had. He would always reply very positively that this or that shop had them, and no other shop. The vogue frequently changed, and he always followed it. If the place to buy neckties was Ginsberg's he went to Ginsberg's, but if Ginsberg lost ground to Goldberg, he switched to Goldberg at once.

In his life fashion became a kind of moral compulsion. All rational values were abandoned in favor of one false value. Once when I was visiting him at his place on Long Island, we turned out early one morning for a walk in the vegetable garden. I happened to see a rabbit eating a cabbage, and called his attention to it. He rushed back into the house for his shotgun—and returned wearing a shooting jacket. He couldn't imagine shooting at even a rabbit without the proper clothes on. Incidentally, he missed the rabbit, which was still eating the cabbage. The sound of the shot scared it away, but it was uninjured.

Warner had started out in the magazine business as circulation manager for *Pearson's* magazine, then controlled by Crowe. The story that Nathan and I heard was that Crowe, at that time, was in love with a young woman named Ruth Eaton, but that she preferred Warner, and that Crowe very gallantly submitted to her decision and gave her beau a job. Ruth Eaton actually became Mrs. Eltinge F. Warner, but I have some doubts about the rest of the story. Warner did well as the circulation manager of *Pearson's*, and when, in the course of time, Crowe got control of *Field & Stream*, he was made its publisher, and given a substantial block of stock in it.

Field & Stream was always his favorite, and he not only read every line of its contents, but gave over most of his leisure to practicing the sports it dealt with—hunting, fishing, and so on. In the days when I first knew him he had made a moving picture showing various experts, including himself, engaged in such sports, and frequently ran it off at gun-clubs, fishing-clubs and the like. At least once a month he dressed himself in the appropriate costume and went out to make additional pictures. One day news came in that a school of sharks was off Atlantic City, alarming the bathers. Warner proceeded to the scene immediately, and by a great piece of luck managed to shoot one of the sharks with a pistol. His photographer had the movie-camera aimed at him at exactly the right moment, and the result was a sequence of film that made a great hit in the gun-clubs and fishing-clubs, and brought in many new subscribers to *Field & Stream*.

These adventures naturally interested him in the general subject of movies, which were just taking on the proportions of a large industry in 1915 and 1916, and he made various efforts to horn into that industry. How much they cost him I do not know, but it must have been a considerable sum, for the Jews who were his associates looked to Nathan and me to be very dubious fellows. While the *Smart Set*'s offices were at 331 Fourth Avenue, early in 1916, he was a partner in a movie company that had an office in the same building, and he often dragged us upstairs for a pre-view of one of its pictures. Those pictures were all bad, and we said so. Indeed, we argued that *all* movies were bad, and this annoyed Warner, and set him upon us every time a new masterpiece struck Broadway. I well recall how, in 1919, he insisted that we go to the Casino Theatre to see a new picture called *Broken Blossoms*, starring Lillian Gish. The film was tinted a kind of pink and looking at it was so uncomfortable to our eyes that we left before it was over. The next day we told Warner that *Broken Blossoms* seemed to us to be a fraud, and La Gish a performer without either beauty or talent.

Warner's age I do not know: he omits it from his autobiography in *Who's Who in New York*. I am sure, however, that he is older than I am. When I dropped in on him at his office at 515 Madison Avenue, New York, in November, 1942, after not seeing him for several years, I found that he had grown completely bald and taken on a noticeable amount of weight. He and Ruth were childless when I first knew him, but in 1923 they had a belated daughter, Lois, and she is now grown up. I gathered from his talk that he had abandoned his old yearning for high society, but I note by the New York telephone-book that he lives at 19 East 72nd Street, a very good address.

He is still publishing *Field & Stream* and still enjoying it, though he told me that it now had very stiff competition and is not making as much money as it used to. His only other magazine is a fortnightly pulp called *Ranch Romances*. This was set up some years ago by W. M. Clayton, the bastard son of Colonel Mann. When Clayton went broke and his properties were put up at auction, Warner bought *Ranch Romances* for $30,000. He told me that he had received a tip that it was the only profitable magazine in the Clayton string. Its success, he learned, was due to a woman editor, and he took over the editor with the magazine. He ushered me to her office to introduce me to her—a slim, pale, quiet blond, apparently beyond her first youth.

Warner's doings during the war brought Nathan and me to the unhappy conclusion that he was not only an ignoramus, but also something of a bounder. His view of international affairs was exactly that of the Long Island *noblesse* he so innocently admired, and as a result he became a violent Anglomaniac at the outbreak of World War I. But though he knew that Nathan and I were of opposite opinion he did not try to influence our editorial policy, and we held resolutely to our decision to keep the war out of the *Smart Set*. In so far as we alluded to it at all, in our review articles, it was with scarcely concealed derision for the great crusade to save humanity.

Even after the United States entered the war we refused to throw open our editorial pages to propaganda, and only once, so far as I can recall, did we ever let Warner pollute them with any of the patriotic canned goods he was printing in the advertising section.

When the Plattsburg training-camp for reserve officers was set up in 1916 he went there for training, and even before this he had been drilling with Squadron A, a fashionable outfit to which he had somehow got admitted. But when the war came home at last he did not volunteer for service; instead he joined the American Protective League, an organization of stay-at-home patriots devoted mainly to spy-hunting. He had a hand in the wholesale round-ups of pedestrians that were made in 1918, ostensibly for the purpose of collaring draft evaders, and at other times he took part in raids on German nationals. Most of the latter were poor and harmless nonentities—waiters, dish-washers and so on—and the sport of harassing them was a sorry one. But Warner gloated over it, and once, I remember, he entertained Nathan and me by describing how terrified some of the victims were when he and his gallant associates asked them where they wanted their bodies sent. He was somewhat taken aback when Nathan and I let him understand that we thought such poltrooneries were disgusting.

Early in March, 1918, he came to me with the news that the A.P.L. had received an anonymous complaint against me, and that he had been told off to investigate it. He showed me a copy of the complaint. It was a half literate document denouncing me as "a friend of Nitzky, the German monster," alleging that I was an intimate of Captain Paul Koenig, commander of the German U-boat *Deutschland*, and hinting that my trip to the German war-front in 1916–17 had had some sinister (but unnamed) purpose. This complaint greatly upset Warner, for all he knew about Nietzsche was what he read in the New York *Times* and *Herald-Tribune*,[1] and that was mainly inflammatory. He had never read my book, *The Philosophy of Friedrich Nietzsche*. When I told him that Nietzsche had died in 1900 and had been *non compos mentis* for ten years before, he was greatly surprised, and also much relieved. In the end he asked me to draw up a report upon myself to be submitted to the A.P.L. as his own, and this I did.

Warner turned in the document a few days after I drafted it, and we both assumed that the case was closed. But soon afterward he was

1. Mencken is here incorrect. The *Herald* and the *Tribune* did not merge until 1924.

prodded afresh by his superiors in the A.P.L.: they had received new complaints about my connection with Nietzsche, who had by now become a really horrendous bugaboo to all 100% Americans. At Warner's request I drew up a statement about my book, showing that Nietzsche had been dead for eight years when it was published, and denying that I had ever had any personal dealings with him. After the higher functionaries of the A.P.L. had marked and inwardly digested the foregoing they subsided, and Warner was no longer harassed with complaints about my relations to Nietzsche.

Meanwhile, however, he was somewhat fevered by my refusal to buy any war bonds. I had made up my mind that I should not do so save under irresistible pressure, and the pressure brought to bear on me, whether by Warner or by others, was never quite irresistible. Once he begged me as a friend to put down my name, if only for a $50 bond, for he was eager to obtain a 100% subscription in the *Smart Set/Field & Stream/Parisienne/Saucy Stories* office, and so be able to fly the flag that gave notice of such unanimous participation. Nathan succumbed to his pleadings, but I refused. The next time I got to New York, however, I noted that the flag was flying from an office window. Whether he simply ignored me, or subscribed to a baby bond in my name—this I did not ask and never learned. I bought no war bonds, in fact, until after the war was over, and then I got them at prices substantially below par.

It was part of Warner's duty to see to the printing of the *Smart Set*, but he gave the business little attention, and as a result the magazine gradually degenerated in appearance. In the days of Mann and Thayer it had been printed on good paper, but Crowe, when he found us at his mercy, began delivering worse and worse. After the beginning of 1917 he actually sent us a grade that was hard to distinguish from common newsprint, though it was thicker. Worse, he often put in a lot that was tinted pink—apparently a left-over from the order of some other customer. But no matter how villainous the paper, Crowe kept the price at the old mark—ten cents a pound. Nathan and I protested against this imposition, and urged Warner to refuse to submit, but he was too timorous to tackle Crowe. We therefore did it ourselves, but Crowe refused to budge. We were lucky, he argued, to get any paper at all in such times, and the fact that we did so was due only to his enormous fondness for us. So the magazine continued to look like a scarecrow, and that fact, along with its absurd name, helped to wear down our interest in it.

CHAPTER VII

Looking back to our days on the *Smart Set* after we had abandoned it, Nathan and I always agreed that our happiest year as editors ran from the spring of 1915, when we moved out of our crowded first quarters at 456 Fourth Avenue to 331 Fourth Avenue, to the early summer of 1916, when we went into a barn-like office in the new Printing Crafts Building, at Eighth Avenue and 34th Street. The building at 331 Fourth Avenue was a small one, but with *Field & Stream*, we had the better part of a whole floor of it, and it was convenient and comfortable. A few days after we moved in Nathan discovered that there was an excellent German restaurant, the Kloster Glocke (Monastery Bell) next door, and there we had lunch together whenever I was in New York—that is, whenever we could throw off Warner, his gold leadpencil and his silly figuring on the tablecloth.

The proprietor, whose name I forget, was a devoted fisherman, and twice a week he arose before dawn, went down to fish off Long Beach, and returned in time for lunch with a fine string of mackerel, rock and bluefish. These noble ornaments to *Pisces* we devoured with great satisfaction, along with plenty of noodle soup, boiled potatoes, rye bread and dill pickles. We never told Warner about the place, for fear that he would insist on coming along, but there was probably no real danger of that, for he avoided German eating-houses. Now and then we entertained a favorite contributor to the magazine, but not often, for we wanted to keep Nathan's find to ourselves. As a matter of fact, we seldom saw most of our contributors at all, for we clung to the theory that it was better to deal with authors by mail.

Our only office assistant was the Miss Stella Golde I have already mentioned—a truly appalling specimen of the Brooklyn Jewess. Her face was heavy and expressionless, with no visible chin, she had a dumpy figure and fat legs, and in her speech were frequent traces of the Brooklyn diphthongization of *er*. Nathan, when he was alone, spent no more than an hour a day at the office, usually in the late morning, but when I was in New York we returned after noon and sometimes came back again at night. When callers were announced, Miss Golde was sent out to get rid of them. This she did in a series of set speeches that she had memorized: they were made up of phrases that she had picked up from Nathan and me, and assumed to be literary. Sometimes we eavesdropped on her for the pleasure of it. She did all her routine work very well, and, as stenographers ran in New York, was not a bad one. But it was impossible to entrust her with anything calling for information or judgment, for she had neither. Nathan and I, on idle afternoons, put in a good deal of time carrying on preposterous conversations for her benefit—say, to the effect that one or the other of us had been offered the editorship of the *War-Cry*, or that Warner was about to buy a $250,000 palace on Long Island, or that some rich and beautiful actress had got mashed on old Lloyd, the dog man.

When Warner decided that we ought to have a rug in our office we sent Golde to a Brooklyn department-store that she recommended as elegant, with instructions to buy the best rug she could find for $12.50. She returned with a Turkey-red one so dreadful that we could not help howling with delight when we saw it. Once it was on the floor we decided that the office deserved decorations to fit it, and thereafter gave over our leisure to amassing them. One of the principal items of the wall *décor* was a series of posters issued by the French Association Against Alcohol, showing the effects of alcohol upon various organs of the body—full size and in full color. To them we added photographs of a dozen or more of the most abhorred characters of the time—for example, Lieutenant Charles Becker[1] and the German Crown Prince—each purportedly inscribed by the subject to either Nathan or me. On our desks stood plaster statues, hideously colored, of the sort that Italian vendors used to sell on the street, and above Nathan's desk hung the pennants of various colleges, beginning with his own Cornell and Warner's Princeton, and running down to

---

1. Becker was a notorious New York police officer.

the Ohio Wesleyan, the Texas Christian and Tuskegee. Warner's office was decorated with the originals of the covers of *Field & Stream* and the stuffed carcasses of fish that he had caught, so we hung the covers of the *Parisienne* in ours and added a couple of stuffed fish that Nathan bought at a junkshop in Third Avenue. In the course of a few months the walls were covered up to the ceiling.

Warner, of course, viewed this buffoonery with disfavor: he believed, and said, that the office of the *Smart Set*, a magazine aimed at intellectuals, should be very dignified, but we replied that intellectuals also loved art. When we moved to the Printing Crafts Building in 1916, we had to abandon most of our wall decorations, for the office partitions there were of glass, but we took the rug along, and it followed us when we moved to 25 West 45th Street at the beginning of 1919. So did my large brass spittoon. The spittoon, in fact, accompanied me from the *Smart Set* office to the *American Mercury* office at the end of 1923, and there it served me faithfully during the ten years of my editorship.

As I have said, Nathan and I let Miss Golde get rid of most of our callers, but there were some that we saw, and a few of them were permitted to become more or less regular visitors. One of these was Harry Kemp, the tramp poet, then a very conspicuous figure in Greenwich Village. Kemp was a robust, noisy fellow who went bareheaded all the year round—that was long before it became fashionable among college boys—never combed his long but thinning hair, oscillated between open shirt collars and florid Windsor ties, and wore invariably the same suit of shabby corduroy. He operated what he called the Thimble Theatre, first in a dilapidated stable in the Village and then at Fifth Avenue and 8th Street, opposite the Brevoort Hotel, and wrote nearly all the plays he presented. He had some talent and we bought all sorts of things from him—lyrics, plays, short stories and briefer sketches—most of them for the *Smart Set*, but also some for the *Parisienne* and *Saucy Stories*. He was an assiduous kicker, and most of his visits were for the purpose of protesting against the smallness of the checks that Nathan sent him. Nathan always listened to him gravely and promised to do better the next time. Kemp, who had no sense of humor whatsoever, would leave convinced that his next check would be at the rate of five cents a word, and when it turned out to be at the rate of two cents a word, or even less, he returned to make another protest.

Whenever I happened to be in the office Nathan and I put in a pleasant hour spoofing him. One of our devices to that end was to address each other as "Mister," and to pretend to be on the most formal terms otherwise. Whenever Nathan arose from his chair I would arise, and *vice versa*. Meanwhile, Miss Golde, instructed in advance, would go out to the reception room—a cubbyhole not more than ten feet each way—and then return with the news that Charles Evans Hughes, John D. Rockefeller, Jr. or some other such bigwig was waiting to see us. We pretended to be greatly interested in the life of Greenwich Village, and pressed Kemp for confidential news about its authors and artists. Virtually all of them save Dreiser, Sinclair Lewis and Eugene O'Neill were frauds; indeed, the Village, like the Paris Left Bank, was much less literary or artistic than sexual, and most of its male denizens lived on women. The typical ménage consisted of a widow or spinster from some small town in the Middle West, come east to spend her dead husband's or father's money and see life, and a bogus painter or pulp-magazine fictioneer who let her feed, clothe and love him. Kemp was always trying to induce us to buy the poems or stories of such quacks, but the specimens he produced were seldom fit to print.

The chief entrepreneur of the Village in those days was one Guido Bruno, a Jew masquerading as a Hungarian. He operated a small magazine and brought out occasional pamphlets of bad poetry—always at the expense of the ladies keeping the authors thereof. I never met him, but he sometimes sent us manuscripts, chiefly the work of his customers and always sorry stuff. In the end he became so bold in his operations that the police took an interest in him, and he had to shut down his business and leave New York. One of his last victims was a poor woman who appealed to me to help her get redress. She was a servant girl in a New Jersey suburb, and had saved $3,000. Also, she had nursed literary ambitions. Bruno, hearing of her, professed to believe that her banal compositions were masterpieces, and by the time she discovered that he was a swindler all her money was gone. I could, of course, do nothing to help her, for when she first wrote to me he had already vanished, but I well recall her pathetic letters.

As a means of kidding Kemp, Nathan and I pretended to a vast interest in the Village, and one day asked him to take us there and show us the sights. He accepted eagerly, and we walked all the way from 331 Fourth Avenue. Whenever he pointed out a celebrity—say, for example, Bobby Edwards, a loafer who held himself out, in succession, as painter, photographer, musician, novelist and even publisher, but lived on women all the while—we would stop short, stare fixedly, and make a show of being tremendously impressed. Finally, almost with bated breath, Kemp indicated a second-story window in a ramshackle house, and said: "When Oscar Wilde was in New York his girl lived there." "His *girl*?" demanded Nathan. "What in hell, Mr. Kemp, was Mr. Wilde doing with a *girl*?" For some reason unknown, this greatly upset Kemp, and he spent half an hour trying to convince Nathan and me that, in addition to his homosexual practise, Wilde also indulged in more normal sin. We professed to regard it as a slander upon his principles, and denounced Kemp for spreading such stories about a dead and defenseless man. He then got into a considerable lather and proposed to produce the woman, but we begged him to say no more about a painful subject.

Another time, when he was in the office and Nathan and I were about to set out to Lüchow's in 14th Street for lunch, he asked if we would object if he walked with us, for he was bound for the Village beyond. "Not at all, Mr. Kemp," answered Nathan with great formality. "On the contrary, we'll be very much honored." "But maybe you forget," suggested Kemp uneasily, "that I wear no hat. Do you object to that?" "Not at all, Mr. Kemp," answered Nathan. "Certainly it is better to walk with you wearing no hat than to walk with you wearing the sort of hat you would wear if you wore one." Kemp, as incredible as it may seem, saw only a kind of compliment in this. He was, in fact, greatly pleased, and as we swung down Fourth Avenue to 14th Street gave us to understand that he regarded both of us as men of talent. But we did not invite him to join us at lunch. Instead, we bowed to him profoundly when we got to 14th Street, and saw him stalk off toward the Village.

He was, in those days, the epitome of the Village, and spent a large part of his time whooping up its *vie de Bohème* and trying to convince all comers that its pretenders were geniuses, but he did not actually live within its bounds. This fact was not known to most of his followers, but it was a fact nevertheless. Sometime in 1914 he had encountered a visitor from uptown—a lovely Irish girl named Mary Pyne, the daughter of a well-to-do lawyer—and she had succumbed to his Gothic beauty and loud talk. On February 28, 1915, they were married—and he and she took up quarters in her father's large apartment at 885 Park Avenue. There, with the wicked rich on all sides of him, the king of the Village slept and breakfasted—a kept man like nearly all its other notables. Nathan and I knew this, but Kemp asked us to keep it quiet. He got his mail at his theatre, and went down to the Village every morning for his all-day and all-evening labors as poet, fictioneer, dramatist, stage manager and oracle. He often invited us to Village functions of one sort or another, but we never went.

Those were the first days of author's teas, and some time in 1916 we gave one in his honor at the *Smart Set* office. A little before this, in visiting Warner's projection-room upstairs, we explored the roof, and there found a thin slab of marble, perhaps 18 inches wide and three feet long. This we had brought down to our office, and there put it across the backs of two chairs. From the Kloster Glocke next door we got in half a loaf of rye bread, a couple of marinated herring, a large dill pickle, a handful of pretzels, and three bottles of Schaefer's beer, then the worst in New York. These things constituted the materials of the tea. To the back of one of the chairs was fastened a bar towel, borrowed from the Kloster Glocke. Kemp came in in a new Windsor tie, and we received him very formally and bade him fall to. He ate and drank heartily. We explained our own abstention on the ground that we had got overdoses of champagne the night before at a party given by J. Pierpont Morgan the younger, and were suffering from gastritis, and the absence of other guests on the ground that we could think of none worthy of being invited to meet him.

The talk, which was somewhat stiff, was all about Kemp's work, as it invariably was when he was present. He complained that his theatre was running at a loss and that the poetry business had been badly hurt by the war. We advised him that he was foolish to waste his masterpieces on magazines. The thing to do, we said, was to take billboard space in downtown New York, and have them painted thereon in letters two or three feet high. By that means he would acquire a really large audience, and become a powerful influence on public opinion. Moreover, he would be doing something revolutionary, and making for himself a secure place in the history of literature. He was greatly taken by the idea, and for months afterward dropped in on us to report progress. It was easy to write poems for the billboards: they were mainly denunciations of the capitalistic system, for

Kemp was then both a Socialist and a Single Taxer. Unhappily, all the sign-painters he could find demanded wages for their work, and Wall Street had cornered all the billboards, and exacted a merciless rental for their use. But he kept on mulling the project for months.

At the beginning of the theatrical season of 1916–17 he came in to announce triumphantly that business at his theatre was picking up, and that if all went well he would soon be paying his actors $15 a week apiece. Before the end of the winter, however, things took an unfavorable turn, and he had to close. Like Warner, he was violently pro-English, or, more accurately, pro-French, and ranted and raged against the Germans until the United States declared war. Then he cooled off very quickly, and made no effort to enlist, though he was in robust health and but thirty-four years old, and his wife was supported by her father.

About this time he protested bitterly against one of the recurrent outrages of Nathan, who had bought a short story from him for the *Parisienne*, changed its locale from Greenwich Village to Monte Carlo, and signed it with some such *nom de plume* as Count Raoul François de Montmartre. When he sent in a letter full of grief and threats, Nathan replied with a long answer in the English of a stage Frenchman, and signed with another bogus French name, ostensibly that of the editor. In this letter the imaginary editor expressed great surprise that such a lover of the French nation, character and civilization as Kemp, who was known to be preparing to offer his sword to suffering France, should object to using a French pseudonym and contributing his mite toward the glorification of the French *Kultur*. After this Nathan and I called him Kempf and insisted that he was a German. We even spread a story to the effect that he had served three years in the German army. In his innocent way he helped along this fiction by airing his German, which he had picked up during a year or so at the University of Kansas.

A brewer friend in Baltimore, Frederick H. Gottlieb, had given me a couple of dozen bonds of the Maryland Brewery Company, an amalgamation of breweries there that had gone bankrupt before it had paid the first coupon, and I kept them in the *Smart Set* office. They were printed in golden orange ink and very elegantly engraved, and looked like real money. Nathan sent Kemp one of them whenever his protests against our rates of pay became clamorous, and he apparently kept them in the hope that they would one day resume payment of interest. First and last, he must have got $8,000 or $10,000 worth of them. His first appearance in the *Smart Set* was with a short story, "The Mistress," in the issue for January, 1915, and thereafter we printed him almost every month—poems, sketches, one-act plays or other short stories. We refused at least three-fourths of the stuff he submitted, but nevertheless the total accepted and printed was pretty large.

I bought all the poetry for the *Smart Set*, for Nathan pretended to have no taste for it; in our average number there would be eight or ten poems. Those were the high days of *vers libre* and the Imagist movement, but in the main I stuck to conventional metres and themes, though now and then I let in an apostle of one of the new evangels—for example, Amy Lowell, who was in our April, 1916, issue with an eleven-line poem called "Summer Rain." La Lowell, from her ivory tower in Boston, had sent in three poems in January, unsolicited, but we took only "Summer Rain." She complained that her check for it (spelled *cheque*) was "rather small," but we sent her no addition to it. In my May, 1916, review of the current poets I mistook a volume of Imagist verse, dated 1916, for another one dated 1915—certainly an excusable error, for there was little visible difference between them. La Lowell wrote to me on June 10 suggesting that I print a rectification. I replied politely, but printed nothing. I had given her *Sword Blades and Poppy Seeds* a friendly notice in the *Smart Set* for May, 1915, and was to give her *Pictures of the Floating World* a very brief but even friendlier one in June, 1920, but though her actual verse was not abhorrent to me, I was repelled by her public posturing, and so let my contact with her lapse. I never met her.

The other poets of our early string I saw very seldom or not at all, for I was convinced that listening to them would be a waste of time: what I was interested in was their manuscripts, not their personalities. One of the best of the lot, as a craftsman, was Robert Loveman, but he was then living, happily enough, in faraway Dalton, Georgia, and spent most of his time in the Southern Bible country, giving author's readings. I had reviewed his *The Blushful South and Hippocrene* in the *Smart Set* for October, 1909, and his *On the Way to Willowdale* in April, 1913, and we fell into a desultory correspondence before Nathan and I took over the magazine.

It seemed to me then, and it still seems to me today, that Loveman was one of the best lyric poets of his generation in America. To be sure, his limitations were very narrow—as I said in my notice of October, 1909, his verses were "triumphs of verbal gemcutting—and nothing more"—but within those limitations he was really superb. I am still convinced, indeed, that nothing better than his "Rain Song" has ever been done, in its class, in the United States. I naturally asked him for contributions when I became responsible for the *Smart Set*'s poetry, and he responded with some excellent stuff. In 1915 he was complaining (alas, like most of our poets) that we were paying him too little, but we remained on good terms and he continued to contribute. Soon after this the poor fellow apparently lost his reason, for I began to receive letters from him purporting to have been written from the European war zone, though they were posted from Dalton.

I was also interested in Bertha Bolling, a dainty, Dresden china little old maid who was the sister of Mrs. Edith Bolling Galt who married Woodrow Wilson on December 18, 1915. She sent me a short poem called "Yellow" early in 1916, and we printed it in the *Smart Set* for March. In the form in which I first saw it it was amateurish and feeble stuff, but Miss Bolling gave me permission to omit its last stanza and edit it a bit, and so I made it printable. It was surely no great shakes, even then, but Nathan and I were amused by the stunt of publishing Wilson's sister-in-law, and we encouraged her to send in more. She did so from time to time until her health broke down in 1921, and we took a piece occasionally.

We did not print notes on authors in the *Smart Set*, but Miss Bertha's identity was soon recognized, and she began to be beset by composers eager to set her somewhat austere little lyrics to music, and by other editors ambitious to print her. One of the latter was Burton Rascoe, then a scout for *McCall's Magazine*, and always a cuckoo. She told me of most of these approaches and I advised her as best I could. One of the magazines that printed her was *Scribner's*, of which Alfred S. Dashiell, also a cuckoo, was then assistant editor. So late as July 15, 1936, she was asking me to read two manuscripts— one her own and the other by one of her Washington friends, John B. Sharpe. I was busy at the time with the two national conventions and their aftermath, but I must have read them, for I received four very friendly letters from her during August and September.

Some time in 1917 she had invited me to dinner at her Washington apartment, then in the Powhatan Hotel. The only other persons present were her mother and her brother. The talk naturally ran on the war, and the two ladies gave me to understand that they agreed with my view of it, not with Wilson's. In fact, they spent most of the evening telling me of the happy days they had once spent in Munich, and praising the German *Kultur*. It was easy to see that they were not especially proud of their daughter and sister's marriage to Wilson, though he was President of the United States. They belonged themselves to the authentic First Families of Virginia and claimed descent from Pocahontas, and by their standards Wilson was hardly a gentleman, for he came from the Western part of the state and was the son of a Presbyterian preacher. The Tidewater Virginians all regarded Presbyterians as but little removed from Methodists.

Why Bertha never collared a husband herself I could not make out. She was petite in figure and very graceful, and had the smallest feet I have ever seen. Nor was she ill-favored in the face. Maybe her ill health was to blame. On November 11, 1921, she wrote to me that she had had a severe heart attack, followed by what she described as a "hemorrhage from the heart," and thereafter she spent a large part of her time at Galen Hall in Atlantic City. She and her mother invited me to visit them again, and on various occasions I invited them to lunch, usually on their visits to New York, but we never actually met. Mrs. Bolling died in 1925, and Bertha on September 20, 1937. I heard no more from her after 1930. She had no talent, but was, despite her prim spinsterishness, an interesting and pleasant woman.

By the time Nathan and I took over the *Smart Set* my book reviews had been running for nearly six years, and had made me known to a number of authors of some importance at the time, among them, Dreiser, Huneker, Hergesheimer, Frank Harris, Hugh Walpole, W. L. George and Harry Leon Wilson. I naturally undertook some effort to recruit these and other such men for the magazine, for even if they did not send in their best stuff their names would help to get it notice. Unfortunately, its funds were too low to meet the prices that many of them were commanding in the open market, and I was reluctant to attempt to cash in on their good will by offering them less. I managed, nevertheless, to obtain contributions from Dreiser, Huneker, Walpole and Harris before the end of 1916, but both Harris and Dreiser demanded honoraria that were above our means, and the other two were producing little that would fit into our scheme.

I HAD REVIEWED three of Harris's books in the *Smart Set* before I came into contact with him in 1915. I made short shrift with *Montes the Matador*, dismissing Harris as "solemn and a bore." But by the time I came to *The Women of Shakespeare* I was more favorably inclined toward him, and confessed that his effort to reconstruct Shakespeare from the plays had begun to fill me with "considerable conviction." He had been living in London for many years when World War I began, and as editor of the *Saturday Review* had become a salient figure in its literary and political life. But when it turned out that he was skeptical about the English itch to save humanity things were made very uncomfortable for him, and late in 1914 he came to New York. Soon after landing he printed his *England or Germany* and sent me a copy for review. So far as I can recall, I printed no review of it, but the doctrine preached in it was naturally grateful to my gills.

I don't recall how Nathan came to meet him, but I suppose it was through his efforts to sell something to the *Smart Set*. He was hard up and eager to get some money, but what he had to offer was mainly outside our field. We finally decided to take a four-page (and characteristically egoistic) paper entitled "How I Discovered George Bernard Shaw," and it was printed in our issue for July, 1915. Harris demanded five cents a word for it—a high price for us in those first days of our editorship—and I remember that we debated whether it would be worthwhile to yield to him. In the end we did so, but we decided privately that he was too expensive for us, and he never appeared in the *Smart Set* again.

He had made plans, when he came to the United States, to set up a new *Saturday Review* in New York, but just as he was about to bring it out he was offered the editorship of *Pearson's* magazine, of which my and Nathan's partner, Eltinge F. Warner, had once been circulation manager. His first issue of *Pearson's* was that for September, 1916, and it must have been soon afterward that I had my first meeting with him, for I recall that it was at the office of the magazine in lower Fifth Avenue. Harris, who was something of a gourmet, had been to lunch just before I dropped in on him, and it took no Hawkshaw to detect that it had included scallions and whiskey.

Our talk was principally about the war, and in general we were in agreement. Harris disliked the English and was not backward about treating them realistically in the first issues of *Pearson's* under his editorship. When the United States horned into the war, early in

1917, he was in a difficult position, for he had already aroused the enmity of the Anglomaniacs, and they now proposed openly that he be suppressed. He circumvented them by the simple device of whooping up Woodrow Wilson. In every issue of *Pearson's* Wilson was hymned as the greatest leader of humanity since Peter the Hermit—and under cover of this anointing there followed page after page of tart flings at the English. It was a transparent trick, but it worked, for Wilson's susceptibility to flattery was only equalled by his appetite for it, and his goons dared not molest an editor who gave him such heavy doses.

I saw Harris off and on during the war years, and we continued in agreement, but I never became one of his intimates, and in fact I had more truck with him after he left the United States at the beginning of 1922 than while he was here. He was an extremely smart fellow, but there was always something dubious about him, and even a touch of the sinister in his appearance. He was short of stature, had hair that grew far down his forehead, and wore a curled moustache that was obviously dyed and showed the traditional gun-metal finish. He paid much attention to his dress, and had a somewhat horsey appearance. His talk flowed in a gushing stream, and was generally amusing, for he had known a great many interesting men at close range and was full of salacious anecdotes about them. Much of what he had to say was far from convincing, but nevertheless it was not dull, so I listened to it willingly, as I listened to the less malicious but even more amusing gossip of Huneker. He gave ready support to my effort to organize opposition to the Comstocks' attempt to put down Dreiser's *The "Genius"* in 1916, but had to proceed somewhat warily. "I do not like to put myself in the forefront of the fight here," he wrote to me on August 15, 1916, "as I had to do in England. There I was better known and it was perhaps excusable; here I think it perhaps would be resented, yet I think we should all fight for freedom from such puritanical nonsense."

The Comstocks made an effort to suppress his *Oscar Wilde*, but in vain, and I judge from a note dated January 22, 1918, that he was thinking of proceeding against them for revenge. In the same note he told me that he had resigned from the Authors' League because he believed it had not shown proper diligence in aiding Dreiser. During the summer of 1918 he acquired complete control of *Pearson's*, and on October 19 he wrote to me that he had reduced its monthly cost of operation from $7600 to $3500, and was hopeful of making it pay. At the beginning of 1919 I suggested to him that he should write his autobiography, and on January 8 he replied that it was impossible, first, because "America keeps me with my nose to the grindstone trying to earn bread," and second, because "If I write my reminiscences I want to do what Shaw says is impossible—write the whole truth," but the suggestion must have stuck in his mind, for after he reached France at the beginning of 1922 he actually began work on *My Life and Loves* and the first volume was published in Paris late in the same year.

Late in 1922 he quit New York for France, and I heard nothing more from him until the early days of 1923, when he wrote from Paris under date of January 1 that the first volume of *My Life and Loves* was finished and that a copy of it would reach me anon. "I had infinite difficulty," he said, "in getting the permission to export it. . . . What you will think of it I can't imagine; your judgment on my stories was so *renversant* that I can only wait and cease to conjecture. But you are an honest critic and that gives me some faint hope. I am minded now to produce a new volume each year."

The book reached me in February, and I reviewed it in the *Smart Set* for June, 1923. It bore a Paris imprint, but was actually dispatched from Berlin, for Harris had been on a visit there. The German export permit accompanying it was dated Berlin, January 5, and gave his address as the Hotel Furstenhof. The German inflation was then in full blast, and the value of the book was given as $2—or 11,800 marks! Unhappily, Harris apparently encountered difficulties at the Berlin export office, which was manned by young women ("Suspecting that girls might be frivolous," he wrote to me on February 2, "I gave largess in many thousands of marks, and bade the *Backfische* and *Flussfische* to be extra careful") and in his confusion he sent me a copy inscribed for an English friend living in France, Herbert Vivian by name, and dispatched my copy to Vivian. He learned of his error from Vivian and promised to send me another copy, but that second one never reached me.

The volume was anything but attractive in appearance. It was, in fact, badly printed and very crudely bound, and Harris himself had helped to make a mess of it by inserting a number of silly full-page illustrations—all of them portraits of voluptuous women. How my copy got through the American customs I do not know. He had made good his promise to be completely frank: his accounts of his youthful love affairs left nothing whatsoever to the imagination, and when they culminated in sexual intercourse, which was usually, he described his sensations with the utmost particularity, and also tried to describe those of the ladies. There was, however, very little mere pornography in these passages; on the contrary, he seemed to be animated by a scientific frenzy rather than by lustful recollections, and more than once he paused to discuss gravely the anatomy and physiology of coitus. I recall one such discussion especially, for it maintained the doctrine that, after the first ejaculation, the semen of the male is free from spermatozoa—a complete imbecility. But the book was by no means a treatise on the pleasures of the bed, and nothing more; on the contrary, it was mainly given over to quite decorous recollections of Harris's school and college days in Kansas, and included a moving and obviously sincere tribute to a pedagogue who had had a large influence upon him, one Byron C. Smith.

Harris asked me to write nothing about the book until March: he wanted all the copies he had sent to American friends to get past the customs before the inevitable outcry. He would never, he said, return to the United States himself. "Sing Sing," he said, "has no attractions for me, and they'd put me in some penitentiary promptly could they get their foul paws on me. . . . I've never been able to understand how Whitman kept out of prison; but imagine it was the verse-form that saved him, as it certainly helped Swinburne. The average Anglo-Saxon lawyer believes that poetry and music in themselves are low forms of self-indulgence, practised usually by the sub-normal." I wrote to him at length about the book, and received a reply dated Nice, March 21, 1923. "Your letter," he said, "ranks with one from Bernard Shaw as about the only sensible letters that have reached me on this first volume. Strange to say, you both agree about the illustrations, and stranger still, I had come to the same conclusion—they were better away. But what would you when revolt is imperative: it is difficult not to put your fingers to your nose in derision." On April 22 he wrote to me again, this time saying that my letter was "better than Shaw's."

In the letter of March 21 he had told me that he was sending me articles on John Ruskin and Wilfrid Scawen Blunt and had asked me to make him "an offer of so much for 20 pages a month for the next year or two," and in that of April 22 he proposed that I pay him

$250 a month for a series of contributions to run indefinitely, and to include both character sketches of various English personalities and reports of his observations in different parts of Europe. "I'm going," he said, "to see Mussolini and the little Italian king in Rome and the literary remains of Casanova at Dux, and I've already met most of the Germans who count." Among his English sitters were to be Sir Charles Dilke, King Edward VII, Parnell, Cecil Rhodes and Lord Randolph Churchill, the father of Winston. "Lord R.C.," he said, "went mad at 40 through syphilis, which I shall call 'that nameless disease.' " The price he named for these pearls was too high for us; moreover, the subjects were not likely to interest our readers. Thus I had to decline his proposal, and we never, in fact, printed anything more of his. On May 21 he wrote from Nice that many copies of *My Life and Loves* had been confiscated by the American customs. On May 30 he asked me to print a notice in the *Smart Set* saying that the book could be obtained from him in care of the American Express Company, Paris or Nice, but this, of course, I had to refuse to do, for it would have brought the Comstocks down on us. In the same letter he told me that, despite his fear of jailing in America, he was thinking of returning to help "an English miner and explorer" work a mining claim "on the Canadian frontier of the Northwest," and so make some sorely needed money, but nothing came of this.

He continued hard up until his death at Nice in 1931. He got some revenue, from time to time, from successive editions of his life of Wilde, but it was spread over a long period of time, and was probably never very large. At all events, he was always complaining of lack of money, and he made frequent efforts, to my knowledge, to raise it by bootlegging copies of the first edition of *My Life and Loves*. On July 5, 1923, he sent me a carbon copy of a letter he had written to an acquaintance of his and mine, Harry Rickel, of Mt. Clemens, Mich., saying that one third of the first issue of Volume I had been confiscated by the American customs, that the French police had collared another third, and that the remainder had been barred from Italy, where he had planned to send them for safekeeping—and, I have no doubt, bootlegging. In the same letter he offered to send Rickel one for "$25, or whatever your purse can afford." The price at the start, he said, had been $15, and he hinted that it would probably be beyond $25 in the not distant future.

Harris died on August 26, 1931. He left virtually no estate save his interest in his books, most of which were either out of print or earning very little. His widow, Helen O'Hara (Nellie), remained in Nice, and news reached me from time to time that she was making very heavy weather of it. But in 1941 she returned to New York to walk into a windfall. This took the form of damages from the authors and producers of a play called *Oscar Wilde*, presented there during the season of 1938–39 with great success. Substantial parts of the dialogue of this play were lifted from Harris's life of Wilde, and the widow's lawyer, Arthur Leonard Ross, convinced the court that they were Harris's inventions, and so protected by his copyright.

On November 7, 1941, Ross asked me to testify in the case, and in particular to say that I had once described the book as "the best biography ever written by an American." "Your opinion and Shaw's," he wrote, "are the two opinions which I am trying to introduce into evidence at the hearings now going on before the special master." I had to reply that what I had actually said was "Harris has written, among other books, *perhaps* the best biography ever done by an American," and Ross did not call me. When in 1942, Julian P. Boyd proposed to do a volume of my letters, I tried to recover those to Harris from Mrs. Harris through Ross, but he could produce but one. Two had been included in a collection of letters that the widow had sold through the Panurge Press, 151 Fifth Avenue, but the rest had disappeared.

Harris's book on Wilde not only brought the Comstocks of England and America down on him; it also exposed him to a violent attack from Wilde's old girl, Lord Alfred Douglas. This Douglas was a vain, quarrelsome and litigious fellow, and made frequent appearances in the English courts. In 1914 he published a book, by title *Oscar Wilde and Myself*, in which he denied categorically that he had ever engaged in homosexual practices with Oscar. Harris naturally challenged this palpable lie in his own *Oscar Wilde: His Life and Confessions*, published two years later; in addition, he handled Douglas roughly in other ways, and accused him *inter alia*, on the authority of Robert Ross, of deserting Wilde in Wilde's last miserable years. The last charge rankled in Douglas's gizzard, and he tried to persuade Harris that it was untrue when the two happened to meet in Nice in 1925. Harris professed to be convinced, and accordingly drew up a new preface for use in subsequent editions of his Wilde, apologizing to Douglas and denouncing Ross as a liar. But he seems to have neglected to get this new preface into print quickly enough to satisfy the choleric Douglas, who presently brought it out as a pamphlet on his own account.

A few years later, in 1929, he published an autobiography in which he admitted at last that his denials in *Oscar Wilde and Myself* had been false—that he had actually engaged in homosexual practices with Wilde, though still denying that he had played the passive part in sodomy. I had reviewed *Oscar Wilde and Myself* in the *Smart Set* for November 1914, but I had never met Douglas or had any communication with him, and had no desire to do either, for he seemed to me to be not only a filthy homo, but also a public nuisance. But when I was in London early in 1930, helping to cover the Naval Conference for the Baltimore *Sunpapers*, he heard that I was in town and wrote to me. His letter, dated Hove, Sussex, February 9, was as follows:

> I gather from a Sunday newspaper that you are staying at the Savoy Hotel, so I take this opportunity of tackling you on a subject which may or may not be of importance or interest to you. I mean that some years ago you wrote in a New York weekly paper, the *Nation*, an article about me which for sheer abuse, libel, and malignance surpassed anything else that I have ever read. At the time when the article appeared I was staying in Nice where Frank Harris (whose grotesque perversions of the facts were evidently your chief source of information when you wrote the article) had just completed his new preface to *The Life & Confessions of Oscar Wilde*. In this new preface Harris admits that practically every word about me in his life of Wilde is false, & he expressed his deep contrition for the "grievous wrong" he did me & his determination to do me "tardy justice." I showed your article to Harris & asked him his advice about it. His reply was that he would write to you & send you a copy of the preface & that as you were an "honest man" you would certainly make amends when you found how grossly you had been deceived.

This puzzled me very much, for I could recall writing nothing about Douglas in the *Nation*. I remembered my review of *Oscar Wilde and Myself* in the *Smart Set* sixteen years before, but only vaguely. I was thus constrained to reply to Douglas somewhat warily, for if he set his lawyers upon me in London I would be in a difficult position. I have no copy of my letter, but I must have denied that I had ever written against him in the *Nation*.

Soon after this I sailed for home, and aboard ship I read Douglas's autobiography. It turned out to be an extremely bad job—whining, badly written and obviously disingenuous—and I decided that it was not worth reviewing in the *American Mercury*. If I told the truth about it Douglas would make one of his usual uproars and probably try to intimidate the news-agents who handled the magazine in England; and I was certainly not inclined to deal with it leniently, for the author disgusted me. On May 3 he wrote to me inquiring when a notice of it was to be printed and saying "I am anxious to have your opinion of it." I gave him that opinion with frankness, and on June 8 he wrote to me from Paris in a considerably chastened mood, for, like all such literary ruffians, he could coo as well as bellow.

Douglas's allegation that I had heaped "abuse, libel and malignance" on him in a review in the *Nation*, in 1925 or thereabout, puzzled me, for I could recall no such review. On my return home I made a search for it, but failed to unearth it. Plainly enough, he must have had in mind my review of his *Oscar Wilde and Myself*, published in the *Smart Set* for November, 1914. Maybe Harris handed him a copy of it when they met at Nice in 1925, and told him (with characteristic mendacity) that it had lately appeared in the *Nation*. That theory is borne out by the fact that the review mentioned Harris himself in a way that must have wounded his vanity. Thus: "Douglas, I daresay, knew Wilde better than any other member of that queer bodyguard which slobbered over him and buzzed around him his days as a London celebrity—certainly better than Frank Harris, or Robert Sherard, or Walter Pater, or André Gide, or even Robert Ross." This sentence unquestionably offended Harris, who always alleged that he was Wilde's one real confidant, and it was like him to try to divert Douglas from proceeding against his own book by baiting him with something worse than the libels picked up from Ross.

After 1930 I heard no more from Douglas, greatly to my relief. But he had hardly subsided before I began to be bombarded by another old Wildista, Robert H. Sherard. Sherard was then living in Corsica, and, like Douglas, was filled with venom against Harris. He also hated André Gide, who had likewise written what he regarded as lies about Wilde. No one, apparently, would publish his diatribes on the subject, so he had them printed in Corsica and circulated them as pamphlets. Under date of September 27, 1933 he sent me one of these pamphlets: its title was *Oscar Wilde: 'Drunkard and Swindler'*, and it was aimed at both Harris and George Bernard Shaw, who had praised Harris's life of Wilde. On October 25 of the same year he sent me another—*André Gide's Wicked Lies About the Late Oscar Wilde*. Simultaneously he informed me that he had completed a larger work on the subject, with the title of *George, Frank and Oscar*, and asked me to bring it to the attention of my publisher, Alfred A. Knopf. I did so, but Knopf was not interested.

In 1936 Sherard sold the book to the English publisher Werner Lauri, and in 1937 it was brought out in London under the title of *Bernard Shaw, Frank Harris and Oscar Wilde*, with a preface by Douglas. I was not interested in this controversy, which by now had grown four- and five-cornered, but I had to be polite to Sherard, who was by 1936 a man of seventy-five, and he continued to write to me for several years afterward. He returned to England in that year, apparently with the purpose of resuming journalism, which had been his trade earlier in life, but no paper in London wanted him, and he was reduced to printing his reminiscences and fulminations in the *Border Standard*, a small weekly published at Selkirk, in the Scotch Lowlands.

THE OTHER IMPORTANT AUTHORS, for one reason or another, eluded my snares, so we were thrown upon authors of less celebrity, and in the long run that fact probably benefited the *Smart Set*, for our eager search for unknowns unearthed a number of considerable talent, and printing them got us a reputation for fostering and indeed wet-nursing the national letters. We never had any such air: our sole purpose, then as always, was to maintain a free platform for ourselves: everything else was only afterthought and *lagniappe*. Neither of us, in fact, enjoyed the everyday work of editors, and I enjoyed it even less than Nathan. But it was nevertheless pleasant, in the midst of my tedious searching through bad manuscripts, to encounter an occasional newcomer of genuine skill and originality, and now and then my surprise and delight took on the proportions of a thrill.

Of these discoveries I recall especially two—both Jewesses—for they became standbys during the first years of the Nathan-Mencken *Smart Set*. One was a woman calling herself Lilith Benda and the other was Thyra Samter Winslow. La Winslow made her debut in our first number, that for November, 1914, with a short story called "The Case of Lou Terry," and La Benda followed in October, 1915, with a half-page sketch entitled "Donna è Mobile." It was apparent instantly that both were smart girls, with a lot in them that would be useful to us, and I accordingly arranged meetings with them at the office. No two women could have been more unlike in manner and appearance. Benda was tall, slim, shy and fragile, with a low, musical voice and the narrowest shoulders I have ever seen on a human being; Winslow, at the opposite pole, was short and chunky, with the ingratiating smile of a child and a voice full of the accents of her native Arkansas.

Benda followed her debut in the *Smart Set* with a one-page sketch in December, 1915, and then produced a full-length short story, "The Laugh of Dolores," which we printed in January, 1916. Thereafter, for a year or so, she was in our table of contents almost every month, and in the September, 1916, issue she had a novelette, "The Art of the Wife." No more original fiction was printed in the magazine in my time as editor. There was little overt movement in it, but it was packed with sharp observation and searching understanding, and there was a fine surface to the writing and a keen sense of the music of words. Nathan and I accepted everything she wrote, and were always glad to see her at the office, for she seldom came in without a manuscript in her handbag, but our interest in her work was scarcely greater than our curiosity about her strangely elusive personality.

She said very little, and always seemed to be scared. We heard from various (probably unreliable) sources that she had been married to a man named Rosenberg and divorced from him, and that her father, Bronder by name, was a professional gambler. One day she astonished me by inviting me to come to dinner at her home in Brooklyn. I accepted with alacrity and a day was fixed at once. The place turned out to be far out in the eastern suburbs of the town, not far from Coney Island. It was a comfortable and well-furnished one-family house, and showed signs that the family was pretty prosperous. Her father, who joined us at dinner, was her precise antithesis—a stout, hearty fellow in a closely-cropped Van Dyke beard, with a loud laugh and an obvious taste for alcoholic stimulation. He put a quart of brandy on the table as the meal began, and before we finished he had got down at least three-fourths of it. Of his talk I remember nothing save that it was boisterous and hollow. His daughter (whose actual given name, I found, was Lucia) said almost nothing, and her mother did not appear at all. I was given to understand that the mother had cooked the excellent dinner before us, but that she was so shy that she never met visitors. After the meal ended the father departed and Lucia invited me to her workroom under the eaves of the house. It was a curious apartment with walls that changed direction every few feet, and all over those walls were shelves of books. We talked therein for an hour or two and then returned downstairs, but I got no more from my hostess about herself than I had got at the *Smart Set* office, with Miss Golde listening in and the horrible decorations glaring down at us.

I met her often after that, usually at lunch in New York, but never learned any more about her. That she was Jewish I could see by looking at her father, whose appearance (despite the report that he was a gambler) was precisely that of a Jewish quack doctor, but in her own aspect, though she had dark hair and eyes, there seemed to be less of the Jew than the Slav. Her manuscripts, always written by her own hand, were models of neatness, and as easy to read as typescript. We had a general rule that all copy for the magazine had to be typewritten, but when she revealed an unaccountable but apparently implacable prejudice against the writing machine, we waived the rule gladly, for we were delighted to get her stuff on any terms. We printed, in fact, everything that she sent in, from one-page sketches to novelettes.

Unhappily, she was in indifferent health, and after 1917 her contributions began to drop off. She was in the magazine but three times in 1918, and not at all in 1919, and in 1920 she appeared but once. Her last story, I believe, was "The Prosaic Conclusion," printed in August, 1921. She was busy, then, with a play, but so far as I know it was never produced. I heard a bit later that she had tuberculosis and was going to a sanitarium, but no direct word from her reached me. Many years afterward, in 1941 or thereabout, I had a note from her, written from 37 St. Paul's Place, Brooklyn, saying that she was in desperate straits and asking for the loan of $75. I sent her the money at once, but never heard from her again.

La Winslow was no such shrinking violet. She had been a chorus girl in Chicago in her teens, and had begun to write two years before I became aware of her. She was already married and to what, to a

Jewish girl of her background, must have seemed a swell husband, to wit, John Seymour Winslow, a son of the chief justice of Wisconsin. This marriage was in being and apparently happy when I first met her, but it eventually blew up, and in 1927 she married another *Goy*, one Nelson Waldorf Hyde, from whom she was divorced in 1938. She was, despite her quite un-Benda-like exterior, almost as shy as Benda at bottom, and when she came to the office Nathan and I used to have a little fun by trying to make her blush. After her appearance in our first issues of November, 1914, we heard nothing from her until the late summer of 1915, when she sent in a satirical short story called "Little Emma," which we printed in December. It seemed to me to be an excellent piece of humor, and I wrote to her at once, praising it lavishly and asking for more.

When she was in New York she would come to the office on some day when I was in town, with her handbag stuffed with little pieces of paper, each bearing notes for a story that she had thought of. Nathan and I would listen to her outlines of them, tell her to write this one and that one, and perhaps make suggestions for revising the remainder. She always seemed eager to hear these suggestions, and usually carried them out. Sometimes, in the course of talk, we thought of story ideas of our own, and offered them to her.

Winslow showed a great deal less psychological finesse than Benda, and her writing was inferior, but she had in abundance something that Benda lacked altogether, and that was humor. There were no heroes or heroines in her stories, and there was little pity. Life, to her eye, was mainly farcical, and men and women were predominantly fools. I am convinced that her "Little Emma" was one of the best comic stories we ever printed, and we printed, first and last, a great many good ones. It was not merely an amusing anecdote; it was also a sardonic commentary upon the eternal gullibility of mankind. There was always that note in her stories: they not only presented human beings vividly and plausibly; they also said something apposite and pungent about them. We printed Winslow very often, and very gladly.

WHEN BEN HECHT first appeared in the magazine, in June, 1915, he was but twenty-one years old, but he had already had nearly five years of experience as a reporter on Chicago newspapers. Since 1914 he had been on the *Daily News*, a paper that had long specialized in nurturing of literati. He was a good reporter, with a vivid slapdash style and an eye for the grotesque, and soon after this time he was put to the job of providing a daily article for the *News*, part fact and part imagination, under the title of "Around the Town," with the subtitle of "A Thousand and One Afternoons in Chicago." Most of this stuff, of course, was pretty obvious, for Hecht had to do it in a hurry, but now and then there was something much better. I invited him to send me some prose for the *Smart Set*—his first contribution had been free verse signed *Benjamin* Hecht—and he did so early in 1917. During that year we printed four of his stories, and during 1918 no less than ten. At the end of 1918 the *News* sent him to Berlin as its correspondent, and he had little time for fiction, and when he returned in 1920 he devoted himself to a novel, *Erik Dorn*, and to various business enterprises. Thus we got but two stories out of him in 1919, and none at all in 1920. He returned to the magazine with one story in 1921, and in 1922 he did another.

Finally, during the summer of 1923 he sent in the best comic story we ever printed, and one of the best, I think, ever written. It was called "Rope" and the name of Charles MacArthur was signed to it, but it was plain that Hecht had had a good deal to do with the writing of it. We printed it in November, 1923. MacArthur was also a graduate of the Chicago news-rooms, but he had less talent than Hecht. In 1928 the two of them collaborated on a newspaper farce called *The Front Page* and it was a considerable success. During the same year MacArthur married Helen Hayes, the actress. Soon afterward both he and Hecht disappeared into the maw of the movies, where they made a great deal of money but produced nothing worth remembering. All of Hecht's best work was done before his association with MacArthur began.

He was born in New York in 1894 and was the son of Russian immigrants. According to the biographical material that he sent to me when my *Modern American Short Stories* was under way, his paternal grandparents were born in Persia. His mother, whose maiden name was Swernofsky, was of Christian birth, but became a Jewess on her marriage. She and her husband were both born at Kremenchug, in the Russian Ukraine. The latter was a pharmacist and worked as a drug-clerk in New York, with amateur acting as his recreation. The family moved to Chicago when Ben was eleven years old, and he there grew up. He left high-school at sixteen for a job on the Chicago *Journal*, and in 1914 moved to the *Daily News*. In the days when I first knew him he not only wrote the daily sketch that I have mentioned, but also did a great deal of news reporting.

He was married in 1915, before he was twenty-two, to Marie Armstrong, a fellow reporter, and they presently had a daughter. I visited them at their pleasant home at 5488 Hyde Park Boulevard in 1920, and they seemed to be on the best of terms. Prohibition had come in and Ben had set up practice as a home brewer. I recall that he not only plied me with his product at his house, but also gave me a basket full of bottles, to stay me at my hotel. How I was foully robbed of this very fair beer by Frank R. Kent and a gang of Maryland politicians is recorded in my *Thirty-Five Years of Newspaper Work, 1906–41*.

Unhappily, the appearance of felicity in the Hecht home was only an appearance. Before the end of 1920 Ben wrote to me that he was doing an autobiographical novel, to be called *Erik Dorn*, and when it came out in 1921 I described it in my *Smart Set* review as "the story of a young husband's gradual revolt against domestic normalcy." In the same letter he urged me to try to get something for the magazine from one Rose Caylor, a young woman then living in New York. "She is," he said, "a most magnificent creature, and can write splendidly." Two sentences further on he said: "I've never read anything she's written." "She's embarked," he continued, "on a theatrical career and is about the best non-handkerchief-using emotional actress I've ever seen. She's full of manuscripts, . . . as yet unwritten." This sounded ominous, but there was yet no visible break with Marie. In fact, she was still playing the dutiful wife in 1923, when Ben's book, *Fantazius Mallare*, was raided by the Chicago Comstocks and she wrote to me asking me to be a witness for him at his trial. But soon afterward they parted, and in 1925 he married La Caylor. She was by no means the genius that he whooped up in his letter of 1920. Beginning in June, 1919, she had contributed a few short stories to the *Smart Set*, but they were of only middling quality. After her marriage to Ben she never, so far as I know, wrote another, nor did she come to anything describable as eminence on the stage.

He had a considerable talent, but there was always something cheap and flashy about him, so I was not surprised when he gravitated to the movies. His view of the world was essentially that of the cynical newspaper reporter of tradition, though he was certainly a great deal more than a cynical newspaper reporter. The spectacle of man's imbecility enchanted him, and he delighted, in particular, in the grotesqueries of the battle of the sexes. As a result, a good deal of his writing violated American pruderies, and more than once I had to refuse one of his short stories for the sole reason that printing it would have only brought the Comstocks down on us. Jew-like, he had a touch of the world-savior in him, though he would have denied it earnestly, and in some of his earlier books I detected the note of moral indignation. In *Fantazius Mallare*, as I said in my review of it in the *Smart Set* for February, 1923, he depicted "the whole business of sex as unutterably revolting." "If such works," I went on, "actually cause the reader to plunge into sin, then it must be equally true that portraits of soldiers with their eyes shot out and jaws shot off would make effective recruiting posters in time of war." In this, of course, there was probably some notion of helping him in his combat with the Chicago blue-noses, who were trying to jail him for publishing the book.

Gargoyles, which I reviewed at the same time, was a violent onslaught, in the form of fiction, on these blue-noses. "Hecht . . . is too young," I said of it, "to have his ideas quite in order, and now and then he succumbs to the temptations of mere rhetoric, but even so he is an extraordinary phenomenon, and if he escapes death at the hands of the Ku Klux Klan, the American Legion, the Rotary Club, the Criminal Court of Chicago and other such great engines of the Puritan *Kultur* he will leave a large, zigzag, scarlet mark across the pages of the national letters." He did another novel, *A Jew in Love*, in 1930 (this time with Horace Liveright, the publisher, as his model), and a volume of novelettes and short stories called *A Book of Miracles* in 1939, but they showed no further advance.

By this time, indeed, the movies had pretty well wrecked him. He was enormously successful in Hollywood, and made a great deal of money, but writing for morons diverted him from his gay *jehad* against the imbecility of mankind in general, and he did nothing more of any genuine force or effect. Worse, the movie-lots not only took the sting out of the American Rabelais; they also drove him back to the ghetto. When World War II came on in 1939 his congenital Jewishness began to dominate him, and by February, 1943, he was contributing to the *American Mercury* (now owned and run by Jews) a set of prose dithyrambs upon the woes of Israel, fit almost for reciting at the Wailing Wall.

OF THE EARLY CONTRIBUTORS who managed to make headway against oblivion I recall principally Sherwood Anderson, Christopher Morley, Sinclair Lewis, Howard Mumford Jones, Douglas Goldring, Reginald Wright Kauffman, Richard Le Gallienne, Avery Hopwood, Aleister Crowley and Alexander Harvey, to which list, perhaps, Albert Payson Terhune and Charles Belmont Davis may be added. Anderson had a story, "The Story Writers," in our issue for January, 1916. In October of the same year I reviewed his first book, *Windy McPherson's Son*, and thereafter, down to 1929, I reviewed nine other of his books and maintained a generally friendly attitude toward him, though I did not like him. Morley was in several of our early issues—for example, those of August, 1916, and November of the same year—but I was not much impressed by his whimsy, and neither was Nathan, so we did not print him often. In those days he was working for Doubleday, Page & Company and had published only one book—his juvenile *The Eighth Sin*—but he was already showing the prehensile aggressiveness that later made him one of the most successful literary business men in America.

Howard Mumford Jones, when I first heard of him, was at the University of Chicago, working for an advanced degree under Robert Morss Lovett. He sent in a short story, "Jorgerson's Teeth," which we published in February, 1916, and thereafter he contributed frequently. He put in the years 1919 to 1925 as associate professor of comparative literature at the University of Texas, and then moved to the University of North Carolina as professor of English. He remained at Chapel Hill until 1930, when he moved to the University of Michigan.

In 1928 or thereabout he came to Baltimore to attend a meeting of teachers of English and I met him for the first time. He was a tall, gaunt fellow who looked a good deal more like a cowboy than a professor. I invited him to my house in Hollins Street, along with one of his colleagues, James F. Royster, for a few drinks, and I recall that he was quickly in his cups, and embarrassed Royster by propping his legs on a fine old walnut secretary in my sitting-room. As he got on in the academic world he abandoned the writing of fiction, and gradually took on solemnity. His books are all dull, and one of them, *American and French Culture*, published in 1927, is a really dreadful performance.

I was immensely surprised when, in 1936, Harvard made him a

professor of English and gave him an honorary Litt.D. This was at the time of the Harvard tercentennial, and many of the other men then given honorary degrees were of high and genuine distinction, whereas Jones, at least to me, seemed to be a simply third-rate pedagogue. He has done nothing of any consequence since he dug in at Cambridge. I saw him again on February 15, 1940, when I went to Boston to meet the newspaper men frequenting Harvard on the Nieman Foundation, and he came to the dinner at which I palavered with them. He had little to say on this occasion, and that little was not worth hearing.

Goldring, Terhune, Davis and Harvey I never met at all. Of Terhune about all I knew was that he was an old New York *World* man who was the son of Marion Harland, a famous woman author of the time; he later specialized in the writing of dog stories, and was constantly in the magazines, but so far as I know he never did anything of more than commonplace quality.

Davis was the brother of Richard Harding, and suffered all his life from the latter's greater celebrity. He was a somewhat prissy fellow, and refused to sign the Protest against the suppression of Dreiser's *The "Genius"* in 1917. He died in 1926 and Terhune in 1942.

Goldring was an Englishman and was steered to the *Smart Set* by Ezra Pound. His first contribution was a short story published in October, 1915, and he soon floated out of our ken. He wrote a number of novels that got good notices in England but did not sell very well, and after 1925 he devoted himself mainly to books of travel and to political tracts. He visited the United States in 1927, but I did not meet him.

Harvey, in 1915, was famous for his story "The Toe," published in 1913—the tale of a woman who, on her way to a rendezvous, discovers that there is a tear in her stocking, and is so embarrassed that she turns back. It is a testimony to the innocence of the era that this was then regarded as a daring idea—and that no one thought it odd for a woman suffering from a severe sex orexis to balk at a hole in her stocking. Harvey, in 1915, was one of the editors of *Current Opinion*, and in 1922 joined the staff of the *Atlantic Monthly*. He had been in the diplomatic service and had also done newspaper work. In 1917 he published a little book on William Dean Howells, favorable in intent but devastating in effect. Unhappily, Harvey abandoned both the writing of fiction and the criticism of contemporaries after 1920 and devoted himself to Greek studies. He was a man of parts and is still remembered by survivors of his heyday, though his later work has gone quite unnoticed. He is now (1943) seventy-five years old, and seldom emerges from his retirement at Englewood, New Jersey.

Hopwood, Kauffman, Le Gallienne and Crowley I met off and on during our first few years. Hopwood was a dramatist, and his principal (it may, indeed, have been his only) contribution to the *Smart Set* was a novelette made of a play. It was called "A Full Honeymoon" and we published it in September, 1915. He was a native of Cleveland and a former newspaper man. I met him in 1905, when his play, *Clothes*, written in collaboration with my old acquaintance, Channing Pollock, was a big hit in New York. He followed it with a long series of popular farces and farce-comedies and acquired a great deal of money. When he died in 1928 he was one of the most successful playwrights in the American theatre. A bachelor, he left money to found a fund for the encouragement of young writers. He was a charming fellow and very intelligent.

Crowley, who contributed a short story, "The Stratagem, " to the *Smart Set* for September, 1916, was an Englishman, and something of an eccentric. I never met him until I visited London in 1922. He had by that time taken to mysticism and was surrounded by a group of idiots who regarded him as inspired and almost, indeed, a god. Inasmuch as it was whispered in London that a certain amount of homosexuality was intermingled with the devotion of these disciples, I avoided him as much as possible, but after I got home he began bombarding me with mystical literature, all of it elaborately printed and brought out at his own expense, or that of his followers. He became, in the end, the recognized head of all of the English occultists, and a figure of some consideration in the life of London.

Kauffman also got on very well, and his autobiography in *Who's Who in America* for 1942–43 runs to 62 lines—exactly double the space devoted to Dreiser—but his writings never interested me, and I have not seen or heard from him for years. Le Gallienne's contributions to the *Smart Set* in my early days as editor were mainly of verse, but now and then he wrote a story or an essay. His occasional visits to the office while we were still in Fourth Avenue entertained Nathan and me pleasantly, for he was a fellow of old-fashioned manners, and in dress and barbering looked the perfect poet of tradition. I had been reviewing his books in the *Smart Set*, usually favorably, since 1910, and when he published a swashbuckling romance, *Pieces of Eight*, in 1918, I gave it a really cordial notice, for it amused me to discover that a poet could write such hearty stuff. Le Gallienne is now (1943) seventy-seven years old, and is chiefly recalled, when he is recalled at all, as the father of the actress, Eva Le Gallienne, but he was, in his day, somebody on his own account, and some of his poems survive in the anthologies. He was a figure in the literary movement of the 90's in London, but kept pretty much to himself after his immigration to the United States, and hence got relatively little notice.

Sinclair Lewis's one and only contribution to the *Smart Set* in its first days was "I'm a Stranger Here Myself," a short story, published in August, 1916. There was in it a foreshadowing of *Babbitt* and *The Man Who Knew Coolidge*, but Lewis had not yet found himself, and so it was pretty crude. I did not meet him until 1920, just before the publication of *Main Street*.

THE PERIOD FROM the summer of 1914, when Nathan and I took over the *Smart Set*, to the end of 1916 was overshadowed by World War I, and, for me in particular, by my conviction that Woodrow Wilson would eventually take the United States into it. I predicted that he would do so in my "Free Lance" column in the Baltimore *Evening Sun* early in 1915, if not before, just as I predicted in 1940, in my articles on the editorial page of the *Sunday Sun*, that Roosevelt II would horn into World War II. I had, by 1914, pretty well established myself as a literary critic, and was beginning to be quoted and discussed, but I was eager to bulge out of the field of books into the wider one of life itself, and had, in fact, already made a move in that direction in my articles on American characteristics, begun in the *Smart Set* for June, 1913.

Unhappily, the war made it more and more difficult to speak freely about any of the matters that really interested me, and after the sinking of the *Lusitania* on May 7, 1915, it became virtually impossible. Things were to become worse after the United States actually entered the war, but in 1915 and 1916 they were already bad enough, God knows. I had to live among people whose view of the events of the time seemed almost insane to me, and whose concept of honor, whether national or personal, was violently at war with my own. There were, of course, some exceptions—for example, Dreiser, Wright and

Nathan—but they were few in number: the prevailing winds all roared in the other direction.

I had always made it a point, both in my critical writings and in my journalistic work for the *Evening Sun*, to avoid attacking any man who was not perfectly free to strike back, but now I found that my opponents were not so squeamish. My colleagues of the *Evening Sun*, in the traditional Anglo-Saxon manner, took to hitting below the belt, and in the autumn of 1915 I gave up my "Free Lance" column in despair and disgust, just as I was to give up my writing for the *Sunday Sun* in January, 1941. I lost a great many friends in those days, but though I missed them, for I was always a very gregarious fellow, it would be going too far to say that I regretted them. When, in the days after the war, some of them came trailing back, seeking to resume our old relationships where the bitterness of the war had cut it off, I refused to go along. I learned a great deal in that unhappy time about human stupidity, and a great deal more about human cowardice and meanness, and I believe that the experience, on the whole, was useful to me.

Fortunately, my withdrawal into myself did not leave me without occupation. I had, in fact, plenty to do. For one thing, I put in a lot of hard work on the *Smart Set*, and more on the launching of the *Parisienne* and *Saucy Stories*, and for another thing I threw myself with energy and industry, in 1916, into resisting the attempt of the Comstocks to suppress Dreiser's novel, *The "Genius"*. But these things, after all, were not my principal business in life, and I chafed against the restraints that gradually hedged me in. Thus, for the first and last time in my life, I suffered from a feeling of bafflement. I knew where I was headed, but I had not yet formulated a definite programme of writing; all I was sure of was that when I came to it eventually it would not be the one I was perforce following.

My trip to Europe at the end of 1916, to see something of the war from the German side, was no more than an effort to get some excitement and new experience into a life that had begun to grow unendurably stagnant. I had planned to make this trip during the summer, but the burden of looking after the *Smart Set* and the two pulps detained me, and when I got to the front at last, at the beginning of 1917, it was just in time to be turned back by the breaking off of relations between the United States and Germany, followed quickly by the American declaration of war.

Meanwhile, I had to confine myself to enterprises that did not collide too violently with the savage taboos and inhibitions of the time. The first of them was the putting together of a book of purely literary criticism, but with a background broad enough to take in such adumbration of fundamentals as the current prejudices would permit. The second was the preparation of a couple of books of harmless jocosity, mainly made up of my contributions to the *Smart Set*—some of them under my own name, but most under the various pseudonyms that I had been using. The first scheme was realized as *A Book of Prefaces*, which did not get into print until September, 1917, though most of the material in it went back to the days before the war. The second came to fruit in *A Little Book in C Major* and *A Book of Burlesques*, both of which were published in the autumn of 1916, with the former a little ahead of the latter.

They bore the imprint of the American branch of the John Lane Company of London, whose American manager was J. Jefferson Jones. Jones had lost money for the firm on *Europe After 8.15*, but he blamed that fact on the war, not on its authors, and he was eager to keep me on his list. Thus, when I told him that *A Little Book in C Major* and *A Book of Burlesques* were under way, he accepted them sight unseen, and by July 15, 1916, the manuscripts were in his hands.

A Book of Burlesques, in its first form, was made up almost wholly of things I had written for the *Smart Set* during the first year of the Nathan-Mencken editorship. There were two principal exceptions: the first was "A Genealogical Chart of the Uplift," printed on a sheet more than two feet long, folded in at the end, which had been prepared originally for the Baltimore *Evening Sun*, and the other was "Epithalamium," a burlesque of the manner of Henry James, also first written for the *Evening Sun*. I had, by this time, pretty well ceased to write for the *Smart Set*, save for my monthly book article, but at the last minute I threw in a couple of things done to piece out the book—"A Contribution Toward a List of Euphemisms for *Drunk*," signed James P. Ratcliffe, A.M., Ph.D. (Harvard), LL.D. (Oxon) and printed in June, 1916, and "A Panorama of Babies," signed W. L. D. Bell and printed in August.

A Little Book in C Major was made up of 226 epigrams, all of which came out of my contributions to the *Smart Set*. It made a volume of seventy-nine small pages, was bound in maroon cloth with gilt stamping, and sold for fifty cents. *A Book of Burlesques* made a volume of two hundred fifty-three pages, was bound in the same style, and sold for $1.25. Jones was hopeful that he could work up a profitable sale for both *A Little Book in C Major* and *A Book of Burlesques*, and to that end he spared no diligence. He sent out a canned review that got into many papers, and with it went a portrait of me—the first to appear in any considerable number of them.

Unhappily, the customers did not rise very avidly to his baits. The sales of *A Little Book in C Major*, to the end of 1916, came to but five hundred ninety-four copies, and those of *A Book of Burlesques*, to but three hundred seventy-eight. My royalties to December 31 were $29.70 on the former and $47.25 on the latter, or $76.95 on the two—not a large sum, certainly, but nevertheless I got a pleasant uplift when my check came in on April 6, 1917, for it was the first royalty check that I had ever received.

During the whole of 1918 the sales of *A Little Book in C Major* were but one hundred forty and of *A Book of Burlesques* but sixty-six, and it had become evident that both books were dismal failures. Jones kept them on his list but six months longer, selling twenty-five of the former and forty-seven of the latter during the first half of 1919; then they were taken over by Alfred A. Knopf, who had meanwhile published my *Book of Prefaces* and was preparing to bring out *The American Language*, my translation of Nietzsche's *Der Antichrist*, the first of my *Prejudices* books, and a new edition of *In Defense of Women*, first published by Philip Goodman. We decided to amalgamate the two Jones books as *A Book of Burlesques*, and the new edition came out in January, 1920. To my great amazement, it was an immediate and durable success.

CHAPTER VIII

THE BEGINNINGS OF my relations with Theodore Dreiser have been described. That was in August, 1907, and until October, 1910, when he lost his job as editor of the *Delineator*, we were in constant correspondence about work that he wanted me to do for that magazine. Whenever I went to New York I dropped in on him, and by the end of February, 1909, we were on such terms that we had already dropped honorifics in speaking and writing to each other. On August 29, 1909, I went to dinner at his house—he was then living at 439 West 123rd Street—and met his wife, and at Thanksgiving of the same year he and she came to Baltimore and had Thanksgiving dinner with my mother, my sister and me in Hollins Street.

Sister Carrie had been published (and suppressed) in 1900, eight years before I began to write book reviews for the *Smart Set*, and he published nothing else save a few magazine pieces until the appearance of *Jennie Gerhardt* in 1911, so there was not much chance for me to whoop him up in the regular course of my critical business, but I managed to sneak in references to him from time to time, and in December, 1910, in the course of a review of an indifferent novel by Reginald Wright Kauffman, entitled *The House of Bondage*, I let go for *Sister Carrie*. I described it as "one of the most thoughtful and impressive novels in our latter-day literature," and contrasted it with the Kauffman story, to the necessary detriment of the Kauffman.

"Here we behold," I wrote to Dreiser on March 14, 1911, "not a yearning to please a friend, but honest admiration for an arresting work of art. I look forward eagerly to *Jennie*." Dreiser himself, it appeared, was not too confident. It was now nearly eleven years since

Sister Carrie, but *Sister Carrie* was still remembered, and he knew that *Jennie Gerhardt* would be measured with it, and condemned unmercifully if there was any apparent falling off. He had been putting in occasional licks upon it for a long time, but it was still unfinished. When he lost his job on the *Delineator* he was irresolute, and wrote to me on October 11, 1910, that he was "considering several good things," *i.e.*, other magazine jobs, and hinted that if he accepted one of them it would further delay his writing. "My conscience," he said, "haunts me a little, for first-hand I should finish my book." The new magazine job did not materialize, and during the remaining months of 1910 he not only plugged away at *Jennie* with great energy, but also began its successor, *The Financier*. On February 24, 1911, he wrote to me that *Jennie* was finished at last, but his doubts continued.

"I sometimes think," he wrote to me on March 10, 1911, "that my desire is for expression that is entirely too frank for this time, hence I must pay the price of being unpalatable. The next book will tell. I wish I could see you oftener." Even after *Jennie Gerhardt* was finished, and I had read it and was full of enthusiasm for it, he remained uneasy. "If *Jennie* doesn't sell," he wrote to me on August 8, 1911, after *The Financier* also was done, "I won't hang on to this writing game very long." But during those early years most of our correspondence, of course, had had to do with the *Delineator* and the *Bohemian*, for both of which he was constantly urging me to write. I was, however, not too eager to undertake the projects he suggested, for many of them had an uplifting smack and lay outside my range of interest.

I got on with Dreiser very well, and our relations were easy and even jovial, but it was already apparent that our ideas about various capital matters differed abysmally. He had thrown off, with some ostentation, his childhood's allegiance to the Roman Catholic Church, and frequently denounced it with venom, but there was still a marked religious streak in him, and he had a fundamentally believing mind. In the long years of our association I was to see him succumb to a long series of assorted quacks, ranging from fortune-tellers to Communists. He laid claim to have read Huxley and Spencer, but he was wholly unscientific in his mental processes, and anything that showed a touch of wonder always fetched him. On September 20, 1909, I wrote to him protesting against the tone of an editorial on spiritualism in the *Bohemian*, obviously written by himself. It aroused, I said, "my holy horror. I wish you would . . . tackle some of the late treatises on biology—le Dantec's *The Nature and Origin of Life* for example. I think they would land you in the German camp of violent unbelievers. The notion that the soul is immortal seems to me utterly gratuitous and abhorrent."

In his turn, he objected to some of the stuff I sent in for the *Bohemian*, and refused to print it—for example, an editorial headed "The Decay of the Churches." "You ask," he wrote on November 2, 1909, " 'Why should they [men] by their acts give countenance to the theory that their fate is determined by the arbitrary moods of the gods?' They shouldn't: but how about the fixed rules? And isn't seeking knowledge (scientific) a form of prayer? Aren't scientists and philosophers at bottom truly reverential, and don't they wish (pray) ardently for more knowledge? If you would but add a few lines to this effect in the last paragraph I would say yes—splendid. It's a fine thing as it is, but the truth is men are not less religious—they are religious in a different way—and that's a fact." The banality of this was flabbergasting.

When the *Bohemian* blew up at the end of 1909, "The Decay of the Churches" was still in his hands. On February 6, 1910, I wrote to him to ask for its return, and he sent it back on February 20. So far as I can recall, it was never printed anywhere. With the *Bohemian* off his hands he divided his time between his duties on the *Delineator* and his efforts to write *Jennie Gerhardt*. On March 21, 1910, he wrote to me that he was setting up a men's page on the *Delineator* and asked me to contribute to it. "The contributions," he said, "want to have a basis of serious advice with just a slight undertone of josh."

Dreiser's efforts at humor, alas, were comparable to the connubial athletics of that husband who suggested to Balzac a chimpanzee trying to play the violin, so his Men's Magazine Page (as he finally decided to call it) was pretty dismal, and did not last long. I apparently wrote but two pieces for it—"How to Put on a Collar," printed in July, 1910, and "The Legal Liabilities of the Best Man," printed in August. It occupied the last page of the *Delineator* from July to November, inclusive, and then disappeared.

Meanwhile, Dreiser himself was devoting his scant leisure to *Jennie Gerhardt* and after he ceased to be editor of the *Delineator*, in October, 1910, he gave over virtually all his time to it. On February 24, 1911, he surprised me with the news that he was also "half through" an unnamed successor that eventually became *The Financier*. On March 18 he asked me to read *Jennie* and on April 19, after a delay caused by the fact that one of his women disciples in New York insisted on reading it first, it reached me in Baltimore. I fell upon it at once, and had got through it by April 23. It made a really powerful impression on me, and when I wrote to him on the latter date I was still dazzled by it. My letter was as follows:

> I have just finished reading the MS—every word of it, from first to last—and I put it down with a clear notion that it should remain as it stands. The story comes upon me with great force; it touches my own experience of life in a hundred places; it preaches (or perhaps I had better say exhibits) a philosophy of life that seems to me to be sound; altogether I get a powerful effect of reality, stark and unashamed. It is drab and gloomy, but so is the struggle for existence. It is without humor, but so are the jests of that great Comedian who shoots at our heels and makes us do our grotesque dancing. . . .
>
> I'll return the MS. by express tomorrow morning. Maybe chance will throw us together soon and we'll have a session over *Jennie*. At the moment I am rather too full of the story as a human document to sit down in cold blood and discourse upon its merits and defects as a work of art. I know that it is immensely good, but I have still to get my reasons reduced to fluent words.

I did not confine myself to direct encouragement of Dreiser himself, but also spread the glad news down my lengthening list of literary correspondents. There was more in all this, I need not confess, than mere rejoicing over a great artist come into his own; there was also, and inevitably, a considerable self-interest. Ever since I began to find myself as a literary critic, in 1909, I had been on the lookout for an author who would serve me as a sort of tank in my war upon the frauds and dolts who still reigned in American letters. It was not enough to ridicule and revile the fakers they admired and whooped up, though I did this with great enthusiasm; it was also necessary, if only for the sake of the dramatic contrast, to fight for writers, and especially for newcomers, they sniffed at—always provided, of course, these victims of their intransigent obtuseness really had something to offer.

My standards, as I gradually formulated them, were by no means rigid or pedantic. I believed thoroughly in those early days, as I still do today, that an author should be judged by what he tries honestly to do, not by what anyone else, whether critic or not, thinks he *ought* to do. But I also believed, and still believe, in what someone has called (in an effort to get the thing within Anglo-Saxon patterns) the moral obligation to be intelligent, and when I detected a departure from it I did not stay my hand. Thus, though I was extremely hospitable to H. G. Wells in his great period—which ran from 1909 to 1911 and included *Tono-Bungay, Ann Veronica, The History of Mr. Polly* and *The New Machiavelli*—I belabored him violently when World War I began to make a brummagem messiah of him, full of hollow sophistries. In the same way I praised Upton Sinclair when he wrote plausible novels (which he could do well enough on occasion) and denounced him when he wrote Socialist balderdash.

As I began to gather an audience I discovered, somewhat to my surprise and consternation, that I was becoming known principally as a killer: the truth was that I was far more eager to discover and proclaim merit, however modest, than to inflict blame and punishment, and certainly a good majority of my early reviews were favorable. I carried on what amounted almost to crusades for Joseph Conrad, George Bernard Shaw, John Galsworthy, James Huneker, the non-messianic Wells and the more honest and convincing of the two Arnold Bennetts, and got in many a lick for Nietzsche and Mark Twain. But all these were established men, and of the eight, six were foreigners and two were dead. What I needed was some American, preferably young, to mass my artillery behind, and I gave a good deal of diligence to the search for him.

Unhappily, the likely candidates were few. I thought I had one in 1909, when Henry Milner Rideout published *Dragon's Blood*, for it was an extraordinarily effective performance in the field (but not precisely in the manner) of Joseph Conrad, but when *The Twisted Foot* followed in 1910 there was apparent a sharp falling off, and soon afterward Rideout disappeared into the maw of the *Saturday Evening Post* and was heard from no more. I was quick, too, to hail Owen Johnson, the son of the old jackass, Robert Underwood Johnson,[1] and so early as *The Cords of Vanity* (1909) I began to beat the drum for James Branch Cabell, but Johnson was a humorist and nothing more, and Cabell, it soon appeared, was rather too precious in both his style and his ideas to make much progress with the generality of readers.

What I needed was an author who was completely American in his themes and his point of view, who dealt with people and situations of wide and durable interest, who had something to say about his characters that was not too obvious, who was nevertheless simple enough to be understood by the vulgar, and who knew how to concoct and tell an engrossing story.

When, toward the end of 1909, David Graham Phillips published *The Hungry Heart*, I began to suspect that I had my tank. Phillips was then forty-two years old, with a long and successful newspaper career behind him, and his writing was marked by a magnificent clarity and directness. He had been in his time one of the magazine muckrakers of the Roosevelt era, and his *Treason of the Senate* series had, in fact, inspired Roosevelt's denunciation of the whole sodality. He was an extremely facile and industrious author, and down to 1909 had written and published nearly twenty novels. Unhappily, I lost my tank at almost the precise instant of finding it, for on January 23, 1911, poor Phillips was shot and killed by a paranoic who accused him (falsely) of using his (the paranoic's) sister as a model for the complaisant heroine of *The Fashionable Adventures of Joshua Craig*.

But luck was still with me, for exactly a month after this tragedy Dreiser finished *Jennie Gerhardt* and on April 19 the MS. reached me in Baltimore. *Le roi est mort! Vive le roi!* In November, 1911, my article in the *Smart Set* was entitled "A Novel of the First Rank" and *Jennie* was its theme, and thereafter, for five or six years, Dreiser was the stick with which I principally flogged the dullards of my country, at least in the field of beautiful letters. I used that stick so sedulously that the impression inevitably got about that I was only a sort of fugleman for Dreiser; indeed, flinging the charge at me was the easiest of ways for the dullards to get back at me.

In 1911, with our acquaintance only three years old and the gorgeous phenomenon of *Jennie Gerhardt* just burst upon me, I was

1. Poet, editor of the *Century Magazine*, and prominent figure in the literary Old Guard.

frankly enchanted, and in my review in November I hailed it as "the best American novel I have ever read, with the lonesome but Himalayan exception of *Huckleberry Finn*." "Am I forgetting," I went on, "*The Scarlet Letter*, *The Rise of Silas Lapham*, and (to drag an exile unwillingly home) *What Maisie Knew?* I am not. Am I forgetting *McTeague* and *The Pit?* I am not. Am I forgetting the stupendous masterpieces of James Fenimore Cooper, beloved of the pedagogues, or those of James Lane Allen, Mrs. Wharton and Dr. S. Weir Mitchell, beloved of the women's clubs and literary monthlies? No. Or *Uncle Tom's Cabin*, *Rob o' the Bowl* or *Gates Ajar*, or *Ben-Hur*, or *David Harum*, or *Lewis Rand*, or *Richard Carvel?* No. Or *The Hungry Heart* or Mr. Dreiser's own *Sister Carrie?* No. I have all these good and bad books in mind. I have read them and survived them and in many cases enjoyed them. And yet in the face of them, and in the face of all the high authority, constituted and self-constituted, behind them, it seems to me at this moment that *Jennie Gerhardt* stands apart from all of them, and a bit above them. It lacks the grace of this one, the humor of that one, the perfect form of some other one; but taking it as it stands, grim, gaunt, mirthless, shapeless, it remains, and by long odds, the most impressive work of art that we have yet to show in prose fiction."

I was, of course, not blind to Dreiser's gross and glaring faults—his incapacity for logical planning, his puerile philosophizing, his really dreadful writing. "On the very first page," I noted, "one encounters *frank open countenance*, *diffident manner*, *helpless poor*, *untutored mind*, *honest necessity* and half a dozen other such ancients. And yet in the long run," I went on, "it is this very *naïveté* which gives the story much of its impressiveness. The narrative, in places, has the effect of a series of unisons in music—an effect which, given a solemn theme, vastly exceeds that of the most ornate polyphony. One cannot imagine *Jennie Gerhardt* done in the gipsy phrases of Meredith, the fugal manner of James. One cannot imagine that stark, stenographic dialogue adorned with the brilliants of speech. The thing could have been done only in the way that it has been done. As it stands, it is a work of art from which I, for one, would not care to take anything away—not even its gross crudities, its incessant returns to C major. It is a novel that depicts the life we Americans are living with extreme accuracy and criticizes that life with extraordinary insight. It is a novel, I am convinced, of the very first consideration."

This flaming review was the first long one to be printed, and its positive tone undoubtedly influenced a good many of those that followed. "I see by the reviews," Dreiser wrote to me on November 6, "that you are certainly the bell-weather [sic] this trip." And then, in December: "It looks to me from the drift of things as though your stand on *Jennie* would either make or break you—judging as an outsider. They are tying you up pretty close to it." It seemed a not unreasonable assumption, but I had no doubt that the issue would be favorable to both of us, and it turned out that I was right. I had by this time acquired a considerable following among newspaper reviewers, and had learned by experience that they had very few ideas of their own, and were always willing to follow a resolute lead.

My *Smart Set* review was by no means my only effort on behalf of the book and its author—my new Trojan horse. I wrote another for the Baltimore *Evening Sun* of November 27, 1911, and afterward revised and expanded it for the Los Angeles *Times*, of which Willard H. Wright, one of my most faithful followers, was then the literary editor, and I filled the mails with letters to my growing list of correspondents, urging them to read *Jennie* at once. Meanwhile, the Harpers, who were publishing the book, made use of my *Smart Set* review in their advertising—at first somewhat timorously, with extracts from newspaper reviews running ahead of it, but soon at the top of the column. By a curious irony, D. Appleton & Company, publishers of *The Husband's Story*, by David Graham Phillips, bought space at the same time to print my encomium of the book and its author. But I did not care, for Phillips, poor fellow, was now dead, and I was booming Dreiser.

All this notice, of course, appreciably enhanced my position as a reviewer. Not a few newspapers began to print notices of my reviews every month, and nearly all that did so approved them. Doubleday, Page & Company, always alert to the main chance, seized the opportunity to unearth my praises of Joseph Conrad, and to print them in advertisements along with kind words by H. G. Wells, John Galsworthy, James Huneker, Sir Hugh Clifford and Ford Madox Hueffer (later Ford Madox Ford). As in the case of Dreiser, I was first put at the bottom of the column, but soon I was in first place.

Between the time I read the MS. of *Jennie Gerhardt*, in April, 1911, and the time the Harpers brought it out, in autumn, Dreiser and I were in constant correspondence. He was hard at work until August on *The Financier* and also did some short stories. His doubts and tremors about *Jennie* continued until the book was published, and even afterward.

Dreiser was somewhat unsettled during 1911. Late in 1910, after losing his job on the *Delineator*, he left the apartment at 439 West 123rd Street, where he had been living ever since I first knew him, and moved to 600–08 Riverside Drive, but by May he had moved again to 225 Central Park West, and there he remained only a short while, for by June 18 he was writing to me that his new address would be 3609 Broadway, at the corner of 149th Street, and that it would be "good for over a year anyhow." His mood, in general, was characteristically depressed, but now and then he had his moments of hope and confidence. On August 5 he wrote to me:

> The London *Academy* for May 19 last (as W. J. Locke writes me) had a notice of *Sister Carrie* putting it with the 24 best books of the world, beginning with the Bible. All the other celebrities dead this long time but yours truly. Also putting it above *The Scarlet Letter* here and *Vanity Fair* in England. How's that? Poor old Thack! Well, here's a glass of beer to you.

Three days later he wrote that "book three" was finished, and that "the data for book four—*The Financier*—was "practically finished," and that the proofs of *Jennie Gerhardt* would soon be ready. The Harpers had insisted upon some cuts in the MS., and he wanted me to see what they were. It was now four months since I had read the MS., and I needed another look at the text in order to prepare my review—that is, if it was to be written before the actual book was in hand, as I planned. But the Harpers were reluctant to let me see the proofs, and our correspondence about them went on for weeks.

Finally Dreiser returned the MS. to me, and by September 15 my notice was finished and on its way to the *Smart Set* office. The same day I wrote to Dreiser: "Have no fear about *Jennie Gerhardt*. It is a novel of the first rank—the best ever done in America. The lady critics will discover that fact some time in 1913." On September 20 I wrote again: "My second reading of *Jennie Gerhardt* has increased my enthusiasm for it. Let no one convince you to the contrary: you have written the best American novel ever done, with the one exception of *Huckleberry Finn*. It hangs together vastly better than *McTeague*. It is decidedly on a higher plane. The very faults of it are virtues."

My *Smart Set* review came out on October 15, and two days later Dreiser wrote to me: "I picked up the *Smart Set* today and read your notice. I confess that my cheeks colored some, for I'm not ready yet to believe it. However, I wish you were here in order that we might drown our philosophic woes in good pale beer." On October 20 he sent me an autographed copy of the book and asked me to read it again, "to see whether in your judgment . . . it has been hurt or helped by the editing." "Your review," he added, "has created a real stir over here." On October 22 Arnold Bennett, who was on his first visit to America, broke out in the New York *Times* with unqualified praise of *Jennie* and it was soon on its way.

Despite the unusual length of the book the Harpers offered it at $1.35, then the usual list-price of novels, and in a little while it was selling briskly in the department-stores at $1.08, then the usual cut-rate price. But Dreiser was soon dissatisfied with their handling of it, and I was to learn that this was his habitual attitude toward publishers. He had rows with every one that ever published him, and on his side, at least, those rows were often extraordinarily bitter and raucous. More than once I have heard him allege with perfect seriousness that his publisher of the moment was cheating him on royalties—and keeping two sets of books to conceal the fact. His contract with the Harpers provided that they were to have the refusal of his next two books, but so early as November, 1911, he was writing to me that he was thinking of deserting them for the Century Company. Grant Richards, the English publisher, was then in New York, and Richards and the Century brethren undertook to get him away from Harpers by offering him the European trip which was eventually to produce *A Traveler at Forty* and by certain other shining baits. On November 11 Dreiser wrote to me:

Richards . . . says I have a good chance of getting the next Nobel Prize for literature following Maeterlinck, if it is worked right. He is going to organize the sentiment in England.

Despite the surreptitious negotiations with the Century Company his contract with Harper & Brothers still stood, and he asked me to write to him in care of their London office, 45 Albemarle Street. I was myself planning a voyage to Europe at the time, with A. H. McDannald, one of my associates on the Baltimore *Evening Sun*, as my companion, and I hoped to join Dreiser and Richards somewhere along the way. Unhappily, it was a presidential year and McDannald and I were kept so busy that we could not shove off until April 16, precisely at the time when Dreiser was starting homeward. He sent me a long series of brief notes and picture postcards as he moved about, including a card showing a view of Beer Lane in London, a discovery which delighted him. On the Rhine he visited his father's birthplace and saw the tombs of other relatives—one of them named Theodore Dreiser! With characteristic diligence, he wrote his record of the trip as he went along, and from Florence he sent me some carbons. "For heaven's sake," he wrote, "don't overemphasize the dullness of the Italian section, or you will have every critic in the U.S. yelping your remarks like a pack of curs. They've done it every time and they'll do it again."

At the Grand Continental Hotel in Rome he encountered Mrs. Paul Armstrong II, who had fled abroad with her children, parked them in Munich, and proceeded to enjoy herself in a large and spacious manner. He wrote to me on February 17, 1912 that he now knew her "right well," and later on I discovered that he had launched into a violent affair with her. This continued *diminuendo* after the two returned home, but it was by no means Dreiser's only preoccupation in that department. He was, in fact, a polygamist on a really wholesale scale, and during the years of our association I saw almost as much of his women as I did of him. Nor did I see all of them, by any means, for he was fundamentally a very secretive fellow, and not infrequently he tried to keep me in the dark about this or that affair. More than once he must have been successful, but even so I soon learned that women occupied an enormous place in his life—a place, indeed, that seemed to me, and to many others, to be inordinate. I sometimes wondered how, with four or five intrigues going on at once, he found time for his really heavy stint of daily writing.

But of all this extra-mural activity I had picked up only a few hints down to the time of *Jennie Gerhardt*. I learned in 1911 that he was on very friendly terms with a woman named Eleanora R. O'Neill, but I did not meet her until much later. The others were only shadows on the horizon, and what I heard of them seemed to me to be largely mere gossip, and hence not to be taken too seriously. When he went abroad in November, 1911, Mrs. Dreiser went west to visit her relatives, and on his return in April, 1912, she was still there, so that he got himself temporary quarters at 605 West 111th Street. There he lived with a woman named Anna Tatum, but he went back to 3609 Broadway on Mrs. Dreiser's return to New York.

On October 23 both of them wrote to me from there, inviting me to visit them and stay overnight. I went on October 28, but did not stay the night. After dinner, which Sarah cooked and served, Dreiser made some excuse for going out for an hour, and the moment the door closed upon him Sarah fell upon me with the story of her woes. She was a small and meagrely-made woman, with rusty red hair, and her whole manner suggested the country environment from which she had come, though she had been married to Dreiser since Christmas, 1898, and had been living in New York with him since 1901. Her stable-name, I gathered, was Jug. Her complaint was not of ill-humors, for Dreiser in his rough way seems to have been kind to her, nor of hardship, for though they had been very poor at the time of their marriage Dreiser's income in his *Delineator* days was large for that time; it was simply of infidelity. He was, she told me, an almost comic set-up for designing women. All the loose gals of the *Delineator* staff had had at him, and he was now under pursuit by at least half a dozen head of miscellaneous harpies, including a Jewish vaudeville actress named Lillian Rosenthal.

But to Mrs. Dreiser, of course, there was nothing comic in all this. She was convinced, I gathered, that connubial malpractice was one of the cardinal sins, and her yearning to bring her husband up to decency was apparently inspired almost as much by a desire to save his soul as by a resentment of rivals. She asked me to give her help in this enterprise, and I naturally had to promise, though it was obvious that I could do nothing. I was sincerely sorry for her, for in a competition with more charming and civilized women she was plainly at a great disadvantage. She looked far too forlorn to be laughed at, and in my promise to aid her there was at least a good intention, if not anything properly describable as hope or confidence.

Dreiser's return from his mysterious sally—he had not told me where he was going—broke in on her melancholy discourse, and I found myself feeling so uncomfortable that I cleared out at once. The apartment-house in which they lived, Riverside Court by name, was at Broadway and 149th Street, and after leaving it I walked down the long length of Broadway in the fine autumn night, meditating upon what I had heard. That meditation, alas, led me, not into a resolve to strike a brave if useless blow for poor Sarah, but into a gradually clarifying comprehension of Dreiser's side of it. To be sure, there seemed to be little doubt that he was guilty of the mortal sin of adultery, but already I had begun to formulate my theory that all sins involving torts should be measured, at least in part, by the character of the victims, not altogether by some abstract and rigid yardstick—that it was, for example, a good deal less offensive to humanity, and probably also to God, to shoot a foot-wash Baptist than to shoot a respectable bartender. Sarah, of course, was a worthy woman, and no doubt she had been mathematically faithful, on her part, to her marriage vows, but it was unhappily clear that she had failed dismally in the prime duty of every wife, which is to be charming to her lord.

While I listened to her I noticed a well-thumbed copy of *Science and Health* on the center-table of her little parlor. "How," I asked myself as I plodded on, "would *you* like to be married to a red-haired Christian Scientist from the Great Plains? How would *you* like to go home to her every night, and sit across from her at the dinner-table, and then listen to her *ad libitum?* Was there ever a Christian Scientist who was not a propagandist? And even assuming that she throttled her natural libido for proselytizing in and out of season, what of the day when you picked up a cold, and she looked on with reproachful eyes while you dosed yourself with castor-oil, aspirin, rock-and-rye, bromo-quinine tablets and Dr. Bull's cough-syrup? How now, good Henry? What is your answer to that?"

By the time I got to 125th Street I was wobbling and by the time I came to Columbus Circle I was lost. Without question Sarah had grievances that would inflame any moral theologian—but moral indignation, I liked to think with Nietzsche, was foreign to my nature. If, in the course of that long and gloomy walk, I recalled any scriptural text at all, it must have been Matthew VII, 1. Who, indeed, was I, to pronounce judgment upon a man who was my elder and better—a great artist, and, in the history of the Republic, almost incomparable? If the needs of his extremely difficult and onerous trade required him to consume and spit out a schoolma'm from the cow country, then it was certainly to be lamented—but that was as far as I could go in logic, or in such ethical theory as I subscribed to. In general, I had a prejudice against adultery, if only because it involved a breach of faith, but my prejudices, taking one with another, differed considerably from those of many other men, and I certainly had no desire to inflict them upon the whole human race.

Moreover, there was something else. In listening to Sarah I had picked up something that I was to observe in the years to come in more than one other wife of a literary character, to wit, a pervasive jealousy of her husband's growing fame. She had, I somehow gathered, literary aspirations of her own, and resented the fact that they were coming to nothing. That they were unaccompanied by any ponderable talent was a detail that she had naturally not noticed. Years later I was to see an extraordinarily virulent exhibition of such jealousy in Dorothy Thompson, the second wife of Sinclair Lewis—but Dorothy, for all her nastiness, actually had a certain amount of capacity of her own, whereas Sarah was only too manifestly a mere blob. Thus I dismissed her from my mind with hardly more than formal regret, and took my stand with the devil's party, which is to say, with Dreiser. After all, I was *his* friend and supporter, not *hers*. *She* had done nothing to lift me, or even to interest me; indeed, the most significant thing about her, intellectually speaking, was that she was a customer of Mary Baker G. Eddy, who seemed to me to be on all fours with the Fox sisters and Brigham Young. So far as I was concerned, she was merely a minor and non-essential function of a man whose activities in other directions I greatly admired, and I was thus easily resigned to letting him work his wicked will with her.

It was not long afterward that he ever mentioned his differences with her to me, and then he was very circumspect, for, as I have said, he was a naturally secretive man. I offered him no judgment on the business, but managed to let him understand that I was for him, right or wrong. On her return to New York they resumed living together at 3609 Broadway, and there they remained until the end of 1912, when Dreiser went to Chicago, and there picked up the woman who called herself Kirah Markham, and, on his return to New York in the early summer, took to living with her at 165 West 10th Street. I never saw Sarah again, though at great intervals I exchanged letters with her. She died in 1942.

MY RELATIONS WITH DREISER continued close through 1912, 1913, 1914, 1915, 1916, and I saw him very often. After his return from Europe in April, 1912, he blocked out the volume about his travels that eventually took form as *A Traveler at Forty*, but mainly he devoted himself to finishing *The Financier*. He kept plugging away during the summer, and by August 28 was writing to me that 250 galleys of proofs of *The Financier* were on his desk. On September 14 he wrote that the book ran to 270,000 words and made a volume of 800 pages.

On October 28, as I have related, I waited on the Dreisers at 3609 Broadway, and Mrs. Dreiser told me the story of her matrimonial grievances. When I got home two days later I found a copy of the printed book awaiting me, inscribed by Dreiser and marked, "This is the first copy that I have secured."

The first New York notices, which appeared on Sunday, November 3, objected to the great length of the book, and Dreiser was somewhat daunted by them. "It should have been cut," he wrote to me, "170 pages instead of 77." My *Times* notice was printed on November 10—with a couple of thumping typographical errors. My *Smart Set* notice had got too late for the December issue, out on November 15, and so did not come along until the January, 1913, issue, out December 15; as a result I was unable to lead the sheep as I had done in the case of *Jennie Gerhardt*. But my *Times* notice apparently helped, and after it appeared the tone of the other newspaper notices began to improve. On November 12 Dreiser wrote to me:

> I am wondering, in case I should prepare a codicil to that effect, if you would act as my literary executor in case of my death. I am particularly keen to have someone whose judgment I respect go over the material that is apt to be on hand in the case of a sudden demise and throw out the worthless. You are that one. You will find various things—poems, short stories, essays, a complete novel, over half of a book on my labor experiences, a part of another novel, and of course all my letters. I should want all writings turned over to you, of any kind, letter-files and all, and would expect you to demand them and to examine them without interference and without admitting anyone to consultation unless you felt so inclined. That's a good deal to ask.

I had to accept, of course, though protesting that I hoped the job would be left for "some better fellow, long after I am safely cremated." "But why," I went on (November 12), "let so much good stuff remain unpublished? I think a book of your essays, for example, would help to make plain what you are trying to get at in your novels, and so shut off some of the nonsense that now occasionally gets into print about you. . . . Somehow, I can see *The Financier* only as an overture to the next volume. I have no doubt about that next volume. You have the thing perfectly in hand: you will knock them out with it." It was understood between us, thereafter, that I was to be his literary executor, and from time to time he made a suggestion, usually verbally, about what should be done about this or that MS. in his drawer. But he was too secretive to be quite frank with me, and I have no doubt that he had a good many things in hand of which I never heard. When we began to drift apart, at the turn of the 20's, no more was heard from him about the matter, and after 1925, I suppose, he appointed some other executor.

I also wrote a notice of *The Financier* for the Los Angeles *Times*, and my *Smart Set* review, as I have said, came out on December 15. It began with a recital of the "characteristic faults of the author," and showed a certain amount of sober second thought. But I had begun to realize by this time that Dreiser was Dreiser and that the whole hierarchy of Hell could not change him. His method of getting his effects seemed to me a clumsy one, but he got his effects. "This," I went on, "is the way he chooses to write; and say what you will against it and against him for choosing it, you must always admit that he keeps his story unflaggingly interesting from start to finish, and that he thinks out his characters to six places of decimals, that nothing worth knowing about them is ever forgotten or glossed over or wrongly estimated, and that he achieves in the end an illusion so nearly perfect that it is almost uncanny."

Dreiser went to Chicago immediately after Christmas, 1912— ostensibly and perhaps mainly to gather material for *The Titan* but also in part, I suspect, to get away from his wife. There, on January 1, 1914, he met Kirah Markham, then leading woman of the Chicago Little Theatre, and thereafter, for two years, he was in her hands. When he returned to New York in the spring she followed him, and in June they set up housekeeping together in 10th Street, and she took over the management of his affairs, both personal and professional. My belief is that her influence upon him was predominantly for the bad, but it is not to be gainsaid that she was a woman above the common, with none of the puny ineffectiveness, bucolic stupidity and waspish envy of Mrs. Dreiser. In no department of her diligent and even somewhat feverish activity did she show any really notable talent, and yet she showed talent of a sort in all of them. She was a pretty fair actress, as actresses run in the American theatre; she painted in a respectable and workmanlike manner; she wrote so well that Nathan and I sometimes printed her in the *Smart Set* and were glad to do it; she had more than a little skill as a passable pianist.

Moreover, despite her wholesale artiness, she did not neglect the more orthodox accomplishments of the female. She did beautiful embroidery, she knew how to make her own clothes, and she was a first-rate cook, as I can testify who more than once sat under her in that character. While she and Dreiser lived together his somewhat meagre household was at the peak of its comfort and order. She kept him clean, she flogged him to work, and if only by chasing away most of the other women who swarmed after him she got him leisure and tranquility for it. On the debit side must be set her excessive bossiness and her eagerness to wring kudos for herself out of her association with a man of mark. When she gave a party she invited too many nonentities—her colleagues in the little theatres, third-rate painters, the editors of obscure *Tendenz* magazines, bad poets, worse novelists, and so on—and one of the results was that Dreiser, who had hitherto lived an essentially bourgeois life, became converted into a grotesque burlesque of the Rudolph of *La vie de Bohème* to the mirth of the gods and the embarrassment of his friends. It was, indeed, hard to refrain from laughing at a Rudolph built like a longshoreman or a farm-hand, with clumsiness in his every gesture, huge teeth, and a cast in one of his eyes.

Kirah, like the Lillian Rosenthal who was the subject of Mrs. Dreiser's bitter complaint, was a Jewess, and like La Rosenthal again, came of a well-to-do family. She was born in Chicago, where her father was a prosperous business man—as I recall it, a jeweler. What her actual name was I forget, but I remember that, when I heard it, it seemed to me to be prettier than Kirah Markham. After vain attempts to stagger humanity as a writer, a painter and a musician, she took to the easier art of the stage, and was presently one of the stars of the Chicago Little Theatre, the pioneer little theatre of the United States. Also, she took to fornication, and by the time Dreiser met her she had passed through the hands and beds of a good many other men, including actors, journalists and artists of various varieties.

She was, when I first saw her, about twenty-five years old, and not at all bad-looking, though it would have taken some generosity to call her a beauty. Rather tallish, with heavy chestnut hair, a good figure and noticeable busts, she looked rather sensuous, and that was what she was. That she was faithful to Dreiser while they lived together I doubt very seriously, for his efforts as a lover, though heroic, were hardly enough to content a woman who had been accustomed to the services of a large and assiduous band of men. I am, in fact, reasonably sure that she carried on an affair with an elderly Jewish painter and engraver named Henry Wolf, and I have reason to believe that she also had a fling with Paul Armstrong, to whom she applied (at my introduction) for a part in one of his plays. If this latter surmise is true, then there was poetic justice in her infidelity, for Dreiser, on his part, had had a delirious affair with the second Mrs. Armstrong, Rella Abell, whom he met in Rome early in 1912.

But these divagations did not diminish her devotion to Dreiser's interests, and during the time they lived together she showed all the sedulousness of a conscientious wife, and never forgot his welfare for a minute, though more than once, it seemed to me, she was greatly in error in her notions as to what it was. I visited him in 10th Street rather seldom during her reign, but that was not because I disliked her but because I objected to the kind of parties she staged. She lighted them by arty candlelight, which I detested, and she invited so many guests that there were not enough chairs for them, and many of them had to sit on the floor. Moreover, they included so many bad authors that meeting them was embarrassing to me, for all of them were eager to sell me something for the *Smart Set*. Nathan went to one of the worst of these parties, and came back with the news that it was dreadful indeed. He was backed into a corner by a herd of Greenwich Village poets, male and female, and most of the latter offered him the use of their persons. Inasmuch as it was not the custom, in the Greenwich Village of those days, for women emancipated from bourgeois restraints to wash their hair, he was not tempted.

Dreiser was somewhat dashed by the reviews of *The Financier*, and even my own gave him a shock, but his trip to Chicago and his meeting with Kirah bucked him up, and when he started back for New York on February 10, 1913, he was determined to push *The Titan* to a finish. He stopped off in Baltimore on his way, and we had a long palaver. In New York he resumed living at 3609 Broadway, but his marriage with poor Sarah was by now in its terminal stages, and by the summer it was done for, though he continued (in his mystifying way) to receive mail at the old address until 1914. Kirah had filled him with an enthusiasm for the theatre, and he soon began work on *The Girl in the Coffin* and other plays. On February 17, 1913, he wrote to me from New York urging me to write "a radical one-act play—something remote from the courage of the average stage," but all my ideas in that field ran to farce, and I had to say no.

Kirah moved in in June, but with characteristic secrecy Dreiser told me nothing of it, and it was not until toward the end of the year that I met her. He and I met often in New York but she was never present, and he said nothing about her in his letters. Meanwhile, I went on serving him as chief fugleman and father confessor. He sent me MSS. to read, chiefly of plays, and I advised him about markets, and kept on the lookout for references to him in the newspapers and magazines. In July, when he sent me *The Girl in the Coffin*, I forwarded it to Willard H. Wright, who had become editor of the *Smart Set*, and urged him to print it. Wright, at that time, was also doing the literary reviews for *Town Topics*, and on August 1 I sent Dreiser his notice of Daniel Carson Goodman's *Hagar Revelly* in which Jennie Gerhardt was spoken of as one of the "unforgettable heroines." But Dreiser did not like Wright, and refused to be grateful. He was dissatisfied with his publisher, Harper, and looking for another: in fact, he was already beginning that dismal flitting from publisher to publisher which was to mark all the rest of his writing career.

The proofs of *A Traveler at Forty*, which was committed to the Century Company by the arrangement with Richards, reached me on November 11, 1913, just too late for my January, 1914, book article. It let me down considerably, for it was full of Dreiser's dull, undistinguished writing, and large sections of it were almost unreadable. But I put the best face upon it that I could. My review of *A Traveler at Forty* came out in the *Smart Set* for February, 1914. I also wrote a review for the Baltimore *Evening Sun*, published on January 3. Dreiser thanked me for the latter on January 8, and asked me for some copies for distribution. "Do you suppose," he wrote that day, "I will ever reach the place where I will make a living wage out of my books, or is this all a bluff and had I better quit? I am getting ready to look for a job."

I tried to reassure him on January 11, but without too much confidence, for *A Traveler at Forty* would plainly do little to enhance his reputation, and I feared that he would have trouble with the Harpers over *The Titan*, as turned out to be the case. I had not seen the MS. of the latter, but I knew pretty well what was in it, and I feared that the prissy Harpers, who had urged Dreiser to make radical cuts in *The Financier*, would insist upon even more drastic ones in its sequel.

My *Smart Set* review of *A Traveler at Forty* was anything but enthusiastic. There was, to be sure, some excellent stuff in the book, but there was also a great deal of almost unendurable stuffing, and though I was eager to help Dreiser as much as possible the principle of *Amicus Plato, sed magis amica veritas* had to prevail. The best I could do was to take refuge in the fact that the book at least attempted a more or less coherent statement of Dreiser's fundamental philosophy, the cardinal articles of which, as I noted, appeared to be: "I. I do not know what truth is, what beauty is, what love is, what hope is. II. I do not believe anyone absolutely and I do not doubt anyone absolutely. III. I think people are both evil and well-intentioned."

My review, of course, must have been disappointing to Dreiser, but if so he did not complain. Instead he took refuge in silence and I can find no reference to it in his letters. Meanwhile, I was busy with plans to rescue him from the Harpers, who had first rights to *The Titan* under the contract for *The Financier*, but were obviously not the right publishers for it. At the start I was strongly in favor of a switch to George H. Doran, who had made a considerable stir as a publisher of fiction and was reputed to be relatively courageous and enlightened. In February, 1914, I began to discover doubts about him and communicated them to Dreiser, but in the end I concluded that he was the most likely publisher in sight.

While negotiations with him were going on Dreiser suddenly disappeared from New York and when I next heard from him he was in Chicago. What he was doing there I did not know at the time, for all the Chicago material for *The Titan* had been gathered, but later on I learned that the trip had been inspired by Kirah. She had some hope, it appeared, of getting a theatrical engagement in her old home town; moreover, she was eager to show off her latest man to her friends. On March 8, out of a clear sky, I received the following almost telegraphic letter from Dreiser, dated Hotel Bradley, Chicago, March 6:

> Harpers, after printing a first edition of 10,000 copies of *The Titan*, have decided not to publish. Reason: the realism is too hard and uncompromising and their policy cannot stand it. Doran is considering at present. Result uncertain.

This was astounding, surely, and also very disquieting. I had heard nothing whatsoever of the antecedent dispute, and could only guess that it must have been raucous. It was entirely characteristic of Dreiser that he sent me no details of this major disaster, and especially that he did not tell me that Anna Tatum had been left in charge of the negotiations with Doran in New York, with such help as she could get from his former secretary on the *Delineator*, Will Lengel. Why he had made her his agent I did not know, nor what his current relations with her were. It is likely that he had been carrying on with her all the while, despite his living with Kirah, but of this I had no evidence. All I could make out was that he had apparently put her to work as he so often worked his women, and he had given her rather large powers.

Under date of March 15 I received a fourteen-page hand-written letter from her telling me precisely what was going on. There had been stormy times in the Harper office, it appeared, when the MS. of *The Titan* came in. Ripley Hitchcock and Van Tassel Sutphen, then the principal readers for the firm, were scandalized by the wholesale veneries described in the first half of the book, and urged Dreiser to make some cuts. But he was in one of his bellicose moods and refused profanely to do so, and it went into type as written. When the first copies came off the press Frederick A. Duneka, then the head of the literary department, gave one of them a hasty overnight reading and was so shocked that he forbade its publication. It was in the midst of this uproar that Dreiser cleared out for Chicago with Kirah, leaving Tatum and Lengel to wrestle with the situation.

Tatum was in favor of turning over the book to Doran, and approached him to that end, but he developed the same dubieties that Hitchcock, Sutphen and Duneka had brought up. He professed to be interested in Dreiser, but said that he believed it would be a mistake to start publishing him with a book so full of salacity. Lengel preferred J. Jefferson Jones of the John Lane Company to the Harpers, and had opened negotiations with him. La Tatum now asked me to write to both Jones and Doran, urging them to take on the book. Jones was about to publish a book in which I had had a hand, *Europe After 8.15,* and was destined to do two more of mine in 1916, but I preferred Doran for Dreiser, and so refused to write to Jones. But I wrote to Doran, and under date of March 18 received the following reply from him:

It has been a matter of very much regret to me that we have not seen our way to take up *The Titan.* I am sorry for the position in which Mr. Dreiser finds himself with his present publishers, but I have already advised both Mr. Dreiser and Miss Tatum that *The Titan* was an utterly impossible book upon which a publisher could make a fair start in handling Mr. Dreiser and all his works.

On March 18 La Tatum wrote to me (on authority of Lengel) that the real reason why the Harpers decided not to print the book was not that it was pornographic, but that it dealt too harshly with what were then called the Interests. The firm, at the time, was bankrupt and in the hands of J. Pierpont Morgan & Company, and Duneka, who was Morgan's agent, feared protests (and perhaps even penalties) from 23 Wall Street. I had, meanwhile, not read *The Titan,* for Dreiser had not sent me the MS. An unbound copy reached me from Miss Tatum on March 18 and I read it at once. The next day came a telegram from her reading: "Doran and Century decline. Lane probably accepts Titan." On March 23, though I had heard nothing whatever from Dreiser about the business since his bombshell note of March 6, I wrote to him as follows:

I have just finished *The Titan.* Believe me, it is the best thing you have ever done, with the possible exception of *Jennie Gerhardt,* and the superiority there is only the greater emotional appeal. *Jennie* is more poignant—but *The Titan* is better written. In fact, some of the writing in it is far ahead of any of your past work—for example, the episode of the honest mayor snared by the wench. I am delighted that you are striving hard in this department. You are more succinct, more dramatic, more graceful. In brief, you are superimposing a charm of style upon the thrill of narrative.

On March 25 Dreiser was back in New York, without Kirah, and wrote to me at some length, giving me details of the business that La

Tatum had either overlooked or didn't know—most probably the latter. The John Lane Company, he said, had accepted the book and agreed to give him an advance of $1,000 and 20% royalties.

I sailed for Europe April 11, 1914, and did not see Dreiser before my departure. In March he had sent me the really amazing news that the Harpers, despite their efforts to suppress *The Titan*, were asking him to let them do *The "Genius"*, which was already well advanced. Meanwhile, Small, Maynard & Company had offered to take him over, and a little while later he also received overtures from Rand, McNally & Company. The John Lane Company planned to publish *The Titan* on May 10, but the Harpers refused to let go of *The Financier* save at an almost prohibitive price.

When I got back in June I found a copy of *The Titan* awaiting me. As a result of my absence my review of it was delayed until the August *Smart Set* and a great many newspaper reviews got ahead of it. *The Titan* had made a really powerful impression upon me, and in my *Smart Set* review I discussed it and Dreiser to the length of 3,000 words. This was the substance:

Four long novels are now behind him, and in every one of them one sees the same grim fidelity to an austere artistic theory, the same laborious service to a stern and rigorous faith. That faith may be put briefly into two articles: (a) that it is the business of a novelist to describe human beings as they actually are, unemotionally, objectively and relentlessly, and not as they might be, or would like to be, or ought to be; and (b) that his business is completed when he has so described them, and he is under no obligation to read copybook morals into their lives, or to estimate their virtue (or their lack of it) in terms of an ideal goodness. In brief, the art of Dreiser is almost wholly representative, detached, aloof, unethical: he makes no attempt whatever to provide that pious glow, that mellow sentimentality, that soothing escape from reality which Americans are accustomed to seek and find in prose fiction. And despite all the enormous advantages of giving them what they are used to and cry for he has stuck resolutely to his program. In the fourteen years since *Sister Carrie* he has not deviated once, nor compromised once. There are his books: you may take them or leave them. If you have any respect for an artist who has respect for himself you may care to look into them; if not, you may go to the devil.

On the whole *The Titan* got bad notices, and its sale, like that of *The Financier*, was much below that of *Jennie Gerhardt*. Meanwhile, Dreiser was plugging away at *The "Genius"*—and making heavy weather of it, for it was not until the end of November that he sent me a typescript of the first sixty-six chapters. He was also trying his hand at one-act plays, and on July 29 he wrote to me from 165 West 10th, where he and Kirah were once more settled: "Can I get you to read a two-part philosophic article and three one-act plays which I have just completed?"

I replied on July 30, asking him to send them along and saying that I had "a particular reason for wanting to see them." That reason was that John Adams Thayer was pressing me to take over the editorship of the *Smart Set* and showing preliminary signs of the panic that was to descend upon him at the outbreak of the approaching war, and lose him control of the magazine.

By the time the three plays reached me Crowe, Warner, Nathan and I were preparing to take over, and I asked Dreiser to give me an option on them for two weeks. "The reason," I wrote on August 11, "must be kept confidential. I am at work on a plan which may give me editorial control of the *Smart Set*, and I want to blaze out with some Dreiser stuff. The chances, at the moment, are against success, but I am hanging on, and may know the result in a day or two. George Nathan is with me. He is, in fact, doing all the final negotiating. If the thing goes through there will be a future in it for both of us. The S.S. is losing very little money, and the cutting off of certain excessive overhead expenses—high rent, extravagant salary to Thayer, etc.—will quickly make it self-sustaining. And we are associated with a truly excellent man of business [Warner]—one who is no mere talker, but has actually made a success elsewhere. Thayer is a sorry quitter. He got into a panic at the first firm." Dreiser gave me the option on August 12, and Nathan and I took it up, after the unpleasantness to be described, as soon as we were in full charge of the magazine. We published *The Blue Sphere* in our second issue, that for December, 1914; *In the Dark* in January, 1915, and *Laughing Gas* in February.

A little while before this, in July, 1914, I had made a trip to Washington to see Herbert Putnam, the librarian of Congress, on some business that I forget, and in the course of lunch with him had suggested that he ought to try to get the MSS. of Dreiser's books for the library. Putnam expressed great interest, and on August 2 I wrote to

Dreiser. On August 3 he replied: "I have all the MSS.—originals. I may be very glad to turn them all over if they will keep them together, the trilogy especially. I will add something to this statement a little later." On August 10 he astonished me with the following: "I hereby offer you the original pen copy of any one of my MSS.—*Sister Carrie*, *Jennie Gerhardt*, *The Financier*, *The Titan*, *The Genius*, (when done with), *A Traveler*, or this set of one act plays. The trilogies ought to be kept together." I replied on August 11: "You overcome me with the offer of one of your MSS. There is nothing I'd be more delighted to have: it would be the arch of my collection of Dreiseriana. But can it be that you really mean it? Trying my damndest to think evil of no man, I am filled with suspicions that you have taken to heroin, Pilsner, formaldehyde. Purge your system of the accursed stuff—and then offer me *Sister Carrie*. And see me jump!"

The MS. was in storage, and it was some time before he exhumed it, but he eventually did so, and then gave it to me. It was, of course, a royal present, and I was duly appreciative. It was done, mainly in pencil, on fifteen-hundred-odd half sheets of copy paper, and made a bundle seven or eight inches high. I undertook to collate it with the published text of the novel, and found at once that there had been some considerable cuts (most of them, it seemed to me, for the better), but the paper was so yellow and fragile that handling it threatened to damage it, so I gave up the business. I kept the MS. in a trunk stored in the silver vault of the Metropolitan Savings Bank, Baltimore, along with various other MSS. and books, but some years later transferred it to a concrete vault that I had built with my own hands in the cellar at 1524 Hollins Street. There it lay until 1935, when the thought occurred to me that it would have to go to some public library at my death, and had better be sent at once.

At some time in the interval Dreiser had written to me saying that Belle DaCosta Greene, librarian of J. Pierpont Morgan's library in New York, had offered $10,000 for it, and proposing, with characteristic lack of tact, that he and I accept this somewhat incredible offer and divide the money. I replied, of course, that I could not be a party to any such arrangement, but if he was hard up and actually needed the money I'd return the MS. to him at once. The negotiations went no further, and I now felt myself free to dispose of it as I pleased. Because of my discussion with Herbert Putnam in 1914 the

Library of Congress naturally suggested itself, and one day I dropped in on Putnam at his office. He professed to be eager to have the MS. and took me to Dr. John F. Jameson, the chief of the library's manuscript division, to arrange the details. Jameson, who was then seventy-six years old, was a specialist in American history, and it turned out when Putnam left us that his interest was wholly confined to political history. He had never heard of *Sister Carrie*, nor even of Dreiser, and my somewhat embarrassed explanations left him plainly dubious.

Finally, with the air of doing me a favor, he told me that, though the MS. I described seemed to have no importance to American history, he *might* accept it as throwing a sidelight on the cultural life of the country, just as he occasionally accepted, so he explained, the books of account of some old firm. I left him chuckling at his imbecility, and in 1937 offered the MS. to H. M. Lydenberg, librarian of the New York Public Library. Lydenberg accepted it instantly and with great alacrity, and it was soon in his hands. He agreed to mount it on rag paper, to treat it with a fixative, and to have it suitably bound. I warned him, remembering the Belle Greene episode, that Dreiser might descend upon him at any minute and ask for its return, and he agreed to surrender it in that event, but also to make hard efforts to "placate him and retain physical possession." It was further agreed that the gift of the MS. should not be announced during Dreiser's lifetime or mine without our express permission, nor should anyone have access to it. I told Dreiser of this arrangement sometime later on and he consented to it.

CHAPTER IX

IT TURNED OUT to be a mistake to print the Dreiser plays in the *Smart Set*, as Nathan and I might have expected and soon found. I had no compunction about asking Dreiser for an option on them, and then suggesting (as I did on August 17) that he make his price "as cheap as possible," for they were not the sort of thing that would have a ready market elsewhere. I soon learned, in fact, that an agent had been trying in vain to sell them. Dreiser responded cordially enough, and added a short story, "The Lost Phoebe," to the plays and also a thing called "The Born Thief" that he had written for the movies; however, he accepted our offer of $100 apiece for the first serial rights to the plays.

But on September 11 he wrote to me that he had accepted "with one mental reservation—that the ten per cent. which I shall have to pay my dear, useless agent be added—otherwise I should only clear $90, and I need such cash as I can get." I responded that we also needed cash—that the *Smart Set*'s accumulated indebtedness was absorbing nearly all the money we could squeeze out of it by our drastic reduction in its operating expenses—but Dreiser insisted on his mental reservation, and in the end we agreed to pay him $110 for each play. These negotiations were very far from pleasant, and Nathan and I decided to be wary of him in future.

At one stage of them, after *The Blue Sphere* was already in type, he demanded raucously that we return all three plays, and a bit later on he showed a good deal of heat when we decided that we didn't want *The Lost Phoebe* and the movie scenario, *The Born Thief*. I explained to him that the things he was sending us were insufficiently characteristic of him; that, in our first stages at least, we should be printing genuine and easily recognizable Dreiser stuff, and not a series of vague and murky experiments. I even suggested that he let us print an episode or two from The "*Genius*", which was now approaching a conclusion, or anything that may have been left over when *The Titan* was cut.

We were learning, alas, that his common reputation as a baiter of editors and publishers was only too well justified, and we resolved to avoid him as much as possible after printing the three plays. He had sent in two more, *A Spring Recital* and *The Light in the Window*, but we refused them. His situation between the summer of 1914 and the end of 1915 was anything but agreeable, for the $3,000 that the Harpers had demanded for releasing *The Titan* was more than the book was earning, and he was hard put to it to boil the pot. On August 10, 1914, he wrote to me that he was "half way through Vol. I of a three-volume 'History of Myself'—Vol. I ends naturally at 20; Vol. II at 40, and Volume III will be written and end chance knows when" and that he proposed to finish it by September 2 and tackle *The Bulwark*, but on August 22 he reported that he was already at work on *The Bulwark*, needed $1,000 to pay his way to the end of it, and had various schemes for raising the money. Soon afterward he abandoned *The Bulwark* in its turn for *The "Genius"*, but his need, of course, continued.

I was naturally very sympathetic, and if there had been any considerable amount of money in the *Smart Set* till I'd have been glad to give him a substantial part of it, but Nathan and I were just starting and there was still very little, and on that little there were many other demands. I had to be extremely polite to him, for I was eager to avoid offending him, but sometimes it was difficult to refrain from inviting him to go to the devil. Our exchanges, it soon appeared, left some soreness on his side as well as on mine, and when I very imprudently wrote to him on April 6, 1915, suggesting that he give "the resurrected *Smart Set* a glance," and, if he could do so "without injury to conscience," "dash off a few lines saying that it has shown progress during the past six months," he waited two weeks to reply, and then sent in a long and extremely unfriendly criticism.

This was so ill-natured that it was easy to read into it a good deal more than sober literary judgment. Nevertheless, there was also a considerable plausibility in parts of it, and I believe that it had some influence on my editorial votes and projects during the remainder of the year. In our effort to take the smell of both Wright's *heliogabal-isme* and Luther's and Boyer's puerility off the magazine, Nathan and I plunged rather heavily into satire, and it was certainly not unreasonable to argue that we were going too far. It was already evident, indeed, that our tastes were not precisely alike—that Nathan had a great deal more of Broadway in him than I had—and this difference was to come to a head in 1924, after we launched the *American Mercury*, though I agreed with him that, for the present at least, we should stick to a very light tone. But I was eager to strike a more serious note as soon as possible, and I managed to do so after we began to flush such newcomers as Lilith Benda.

There was more behind Dreiser's choler than resentment of my refusal of *The Lost Phoebe* and all the plays after *Laughing Gas;* he was also upset by my skeptical attitude toward his removal to Greenwich Village and his arty life there with Kirah Markham. While he lived uptown with Sarah he led a thoroughly bourgeois life, and there was no sign in his carriage of the Bohemian, though he was already practicing a Latin Quarter promiscuity, but once he got down to 10th Street he took to the life of art, and was soon a painful figure to his old friends. All this was due to the precept and example of Kirah, who had come up in the Little Theatre atmosphere of Chicago, and was eager to make her new man a great figure in her brummagem world. Kirah was not unintelligent, and, as I have said, she had some talent, but there was always something third-rate about her, and she came very near making Dreiser third-rate too.

An innocent and confiding fellow at bottom, despite his chronic suspiciousness, he let her lead him into a circle of writers and artists who were almost unanimously mountebanks, and when, in 1916, the suppression of *The "Genius"* brought him to a time of serious trial their efforts to make capital out of him came near being disastrous. I was really fond of the old boy, and after the outbreak of World War I we had a new interest in common, for he was against the English just as I was, but I couldn't conceal from him the fact that the Greenwich Village into which he had been sucked seemed to me to be wholly bogus and silly. Nor could I resist the temptation to poke frequent fun at his own grotesque transmogrification—a German peasant turned Bohemian. This irked him and it irked Kirah still more, so I began to see him less often than I had seen him before she collared him, though I did visit them now and then in what Kirah had taught him to call their "studio," and more than once I enjoyed Kirah's excellent cooking.

It began to be understood that when I came none of her arty friends were to be invited; if there were any other guests I took them myself. Looking about the place, I could not help contrasting it with Sarah's folksy flats in 123rd Street and upper Broadway. It was the ground floor of an old and somewhat decrepit three-story house, and the two parlors had been thrown into one. The furniture was all arty and half a dozen paintings by Kirah hung on the wall. I was, and have always been, in favor of bright illumination at meals, but Kirah insisted on lighting the huge and dismal room with candles, and they threw insufficient light and were always guttering and going out.

The neighborhood was in an advanced state of decay, and getting to the place in bad weather was not pleasant. Such of the neighbors as were not professional Bohemians were mainly poor Italians. Shortly after Kirah's exit in 1915 work began on the 7th Avenue subway, and in a little while there was a huge excavation behind the house, and the clatter of pneumatic drills went on day and night. The plumbing was often out of order, and there were times when poor Dreiser had a hard time getting fuel delivered for his open fireplace.

One day in 1916 or 1917 two detectives came to the door and asked him if he knew anything about his neighbors in the basement. He replied that he knew nothing about them save that they were Italians and appeared to be very industrious people, for they kept a sewing-machine going nearly all the time. The cops then told him that this sewing-machine was actually a machine for making counterfeit quarters, and that they proposed to raid the Italians at once. All this palaver took perhaps ten minutes. When it was over the cops proceeded to the raid—and discovered the Italians had got wind of it and escaped by way of the subway excavation, taking their counterfeiting machine with them! Dreiser, whose humor was predominantly of an oafish type, told this story over and over again, and cackled fit to choke every time. When the cops, baffled, went away, he descended to the basement to see if he could find any counterfeit quarters, but the wops had taken their stock away along with their machine.

In June Dreiser and Kirah separated, and in August he went to Indiana with Franklin Booth on the automobile trip that was to produce *A Hoosier Holiday*. The first printed copy of *The "Genius"* reached me on September 29, too late for me to review it in the November *Smart Set*. Thus, as in the case of *The Titan*, my notice followed instead of preceding the newspaper notices, and when they began to appear I saw that the book was in for pretty rough handling. I must have made it plain to Dreiser that I was not much taken by it myself, for on October 9 he wrote to me with somewhat heavy sarcasm: "Favorable reviews in this case no doubt indicate the inherent weakness of the book to you—and no doubt you are right. The applause of boobs is the proof of a failure. I, most of all, am aware of that." There was, alas, very little applause, even from boobs. The climax came on December 2, when Stuart Pratt Sherman gave over nine columns of the *Nation* to a furious denunciation of both *The "Genius"* and Dreiser, closing as follows:

> A realistic novel is a representation based upon a theory of human conduct. If the theory of human conduct is adequate, the representation constitutes an addition to literature and to social history. A naturalistic novel is a representation based upon a theory of animal behavior. Since a theory of animal behavior can never be an adequate basis for a representation of the life of man in contemporary society, such a representation is an artistic blunder. When half the world attempts to assert such a theory, the other half rises in battle. And so one turns with relief from Mr. Dreiser's novel to the morning prayers.

This banality was quite in line with the academic criticism of the time. The professors believed that they had disposed of a work when they pasted a label on it and filed it away in a drawer, and Sherman was then the archetype of the species. His disingenuous and cowardly attempt to set the Anglomaniacal press upon Dreiser was also characteristic of the man. Later on, after he moved from Urbana, Illinois, to New York and fell under the influences of Carl and Irita Van Doren and other civilized persons, he changed his tune completely and took to praising Dreiser. The vituperative tone of his *Nation* review was imitated by many other reviewers, and it soon became evident that *The "Genius"* was a flop and that Dreiser would be lucky if it brought him nothing worse than bad notices and did not lead to an investigation of him as a German spy. He was at work at the time upon *A Hoosier Holiday* and trying to piece together the text of *Plays of the Natural and Supernatural*, but his literary prospects seemed pretty dark, and even before the Sherman billingsgate appeared he wrote to me that he was thinking of taking a job as director "in a new and somewhat imposing film corporation." "I can't begin," he said, "by ramming naturalism down their throats—not, at least, until I get my hand in, but I can make such incidents as will go over appealing."

But nothing came of this movie enterprise, and a little while later Dreiser was trying to sell me another one-act play and also a sequence of poems in free verse. The play was called "The Scavenger" and seemed to me to be so bad, at least in the form in which I then saw it, that I had to refuse it. The poems turned out to be seven in number. They reached me on Christmas Day, 1915, and I rejected them. At Dreiser's request I returned the three rejected poems on January 4, 1916, and at the same time offered him 50 cents a line for the remaining four—our regular rate. He protested that this was too low, and I replied from Baltimore on January 21: "The market price for first-class verse, dear heart, is 50 cents a line. At this rate we are offered endless consignments of such goods by the best firms in the business. But the finances are up to Nathan and if he finds it in his heart to throw away money I'll go with him." But Nathan was still out of humor with Dreiser on account of the unpleasantness over the plays, and refused to yield. Dreiser had meanwhile gone to Savannah, Georgia, on a mysterious mission, and from there he wrote to me on February 4, offering to give me the four poems for nothing "with my compliments and paternal blessing." Nathan, who saw this offer as no more than a bluff, advocated accepting it, but I insisted on sending Dreiser $25, which worked out to sixty cents a line. We published them in May, 1916. I liked two of them very much, but they apparently made no impression on the customers.

My review of The "Genius" was published in the Smart Set for December, 1915, under the heading of "A Literary Behemoth." If it had been written after instead of before Stuart Sherman's poltroonish attack in the Nation I'd probably have undertaken some sort of defense of it, however speciously; as it was, I was worn out by the weariness of trying to plow through its more than 300,000 of undistinguished words, and something of my boredom got into my notice. The best I could do, as in the case of The Financier, was to argue weakly that Dreiser was Dreiser, and should be allowed to choose his own weapons.

The book naturally did badly—and certainly not only because the reviews were generally caustic. Dreiser, in the way now become familiar to me, put all the blame upon Jones of the John Lane Company. On January 19, 1916, he wrote to me asking me to find out "from the one or two leading book-stores in Baltimore the exact number of copies sold to date." He led me to assume that only the natural concern of an author was behind this request, but a little later on, when I asked him for a report on the Lane Company (which was soon to bring out my two books, *A Little Book in C Major* and *A Book of Burlesques*), he replied that Jones was "apparently not a bad fellow in his way," but hinted broadly that the Englishmen in charge of "the financial department" were rogues. This charge that his publisher kept two sets of books was one that he was to make often in the years to come, and as he got further and further down the scale of Barabbases there were probably times when it was true.

Dreiser returned from his mysterious trip to Savannah by way of Washington and Philadelphia and was back at 165 West 10th Street by April 10, 1916. Kirah had meanwhile returned there from Chicago, but her stay was destined to be short, and soon afterward she and Dreiser parted for good. She had now abandoned, it appeared, her hopes for a stage career, and was concentrating on literary endeavor and the graphic arts. On April 18 she sent me some of her poems, and, as I have recorded, I printed one of them, an eleven-line piece called "Mid-Summer," in the *Smart Set* for August. She also proposed to do some line drawings for the magazine, having heard that Nathan and I were toying with a plan to illustrate it. "I am returning for a brief period in May," she said, "to the paternal roof, and I am trying to find plenty to keep me busy, particularly during that time." While she was on that visit to Chicago she met Frank Lloyd Wright, Jr., son of the architect, and soon afterward she married him and 165 West 10th Street saw her no more.

Dreiser, on his return from Savannah, put in the finishing licks on *A Hoosier Holiday*, and toward the end of June he sent me the typescript. At about the same time he wrote to me that he had handed Vol. I of *The History of Myself* to Jones, and asked me to take charge of it in case of his death before its publication. "If it ever fell into the hands of Mrs. Dreiser or some of my relations," he explained, "I am satisfied that they would destroy it at once." I accepted this commission, and told him on June 26 that I'd try to find someone to handle the business in case of my own death. "It is conceivable," I said, "that we may enjoy the felicity of dying together—for example, in battle for the Republic."

I found *A Hoosier Holiday* interesting, but in reporting on it had to add: "I am constantly outraged, however, by banalities, and it seems to me that they should come out. My hands itch to get at the job. . . . It must run to 200,000 words or more—too much for such a book." I also objected, like Grant Richards, to some of the passages dealing with living persons, as in bad taste, and we had some correspondence regarding one dealing with Day Allen Willey, a Baltimorean. In the end, he let me have my way, and on July 5 I returned the edited typescript. "Most of the changes," I wrote on that day, "involve the excision of repetitions: your discussion of the nature and meaning of life, for example, is repeated a dozen times, and often in very similar words. Again, there are many smaller repetitions. Yet again, certain words are overworked—for example, *secure*—and I have substituted synonyms. Yet again, I have performed some discreet surgery upon the Day Allen Willey episode, and upon others of its sort. In the main, I have let the discussion of the Catholic Church stand. They are against you anyhow. Why not strike back?"

Aside from these blemishes, the book was certainly not bad. "It contains," I wrote to Dreiser, "the best writing you have ever done. A genuine feeling for style is in it." He agreed to all my proposed cuts save one or two. The book was scheduled for publication in the early autumn, and I fell upon my review at once. It was printed in the *Smart Set* in October, 1916, and I devoted most of it to a general consideration of Dreiser and his ideas, for I planned to use a considerable part of it in *A Book of Prefaces*, which Alfred Knopf was preparing to bring out in September.

I did three articles on Dreiser for the Baltimore *Evening Sun* during the summer of 1916, and like my *Smart Set* reviews they entered into the section on him in *A Book of Prefaces*. I sent them to Dreiser as they came out, and he made various suggestions for minor changes. Along with the first article there was a note cautioning him not to show it to Jones of the John Lane Company, which, under the contract to *A Little Book in C Major* and *A Book of Burlesques*, had the refusal of the new book. "There are several references in it," I explained, "that may excite his patriotic ire, and he may want to cut them out of the book. It will be easy enough to slip them into the actual book MS. I believe that Jones never reads a book MS."

All these pleasant exchanges and negotiations were broken into at the end of July by the news that the New York Comstocks had filed a complaint against *The "Genius"*. This, of course, was not wholly unexpected, for many of the newspaper reviews had denounced the novel for salacity, and I was well aware that John S. Sumner, the new head of the Society for the Suppression of Vice, was eager to make his mark with a prosecution that would get attention in the newspapers. Characteristically, Dreiser sent me the news quite casually. "In passing," he wrote to me on July 27, 1916, "the censor has descended on *The "Genius"* and ordered Jones to withdraw it from the market. He claims complaints have been filed in New York and Cincinnati. Don't write Jones concerning this, or say anything until I get further details. Jones is apparently anxious to compromise, and I do not intend that he should unless I have to, but I have promised silence until the specific directions are laid down. So far they are 'blasphemy' and 'immorality.' You may be called upon as an expert, later. . . . This book was selling the best of any and now this cuts me off right in mid-stream. Don't it beat hell?"

My experience with the *Parisienne* case convinced me that the situation was more serious than Dreiser seemed to think. What I was mainly uneasy about was the Stuart P. Sherman article in the *Nation*. If Jones and Dreiser put me on the stand for the defense, or any other critics willing to testify, the prosecution would undoubtedly put on Sherman, and he would not only denounce the book as grossly immoral, but also try to raise anti-German prejudice against the author. Moreover, he would have the support of a great many other Pecksniffs of his kidney, for the notices of the book, as I have said, had been predominantly unfavorable, and not a few of them had suggested that it ought to be suppressed. Jones, meanwhile, had left New York, apparently on a holiday, and the situation became increasingly murky. On August 4 Dreiser wrote to me:

> If it were a question of a few changes I would say fine. But consider! And each one is enough, according to Sumner, to suppress on. A fight is the only thing, and I want Lane to fight. I hope and pray they send me to jail.

All this was very well, but it seemed to me to be foolish to take on a head-long fight with the changes running so heavily in favor of the Comstocks. Most of the articles in their complaint against the book, of course, were silly, but there were a dozen or more passages that would undoubtedly strike any jury as obscene, especially if done by a German, for the Germans were being depicted by the English propaganda which filled the newspapers as wholesale and incorrigible immoralists. But if Dreiser was determined to demand his day in court, despite the heavy odds against him, there was nothing for me to do save go along.

Dreiser was full of the idea of going to jail as a martyr to free speech, and there was no holding him. His reports about the attitude of Jones varied from day to day. One day Jones was hot to fight and had hired lawyers and the next day he was sulking. In all this I began to see something more than Dreiser's own hand. Kirah, as I have related, had pulled him down into the quagmire of Greenwich Village, and now some of its quacks were operating on him. They had, of course, no real interest in him, or in his book, or in the freedom of American letters; they were simply trying to get publicity out of the row.

In a little while I heard that he was exhibiting himself at the Liberal Club, the hang-out of all the more radical of them, and even making a speech. Also, he began to give out interviews sneering at Jones, whose cooperation he plainly needed very badly, for he had no money and could not fight the Comstocks on his own. He even talked of applying for an injunction restraining Jones from suspending the sale of the book. I warned him against the Greenwich Village radicals on August 9 and against antagonizing Jones on August 22. "Your talk about injunctions," I said on the latter date, "is absurd. If the book is ever barred from the mails Jones's obligation to print it will cease at once, all contracts to the contrary notwithstanding. It is impossible to enforce a contract which involves the performance of an unlawful act. This is one of the primary axioms of the law."

The only sensible idea that emerged from all this fustian and poppycock was a plan for a manifesto by American authors, protesting against the attempt to suppress *The "Genius"* by what amounted to a process of blackmail. It was at first proposed—by whom I do not know—that a Committee of One Hundred be formed, and by August 11 I was already writing to various authors of my acquaintance, trying to induce them to join, and also undertaking to enlist the aid of the Authors' League of America. To that end I drew up a proposed text for the manifesto, and proposed that Jones have it printed. "I think the best way to go about it," I wrote on August 22, "will be to print a hundred or so copies and then put them into the hands of four or five men who will personally besiege the leading authors of the country. By leading authors, of course, I mean those best known to the public. The signature of such an old ass as Brander Matthews will be worth a great deal."

Unhappily, Dreiser's bellicose attitude alarmed Jones, and in the end the business of handling the manifesto fell to me. Sending it out involved a great deal of clerical work, and Dreiser had no money to pay for the necessary postage and secretarial assistance. I had, a little while before, acquired a competent secretary in Baltimore, Miss Addie B. Deering, and by the end of August she was already hard at work. There was not too much time to spare, for I was planning to go abroad at the end of the year to see something of the war, and could only guess when I'd return. So Miss Deering and I put in long hours on the business, and by the time I sailed a great many signatures had been rounded up.

THE TEXT OF what came to be known as the Dreiser Protest, as I drew it on August 20, 1916, or thereabout, was as follows:

A PROTEST

We, the undersigned, American writers observe with deep regret the efforts now being made to destroy the work of Theodore Dreiser. Some of us may differ from Mr. Dreiser in our aims and methods, and some of us may be out of sympathy with his point of view, but we believe that an attack by irresponsible and arbitrary persons upon the writings of an author of such manifest sincerity and such high accomplishments must inevitably do great damage to the freedom of letters in the United States, and bring down upon the American people the ridicule and contempt of other nations. The method of the attack, with its attempt to ferret out blasphemy and indecency where they are not, and to condemn a serious artist under a law aimed at common rogues, is unjust and absurd. We join in this public protest against the proceeding in the belief that the art of letters, as carried on by men of serious purpose and with the cooperation of reputable publishers, should be free from interference by persons who, by their own statement, judge all books by narrow and impossible standards; and we advocate such amendments of the existing laws as will prevent such persecutions in future.

The business of soliciting signatures for this manifesto was thrust on me rather against my desire, though I was eager to help Dreiser as much as possible. It was hardly prepared before I became involved in the onerous and wearying effort to sell Nathan's and my share in the *Parisienne* and *Saucy Stories* to Crowe and Warner, and presently I was trying hard to advance my *Smart Set* and other routine work sufficiently far to enable me to sail for the war. Moreover, I was beset by an extraordinarily severe attack of hay-fever on August 25, and on August 28 went to Long Beach, Long Island, in hope of relief, and, as I wrote to Dreiser on that day, planned to proceed to New Hampshire in case I didn't find it on Long Island. My hope was that Jones's office would take over the job of canvassing authors, with such help as it could get from the Authors' League, the secretary of which, at the time, was a young man named Eric Schuler. Schuler was an energetic fellow and very sympathetic to Dreiser, but he was only a paid employe, and he hesitated to take any active hand until he was sure that the majority of members of the League, and especially of its board, were solidly behind him. The board held a meeting on August 24 to discuss the matter, and it appeared that the prevailing sentiment was favorable to lending Dreiser a hand. The next day the executive committee met and adopted the following minute:

It was the sense of the meeting in discussing the proposition involved in the proceeding pending against the John Lane Company and Theodore Dreiser *in re* the suppression of The *"Genius"* that the book complained of by the Society for the Prevention of Vice is not subject to condemnation by it, and that the same is not lewd, licentious or obscene, and it is further the sense of the meeting that the test ordinarily applied in such cases is too narrow and unfair, and that it may, if not modified, prevent the sale of many classics and of much of the serious work which is now being offered, and it is further the sense of the meeting that the League take such action as may be possible to prevent the suppression of the work complained of.

To this document was appended the notation: "Mr. Dreiser is not now and never has been a member of the Authors' League of America." The moving spirit in the action was Harvey J. O'Higgins, a member of the board but not of the executive committee. It was mainly because of his energetic agitation that the League proceeded to implement the minute of the executive committee by appointing one of the young men on its office staff, Harold Hersey, to send out copies of the Dreiser Protest from its office and to gather signatures. Hersey, alas, was a poor fish, and in the end the main burden of rounding up the literati fell upon me. Meanwhile, Jones was showing such alarms that Dreiser began to fear that he would try to placate the Comstocks by surrendering the plates of The *"Genius"*, and on August 28 I agreed to let them be shipped to me in Baltimore, though I was well aware that the Comstocks could easily trace them. In the end they were sent over the North river into New Jersey for safety, and there they remained until the uproar was over.

The first response received to the protest itself was a refusal to sign it. This came from Churchill Williams, then a member of the staff of the *Saturday Evening Post*. His letter, dated Philadelphia, September 12, 1916, was addressed to Hersey and was as follows: "Without personal knowledge of the attempt to suppress the work of Theodore Dreiser. . . . I would rather not sign the Protest. . . . Speaking for myself, however, Mr. Dreiser's work has always interested me deeply, and I would have no sympathy whatever with any movement to suppress those writings."

There was silence from many others to whom I had sent copies of the Protest, and in the early days of September the prospects of getting together a really formidable body of signers seemed pretty blue. But on September 13, Jones received the following cable from London, and rushed it to the newspapers, and after that the sledding was easier:

> Convey to Dreiser and Authors' League following message: We regard The *"Genius"* as a work of high literary merit and sympathize with the Authors' League of America in their protest against its suppression.
>
> Arnold Bennett
William J. Locke
E. Temple Thurston
H. G. Wells

The name of Hugh Walpole was presently added to this pronunciamento. It naturally had a powerful effect, for English example is always followed sedulously in the United States, and it was never more potent than in those war days of 1916. After September 15 signatures began to pour in, not only to me but also to the Authors'

League and to others who had volunteered to send out copies of the Protest. Reginald Wright Kauffman, who was in Maine, not only signed himself on September 16, but proceeded to round up a number of other signatures, and Frank Harris, then editing *Pearson's* maga-zine in New York, resigned from the Authors' League because it had not "taken the energetic action" he "desired and expected," and of-fered to contribute to a fund for Dreiser's defense. Alexander Harvey, after signing, addressed a letter direct to Sumner, and got from him under date of September 19, 1916, the following statement of the Comstocks' case:

Authors taken as a whole may be very good judges of the ar-tistic attributes and the literary merits of any particular writing, but as judges of the tendency of that writing on the manners and morals of the people at large they are no more qualified than are an equal number of mechanics of ordinary education. The term "indecent" is a word of common significance. Its meaning is known to all persons who have reached the age of discretion. It is not for any limited group of individuals to attempt to force upon the people in general their own particular ideas of what is decent or indecent. It seems to me that this is what your associ-ates are trying to do, as distinguished from our position which is based upon the decisions of courts representing the sentiment of the people through a great number of years to the present day in every section of the country. We believe that American Letters can survive and hold its place in the literary world without the necessity for a descent by authors into the vicious side of life for material for their productions. Of course, you and I do not agree in this matter, as was very apparent yesterday when you stated that the people of this country should assimilate the ideas of the foreign element coming to this country in the way of art and literature, such as is exemplified by the writing now under dis-cussion. We need to uphold our standards of decency more than ever before in the face of this foreign and imitation foreign in-vasion rather than to make those things which are vicious and indecent so familiar as to become common and representative of American life and manners.

Dreiser sent me a copy of this letter, with "How about the gang which Mr. Sumner represents?" written in the margin beside the sentence beginning: "It is not for any limited group." He also favored me with the first draft of an open letter that he proposed to publish, and I had to drop my work on the Protest to dissuade him. "I am full of doubts," I wrote to him on September 22, "that it should be published in its present form." And then:

The enclosed leaves me in very serious doubts. It would do you no good whatever and it might conceivably do you much harm. On the whole, I think it better for you to keep quiet till the result of the fight before the Post Office is determined.

What have you done in the direction of getting signatures to the protest? You once mentioned several well-known men who would probably sign at your request. Have they been approached? I have sent out many letters and got a number of signatures, but it is necessary that there be concerted action. Moreover, it must be done quickly. Has Howells been approached?

Howells, as a matter of fact, refused to sign, and so did many others, including William Lyon Phelps, Ellis Parker Butler, Bliss Perry, Kate Douglas Wiggin, Caroline Atwater Mason, Agnes Repplier, Arthur Sherburne Hardy, Mary Johnston, Ellen Glasgow, Brander Matthews and George Horace Lorimer, not to mention Corinne Roosevelt Robinson, Arthur Brisbane, Henry Sydnor Harrison, Mark Sullivan, Dr. Frank Crane and Joyce Kilmer. Some of these explained that they had not read *The "Genius"*; a few said that they had not read anything by Dreiser. Francis Hackett, then literary editor of the *New Republic*, undertook to tackle four recalcitrants he happened to know—Howells, Cale Young Rice, Hamlin Garland and John Kendrick Bangs. Bangs and Rice succumbed and signed, but Howells continued to refuse, and so did Garland.

Garland, in fact, undertook to start a movement against Dreiser within the Authors' League, and O'Higgins and Schuler had a hard time holding him down. He was an extraordinarily hypocritical fellow, and had blown, in his time, both hot and cold. One of his own early books, *Rose of Dutcher's Coolly*, was belabored by the Comstocks, and he posed in Chicago, where he was then domiciled, as a stern realist and even as a literary revolutionary. But after he moved to Boston and began to frequent its more elegant literary circles, he embraced its Puritanism, at least as a sort of half-way station on the way to the spiritualism that filled his declining years. I plastered his

The Shadow World in the *Smart Set* for February, 1909, and sneered at his *A Son of the Middle Border* in December, 1917, and he responded by denouncing me in *My Friendly Contemporaries* (1932). There was always something offensive to me about him, and I was thus not surprised when he tried to stab Dreiser in the back. His *A Son of the Middle Border*, I said in my review, was the "autobiography of a man who spoiled a possibly useful life by going in for literature. He should have stuck to the Chatauqua, his first love. In the world of beauty he is as forlorn a stranger as a Methodist deacon at a *Kommers*."[1]

The refusal of Howells to sign the protest was a serious disappointment, but hardly more surprising than Garland's knavery, for Howells was a notorious coward and everyone remembered his poltroonish conduct at the time of Maxim Gorky's visit to the United States in 1906. Many of the other eminentissimos of the time signed, and some of them needed no urging. Ezra Pound, by this time, was hard at work furthering the good cause in England. I had long correspondences with various authors who refused to sign, for example, Henry Sydnor Harrison and Mark Sullivan, and I set Miss Deering to work on a series of follow-up letters to harass others. James Lane Allen and the American Winston Churchill came in in October or November, and I used their names with considerable effect, as I did those of Booth Tarkington, Bliss Carman, Gertrude Atherton and the Englishmen. I figured, when the business of rounding up the hesitant and recalcitrant was over, and I sailed for Europe at last, that my expenditures for postage, stationery and secretarial aid came to at least $300. Happily, I was in funds, and was glad to lay out the money for Dreiser, who was very hard up himself.

The aid that he undertook to give himself was usually embarrassing, and sometimes almost disastrous. I have already mentioned the imprudent open letter that he proposed to publish in September. Before Jones circulated a printed copy of the protest, with signatures, in October, Dreiser set afloat various mimeographed copies, and on October 8 one of them fell into my hands in Baltimore. I was astonished to discover that the names of a number of important signers— for example, George Ade and Winston Churchill—had been omitted, and that those of a number of Greenwich Village radicals had been

---

1. German for a noisy student beer party.

added. I had warned Dreiser against succumbing to the latter only a little while before, and was naturally upset to find him yielding to their flattery.

He was, in such matters, a singularly naive fellow, and accepted most of the preposterous flatterers who sought him out, seeking to get *kudos* out of his notice, at their own valuation. It was in this way, precisely, that he succumbed to nearly all of the women who had at him—a few of them, to be sure, intelligent and more or less presentable, but the rest ranging down to vaudeville actresses, pulp writers and mere *Schwärmin*. Despite all his fine denials, the names of many such preposterous wenches were on the protest lists that he assembled, and with them were the names of male pinks, chiefly Jews, of the most puerile sort.

Obviously, such names could add nothing to the authority of the protest; they would only dispute it, and some of them—for example, that of Margaret Sanger, the birth-control propagandist—would seriously weaken it. But it was not possible to engage in a pitched battle with Dreiser in the face of the enemy, so I had to forget my discontents and go on. He had some fresh scheme every few days, and nearly all of them were bad. Once he informed me with great satisfaction that a debate had been arranged between B. W. Huebsch, the publisher, and Sumner, the head Comstock, before a mysterious organization called the Twilight Club, and asked me to send Huebsch some material for his argument. Inasmuch as it was plain that a defender of free speech who needed help would never be able to stand up to Sumner, who argued for the other side every day, I refused. But such foolishness naturally irked me, and I was glad that I'd be clearing out at the end of the year. On October 21 he wrote to me that Jones had begun to show signs of quitting, and that he (Dreiser) proposed to get hold of a good lawyer, and proceed on his own. He mentioned two such lawyers—John B. Stanchfield and John Quinn—and said that either would be willing to take the case for "a moderate consideration." Where that consideration was coming from he did not say.

On October 25 I wrote to Dreiser offering to make a contribution toward the defense fund, and reported that Harry Leon Wilson was eager to contribute too. On October 26 Jones wrote to me that Schuler, of the Authors' League, had been to Washington to see one Sutherland, apparently of the legal staff of the Post Office, and that

Sutherland had told him that the Post Office would not proceed in the case unless a formal complaint was filed by some responsible person, and that no such complaint had yet come in. "This report seemed so encouraging to me," said Jones, "that I advised Dreiser to let his attorney, Mr. Stanchfield, 'loosen the dogs of war' on Sumner and his crowd at once." In other words, Jones was passing the buck to Dreiser, and where Dreiser was to get the money for loosing the dogs of war did not appear.

The next day I received a letter from James Hay, Jr., a Washington newspaper man, saying that he had been to see W. H. Lamar, solicitor to the Post Office, and that Lamar had promised to read *The "Genius"* and let Hay know whether, in case it reached him officially, he would rule against it. "Lamar," I wrote to Dreiser on November 1, "agreed to . . . prepare his decision in advance of any possible official action. The advantage of this scheme will be that Hay will have a chance to get at him and beat him into line before anything is done. Lamar is a Maryland politician of an extremely dubious type, and if the worse comes to the worst I think I can bring some pressure to bear on him here. In such matters it is always better to deal with a professional politician than with an ass who is full of the uplift and believes that he is a modern Jesus."

A couple of days later Hay went to New York, saw Dreiser, and told him that Lamar had promised him, if a phoney complaint against the book could be arranged, to advise the Postmaster-General, Burleson,[2] that it was harmless, which opinion "could be given out to the press generally and used as an adv."—this before he had even seen the book! On November 4 Dreiser wrote to me that Stanchfield had got a written opinion from R. Snowden Marshall, the federal district attorney in New York, that *The "Genius"* was not actionable. Simultaneously, one of Stanchfield's associates had got to Swann, the state district attorney, and Swann had told him that Sumner was an ass, and that he (Swann) "would have nothing to do with the case." Stanchfield and his partner, Levy, now proposed to go into the state courts and ask for an injunction restraining Sumner from interfering with the sale of the book.

Jones, it appeared, was in favor of this, but refused to pay the costs. He also refused to take the risk of selling the book, which re-

2. Albert S. Burleson.

mained suppressed. He even refused to give Dreiser a few copies for use in propaganda. "My estimate of him," Dreiser wrote to me on November 4, "is now so low that I can scarcely bring myself to talk to the man any more. He has broken his word in every matter concerning which we had a specific agreement"—for example, to the effect that he would release the book "if the government did not act inside two months." On November 8 Sumner applied to Jones for ten copies of the printed Dreiser Protest, with names, but on the advice of Stanchfield, Jones refused to send them. Meanwhile, he proceeded with *A Hoosier Holiday*, and it came out while *The "Genius"* case was roaring on.

I was so busy with my own affairs in December, 1916, that I could devote but little time to Dreiser's. The Dreiser Protest was now completed, and I was glad to get it off my hands. In the midst of my preparations for clearing out we fell into another row. This one started when he sent me the MS. of his play, *The Hand of the Potter*, on December 13, and hinted that he proposed to print it forthwith. Inasmuch as it dealt with sexual perversion, and seemed to me to be a poor piece of work otherwise, I was violently opposed to this, for its publication would give the Comstocks another whack at him and probably alienate a good many of the authors who were supporting him in the matter of *The "Genius"*. What Jones thought of *The Hand of the Potter* I never heard, but plainly enough he did not believe that printing it would help *The "Genius"* case, for it did not come out until 1919, and then it was done by another publisher.

On December 27 Nathan and I had dinner with him at Lüchow's. Three women were with us, and we had a gay and somewhat boozy evening. I heard no more about *The Hand of the Potter* from Dreiser for a long time. I sailed from Hoboken on December 28, 1916, in the Danish steamship *Oscar II*, and was soon out of sight, hearing and mind of Dreiser and his troubles. When I got back in March I found that he was preparing, through Stanchfield and Levy, to sue the John Lane Company for breach of contract. I had warned him against the hazards of this method of proceeding, and he had disregarded my advice. But he was soon to discover that it had been sound, for when the case reached the Appellate Division of the Supreme Court—First Department—in May, 1918, Sumner dropped out, leaving Dreiser and Jones to fight it out between them, and the five learned judges, eager to get rid of a headache, decided that a *bona fide* case was not before them, and refused to say whether or not *The "Genius"* violated the law. Dreiser had no money for an appeal, so *The "Genius"* remained ignominiously in the doghouse until 1922, when I volunteered to see Sumner and try to induce him to agree to release it with a few cuts.

CHAPTER X

A *Book of Prefaces*, which came out in September, 1917, was the most important book, in its effects upon my professional career, of any in my long line. It had been gathering form and direction in my mind ever since I first began to feel my oats as a literary critic, and there were parts of it that dated back to my first writings about Joseph Conrad in the 1909–13 era, to my whooping up of Huneker at the same time, and to my ardent championing of Dreiser from 1911 onward. Not a little of the material that I had gathered for my "American" articles in the *Smart Set*, from June of 1913 onward, went into it, and also a great deal of stuff from my contributions to the Baltimore *Evening Sun*—not always, to be sure, in the original form, but nevertheless in essence.

I had become convinced early in my newspaper days, and even before, that the distinguishing mark of the normal Americano was his essentially moral view of the world, his tendency to color all values with concepts of rightness and wrongness, his inability to throw off the Puritan obsession with sin. There had been, of course, a revolution against Puritanism in New England, and it had gone so far on certain levels that the Boston area had been distinctly ahead of the country in general, intellectually speaking, for two generations, but even in the Boston area there were still plenty of surviving evidences of the old madness. Elsewhere, save on the Pacific Coast and in what I came to describe as "a few walled towns," it was raging almost without challenge, and especially in the South and the agricultural parts of the Middle West.

Both of the latter regions, in the first years of the new century, seemed to be virtually lost to civilization. In the South the Civil War had either killed off or driven out all save a small minority of the old gentry, and there remained only a rabble of poor whites preyed upon by a new class of barbaric exploiters, and in the Middle West the descendants of the pioneers were offering massive proof that the stock from which they had sprung, whatever its fitness to withstand heat, cold, thirst, hunger, insect bites and physical fatigue, had not left them any heritage of sense. The time was one of almost unimaginable intellectual backwardness—a low point in the always dipping curve of American imbecility. There were, of course, some points of light in the pervading gloom—the Johns Hopkins University, what remained of Charles A. Dana's New York *Sun*, the *Bookman* edited by Harry Thurston Peck, William Graham Sumner, James Huneker, George Ade and his fables in slang, the Stone & Kimball publishing venture in Chicago, the music of Reginald De Koven, the occasional flashings of the Adams family, *et sic de similibus*—but they were only points, elsewhere the murk was a solid black.

It was the heyday of some of the most banal eminentissimos that even the United States, up to that time, had ever known—William Jennings Bryan, T. DeWitt Talmage, Orison Swett Marden, Hamilton Wright Mabie, Lydia Pinkham, James Munyon, William Dean Howells, Edward Bok, David Belasco, and so on and so on. The spectacle they provided was a gaudy one, and I surely enjoyed it as much as most, but meanwhile my hand itched for a club to belabor them to the glory of God. I had, I believe, no more public spirit than a policeman or an archbishop, but I was full of lust to function, and before I was twenty-five it was already plain that my functioning would take the form of a sharp and more or less truculent dissent from the *mores* of my country. By the time I set to work on my Shaw book I was already becoming known, in the narrow circle I then inhabited, as one to whom the American spectacle, American ideas and ideals, the great body of Americans themselves, were predominantly more amusing than inspiring, and less admirable than obscene.

I doubt seriously that my German blood had anything to do with this reaction, at least on the conscious level. I had, before my first trip abroad in 1908, when I was already nearly thirty years old, little contact or sympathy with Germans, and my acquaintance with German literature, and even with German history, was of the meagerest. I recall well how, in preparation for my Nietzsche book, I had to bone up on German philosophy, and how dull I found most of it, not to say repulsive. My reading had been almost wholly in English literature, even at the expense of American, and I was so soaked in it that the high point of my first trip abroad was not my visit to Leipzig, the old home of my family, but that to London, where I was genuinely thrilled when George Fawcett took me down the Strand to the Temple and showed me the haunts of Thackeray and the grave of Oliver Goldsmith.

My Grandfather Mencken, as I have recorded in *Happy Days*, held himself aloof from the other Germans of Baltimore, and my father had an active distaste for them. My mother, who was pure German, spoke the language more or less, but it was not often heard in our house, and I had only the sketchiest knowledge of it when I entered F. Knapp's Institute in 1886. The teaching there was done by the old-fashioned method of endless repetition, and though it made me familiar, if only by a kind of osmosis, with the sounds of the language, it certainly did not give me anything properly describable as a command of even its elementary grammar. Whatever real acquaintance with it I acquired later on was picked up from German servant-girls.

My grandfather, if he had lived, would have interested me in the Mencken family, if not in the German *Kultur*, but he died before I was twelve, and my father showed no concern about such things. It was not, indeed, until after his death in 1899 that I so much as examined the family documents and souvenirs that were kept in the bottom compartment of his old walnut secretary, and not until after World War I that I made any serious effort to find out who the early Menckens were and what they had done. The point of view that was to color all my writings probably came, in its essence, from my father, for he was a natural skeptic, and hence had a low opinion of the prevailing American scheme of things, but I don't recall ever hearing him connect it specifically with the Puritan demonology. Thus I got nothing save a sort of framework from him: all the rest had to come out of my reading, and, once I had taken to journalism, from my observation of the American scene at first hand.

I believe today that the most powerful influence ever exerted on my thinking was that of Thomas Henry Huxley, who taught me to distrust moral certainty, and, in particular, to be very suspicious of those who had it. But I also got a lot from Thackeray and from many another English writer, and perhaps even more from Mark Twain.

It was Mark, and not any racial or family interest, that turned my curiosity toward Germany and the Germans. When I first visited Germany, in 1908, *A Tramp Abroad* was my guide-book, though I did not carry it with me, and on my subsequent visits, ending in 1938, I covered nearly the whole of the route it lays down.

But in the years before 1912 I certainly did not think of myself as a German, though I was already conscious of my differentiation from the common run of Americans. If I ever pondered that differentiation at all, I probably thought of it, in the egoistic way of youth, as no more than an evidence of my superiority as an individual. This superiority, in the narrow world that I then inhabited, was certainly not all imaginary: I actually got on much better than anyone else I was close to, and if good luck had something to do with it, then hard industry and an undeniable competence also had something to do with it. As for the common run of Americanos, I disdained them, not as members of a different species, but as inferior members of my own species.

Two things, I believe, served as the immediate catalysts of my dawning race consciousness. The first was my intimate contact with Percival Pollard in 1911, at the time he was writing his *Masks and Minstrels of New Germany*. He was a thorough-going Germanophile, and in our long talks he greatly widened my information about German ideas and doings and my understanding of the German character. When I reviewed his book in the *Smart Set* for August, 1911, my enthusiasm for the author was a great deal more visible than my sympathy for his theme, but all the same the foundation was laid, and when I. A. R. Wylie's *The Germans* followed in 1912 my review in March of that year resolved itself into a general defense of the Germans against the libels of English propagandists and the ready credulity of American dupes. I discovered, reading it, that the dominant German ideas were also my ideas, and when they were attacked (as it seemed to me, ignorantly and viciously) by Price Collier in his *Germany and the Germans* in 1913, I fell upon both book and author with a good deal of heat (September, 1913). As I have said, Pollard laid the foundation for all this, but at least a part of it went back to my early enthusiasm for Mark Twain, and both influences were strongly reinforced by my second visit to Germany, in 1910.

But it remained for the shock of World War I to carry me all the way. Even in its preliminary rumblings I saw the beginnings of an inevitable struggle to the death between the German *Weltanschauung* and the Anglo-Saxon *Weltanschauung*, and it was quickly apparent which side I was to take myself. I, too, like the leaders of Germany, had grave doubts about democracy. I, too, felt an instinctive antipathy to the whole Puritan scheme of things, with its gross and nauseating hypocrisies, its idiotic theologies, its moral obsessions, its pervasive Philistinism. It suddenly dawned on me, somewhat to my surprise, that the whole body of doctrine that I had been preaching was fundamentally anti-Anglo-Saxon, and that if I had any spiritual home at all it must be in the land of my ancestors.

When World War I actually started I began forthwith to whoop for the Kaiser, and I kept up that whooping so long as there was any free speech left in the United States. That period, unhappily, was not prolonged. By the spring of 1915 it was obvious that Wilson would take his American lieges into the war soon or late, and by the autumn it began to be evident that an honest discussion of the issues would presently be impossible. I thus quit my job on the Baltimore *Evening Sun* and made plans to go abroad, to see something of the German Army in action before it would be too late.

Unhappily, it was impossible for me to break away from my new and increasing magazine duties until the end of 1916, and when I returned in March, 1917, free speech was completely suspended, and for two years I was pretty well hobbled. As I have recorded, I refused absolutely to acquiesce even formally in the current American balderdash about the causes, purposes and ultimate aims of the war, and I even managed, from time to time, to sneak sneers at them into my book reviews and other writings, but in the main I had to mark time. This marking time, of course, was extremely disagreeable, and I was by no means disposed to take my disabilities lying down. Back in the first months of the war I had begun to think of a book that would set forth my objections to the whole Puritan *Kultur* in a large and positive way, and before I went abroad at the end of 1916 I put most of it together. When I returned in March, 1917, all that remained was to make it printable in war time.

This was *A Book of Prefaces*. Not a little of it, as I have recorded, went back to the time of my first championing of Dreiser, and even beyond, and substantial parts of it came out of the book to be called *The American*, which I began serially in the *Smart Set* in June, 1913, and then abandoned. The chapters on Conrad, Dreiser and Huneker were easy to assemble, for I had written and printed a great deal more about all three men than I really needed, and the necessary rewriting did not involve any fresh study. To the Dreiser chapter, however, I resolved to add some statistics showing the distribution of Dreiser's books in American public libraries, and to that end I began to send out letters of inquiry in May, 1917.

The response from the librarians was ready, and, on the whole, surprising and gratifying, for the libraries in most of the principal cities reported that they had shelved virtually the whole canon. *Sister Carrie* was in seventeen of the twenty-five libraries reporting, *Jennie Gerhardt* was in sixteen, *The Financier* was in fourteen, *The Titan* was in twelve, and even *The "Genius"*, despite the uproar over it, was in eleven. The plays and travel books were even better represented, and only two public libraries, those of New Orleans and Providence, both intellectual slums, reported that they had no Dreiser books at all. I was disconcerted to learn that the Enoch Pratt Free Library in Baltimore had only one, to wit *A Traveler at Forty*, but certainly not astonished, for its librarian in those days was an imbecile named Bernard C. Steiner, who devoted most of his energies to Y.M.C.A. work.

The fourth essay in the book, "Puritanism as a Literary Force," gave me more concern, for I knew I had to make it accurate and I hoped to make it devastating. I had set down the first sketches for it back in 1913, when I was at work on *The American* series for the *Smart Set*. When the second of the series, "The American: His Morals," appeared in the magazine in July, 1913, Dr. James W. Bright, professor of English literature at the Johns Hopkins, was so pleased with it that he sent a copy to Henry Holt, the publisher, who was preparing to bring out the first issue of a new review, the *Unpopular*, as of January, 1914.

Apparently Bright suggested that I might make a good contributor to the *Unpopular Review*, for on September 12, 1913, Holt, who had published my *Men vs. the Man* in 1910, sent me a dummy of the magazine and proposed that I attempt something for it. He was then seventy-three years old, and September 12, 1913, was my thirty-third birthday. "Most every man to whom I have sent this dummy," he wrote, "is old enough to be your father; so I am running . . . risk of spoiling you . . . in telling you that I wish you would write for me an article on 'The Greek and the Puritan' which has been rattling about in my head for some time. But I have got enough else to do, and probably wouldn't do it as well as you anyhow. And now to counteract some of the tendencies to spoil you, and for other reasons, I must tell you that although the style of your article was pretty well adapted for the *Smart Set* (in which, also in the direction of anti-spoiling, I will tell you I think it is a disgrace for any man to appear), I should want you to consent to do the one for the *Unpopular Review* in a rather different style, though I shouldn't want you to do it with any less humor. *Verb. sap. sat.*,[1] I guess. If not, ask further particulars if you care to. The *Unpopular Review* will of course have a limited circulation, though I hope it will be read by people whose reading of one is an honor. Of course, such things can't compete with the *Smart Set* in prices paid for articles. The *Atlantic* manages to get itself filled up on $15 a thousand words—at least, that is what it has always paid me; but if there is so little unpopularity about you that must have more, pray let me know how much more, and I will think it over. Several very eminent men have pronounced the *Atlantic* terms satisfactory, but they have independent incomes from professorships and that sort of thing."

The pedagogical (and patronizing) tone of this was not reassuring, and I still remembered unpleasantly the trouble I had had with old Holt while *Men vs. the Man* was under way, but I was well aware that getting into so respectable a review as he seemed to have in mind might do me some good, so I fell on the proposed article at once and by the end of October had finished it. While it was being written Holt favored me with various admonitions. "It will certainly be more effective," he wrote to me on October 9, "the more you hold yourself in—not meaning necessarily that you should suppress anything worth saying; but the manner of saying and the degree of avalanche-like rush can of course influence the effect." By October 13 he was already so full of fears that he was talking of placing the article elsewhere—"if we can't agree on modifications, should I regard any as desirable." But by October 18 he was taking heart, and urging me to write "5,000 words or even more, if they come out naturally without padding."

By this time I had pretty well concluded that he would never print the article, but when it was finished I nevertheless sent it in, and at once my expectations were borne out. He not only had at me with a

---

1. *Verbum sapienti satis est:* a word to the wise is sufficient.

long letter on November 4, setting forth at least a dozen puerile objections to my argument; he also returned the typescripts with scores of even worse annotations. I refused, of course, to let him tell me how to write the article, and after a brief exchange of letters asked him to send it back. I preserved the annotated typescript for many years afterward as a shining example of editorial impudence and folly, but now (1943) it seems to have disappeared, for I can't find it.

I sent a carbon to the *Smart Set* at once, and Wright printed it in February, 1914 (probably the last issue of his editorship) as "The American: His New Puritanism." But it fell far short of satisfying me as it stood, for Holt's fears had stayed my hand while it was under way, and when the time came to put *A Book of Prefaces* together I greatly expanded it, and reinforced it with material from other *Smart Set* articles and from my newspaper stuff, and with a lot of fresh material. In its final form it was the most headlong and uncompromising attack upon the American *Kultur* ever made up to that time. I had, of course, to be careful about the present applications of my argument, for the United States was now in the war, but I nevertheless managed to make it plain that I had no belief in the so-called ideals that Wilson alleged to be at the bottom of the holy crusade.

Under my contract with the John Lane Company for *A Little Book in C Major* and *A Book of Burlesques* it had the refusal of *A Book of Prefaces*, and J. Jefferson Jones gave me to understand that he was ready and eager to do it. But in view of his pusillanimous course in the manner of *The "Genius"* and other good and sufficient considerations I was determined to escape from him, and soon a way to do so suggested itself. His principal author, at that time, was William J. Locke, the English novelist. I had nothing against Locke; on the contrary, I greatly enjoyed his amusing if insubstantial tales, and had frequently praised them in the *Smart Set*. Moreover, he was one of the Englishmen who had joined in the Dreiser Protest, promptly, without reservations and to the consternation of the American bluenoses, and so I had a special tenderness for him. But now I began to discover grave defects in him, and, what is worse, found that my critical conscience forced me to make note of them in my book—as I recall it, in the chapter on Dreiser.

I directed Jones's attention to the passage, telling him that I had heard that he never read MSS. if he could help it, and that I didn't want to let him print unwittingly anything that might get him into trouble with his London headquarters. He thanked me for my politeness, and after giving the passage a careful reading told me that he simply could not print it. Locke, he explained, was the chief glory and meal ticket of the house of Lane, and it would be insane for the American branch to print and countenance a violent attack upon him. He might, at worst, jump to some other publisher, and even at best he would be greatly offended. I told Jones that I appreciated the delicacy of his position, and sympathized with him in his difficulty, but that my own dignity had to be considered. Could I subject to the censoring of a serious work for reasons of business? Obviously not. If any other reasons for omitting the offending passage had been adduced I might have yielded quietly and forgotten it, but now I was on notice and could not do so.

Jones was much distressed, but granted in the end that I was within my rights. The whole negotiation was carried on in the manner of ambassadors, and Jones and I remained on good terms for years afterward. But in the end he had to hand me back my MS. I thereupon took out the onslaught on poor Locke, and turned the book over to Alfred A. Knopf, with whom, after long consideration and plentiful doubt, I had resolved to throw in my publishing fortunes.

I had known Knopf since the early part of 1913, and we were already on friendly terms when he launched out as a publisher on his own account in 1915, but I had been somewhat wary about joining him, and hence both of my 1916 books went to the John Lane Company. My doubts rested on various grounds. For one thing, there was his extreme youth—he was only twenty-three years old in 1915 and though he looked older he was still somewhat vealy. For another thing, his experience in publishing had covered but three years, and there were large and important gaps in his knowledge of the business. For a third thing, it appeared that he had no money of his own, but was dependent on the backing of his father, whom I had never met and of whose resources and ideas I knew nothing.

Finally, there was the fact that he was a Jew. I had little if any prejudice against Jews myself, and in fact spent a great deal of my leisure in their company, but they were rare in the publishing business and rather resented by the *Goyim*, and there was little indication that they would ever be successful. Knopf had what seemed to me to be excellent intentions, and we had in common our great enthusiasm for Joseph Conrad, but it also seemed to me, in the early days of our acquaintance, that he showed a certain amount of the obnoxious tact-lessness of his race, and on March 27, 1914, I warned Dreiser to be careful in dealing with him.

But all these dubieties began to wear off as I came to know him better, and when he actually got under way and I began to see what sort of books he was trying to print, I resolved to go along with him. My experience with three Christian publishers—Schaff, Holt and Jones—had not been too happy, and I was eager to arrange more comfortable connections. If the Scribners, Macmillan or even the Harpers had made overtures to me in those days they could have had me, but none of them did. The only overtures came from Houghton Mifflin, Little Brown and Knopf—and after lengthy and somewhat painful consideration I decided to go to Knopf. During the year fol-lowing, 1918, I allowed another publisher, Philip Goodman (also a Jew) to do two of my books, but that was only an interlude, and thereafter I stuck to the Borzoi banner.

Knopf, in 1917, was a tall, slim, but well-built and not unhand-some fellow, with large dark eyes and a small black moustache. He was enormously interested in publishing, and threw into it a really immense amount of energy. No detail of his business was too trivial for his personal attention. He spent long hours toying with the design of his books, and devoted himself to acquiring a sound knowledge of printing, paper and binding, but he was by no means arty, for he also put in a great deal of hard work upon selling. This enthusiasm dated from his college days at Columbia, and when he was graduated *in absentia* in February, 1912—he had gone abroad before com-mencement—he was fully resolved to try his luck at publishing. He remained abroad until August, 1912, and on his return tried at once to get a job with some established house.

This, it turned out, was by no means easy. There were dozens of applicants for every opening, most of them also college graduates, and it quickly appeared that there was a considerable anti-Semitism among the Barabbases. But after two months of effort Knopf finally found a meagre opening at Doubleday, Page & Company's large new plant at Garden City, Long Island, opened but two years before. He got it through the influence of his father, who happened to be a business acquaintance of Ralph Peters, the president and general manager of the Long Island Railroad. The Doubledays, at the time, were trying to induce the railroad to establish a new station at its plant, and Peters was reluctant to do so. The elder Knopf undertook to convince him in return for a job for Alfred, and this rather curious arrangement went through. Alfred's welcome, even so, was not too hearty. He was put to work operating an adding-machine in the accounting department, and paid $8 a week. This post, of course, ill befitted the dignity of a B.A. of Columbia and he was soon agitating for a better. Some time in 1913, in response to this clamor, he was transferred to the promotion department and his wages raised to $12. This was the largest emolument he ever received from the Doubledays, for the head of the firm, Frank N. Doubleday, was an extremely stingy fellow, and, moreover, did not like Jews.

The firm had brought out an expensive edition of the works of Rudyard Kipling, and Knopf was sent on the road to make propaganda for it. Eugene F. Saxton, who was then on the staff, knew that I was (or had been) a Kipling enthusiast, and suggested that he call upon me at the *Sun* office in Baltimore, in the hope that I might be able to give the enterprise a lift in the *Evening Sun*. It must have been early in 1913 that he came to see me, for he left the Doubledays soon after the beginning of 1914, and by that time we were good friends. He found that I had begun to lose my old ardor for Kipling, but we quickly found a source of common interest in Joseph Conrad. I had been whooping up Conrad in the *Smart Set* ever since I began to write its reviews in 1908, and was about to print a florid eulogy of him in the issue for July, 1913.

Knopf, years later, told me that he had first heard of him from a clerk named Simpson in Scribner's old downtown bookstore in New York, and that his enthusiasm had been fanned by a visit to John Galsworthy on his trip to Europe in 1912. He was already full of plans to assemble all the scattered books of Conrad and bring them out under the Doubleday imprint in a dignified format, and I was naturally hot for it. He told me that Frank N. Doubleday, who already had four of them, was less than lukewarm. But Knopf had written to Conrad direct, had found him interested, and was full of enthusiasm. He finally induced Doubleday to consider the project seriously, and when it was finally decided to go on with it prepared a pamphlet to promote it.

Later on Doubleday took all credit for it, and began to pose as the champion of Conrad, but he actually had nothing to do with it until Knopf heated him up. The whole idea was Knopf's and no one else's, and it is a pity that he did not keep it *in petto* long enough to execute it himself, for he would have done so much better than Doubleday. By the time the Doubleday collected edition began to come out Knopf had left the employ of the firm.

He quit his Doubleday job in March, 1914, and went to work for Mitchell Kennerley, then the least conventional and most venturesome of the younger publishers in New York. His salary was $25 a week and his duties covered a wide range, and among other things he had dealings with the authors on the Kennerley list. One of these was Joseph Hergesheimer, whose first novel, *The Lay Anthony*, he brought out in 1914. Hergesheimer and Knopf soon became friendly, and when, at the end of 1914, Knopf let it be known that he was thinking of setting up as a publisher on his own account, Hergesheimer, who was dissatisfied with Kennerley, agreed to go with him. Unfortunately, Hergesheimer's second book, *Mountain Blood*, was already in Kennerley's hands, but *The Three Black Pennys*, his first really first-rate work, went to Knopf. It came out in the autumn of 1917, simultaneously with *A Book of Prefaces*, and thus we were launched together as Knopf authors. Unfortunately, Knopf's negotiations with Hergesheimer got him into an unpleasant row with Kennerley, who had a female spy in his office, passing under the guise of his secretary. This fair creature found a letter from Hergesheimer to Knopf on the latter's desk, and rushed it to Kennerley, who accused Knopf of treason and fired him forthwith. This was in May, 1915, and the two did not speak thereafter for twenty years.

Knopf was not yet ready to begin business on his own, but the loss of his job forced him to do so, and by the summer of 1915 he was on his way. On April 4, 1916, he married Blanche Wolf, and she was presently hard at work in his office, recording orders, wrestling with printers and binders, and even wrapping up books. He had no backing save $5,000 that his father, Samuel Knopf, had agreed to lend him if he needed it, but he did not need it. Working day and night himself, and exercising the utmost economy in all his operations, he paid his way from the start. His first really big success was *Green Mansions*, by W. H. Hudson, published in the spring of 1916; after that he was in easy waters, and he remained in easy waters until the Great Depression overtook the publishing business in 1933.

Immediately after their honeymoon Knopf and Blanche took a house at Hartsdale, near New York, and there I often visited them.

In it their only child, Alfred, Jr., was born in June, 1918. In September of the same year they left Hartsdale and leased a house in West 95th Street, where they remained until 1924. I was greatly interested in their publishing schemes, and even before I was on their list myself began diverting authors their way—for example, Louis Wilkinson, John McClure, and my associate on the *Smart Set*, George Jean Nathan.

Knopf not only made efforts to get together a list of good books; he also undertook innovations in printing and binding, most of them good ones. The average trade book of the era, forgetting those of Kennerley, was a dreadful botch; the printing was left to the printer and the binding was usually hideous. Knopf, whose own tastes were somewhat florid, tried to produce more appropriate and sightly investitures, and he succeeded so well that within a few years all the other publishers of New York, including such old-timers as the Harpers and the Scribners, were imitating him. He had his eye on German models, and they were good ones, for the German publishers of that era were completely revolutionizing book design. When he adopted the Russian wolf-hound, the *borzoi*, as his trade-mark, and began to advertise Borzoi Books, Nathan and I spoofed him a bit, but we believed that, at the bottom, it was a sound idea, and so it turned out to be. In a little while he had the refusal of work by authors who were already lodged with other publishers, but harbored discontents of one sort or another. One of these was Willa S. Cather, who walked in unannounced in 1917 or 1918, and asked Knopf to take her over from the Houghton Mifflin Company. It was not, however, until 1920 that the transfer could be arranged. The first of her books to appear on Knopf's list was *Youth and the Bright Medusa*, published in that year, and at once a success.

Some time in May, 1917, I wrote to Dreiser: "I have been rewriting my preface book from snout to tail—a fearful job. But there is now some very good stuff in it. I tell the truth about you, and discover to my astonishment that much of it is almost creditable to you." A few days later I sent him word that it was finished. "A week or so of polishing, *i.e.*, of changing all intelligible English into fantastic and mystical balderdash, and it will be ready for Jones. It is my hope that he will gag at it." How and why he gagged at it I have related, and also the reasons for my decision to give it to Knopf. Some time before the end of May, I told Dreiser of that decision and also sent him a carbon of the chapter on himself. So far as I can recall, he made no objection to anything in it, though after it was set up he seems to have been persuaded by Merton S. Yewdale, a minor functionary in the John Lane Company, that my discussion of him was too frank and would probably injure him.

At the last minute, however, I was forced to make a good many changes in the text, for the United States declared war on April 6, 1917, and immediately thereafter the very drastic and extravagant Espionage Act, finally passed on June 15, came before Congress, and it became apparent at once that any author essaying to deal realistically with American institutions and ways of thought would have to watch his step. Knopf, in fact, became somewhat alarmed when he read my MS., for it would certainly never pass as a piece of 100% American propaganda. I forget precisely what it was that he objected to, but I recall that I resisted him on some points and yielded to him on others. This revision and re-revision occupied me until July. Even after the book was set up I continued to tinker with it, and five years later, in the introduction I wrote to a new edition of *In Defense of Women*, I recorded that I had had to change the plates of "a book of purely literary criticism, wholly without political purpose or significance, in order to get it through the mails." There was, of course, intentional irony in this description of the book, and perhaps there was also some rhetorical exaggeration in my statement about the mails, but I remember clearly that there were some passages, even in the text as revised, that kept me in some anxiety and Knopf in much more.

The contract with Knopf for *A Book of Prefaces* was signed on July 9, 1917. It provided for royalties of 10% of the retail price on the first 2,500 sold, 12½% on the next 2,500, and 15% on all above 5,000. Knopf fixed the price of the book at $1.50, printed it in Bodoni type, then something of a novelty, and bound it very neatly in dark blue, with gilt stamping. It made a volume of two hundred eighty-three pages and was very attractive in appearance. There was no index, but this was supplied when the second edition came out, in September, 1918. Under my name on the title page appeared "Opus 13," but this was mere blague, for a list of my books facing the title showed only nine titles, and all reference to opus numbers was omitted with the third edition, in August, 1920.

The book was to have been published in September, 1917, but my changes in the text apparently delayed it a bit, for Knopf's first advertisement of it did not appear until October 28, and most of the reviews were delayed until November, December and beyond. The first, however, appeared on October 11. It was in the Springfield *Republican*, and started out by describing me as "an American critic of alien race." The rest was mainly a denunciation of Dreiser for "his habit of dwelling on the sensual phases of human nature, very largely to the exclusion of all others," and a defense of the Comstocks who had suppressed *The "Genius"*. "The mere fact," said the anonymous reviewer, "that there is a common sense precaution against the circulation of obscene books proves nothing, and while the work of Mr. Comstock's society has on a few occasions been absurd, it has been on the whole salutary." The same notes were soon struck in other reviews.

But of all the attacks upon the book and its author the most violent was that of Stuart P. Sherman in the *Nation* of November 29. It was headed "Beautifying American Literature" and was devoted largely to turning upon me the current German spy scare. The *Nation* had not yet been taken over by Oswald Garrison Villard, and it was still the chief critical organ of the orthodox American *Kultur*. Thus Sherman had a free hand, and he took every advantage of it, hitting below the belt with great enthusiasm. It was violent stuff, indeed, and it gave Knopf a considerable scare, but I was well aware that, in the long run, it would get me a great many more friends than enemies, and so I took it with equanimity. It was a studied attempt to be unfair, and yet it was certainly not as unfair as Sherman's onslaught on Dreiser had been. I had, in fact, taken an open and active part in the debate which went on before the American entrance into the war, and was known to everyone who had heard of me at all as pro-German, and I had only lately offered fresh affront to the Anglomaniacs with my article on Ludendorff in the *Atlantic Monthly* for June, 1917.

There was thus some excuse for trying to raise the bitter prejudices of the time against me, however irrelevant it was to a literary discussion. But Sherman's attack on Dreiser was wholly without justification, for Dreiser had printed nothing whatsoever on the subject of the war, and the only way he could be connected with it was through his German name. To be sure, he was ardently pro-German in private, but that was only in private; he had not, so far as I knew, uttered a word on the subject in public. This was my reason, and not his attack on me, for my refusal to meet Sherman during the years following, even after he had changed his tune about Dreiser and was obviously eager to cultivate me. It seemed to me that his attempt to raise the professional patriots against Dreiser was cowardly and ig- nominious, and I was not disposed to forgive and forget it.

His conversion followed his removal to New York in 1924, to be- come editor of *Books*, the literary section of the *Herald-Tribune*. There he came under the influence of Irita Van Doren, who was his second in command, and of her husband, Carl, and in a little while he was singing a wholly new tune, and actually praising Dreiser. His readiness to yield to Irita's more civilized point of view was not due entirely, nor even mainly, to intellectual conviction; its main source was the fact that he had fallen violently in love with her. This affair made a great pother in the literary circles of New York in the 1924– 26 period, but so far as I know it remained quite innocent and cer- tainly nothing came of it. Irita, who was a very charming woman, made various efforts to bring Sherman and me together, and so did Carl, but I always declined. Once, when we were both guests at a dinner in honor of Jimmie Walker, and there was a considerable flow of bootleg beverages, other friends made the same effort, but though Sherman was willing and eager I was not.

His own efforts to break down my hostility to him were frequent and pathetic. On April 20, 1925, for example, he wrote to me that he had unearthed "a brilliant young woman" who reported that she had been "wading through literature with Mr. Mencken strapped to one leg and Mr. Sherman to the other." I replied to this only too obvious overture politely but coldly, and six months later, when Sin- clair Lewis arranged a party with Sherman's connivance and pressed to me to come to it I refused. I never, in fact, met him. He was fundamentally a yokel, despite his transformation in New York, and hence a bounder, and I had a pretty firm (and probably sound) feel- ing that I could never get on with him.

His bitter denunciation of me in the *Nation*, like his denunciation of Dreiser in the same place two years before, naturally delighted the Anglomaniacs of the time, and the violently pro-English New York *Herald-Tribune*[1] reprinted it *in extenso* on December 16, under the

1. See the footnote on p. 90.

heading of "What H. L. Mencken's 'Kultur' is Doing to American Literature." This alarmed Knopf all over again, but I was a good deal less upset, for I could see clearly that attacks from such sources were making me the leader of the forces arrayed against Sherman, Paul Elmer More, Babbitt and company, and I was confident that, in the long run, my gang would prevail. Not a few of the newspaper reviewers, in fact, were already choosing sides, and mine was getting the smarter ones.

Despite the fact that *A Book of Prefaces* came out at the high point of the hullabaloo over the war, it did fairly well. Knopf was cautious and printed a first edition of but one thousand copies. He had sold seven hundred thirty-eight by February 1, 1918, and by August he had sold two hundred fifteen more, so that a new printing was needed in September. My royalties down to August amounted to $140.77— the largest income I had got from a book so far. Thereafter the book sold pretty steadily until August, 1920, when Knopf brought out a third edition and raised the price to $2.50. The sales dropped a bit thereafter, but not badly. In January, 1922, there was a fourth edition and in February, 1924, a fifth, and at the end of 1927 Knopf added the book to his series of Pocket Books, selling at $1. At about the same time the Garden City Publishing Company, a subsidiary of Doubleday, Page & Company, bought the right to issue five thousand copies in its series of $1 reprints, and before the end of 1928 it had added five thousand more. Meanwhile, the fourth regular edition of 1922 had been issued in England by Jonathan Cape. It was not until the end of 1931 that the book ceased to sell, and even after that there were a few sales of the Pocket Edition. When it went out of print at last, in 1933, and the plates were melted, the sales of the regular edition to date had been 5,272 and of the Pocket Edition 1,324, or 6,596 altogether. In addition, Doubleday had sold the ten thousand copies of his reprint, so that the grand total came to 16,596.

This was certainly not a bad circulation for a book of literary criticism. My receipts, first and last, were only $1,863.73 in cash, but the indirect benefits that I derived from the book were enormous. It gave me a kind of authority that I could never have got from my *Smart Set* reviews alone, and brought me a large number of new readers. The discussion of the ideas in it went on for years, and some of them are still quoted and debated to this day. It will probably be a long while before anyone will be able to write a history of American literature without mentioning it, or, at all events, stealing from it. It shook the professors as they had never been shaken before, and one of those it shook the most, in the long run, was Sherman. Moreover, it got me notice abroad, and brought me that of many persons at home whose interest in the matters it discussed I had never so much as suspected. It was also of great value to Knopf, for it gave direction to his publishing ventures, and brought him a number of far from bad authors. From 1918 my name was intimately identified with that of his house, and he and I engaged in many ventures together.

CHAPTER XI

ON MY RETURN from the war in March, 1917, I did not resume writing for the Baltimore *Evening Sun*. Under the editorship of John Haslup Adams and the managing editorship of Frank R. Kent both *Sunpapers* had become more and more rabidly pro-English, and after the United States entered the war their editorial pages and their news columns were alike filled with grotesque and indeed almost idiotic fulminations against the Germans. I kept away from both Adams and Kent, for I had a low opinion of their editorial skill and judgment and even certain doubts about their honesty, or, at all events, their candor, and well knew that if I had any truck with them we'd get into vain wrangles.

When Harry C. Black entered the Navy and departed from Baltimore for the duration my palavers with him about *Sunpaper* affairs of course ceased, but I kept in contact with Paul Patterson, and discussed with him, often and at length, his still somewhat vague plans for rehabilitating the papers after the war. His troubles, in 1917 and the first half of 1918, were chiefly of a financial character, for the property was losing a great deal of money, and more than once the question whether it could survive became a pressing one. I still retained the stock that Charles H. Grasty had given me in lieu of a salary increase, but it paid no dividends and was virtually worthless. Patterson, as business manager, had no voice in editorial affairs, but he was a competent newspaper man, and hence was well aware that Kent was a sorry failure as managing editor of both papers, and that Adams was not much better as their editor. He saw clearly that, if they ever got upon a paying basis, it would be necessary to reorganize editorially, and he and I put in a good many evenings discussing ways and means to that end.

Patterson's sympathies ran toward the English and he knew that I was implacably pro-German, but we remained on good terms nevertheless, and he realized that the war would be over soon or late, and that when its violent feelings began to abate there would be need for the exercise of a cooler judgment and a bolder imagination than either Kent or Adams could offer. He appeared to believe that I had both, and so I became his confidant, and had a considerable share in the radical editorial reforms that began in 1919. But in 1917 and down to the Armistice in 1918 there was nothing to do save to wait for better times and more favorable auguries with as much patience as we could muster. Meanwhile, it was at least possible to give Van Lear Black some assistance in his heroic effort to reorganize the business office and pull the property out of the red, and this Patterson did with great energy and competence.

He had joined the *Sunpapers* as an editorial executive in Grasty's time, and Grasty, who was always trying out editorial men in the business office, had sent him there. Another sent the same way was John E. Cullen, a young Irishman who joined the staff in 1907, had been a reporter, Sunday editor, city editor and (for a brief time) managing editor upstairs, and was now in the advertising department. In the last months of 1914, after Grasty had been ousted, Cullen told me that he had begun to fear that the *Sunpapers* would be a long, long time working out of their morass, and that he thought he'd like to take a chance in some more promising field. He asked me to look about in New York for a likely job for him, and after a considerable search I found one for him on the New York *Evening Mail*. This must have been in June, 1915, though *The Sunpapers of Baltimore*,[1] apparently on Cullen's authority, says that it was "at the end of 1914," for I recall distinctly that my negotiations were with Dr. Edward A. Rumely, and Rumely did not take over the *Evening Mail* until June 1, 1915.

Rumely was a medical man who had inherited a farm tractor plant in Indiana and was reputed to be rich, though as a matter of fact the family corporation had gone bankrupt before he acquired control of the *Mail*. Born in La Porte, Indiana, he had taken his medical degree at Freiburg im Breisgau, and was pro-German in sentiment, and during the two years before the American entrance into the war he

1. A history of the Baltimore *Sunpapers* by Gerald W. Johnson, Frank R. Kent, Hamilton Owens and Mencken, and published in 1937.

tried to make the *Mail* a spokesman for the German point of view, which had no other voice among the New York dailies. Inasmuch as my own attitude toward the war was virtually identical with his, he naturally made an effort to recruit me for his paper, and I remember that while I was trying to get a job from him for Cullen he was pressing one on me. But in those days I was still writing for the Baltimore *Evening Sun*, and so refused. We kept up, however, a tenuous contact, and after Cullen had worked for a while in the business office of the *Mail*, as advertising and promotion manager, I suggested to Rumely that he be transferred to the editorial department, which sorely needed his energy and enterprise.

In April, 1917, he was duly sent upstairs as managing editor under Frank Parker Stockbridge, then the chief editor, and in that character he was soon urging me to give him some aid. Inasmuch as I had, by this time, ceased to write for the *Evening Sun*, I yielded to his persuasions, and we came to an agreement. It provided that I was to do an indefinite number of articles, at the rate of say two or three a week, and at the flat price of $15 apiece. By this time, of course, the United States was in the war and the Espionage Act was on the books, and we had to agree between us that I should avoid the war issues. But though I could not attack directly the blather that Wilson and his parasites were unloading upon the country, it was still possible to get in some practice upon the persons and groups who swallowed it, and this I did frequently.

One of my targets was the ex-Confederate—the easiest of all the easy marks for the balderdash of the time, ranging from Prohibition to Woodrow's scheme to save humanity by going to the rescue of England. This ex-Confederate seemed to me then, as he seems to me now, to be the bell-wether and archetype of all the worst varieties of American imbecile, and I had been sniping at him in the *Smart Set* since the first days of my book reviews. Almost at the precise moment I took the *Evening Mail*'s shilling I emptied a whole load of bricks upon him in an article entitled "Si Mutare Potest Aethiops Pellum Suam?" This caused a considerable uproar south of the Potomac and I was belabored with great ferocity by the Southern papers. This, of course, delighted me, for it had been my hope and intention to gall the jade to the wincing point, and as soon as I settled down on the *Evening Mail* I resolved to make another attack.

This took the form of an article headed "The Sahara of the Bozart" and printed on November 13. It was done with some finesse, appealed artfully to the South's pride in its glorious past, and appeared to show sorrow more than anger. But my actual object, of course, was to outrage the professional Southerners, and that object was very successfully attained. Though the thing was printed in a newspaper that ordinarily was never read, nor even heard of, outside the New York area, they had read it within a few weeks of its publication, and thereafter, for months on end, I was the subject of their violent counter-attack. That attack, in fact, went on for years, and occasionally revives even to this day. With the dawn of the 20's there arose a faction of young Southerners who discovered that my main allegations were perfectly sound, and since then there has appeared another faction which argues that their effect was salutary—indeed, that I am, as their author, a sort of savior of the Confederate *Kultur*, though unquestionably an unpleasant one. As a matter of history, the article probably did have a great deal to do with the revolt against the old Southern stupidity which got under way after World War I, with the result that the South began to be extremely conscious of its shortcomings and to produce such effective self-critics as Julian Harris and Grover C. Hall, William Faulkner and Erskine Caldwell.

Cabell and Ellen Glasgow were already in being, but I think "The Sahara of the Bozart" helped to liberate and hearten them, indeed, they have both told me so. I began, after 1902, to receive frequent communications from the young Southern rebels, and from them got a lot of useful communication for my subsequent onslaughts. All this issued, not from "Si Mutare Potest Aethiops Pellum Suam," but from "The Sahara of the Bozart." The epithet in the title stuck, and even after I had displaced it with the Bible Belt, it kept on sticking. Nor did I confine myself to the direct attack: I also afflicted the Confederates by heaping praises on the authors of other regions, by calling attention (invidiously) to the rising achievements of their own blackamoors, and even by singling out for encomium white Southerners who were neither Methodists nor poor white trash.

Another *Evening Mail* article that was a great success was "A Neglected Anniversary," printed on December 28, 1917. It was, in form, a burlesque history of the bathtub in America, but I managed to make it so plausible that its grotesque imaginings were accepted as fact, and have since passed into the folklore of the Republic. When I began to encounter them, not only in newspaper editorials, but even in medical literature and standard reference works, I confessed publicly and repeatedly that the whole thing was a hoax, but it was then too late to stop it, and it still survives. I well recall writing it on a murky morning in December, at a time when Cullen was alarmed by some of my attacks on the 100% Americans of the time and had begged me to be careful. I had slugged, among others, the sex hygienists, the penologists, the Prohibitionists and the suffragettes (though I was in favor of the extension of the suffrage), and all of them had struck back by seeking to make it appear that I was an agent of the Kaiser, told off to breed dissension and bitterness in free America. That, of course, was actually my purpose, though the Kaiser had nothing to do with it.

Early in the summer of 1918 the professional spy-hunters began to make allegations that Rumely, when he acquired control of the *Mail*, had been backed by German government money. He denied this vigorously, and even if it were true it would not have been unlawful at the time it occurred, but the spy-hunters got at him on the ground that he had failed to reveal the alleged fact to the Alien Property Custodian, and in the first days of July, 1918, he was forced to relinquish control of the paper to the bondholders. At the command of the Custodian they put Stockbridge in charge of it—and Stockbridge signified his gratitude by printing a series of cowardly and bounderish attacks upon his late boss in the New York *Herald*. But there was still some doubt in official minds that Rumely was really guilty, and it was not until April 17, 1919, that he was indicted. His lawyers, S. Walter Kaufmann and Norvin R. Lindheim, were indicted with him, and after another delay of more than a year and a half the three were put on trial on November 12, 1920, before Judge William I. Grubb in the United States District Court. The jury found them not guilty on the counts charging them with directly taking German government money, but guilty on the counts charging them with having failed to notify the Alien Property Custodian that some of the backers of the *Mail* were German nationals and probably financed from Berlin. It recommended them to mercy, and the judge sentenced each of them to a year and a day in Atlanta.

Rumely was defended by the redoubtable Max D. Steuer, but the best Steuer could do for him was to have his trial postponed until after the election of Harding, when the spy-fever had begun to abate a bit. He served his term, and then vanished. Ten years later he bobbed up in New York again, this time as the promoter of a fig preparation guaranteed to be full of vitamins. Then he vanished once more, and the next time he appeared in the newspapers it was as the legislative agent of the National Committee to Uphold Constitutional Government, organized by Frank Gannett. In 1938 he refused the demand of a Senate committee that he throw open his books to it, and was threatened with jailing for contempt. But this tempest soon died out, and once more he disappeared. He was an odd fish, and more the dreamer than the intriguer, and he spent a large part of his time and energy on idealistic flubdub. As a young medical man fresh from his German university he founded a so-called progressive school in his native La Porte, and lost a great deal of money on it before it closed its doors. His management of the M. Rumely Company seems to have been largely responsible for its bankruptcy in 1915. His name was dropped from *Who's Who in America* after the 1918–19 edition.

My own departure from the *Evening Mail* was accompanied by a certain amount of unpleasantness. I was not involved in October, 1917, when Willard H. Wright, who had been given the job of literary editor at my suggestion, was heaved out for a gross and embarrassing imbecility, but that was only because Cullen knew that I had nothing to do with, and was, in fact, greatly incensed by it. After the effort to oust Rumely began in earnest I naturally fell under suspicion too, and in a little while Stockbridge was harassing me in various small ways, characteristic of so ignominious a fellow. Rather curiously, he never made any complaint that my stuff was subversive, but contented himself with hinting that it was immoral. I was devoting too much space, he let it be known, to denouncing Prohibitionists, vice crusaders and other such Christian people.

I responded by sending in a number of purely literary articles, but even these literary articles took occasional hacks at Puritanism, now disguised as patriotism. Stockbridge alleged that he was under heavy pressure from the bondholders, who had been put in nominal charge of the paper by the Alien Property Custodian, but this was only baloney, for he was himself an arrant blue-nose. He began to hold up my articles while Rumely was still being "investigated" by the spyhunters, and printed no more of them after Rumely was kicked out. The last appeared on July 8, 1918. I had a contract with the *Mail*, made through Cullen, which ran to September 11, but contracts were nothing to Stockbridge. More, he held up my checks for articles already printed, and I wrote to Dreiser on July 16 that I was probably in for a loss of $500. "It would cost twice as much," I said, "to resist. My pastor counsels prayers." In the end I settled for $250 on August 23.

One of my colleagues on the *Mail* was John Reed, later to die in Moscow in the odor of sanctity: he was, in his *Mail* days, a liberal rather than a Communist. I saw him only a few times, for I seldom went to the office. Another colleague was Zoë Beckley, a very smart newspaper woman. I had little interest in the *Mail*, for though Cullen was a competent managing editor Rumely was only too plainly a fool and Stockbridge a knave. Nevertheless, my year of service was of some use to me, for it not only brought me in $2,155 at a time when I was far from flush, but also enabled me to work off such things as "The Sahara of the Bozart" and "A Neglected Anniversary," and to organize and try out ideas that were later put to work in my books. A large part of the material that went into *In Defense of Women* and *Damn!: A Book of Calumny* first appeared in the *Evening Mail*, and I also tried out in it stuff that was used in *The American Language* and the first three *Prejudices* books. This, in fact, was my common practice. First I used an idea in a newspaper article, then I developed it in a magazine article, and finally I put it into a book. The first book of mine after my Nietzsche that was made up wholly of new matter was *Treatise on the Gods* (1930), and even *Treatise on the Gods* embodied a number of notions that I had long before played with in other forms.

THE *Smart Set* was in a low state when I got back from the war in March, 1917, and I found Nathan considerably depressed. All our hopes of pulling the magazine out of the mud and converting it into a paying property had been dashed. With the entrance of the United States into the war we were worse off than ever, for the people of the country were now reading newspapers, not magazines. Crowe, as I have recorded, took advantage of the rise of prices to work off on us some paper of the very worst quality, and as a result we were still receiving $50 a week apiece as editors, but as a matter of fact these payments were much in arrears.

As a result our enthusiasm and energy began to slacken, and the *Smart Set* slumped editorially as well as financially. The effect was visible in the novelettes we published in 1917—a traditional feature of the magazine. No less than three of the twelve were by a literary drudge named Lillian Foster Barrett—a pale, slim, faded, somewhat dismal woman who lived at Newport and was understood to have fashionable connections. A fourth was by her younger brother, Richmond Brooks Barrett, and no doubt she had a hand in it, for he greatly admired her and sedulously imitated her, and she often helped him with his work. Of the other novelettes that we did in 1917 six were by similar or worse hacks, and only the two remaining showed any skill at writing. Of the latter, one, "Look Upon the Prisoner," published in July, was by Rita Weiman, a Philadelphia Jewess who later made a considerable success as a dramatist. The other was by our standby, Lilith Benda—by title, "The Intolerable Hours," published in November. The rest of our fiction, until toward the end of 1917, showed the same falling off. Now and then, to be sure, we got a little life into the magazine, but not often. In March we resumed the series on American cities with "Blue Boston" by John Macy, but it was hard to get good copy for it, and in April we were reduced to printing an anonymous article on Pittsburgh.

Our prose likewise came largely from tried and true professionals of the time, most of them now forgotten. Who were Patrick Kearney, Harold Cook, John Hamilton, George B. Jenkins, Jr., Van Vechten Hostetter, Mildred Cram, Kingsley Moses, Neeta Marguis, June Gibson, Patience Trask, Lawrence Vail, Maverick Terrel, G. Ranger Wormser and Elinor Maxwell? I find their names over and over again in the disintegrating files of the *Smart Set*, but I can't remember anything about them. They are not even listed in Burke and Howe's *American Authors and Books*, 1640–1940, the huge stud-book of the literati—good, bad and indifferent.

With the passing of 1917 there came a bucking-up, and by March, 1918, we were printing a novelette by Thyra Samter Winslow, followed the next month by one by Hugh Kahler. An even greater improvement was shown in our one-act plays. This last, indeed, began before the end of 1917, for in the October issue of that year we published Eugene O'Neill's *The Long Voyage Home*, a really distinguished piece of work. In May, 1918, we followed with his *Ile* and in August with *The Moon of the Caribbees*. It was ordinarily Nathan's job to rustle for one-act plays, but O'Neill fell to me, and it is my recollection that it was Louis Untermeyer who suggested trying to recruit him. He had published a volume of one-acters, by title

Thirst and Other One-Act Plays, in 1915, but it had made no impression, and he was virtually unknown save in Greenwich Village, where he had recently lived in drunken squalor with Louise Bryant, afterward the wife, in succession, of John Reed and of William C. Bullitt, ambassador to France. He had been married himself, in 1909, to a Greenwich Village belle named Kathleen Jenkins, but they separated soon afterward, and in 1918 he married Agnes Boulton, an occasional contributor to the *Smart Set.* Two of his plays, *Bound East for Cardiff* and *Thirst,* were produced by the Provincetown Players at their wharf theatre in Provincetown in 1916, and later the company brought the former to New York, but, though it showed signs of growing skill it was lost in the welter of one-acters then being put on in Little Theatres centered in and radiating from the Village, and I believe that Nathan had not seen it. At all events, it fell to me to deal with O'Neill and I must have begun negotiations with him soon after my return from the war.

In 1929, having got rid of La Boulton, who carried off his total savings to date, O'Neill married Carlotta Monterey, formerly the wife of Ralph Barton, the artist (and a friend of mine), and so far as I can recall I have never met him since. In 1932, while Sara and I were staying at Sea Island, Georgia, where he had a place on the beach, I one day caught a glimpse of him in his patio, but I did not call upon him, for he was in bad health and a very shy and anti-social fellow, and it was understood that he wanted no visitors.

NATHAN AND I, in those days, had already passed our first youth, but there was still plenty of steam in us, and our pessimism about the situation of the *Smart Set* did not keep us, save for relatively brief intervals, from enjoying our jobs. We had acquired, by 1917, a pretty low opinion of Warner, and this fell even lower when we saw how, after all his loud bawling for the blood of the Hun, he delicately evaded military service. We liked Crowe a good deal better, but Crowe, after all, was much our elder, and moreover, he was so rich that there was a certain strain when we met him on the social level.

We were well aware that the *Smart Set,* however shabby it looked and however difficult it was to get good authors into it, at least offered us a fine outlet for our own writings. In our monthly review articles, despite the inhibitions of the time, we had a very large measure of free speech—and surely a great deal more than any other contemporary writers enjoyed. We insisted that Crowe and Warner pay us $100 a month each for these articles, whatever their delays in paying our salaries as editors, and we were constantly at pains to keep them from acquiring any right, whether prescriptive or otherwise, to issue orders to us, or even to make suggestions.

In brief, we ran our editorial business exactly as we pleased—and we tried diligently to make it as amusing as possible. The buffooneries that began in Fourth Avenue continued after we moved to the Printing Crafts Building in the early summer of 1916 and even after we proceeded to the chaster precincts of 25 West 45th Street at the end of 1918. We arranged all sorts of hoaxes for the roping of Warner, and spent most of the time that we had to put in with him during the war years in laughing at him for his social ambitions and his poltroonery, though he didn't know it. We became adepts at the art of getting publicity (not for the magazine, but for ourselves) and gradually began to collar a lot of it.

Many legends about us got afloat, and not few of them we launched ourselves. One of our devices to that end was the occasional issue of leaflets and pamphlets—ostensibly for the information of authors aspiring to contribute to the *Smart Set*. The first of these, "A Note to Authors," apparently dating from 1916, was an eight-page pamphlet bound in the cadet-gray covers of the magazine.[1] Another, following in 1919, or thereabout, was a four-page expansion of our rejection slip. A third, a sixteen-pager entitled "A Personal Word," signed by me alone, was got out early in 1921, after we had raised the newsstand price of the magazine from twenty-five cents to thirty-five.[2] A fourth, which seems to belong also to the 1921–1922 era, was a four-page leaflet entitled "Suggestions to Our Visitors."[3]

All of these things were highly confident in tone, and probably gave those who read them the impression that the *Smart Set* was a roaring success, and that Nathan and I were very well heeled indeed. If so, then that effect was contrived deliberately, for we had discovered early in our joint career as editors that it paid to be thought rich. When we sold our shares in the *Parisienne* and *Saucy Stories* to Crowe and Warner, in the autumn of 1916, we saw to it that the common

1. See Appendix I.
2. See Appendix II.
3. See Appendix III.

reports of the money we bagged went far beyond the truth, and at all other times we professed to be in very easy circumstances, and beyond any temptation to desert the *Smart Set*. This last was actually based upon a disquieting fear that it might blow up under us at any minute: we wanted to make sure, if we were ever reduced to transferring our flags, that no other editor would dare to offer us anything save very substantial honoraria. We had a lot of fun with these leaflets and pamphlets, which were circulated in large numbers—at the expense, of course, of the office. I wrote all of them, but Nathan made suggestions and was free to edit the copy. I can recall him insisting upon but one change, and that was the deletion of a sentence reading "one of us is a baptized man."

But the most successful of all these pamphlets was not issued by the *Smart Set*: it was published by Knopf. Its title was "Pistols for Two," and it came out in September, 1917. Printing it was my idea, and what I had in mind was to feed and stimulate the notice that both Nathan and I were beginning to get in the newspapers, and in the literary gossip of New York. Hobbled by war restrictions, I was unable to write about the imbecilities of the time with anything resembling complete freedom, but nevertheless I had managed to work out a formula whereby I could deliver enough licks at some of them, and sufficiently hard licks, to acquire a considerable notoriety as an opponent of the American way of life. What was needed was an organization and accentuation of this notoriety, for I wanted to make sure of a willing audience when free speech was restored. I had long been dreaming of a better forum than the *Smart Set*, but I was well aware that I might not be able to find it, and I therefore resolved to make what I could out of the second-rate opportunity that the *Smart Set* presented. In consequence, I had to admit Nathan to my scheme, and "Pistols for Two" was thus divided equally between us.

It opened with a mock-serious essay on biography, written by me, then proceeded to biographies of Nathan and myself, and finished with a sort of epilogue describing how we operated the *Smart Set*. The thing was signed Owen Hatteras, but I wrote all of it save Nathan's biography of himself. We tried to keep the two biographies as plausible as possible, but could not resist the temptation to insert some rather obvious stretchers. One of these, to the effect that Nathan, after leaving Cornell, went to the University of Bologna, was received so gravely that he used it frequently in other pronunciamentoes, and has come to half believe in it himself.

Knopf published the pamphlet because both of us were just appearing on his list of authors. He made a characteristically beautiful job of it, with 42 well-printed pages and charming covers in a sort of dusty pink. How many copies were printed I do not know, but there must have been at least a couple of thousand. They went out to literary critics, to authors of our acquaintance, and to publishers, and presently the pamphlet was getting notice in the newspapers. On September 30, 1917, the New York *Telegraph*, the theatrical daily, reported that Fatty Arbuckle, enchanted by the fact that his habits coincided with some of mine and Nathan's, had got hold of a number of copies for his friends. (This, of course, was before poor Fatty was tried for rape and ruined as an artist.)

Soon after it came out Knopf began to be deluged with requests for copies, and before the end of 1917 he decided to sell the few that remained in stock at fifty cents apiece. Nathan and I had contributed $300 between us toward the cost of the enterprise, for Knopf was just getting on his legs as a publisher and the advantage that we hoped to get out of it was much greater than any he could count on, but when cash sales began he insisted on paying us 2 ½% royalties apiece, and before the last copy was sold I had received $5 on 200. There had been no record before that time of an advertisement paying a cash royalty to its perpetrators, and so far as I know there has been no record since. In the days when American first editions were at their peak copies sold for as much as $15. Even to this day (1948) I occasionally receive a request for one.

The Albany *Knickerbocker-Press*, in a notice printed on November 11, 1917, complained that "Pistols for Two" was marred by the "blotches of bad taste which will always, so long as it is so exploited in their writing, handicap the talents of these two very young and very extraordinary young men." There was some underestimate here, of our ages, for I was thirty-seven and Nathan had passed thirty-five, but the charge that the thing was not altogether genteel was certainly well founded. It was, indeed, full of boasting—about our revenues, about our elegancies, about our lofty disdain of literary society—and though that boasting was meant to be taken as buffoonery, it was still boasting. In one place Nathan said of himself that he had no male familiars save John D. Williams and me—considerable exaggeration, for we also, in those days, saw a good deal of T. R. Smith, then managing editor of the *Century*; Philip Goodman, then just setting up as a publisher; and various others. Naturally enough, most of my time in New York was spent with Nathan, but I also saw all of these others, and in addition several that Nathan did not see, for example, Willard H. Wright.

Williams was a South Boston Irishman who had been put through Harvard by his sister, Hattie Williams, a successful musical comedy star of the time, and on his graduation she got him the job of press-agent for Charles Frohman, who was her manager. He was a very charming fellow, and inasmuch as his view of World War I was substantially my own, I found him a pleasant companion. He and Nathan and I put in many gay evenings together—at Rogers' restaurant at Sixth Avenue and 45th Street, at the Beaux Arts at Sixth Avenue and 40th, at the Kaiserhof at Broadway and 39th, at Lüchow's in 14th Street, at Sherry's on the corner of Fifth Avenue and 44th Street, and at Delmonico's across the street. We would often meet at Sherry's or Delmonico's for cocktails in the late afternoon, and then proceed to dinner somewhere else. Williams was a considerable boozer, and more than once Nathan and I, in his company, came to grief.

Frohman had died in the *Lusitania* in 1915 and Williams was now on his own as a manager. He showed a civilized spirit in the theatre, and was responsible for the production of more than one play of sound merit, including, as I have noted, Eugene O'Neill's *Beyond the Horizon* in 1920. He had read heavily, and there was but little smell of Broadway about him, though he was of it.

Another man we saw often in those days was Edgar Selwyn, once an actor and now a theatrical manager and movie producer and the lover of Kay Laurell. Edgar had a serious crush on Kay and was in fact eager to marry her, but she refused to go under the canopy with him, though she was apparently fond of him. He was a Jew whose family name was Solomon, and he had been a big success as Tony in Augustus Thomas's *Arizona* in 1900, and had afterward starred in various plays on Broadway. In 1912 he retired from the boards and took to management and play-writing, and at the time Nathan and I saw most of him he was in on the ground floor of the movies, and seemingly destined to make a large fortune. There was but little suggestion of the Jewish in his appearance and manner, and I got on with him very well.

He had the first penthouse apartment I ever saw. It was somewhere in the region of Sixth Avenue and 52nd Street, and was very comfortably turned out. On warm summer evenings he and Nathan and I would dine in our shirt-sleeves on his terrace, and discuss the news of Broadway and the world. I recall that the *Vorspeise* was always a *kosher* salami full of garlic, and that we commonly washed down our meal with Rhine wine. After a while Edgar moved to Hollywood and I saw him seldom, but we remained on good terms. He had a raffish brother, Archie, who was the business man of the family firm, but Archie I met only a few times. Edgar was eased out of the really big money when the movies began to flourish in earnest, but he retained a respectable toehold, and became very well to do. Nathan and I also saw Kay Laurell off and on, but never in Selwyn's company, for their love affair was usually going badly.

Another woman we often saw together in the 1914–1918 era was Marguerite Clark, then one of the most successful of movie stars. Nathan had done her some service in the early days of her movie career, and she and her old sister Cora, with whom she lived in Central Park West, sought to repay the debt by giving us frequent dinners. There were never any other guests, and Cora herself, who was somewhat eccentric, always withdrew before the dessert. Marguerite was a small and pretty woman, and though she must have been almost as old as we were, for she had made her debut on the stage in 1900, she looked much younger. She was not remarkable for her brains, but she was nevertheless very pleasant, and I always enjoyed going to dinner at her apartment or riding through Central Park with her in her automobile. Whenever Nathan and I invited the sisters to dinner as a set-off to their constant and lavish hospitality, Cora refused to come and Marguerite chose some cheap French or Italian restaurant, for she did not believe our public pretense that we were rolling in money, and insisted on regarding us as poor literary men.

One of the delights of dining at her house was the table wine—a rich, very dark, Burgundy-like vintage that always appeared in a decanter. It took us a long time to worm its provenance out of her. Finally, she confessed with blushes that it came from California and that she bought it from a German wine-dealer in Hoboken. We demanded and got his name, and in a little while a large shipment was on its way from Hoboken to Baltimore. When the bill came in I was astounded to discover that the cost was thirty-five cents a quart— bottled! I sent in many orders thereafter, and when Prohibition came down in 1920 I had a large stock in my cellar. It was a really excellent wine, and I worked it off as genuine Burgundy at many a party.

Marguerite and Nathan had a phosphorescent love affair that came to nothing. In 1918 she married a bald-headed young man named Harry P. Williams, a rich lumberman from Louisiana, and went to live with him at his headquarters down there, a miserable place called Patterson, eighty or ninety miles west of New Orleans. In 1926, as I was on my way from New Orleans to El Paso by the Southern Pacific, my train was stalled at Patterson and I got a good look at it. It was a ghastly caricature of a town in the midst of a huge wooded swamp, and life in it must have been dismal for a woman used to Broadway and the movie lots. But Marguerite stuck it out bravely, and when she emerged at all, which was seldom, it was usually only to go to New Orleans for a visit to her friend Genevieve Clark, the daughter of Champ Clark[1] and the wife of James Thomson, at that time publisher of the New Orleans *Item*. After a while Williams took to aviation and in 1935 or thereabout was killed in an airplane accident, leaving Marguerite a rich widow. In that character she came northward more frequently, and in 1936 I saw her in Philadelphia, where she was visiting Marguerite Egan, the widow of Nathan's brother Fritz.

She turned out to be in a very fair state of preservation, but she must have been well into the fifties in 1936, and there were some inescapable marks of oxidation upon her. She died on September 25, 1940, leaving all her money to her sister Cora. It ran to a very considerable amount, for it included not only what she had got from her husband but also half of her own far from small savings as a movie star: the other half had always gone to Cora. Cora is still alive (1948). She devotes herself to tracking down youngsters with an apparent talent for the arts of the theatre, and paying for their education, professional training and subsistence. She has announced and brought out a great many discoveries in her time, but I can't recall one that ever made a durable success. Despite her eccentricities, she is a very kindly though far from intelligent woman, and played the mother, manager and protector to her sister with great fidelity. Nathan and I, I believe, always puzzled her, and in a vague way upset her. Marguerite, whose IQ was probably short of 100, would roar over our

1. Speaker of the House of Representatives, 1911–19.

buffooneries when the Hoboken Burgundy began to rise in us, but Cora always looked rather uneasy. I haven't seen her for years.

Nathan's interest in Marguerite, though it never got anywhere, was characteristic of him. She was a very small woman, and she was a conspicuous figure in the world of Broadway—and that was a combination he always looked for in females. A slight fellow, of less than average height, he is intensely self-conscious about his physique, and is at great pains to avoid being seen with women who are not smaller than he is. If they are known by sight to all the Jews and whores who hang about the theatres and nightclubs, so much the better, for though he has denied, in recent years, that he is a Jew himself, a typically Jewish inferiority complex is in him, and it gives him great satisfaction to have some eminent (or even only notorious) fair one under his arm. All the girls he has been devoted to since I first knew him, ranging from Anita Loos and Lillian Gish down to Ann Pennington the *Follies* hoofer, and including even the early stars of café society that he trailed during his days as a social pusher, have met these specifications. I doubt that in his whole career as a dramatic critic he has ever entered a theatre with a woman taller, or as tall, as himself.

This preference for miniatures is also marked in Charlie Chaplin, the movie clown, another small, slight and very vain fellow, and in Chaplin's case it has produced some very lucrative blackmail, including two forced marriages, for female brigands who have yielded to his lechery and then alleged (through lawyers) that they were under the age of consent. Nathan has been a good deal more circumspect, and I have never heard of him being so beset. No doubt that is mainly because he does not demand both youth and smallness, like Chaplin, but is content with smallness. Also, there is the difference that he always tries to recruit women who are somebody, by his standards, on their own account, and hence above the temptation to highjacking.

I have watched this comedy going on for thirty-five years and it still amuses me. The woman need not be intelligent or even beautiful: it is sufficient that the top of her head come no higher than his eyebrows, and that she be recognized as a personage in the lights of Broadway. He has, of course, known taller and less public women, and for some of them he has had a considerable admiration, but he has never willingly appeared in public with them.

I recall, for example, the case of Jobyna Howland, who was at least six feet in height. Nathan found her a very pleasant boozing companion, as I did, but he always saw her behind the doors of some apartment, usually Zoë Akins's. So far as I can remember—and I'd certainly have remembered it if it had ever occurred—he never took her to the theatre, though he met her there constantly. Even his admiration for Lilith Benda, which was very high, never induced him to change his spots. When she had to be taken to lunch, it was always I who took her—for Benda, though surely no giantess like Jobyna, was so slender that she appeared to be tall. The one apparent exception was Kay Laurell, who was quite as tall as Nathan himself, but even Kay was not a real exception, for when he saw her it was usually either at her apartment or at the *Smart Set* office: he never took her to the theatre and whenever the two went to a restaurant together I was always along.

CHAPTER XII

I T WAS THROUGH John Williams that Nathan and I met Philip Goodman, who was to publish two books for each of us in 1918. This was some time in the latter half of 1917, and Goodman and I became friends almost immediately, and remained so until the shattering impact of Hitler made him turn Jewish on me, but he and Nathan were somewhat less sympathetic, and before the end of 1918 had quarreled. Nathan also had a distrust of Willard H. Wright, born of some forgotten disagreement over *Europe After 8.15*, and often warned me to be wary of him. There were, to be sure, certain traits in Wright that I did not like—for example, he was a monumental liar—but on most of the matters that interested me during the early war years his ideas and mine were substantially identical, so I got on with him well enough. I had been in friendly communication with him since 1909, and, as I have related, had got him the job of editor of the *Smart Set*. Two years before this, on the death of Percival Pollard, I had suggested to Charles Bohm, managing editor of *Town Topics*, that he be made Pollard's successor as book reviewer, and after a little delay this was done. I also induced Norman Boyer to invite him to contribute to the "Pertinent and Impertinent" department in the *Smart Set*, signed Owen Hatteras: this was in 1912.

When he came to New York, early in 1913, to become editor of the magazine, he left his wife and daughter in Los Angeles and set up a somewhat bawdy bachelor apartment in 45th Street, a few doors west of Fifth Avenue. There he lived with various women and staged many parties, all of which I attended when I happened to be in New York. Wright, in those days, was an extremely amusing fellow and full of ambitious writing plans. He published *What Nietzsche Taught* in 1914, *Modern Painting* in 1915, *The Man of Promise* and *Modern American Painters* in 1916, and *Misinforming a Nation* and *Informing a Nation* in 1917. I could not follow him into his liking for what has since come to be known as Modernist painting, but his taste in music was orthodox and impeccable, and he read widely and to much profit.

After trying polygamy for a year or so he settled down with Claire Burke, and when Thayer fired him at the beginning of 1914, and he made a mess of an effort to follow Franklin P. Adams as columnist for the New York *Evening Mail*, he went abroad with her, and they lived in Paris until the outbreak of World War I drove them home. During the terminal stages of the row between Wright and Thayer both of them sought my counsel, and as a result I had an unpleasant time of it. There was a contract between them, running until the end of 1914, but on December 14, 1913, Thayer appeared unannounced in Baltimore, and told me that he was determined to break it. I argued with him for hours, but found it impossible to shake him.

Thayer, as I knew, actually had a case against Wright, for Wright's efforts to enliven the magazine had led him more than once to flaunt and defy the Comstocks in a manner that, in those days of their highest puissance, was certainly very far from prudent. A good deal of infantile recklessness was in him, and his chief defect as editor was his lack of sober judgment. I agreed with him, of course, that the Comstocks were vermin, but I had advised him more than once that it was folly to stick his head into their mouths, and he had made some effort, not always whole-hearted or successful, to get the smell of his *heliogabalisme* off the magazine. But as between Wright and his rashness and Thayer and his cowardice, I was naturally in favor of the former. Thayer not only feared the Comstocks with a quaking fear; he also, at bottom, believed in them, for he was a genuine New Englander. As I might have expected, he gave Wright, when he returned to New York, a highly inaccurate account of our palaver in Baltimore. In brief, he made it appear, by paraphrasing me without actually quoting me, that I had advised firing Wright out of hand, contract or no contract. Wright wired me this news, and I had to reassure him.

On December 20 Wright came down to Baltimore to spend the weekend with me. We put in most of the next day discussing the situation, and I convinced him that his only rational course was to

clear out of the *Smart Set*, for Thayer had become completely hopeless. After a couple of weeks of negotiations Thayer agreed to pay
him a substantial sum to surrender his contract—as I recall it, six
months' salary—and the magazine went staggering on under Luther
and Boyer. Meanwhile, I had heard that Franklin P. Adams, who
had been running a daily column on the *Evening Mail* since 1904,
was leaving to join the *Tribune*, and I made immediate efforts to get
the job for Wright. These efforts were successful and he went to work
at the beginning of 1914. I gave him a good deal of help in his first
days, chiefly by digging up contributors to his column, but it soon
turned out that he was not a columnist, and by February 1 he was
in violent conflict with Stockbridge. He poured his troubles into my
ear, and told me also of various other difficulties that were besetting
him—for example, the illness of his wife and daughter in Los Angeles. He told me that he thought of quitting the *Mail* at once and
putting in six months on the writing of books, with the Thayer money
and a small job on *Town Topics* to sustain him.

A few days later Wright quit the *Mail* and by March he was beginning to be pinched for money. Most of what he received from
Thayer had gone, by this time, to pay for the last illness and funeral
expenses of his father, who had died in Los Angeles in September,
1913, and he had only indifferent success writing for the magazines.
We discussed various plans for his future, including settling in Baltimore, and in the end he decided to go to Paris, where he could live
cheaply. He asked me for a loan in March, but I was preparing to
go abroad myself and replied that my own trip would consume all
my available cash. He must have got some money elsewhere, for he
sailed at about the time I did, taking Claire Burke with him.

Nathan was also going abroad, and the three of us met in Paris in
May, along with A. H. McDannald and W. Edwin Moffett, who
were my travelling companions. We had a pleasant week, but the
rest of us had to pay all the checks, for Wright was extremely hard
up, and he and Claire were living in squalid quarters on the Left
Bank and subsisting (as he told me) mainly on some cheap carbohy-
drate on the order of tapioca. When World War I broke out they
were forced to return to the United States, and did so in the crowded
steerage of an English ship. I got home myself before the war began,
and for several months served as Wright's *locum tenens* on *Town
Topics*—only, of course, for book reviews. He resumed his post when

he returned, and in a little while he and Claire were living in an apartment at 787 Lexington Avenue, upstairs of a store. His pay from *Town Topics* fell far short of supporting them, but he pieced out a meagre income by collecting advances from publishers for books that he had in hand or in mind, acting as an agent for various painters, writing occasionally for the magazines, and borrowing money.

His brother, Stanton Macdonald Wright, a painter, hung about the place, and had a hand in his schemes. Stanton was a fellow of some talent, but his paintings were so advanced in manner that he could not sell them, and so he was even more short of money than Willard. A touch of the nefarious was in him, as there was indeed in Wright, and I recall a time when he hinted broadly that he was raising the wind by arranging fake accident claims against the Third Avenue street railway. Wright's apartment had one sizable room, and its walls were hung with the paintings of his friends and clients—most of them extravagant imitations of Picasso. From time to time I lent him money on some of these paintings, which he declared would be very valuable in the course of time, and at other times I helped him by buying a few of them. I have no record of our transactions, but Wright himself recalled some of them early in 1928, after he had become a big success as writer of detective stories, under the pseudonym of S. S. Van Dine.

One day, in that era, I met him on the street in New York and he brought up the matter of his debt to me, and the next day I received a check for $100 from him on account. On February 6 he sent me a further check for $350. In the accompanying letter he explained that $300 of the total of $450 represented a loan to him on the security of a painting by George Of, and $150 a loan without security. He kept the Of painting and apparently sold it at some time before 1927, for I never saw or heard of it after lending him the $300 on it. He also induced me, in 1914 or 1915, to join him in buying a painting by one Russell, another very advanced painter of the time. It was called "Cosmic Synchrony" and was a riot of primary colors. We paid $250 or $300 for it, or, more accurately, I paid my half to Wright. The theory was that he was to hold the painting for resale when Russell's ship came in, and that we were then to divide the profit. But Russell's ship never came in, and in 1928 Wright still had the painting. In his letter of February 6, 1928, he offered to buy my half of it, but I told him that I had long ago chalked off my so-called investment to profit and loss, and refused to take his money.

Another painting that I bought in those days was a small canvas by Thomas Hart Benton, the illustrator of *Europe After 8.15*. Benton was then under the influence of Picasso, like all the other artists of the Wright entourage, and his painting was a whirl of colored bubbles. I paid $50 for it. How much of my $50, if any, went to Benton I do not know. I was not much interested in painting and most of the work of Wright's friends seemed to me to be bizarre and even absurd, but I made the loans and purchases mentioned in order to help him. In 1947 I presented the Benton painting to the Baltimore Museum of Art.

Between the time of his return to New York in 1914 and the summer of 1917 I saw Wright constantly, and we put in many an evening at the apartment in Lexington Avenue, or at one of the nearby eating-houses. Our favorite was a place in a cellar, also in Lexington Avenue, kept by a fat Italian who was his own cook, and worked his current wife as waitress and cashier. This wife changed from time to time, but she was always attentive to us, and the Italian's food was at least eatable. In the Greenwich Village manner, though his place was far from the Village, he offered a *table d'hôte* dinner, with a quarter-bottle of California claret, at sixty cents. Our party usually consisted of Wright, Claire, my girl of the moment and myself. Wright and Claire lived in domestic decorum, and so far as I knew he was quite faithful to her. In fact, he used to argue at great length that monogamy was the only peaceful, rational and sanitary way of life.

Claire was an Irish girl of mysterious origin who had been, before she went abroad with Wright, a considerable figure in Greenwich Village. She had started out, I believe, as an actress in the Little Theatres, but when I first became aware of her she had set up as a publisher under the trade-name of Claire Marie. How she financed this venture I do not know, but there were reports that she was backed by one of her authors, an advanced poet named Donald Evans. She did books by a number of the other Village celebrities of the time, now all forgotten, but the height of her publishing career was reached early in 1914, when she published *Tender Buttons*, by Gertrude Stein. Most of her authors were poets, and I had a lot of fun with them in my annual reviews of the new poetry.

La Stein's book, which was taken quite gravely by most of the reviewers of the time (and is still taken with some gravity by their heirs and assigns), struck me as unmitigated balderdash, and I recall well how Louis Untermeyer and I put in a gaudy evening digging phallic symbols out of it: it was, in fact, peppered with them. I slated it mercilessly in the *Smart Set* for October, 1914, and was equally rough with most of the other Claire Marie authors. After going under coverture with Wright Claire withdrew from the life of a female Barabbas, but her firm went on feebly in other hands, and I kept on making sport of its goods until it blew up at last in 1915.

Claire and I often discussed these books after I got to know her, and she agreed that most of them were rubbish. She was a very intelligent woman, and also good-looking, with small and piquant features, red hair, and a trim figure. Toward the end of her three years with Wright she met a well-to-do but stupid young New Yorker of good family named Schermerhorn, and he fell in love with her and urged her to marry him. After Wright's *debacle*, presently to be described, she did so, but they were soon at odds and before long they were divorced and she married Samuel Hoffenstein, an amiable young Jew who had made a success as a writer of satirical verses. But this marriage also came to grief, and a little while it ended in divorce and Claire remarried Schermerhorn. Thereafter they lived together in reasonable amity until 1935 or thereabout, when he died of drink under Christian Science treatment.

Late in 1942, desiring to obtain some information from Claire for this chronicle, I got her address from Hoffenstein, and on January 20, 1943, George Nathan and I took her to dinner and had a pleasant evening gabbling of old times. She was living at 212 East 48th Street with a woman whom we met but who didn't join us. Claire said that Schermerhorn's last days under Christian Science were rather dreadful. He left her enough money to live on, but only enough, and when taxes began to mount in 1942 she found herself hard-pressed. Always enterprising and resourceful, she got herself a job as a supervisor in the office of the censorship of foreign mail in New York. She knew no foreign languages, but she was a smart gal, and was apparently making a success of managing her share of the 2,000 linguists who worked in the bureau. Claire, by this time, was well beyond fifty, but her figure was still good, her red hair was still bright, and there were only a few marks of oxidation on her face.

Wright led a retired life in Lexington Avenue, and worked hard on various books—*Modern Painting: Its Tendency and Meaning*,

which the John Lane Company published in 1915; *The Creative Will*
and *The Man of Promise* (a novel), done by the same firm in 1916;
and *Misinforming a Nation*, brought out by B. W. Huebsch in 1917.
In writing *Modern Painting* and *The Creative Will* he had the aid of
his brother Stanton and of the other artists he was friendly with, and
they also gave him some help later on with *The Future of Painting*,
which was not published until 1923. But though he thus made use of
them, he apparently got little pleasure out of their society, and about
the only regular visitor in Lexington Avenue, aside from myself, was
André Tridon. Dreiser disliked Wright and would have none of him,
and Nathan was hostile to him too: in fact, both warned me that he
was a dubious character and would do me some hurt soon or late.

Tridon was a Frenchman and a very amusing fellow. He knew
German and had been making a living for years by translating German
medical books into English. He had been in New York most of
this time, but he was still a French national, and when World War
I began he was notified by the French consul general in New York to
return home for military duty. He replied: "I'll be glad to go back to
Paris when the Germans take it, not before." This was a good quip
and it greatly amused Wright, but when the United States got into
the war poor Tridon found himself in serious difficulties, and how he
managed to escape jailing I do not know. His business of translating
German books, of course, had been destroyed by the war, and for
several years he lived in mysterious and perhaps somewhat shady
ways. At about the time of the Armistice he found a new and easy
source of livelihood in the pseudo-science of psychoanalysis, then fast
becoming the rage in New York. He studied all the Freud books in
the original, and presently set up shop as a psychoanalyst, for he
knew enough about medicine to impress the customers, and was
moreover a very plausible and ingratiating fellow, with an impressive
beard and a ready-made professional manner. Also, he undertook a
text-book of the new arcanum, by title *Psychoanalysis: Its History,
Theory and Practice*, and when B. W. Huebsch brought it out in
1919 it was a considerable success. In 1920 he followed it with *Psychoanalysis and Behavior*, in 1921 with *Psychoanalysis and Dreams*,
and in 1923 with *Psychoanalysis and Love*, for by that time the exploration of the subconscious had become almost purely sexual. I saw
but little of him after I ceased to see Wright. He died of cancer of
the stomach before the end of the 20's.

Wright's books of the 1915–1917 era brought him in very little money—in fact, they never earned the advances paid to him by their publishers—and in consequence he was often hard up. As I have recorded, I sometimes lent him money, and he also got a little by trading in pictures, but he needed a steady job and I urged him to look for one. He showed, however, a reluctance to settle into harness, and so I undertook, in the spring of 1917, to find one for him myself. Other friends gave aid, and the result was that, on June 21, he became literary editor of the New York *Evening Mail*, where he had failed as a columnist—certainly not a lucrative or important post, but at least one that gave him a regular income and promised a better one thereafter. Reviewing books was easy for him and he did it well, but the doctrines he preached in his reviews often alarmed the *Mail* administration and in consequence his hold on his job was soon precarious.

During the summer of 1917, he began to show aberrations that upset not only the prissy Stockbridge, but also me. His talk, always voluble, took on a kind of exaltation that inevitably suggested something approaching mental derangement, and he was full of grandiose schemes that obviously had no sense. I heard from Claire, through my current girl, that what I thus noted at our occasional meetings was going on all the time, and from the same source soon came news of the cause. Wright, it appeared, had taken to morphine. He began, characteristically, in mere bravado, probably led by his vile brother, but after a little while he found himself an addict, and though he never, I believe, proceeded to really large doses, he nevertheless reached a sufficient intake to make him a slave to the drug.

Inasmuch as the Harrison Act had gone into effect on March 1, 1915, and was beginning to be enforced, the cost of morphine was increasing, and the habit was a serious expense to a man of small and irregular income. Claire added the detail that his addiction had made him impotent, and thereby produced a rift in the lute of their domestic felicity. I was supposed to know nothing of this, and I therefore never discussed it with Wright, but I could note his gradual deterioration, and after the summer of 1917 I saw him less often than before. In October it led him into a piece of folly so vast and yet so childish that it enraged me beyond endurance, and I washed my hands of him, and did not see him again for ten years.

The origins of this imbecility lay in a book that he had undertaken

toward the end of 1916, to wit, *Misinforming a Nation*, a brief but
very searching and devastating analysis of the eleventh edition of the
Encyclopedia Britannica, which was then being unloaded on American suckers by a campaign of high-pressure salesmanship. I had myself called his attention to the gross inferiority of the new edition,
and especially to its studied whooping up of all sorts of English nonentities, and its corresponding ignoring of important Americans. This
did not make me indignant; it simply amused me, for I saw in the
gravity with which the work was being received in the United States
a hilarious *reductio ad absurdum* of the colonial docility that was
then so marked.

But Wright took the thing seriously and began to make notes for
an exposure of the swindle. I warned him that it would be futile and
probably also hazardous to bring out any such exposure while the
war was still going on, and advised him to keep it until the period of
Katzenjammer sure to follow the peace, but he was impatient to
launch the attack—and also to collect some advance royalties—and
by the early part of 1917, greatly to my surprise, he had duly collected
them from B. W. Huebsch. Huebsch must have been well aware, in
moments of sober reflection, that no such book would have a Chin-
aman's chance after the United States entered the war, but he was
the sort of fellow who seldom indulged in sober reflection: his business was carried on by hunches.

Wright, meanwhile, was plugging away at his MS. and by the late
spring it was in type. When I read the proofs I warned both him and
Huebsch that publishing it would bring them only grief, but they
decided to go ahead, and in the early summer the book came out. I
printed a long review of it in the *Smart Set* for July, seeking to turn
aside the inevitable wrath of the Anglomaniacal reviewers (for example, by showing that the new Britannica actually treated Germans
more politely than Americans), but the passions of the time were such
that my effort failed, and most of the newspaper reviews were violently abusive, and included hints that Wright must be a German
agent. Many booksellers refused to handle his little book, and its sales
quickly petered out to nothing.

But if it was thus soon forgotten by the native viewers with alarm,
the British Secret Service, then operating openly in New York, remembered it, and in September some enterprising functionary therein
undertook to bring Wright to heel. Nothing seems to have been un-

earthed against him that was of any consequence: he was, to be sure, pro-German, but so were many other Americans, and there was no evidence that he had ever got any German money or taken any hand otherwise in German propaganda. Even his connection with the New York *Evening Mail* was quite innocent, for he was only its literary editor and had nothing to do with its editorial policy. But the British decided that he deserved some punishment nevertheless, and accordingly decided to plant an *agent provocateur* on him. This agent took the form of a woman stenographer, who came to him offering to act as his secretary at extremely low wages. If he had been his normal self Wright would have smelled a rat at once, but by this time morphine had begun to fog his brain and he succumbed without a struggle.

I myself, of course, knew nothing of all this: if I had been told I'd have protested bitterly, if only on the ground that Wright could not afford a secretary, however cheap. But I was already seeing Wright less than formerly, and hence did not hear of the business until it was too late. He noticed at once that the woman was acting queerly—for example, prying into the MSS. in his desk and taking her notebook home with her every night—but he had departed so far from sense that he let it pass, and she stayed on. But even in his clouded state of mind her snooping was irritating and he resolved to set a trap for her. The easy way out would have been to fire her and have done, but his cloudiness suggested a more elaborate and dramatic way of getting rid of her.

This took the incredibly imprudent, and in fact downright idiotic, form of dictating a couple of extremely compromising letters to her, in the hope that she would be unable to conceal her perturbation, and that he would thus catch her, so to speak, with her pants down. The first letter was to Stanton B. Leeds, then Washington correspondent of the *Mail*, and the second was to some unknown person—name not given—in the Department of Justice at Washington. The first brought in the name of Rumely and both mentioned Tridon. By the time the dictation of the second was finished the lady from the British Secret Service was almost in hysterics. Wright thereupon denounced her melodramatically as a spy, and demanded that she hand over her notebook, and begone.

Instead, she stuffed the notebook into her bag, grabbed up her hat, and ran out of the place, with Wright after her. He trailed her to a drugstore in Lexington Avenue between 59th and 60th Streets, but she refused to give up the notebook and he could not wrest it from her without risking a yell of "Murder!" and a riot, so he had to stand by while she ducked into a telephone-booth and called up her employers. They must have advised her to summon the police, for immediately afterward she was telephoning to the East 67th Street station, and in a few minutes a cop arrived on the run. The spy thereupon denounced Wright as "pro-German" and demanded that he be taken to the lockup, but the cop apparently had some doubts that a *prima facie* case had been made out, and when Wright explained that he was a newspaper man (*i.e.*, literary editor of the *Evening Mail*) he was allowed to return to his apartment. There he was presently visited by four men of the American Secret Service, which in those days was hardly more than a branch of the British Secret Service, and the rest of the evening was devoted to trying to convince them that the letter was a hoax and he was not actually engaged in espionage. He was a very plausible fellow, and managed to placate the agents, but the next morning the New York papers were full of the story. Before the end of the day he was fired as literary editor of the *Evening Mail*, and then poor Leeds was fired as Washington correspondent, apparently for good measure. Leeds, as a matter of fact, was completely innocent, though, like Wright, he was actually pro-German. He knew nothing of the letter to him until news of it came out in the papers, and he had had no dealings whatever with Wright about political matters, and had seldom so much as discussed them with him, for Wright was densely ignorant of such things.

By some lucky chance I was not mentioned in the letter to Leeds, but this was only an accident, and the whole affair made me very angry. Wright well knew that Rumely was under investigation, and that any suspicious action by a member of the *Evening Mail* staff would do him serious injury. Moreover, there was Leeds to think of— a decent fellow if there ever was one. The investigation of the matter by the Secret Service went on for days, and I was myself called on to tell what I knew about Wright. I tried to persuade the agents that he was a moony aesthete who knew nothing of politics, and had been roped by a woman who had probably had designs on his chastity, and this view of him they finally adopted, aided by a report from the New York City police that he had no police record.

From end to end of the inquiry no cop had sense enough to ask Wright for his draft registration card. If it had been demanded he'd have been in serious trouble indeed, for he had none, though he was but thirty-four years old at the time. It is possible that he had been refused registration because of his addiction to morphine, but this is rather improbable, and he always represented to me that he had simply failed to register. Perhaps the cops were diverted by his florid beard, which made him look at least 40; perhaps they simply missed a bet. Whatever the reason, they did not ask for his card, and so far as I know he remained unregistered until the end of the war. Once he got out of their clutches he sent me a long letter of explanation, but it was full of the maunderings of a man who was plainly not himself, and I did not make any reply to it. I had by this time, in fact, become fed up with Wright. I had got used to his frequent borrowings of money and to all his other failings, but I found it impossible to carry on friendly relations with a drug addict.

A little while after the uproar ceased he parted from Claire and returned to the Pacific Coast, where he presently got a job on the San Francisco *Bulletin*. There he remained for several years, struggling to cure himself of the morphine habit, though of this I knew nothing, for I had no communication with him, and did not hear from him again, in fact, until 1928. Apparently he was successful, for after 1922 he began to do some magazine work and in 1923 he published another book, *The Future of Painting*. In 1926 he followed it with *Modern Literature*, and during the same year, under the pseudonym of S. S. Van Dine, he published *The Benson Murder Case*, the first of a series of detective novels that were an enormous success and made him rich.

In November, 1934, he appealed to me for aid for his second wife, who needed gynecological attention, and I invited him to bring her down to Baltimore to consult Dr. Edward H. Richardson. He came to Baltimore with her on November 18 and they had dinner in Cathedral Street. I received him politely but suspiciously, for I was already convinced that he had had something to do with the libels upon me lately launched by Burton Rascoe. He invited me to visit him in New York, but I never did so. He died of a heart attack on April 11, 1939.

CHAPTER XIII

MY RELATIONS with Dreiser continued friendly in 1917 and most of 1918, but I saw rather less of him than in the past, and for three principal reasons. The first was that I disapproved of the method he had chosen to try to force Jones to release *The "Genius"*. I believed that it would fail, and found it impossible to discuss the case with him without quarrelling. The second was that he had begun to surround himself, despite his denials and disclaimers, with a frowsy bunch of advanced thinkers of one sort or another, most of them plain frauds and all of them seeking to get publicity for themselves out of his troubles. The third was that, following the departure of Kirah Markham, he was shopping around for another girl, and most of the candidates for the situation that I encountered at his place in 10th Street, or heard of from other explorers, seemed to me to be either harpies or fools.

It was almost impossible, in those days, to offer him anything resembling rational advice, for he was always ready to listen to and follow the prehensile messiahs and designing females who swarmed about him. He was in really serious difficulties, for the suppression of *The "Genius"* had cut off the income on which he had planned to live while writing a successor to *The Financier* and *The Titan* and the three volumes of his autobiography, and his income from magazine stories was irregular, uncertain and usually short of adequate. He was hard up and in a very low state of mind. To be sure, he occasionally sold a story and in December he also got some money out of a more or less arty production of *The Girl in the Coffin*, but these revenues were delayed until the end of the year, and in its earlier months he encountered mainly disappointments.

On August 13 he wrote in his diary: "I am horribly blue and sad, feeling eventual failure staring me in the face." Even in the later months he continued depressed, despite the successes just mentioned, for they were accompanied by the rejection of "A Story of Stories" by the *Saturday Evening Post, Hearst's,* and *Collier's,* by other rejections from the *Red Book* and the *American Magazine,* and by the refusal of *Hearst's* to make a serial of a shortened (and denatured) form of The *"Genius",* on which he had set considerable hopes, financial and otherwise. His life throughout 1917 was pretty dismal, for the women who pursued him were all irritants rather than sedatives, and many of his habitual male associates were arrant frauds— for example, Charles E. Fort, the pseudo-scientific quack. He patronized a fortune-teller, worked the Ouija board, and looked for signs and portents as he stalked about the streets of New York, apprehensive and miserable. "My mind," he wrote in his diary for November 18, 1917, "is full of loneliness and need for color and life."

He had now been separated from his red-haired Eddyist Sarah for four years, but she still harassed and worried him. In October, 1917, she sent him news that she had lost a job that had been given to her on the *Delineator,* apparently to annoy him, and demanded that he support her. This resolved him to get a divorce, but when he undertook definite plans to that end they came to a low-comedy conclusion. Kirah, though she had quit him some time before, still tried to exercise her lascivious arts upon him, and he was hard beset, from time to time, by such insatiable nymphomaniacs as Rella Armstrong and Nina Wilcox Putnam.

I had long before suggested to him that he put the basic articles of his philosophy into writing, if only to make them clear in his own mind, and to this business he applied himself toward the end of 1916. But when his pronunciamento came out in the *Seven Arts* in February, 1917, it turned out to be pretty feeble stuff; indeed, most of the facts in it that had any objective existence at all, and most of the ideas of any coherence, had been borrowed from me. But even this performance, as bad as it was, was measurably more intelligent than most of the other enterprises that occupied him during 1917. He continued, with the aid of various parasites, to nurse his committee for discovering and whooping up new literary work of surpassing but occult merit, he allowed sundry gangs of self-seekers to get what publicity they could out of the attack on The *"Genius",* and he hatched a number of grandiose plans of a miscellaneous and preposterous character. All these doings, of course, seemed idiotic to me. Nor could we come to anything even remotely resembling agreement about the management of The "Genius" case, for I was convinced, as I have said, that the lawyers who had taken it over had adopted an ineffective scheme of action, and would eventually get a beating.

Our only real bond in those days was the war, regarding which our notions were much alike. Dreiser was intensely German-conscious, and rooted for the Kaiser with great enthusiasm. He was anything but reticent about showing his sympathies, and on one occasion came near getting into trouble by refusing to arise in a theatre when "The Marseillaise" was played! It is curious to recall, in the light of his alliance with the Communists during World War II, that he was scornful of "the rank and file" in 1917 and believed that an autocracy was needed to keep it in order. He remained confident until the summer of 1918 that the Germans would win, and began to doubt it then only because his favorite fortune-teller discovered indications in the tea-leaves that they would be beaten. His doubt became certainty when one of his raffish visitors told him that there was a plain forecast of the Kaiser's defeat in the Book of Revelation. This may seem incredible, but it is a sober fact.

In June, 1917, he was so hard beset by his troubles that he decided to get out of New York for a while. He wanted to find a place where telephone calls and concupiscent women could not reach him and life and the mails were slow, and finally decided (not at my suggestion) upon Carroll County, Maryland. He remained at a farmhouse there for four or five weeks, and found what he was looking for, for the place was remote, the country victuals were to his taste, and the quiet of the countryside cleared his mind (at least temporarily) and gave him peace.

I saw him several times during this visit. Once he came to Baltimore, and I returned to the country with him for a dinner of home-cured ham and fresh greens. My colleague of the Baltimore *Sunpapers*, Folger McKinsey, accompanied us, and we travelled in my car, with three or four cases of beer in the rumble. A mile or so west of Ellicott City, as we were on a curve, the car began to steer badly, and I had some difficulty keeping it on the road long enough to stop it. When we got out we found that the front right wheel had ground off a too-tight nut and was within half an inch of coming off the axle. If it had done so while we were in motion we'd have been wrecked, and it is quite possible that Dreiser might have been killed. I telephoned in to Ellicott City for a mechanic, and while he made repairs Dreiser, McKinsey and I drank warm beer, and then set the empty bottles on the roadside fence and threw stones at them. Meanwhile, we worked out a suitable funeral service for Dreiser—in case he had been killed. It included speeches by Sumner the Comstock, William Dean Howells and Nicholas Murray Butler (both of them had refused to sign the Dreiser Protest) and Jane Addams, with music by both the Salvation Army and the Sistine Choir.

Dreiser, who was a good deal of a yokel, liked rural Maryland, and before his return to New York hatched a plan to spend a month or two on one of the islands of the Chesapeake. I warned him against this last project. "Avoid the Chesapeake shore," I wrote, "as you would the great pox. It is hell's kitchen." The following summer he spent a few weeks at Havre de Grace, at the head of the bay.

I gave no further attention to the Dreiser Protest after my return from Europe in March, 1917, but there was naturally some overflow from the correspondence that it had set up. On reaching Baltimore, for example, I found a very friendly letter from Brand Whitlock, then ambassador to Belgium, dated Brussels, December 5, 1916. Whitlock said that he had some doubt that, as ambassador, he should sign the Protest, but he volunteered to make strong representations on Dreiser's behalf at Washington, and it is possible that they had something to do with dissuading the Post Office from barring *The "Genius"* from the mails. In March, 1917, the Comstocks descended upon David Graham Phillips's posthumous *Susan Lenox*, and there was a sideshow to *The "Genius"* show. D. Appleton & Company, the publishers of *Susan Lenox*, talked bravely of fighting the case to a finish, but were presently as full of hesitations as Jones, and meanwhile the Authors' League, probably through the machinations of Hamlin Garland, began to grow lukewarm about *The "Genius"*.

Dreiser conferred constantly with his lawyers, Stanchfield and Levy, and listened to various fools who came in with offers of help. He sent me, on May 5, 1917, a brief that Stanchfield and Levy had prepared, and I reported that it was "a very able document," but before the case came to a hearing they had been displaced by their associate, Joseph S. Auerbach, who actually argued it. A few weeks later Dreiser set me a long memorandum prepared by Merton S.

Yewdale, seeking to make out a case for The "Genius" on purely aesthetic grounds. It seemed to me to be no more than a réchauffé of ideas that Willard H. Wright had set forth at length in his Modern Painting two years before, and I said so.

Wright, like Dreiser, had a grievance against Jones of the John Lane Company. His first book, What Nietzsche Taught, had been published by B. W. Huebsch in 1914, but he had taken Europe After 8.15, which he, Nathan and I did together, to Jones, and Jones also published his Modern Painting, The Man of Promise and The Creative Will, but when he finished Misinforming a Nation early in 1917 poor Jones simply could not publish it, for he was only the agent of an English firm. Wright soon found another and willing publisher in Huebsch, but he denounced Jones violently and tried to qualify as a martyr. This irked Dreiser, who disliked him in general and was not eager to see another martyr to book censorship grab away space in the ring.

I was myself growing out of conceit with Wright, and was soon to give him the bum's rush, but this letter seemed to me to be whining and silly, and I did nothing about it. The news that Jones was trying to keep Dreiser on the Lane list was news indeed, but it hardly surprised me, for I knew that the Harpers, who had suppressed The Titan, were trying to lure him back to theirs. Both these precious outfits of Barabbases were destined to fail, for on July 30, having returned to New York, he wrote to me that Boni & Liveright were after him, and after some hesitation he succumbed to their offer to assemble and reissue all his books. While his negotiations with them were going on they stole a march on him by acquiring the right to reissue Sister Carrie without his consent. This upset him, but he eventually succumbed to Horace Liveright's salesmanship, acquired as a customer's man in Wall Street, and Boni & Liveright were his publishers for a long while thereafter. So long as I was in contact with him Dreiser quarrelled with them, and frequently made his familiar charge that they kept two sets of books and were cheating him on royalties, but nevertheless he went on with them. After 1921 the job of handling him fell to T. R. Smith, then the literary head of the firm, for by that time he and Liveright were at daggers' points. I saw Smith often in those days and had to listen to his sad tale of Dreiser's outrageous charges and demands. In the end they quarrelled, and Dreiser was once more without a publisher.

It must have been in the Summer or Autumn of 1917, before the arrangement with Boni & Liveright was completed, that I one day suggested to Alfred Knopf that he might have him if he wanted him. But Knopf declined to consider it. He was not alarmed by the attack of the Comstocks on The *"Genius"*, for they had also attacked one of his own books; what scared him off was Dreiser's identification with the antinomianism of Greenwich Village, and especially his unpleasant reputation as a stalker of women. I well recall Knopf saying to me: "I don't want any author on my list that I'd hesitate to invite to my house." Thus Dreiser lost a publisher who might have saved him most of the difficulties that beset him until *An American Tragedy* suddenly made him rich. But this possibility falls very far short of a certainty, for Dreiser was suspicious of all publishers, the good along with the bad, and the chances are that, if Knopf had taken him over, the two would have fallen out even sooner than Dreiser fell out with Liveright.

When Stanchfield and Levy withdrew from active participation in *The "Genius"* case, Joseph S. Auerbach, who had been associated with them, became Dreiser's trial lawyer. The case was heard on May 1, 1918, before five judges. The instant the issue was joined the imbecility of Dreiser's plan of campaign became manifest. The lawyers for the John Lane Company were thrown willy nilly upon the defense that *The "Genius"* was actually obscene, and in order to support that defense they had to adopt the whole position of the Comstocks.

The learned judges, plainly enough, could not decide the case without deciding at the same time that the book was either obscene or not obscene. But an appellate court was not the proper place for determining such a question, and they got rid of their headache by announcing that they had no jurisdiction, and could acquire none unless and until the case came up to them after a verdict of guilty in a criminal court. Jones, of course, was not eager to take his chances in a criminal court, for if he lost he might be fined heavily and even sent to jail, and Dreiser couldn't do it because the essence of the alleged defense was selling the book, and he had none to sell. Thus the case ended on a dead center, with the Comstocks delighted. Thanks to Dreiser's folly, the John Lane Company had been forced to adopt and argue their case, at no cost to them whatever, and now Dreiser had no recourse save to meet them on their own terms, and before a police magistrate of their choice. They chose to let the matter lie, and lie it did until 1923, with The *"Genius"* gathering cobwebs in Lane's storehouse.

I was, as I have said, strongly opposed to Dreiser's whole plan of action, as unwise in principle and almost certain to lead to disaster. During the months immediately before the fiasco before the five judges I must have set forth my objections with something approaching vehemence, for Dreiser became offended and for some time we were on very distant terms. Meanwhile, T. R. Smith, then managing editor of the *Century*, was more optimistic, and actually began to make arrangements for a public dinner to Dreiser, to be given at the victorious conclusion of the trial. I refused, of course, to have anything to do with this dinner, which had various other promoters beside Smith, including B. W. Huebsch. Huebsch, with whom I was very friendly, was upset by my refusal to join the dinner committee, and apparently ascribed it to the currently bad state of my relations with Dreiser.

I had certainly not paid Dreiser any grovelling devotion, but he was my elder, and, in my judgment, a great artist, and so I always treated him with a decent respect, even when I had to argue that his proceedings were so imprudent as to be almost insane. Two or three things that had nothing to do with our personal relations were sticking in his craw. One was the fact that I refused absolutely to join the Greenwich Village literati in contending that The *"Genius"* was far superior to *Sister Carrie* and *Jennie Gerhardt*; on the contrary, I kept on preaching that the exact converse was the case, and I still believe that I was right. When I tried to tell the truth as I saw it in *A Book of Prefaces*, the more silly of his followers undertook to convince him that the book was really an attack on him, made with malice prepense. Another thing that irritated him was my attitude toward these parasites: I knew very well that all save a forlorn few of them were trying to work him to their own ends, and I said so.

But even more important was a kind of ill-nature that showed in him when *A Book of Prefaces* began to attract attention. Hitherto, I suppose, he had looked upon me simply as one of his disciples—very useful, perhaps, but still only a sort of function of himself; but now I was beginning to make a noise on my own account, and he was peasant enough to resent it. Moreover, he was not interested in most of the ideas I was undertaking to merchant; indeed, the only one of them that got any real response from him was the idea that he was a great novelist.

All this, of course, sounds almost incredibly stupid and little, but the truth is that Dreiser was an extremely ignorant man, with the sort of mind that shied away almost instinctively from realistic thinking. Whenever an obvious fact competed for his attention with a sonorous piece of nonsense, he went for the nonsense. It was thus impossible to get and hold his confidence, for his dark and tortured spirit was constantly retreating into silence and suspicion. I was fond of him in a way, but I could never really come to grips with him, for his oafish suspiciousness constantly irritated me, and I could not conceal the fact.

I was not one to bear grudges, and when he wrote to me after the case was disposed of, seeking to sell me, for the *Smart Set*, a piece called "Phantasmagoria," I was very polite, for I knew that he was hard up. The piece turned out, alas, to be dreadful stuff, and I got rid of him by putting the blame for its rejection on Nathan. At about this time he had a fall and hurt his ribs, and began to talk of going West (perhaps lured by Kirah) to get rid of his multitudinous troubles. But in the end he decided on Havre de Grace, and from there, in June, he sent me the MS. of a whole book of philosophical maunderings and offered me my choice. Unhappily, it was a match in badness for the previous sample, and I had to return it. In July he followed with something ostensibly in the comic line—what it was I disremember—but once more I had to say no, for his humor was of an extremely heavy sort.

Dreiser, as a matter of fact, never appeared in the *Smart Set* again. Nathan and I, remembering our unpleasant adventures with him in the matter of his three plays and his sequence of poems, were not eager to take him on; moreover, he was doing little if anything that fitted into our scheme of things. He and I resumed our old friendly interchanges, but it was with a difference, and I saw him relatively little. On September 3, 1918, knowing that I was always beset by hay-fever in the autumn, he sent me news of a cure he had lately heard of—"A bit of medicated cotton stuffed into the nose to keep out irritating germs." It was characteristic of him that he did not think to inquire what the medication was. "The cure," I wrote to him on September 4, "has merit, but you apply it to the wrong malaise. It helps hay-fever very little, but is excellent for piles. Seriously, it gives some relief to the nose, but at the expense of the throat. Mouth-breathing, its necessary consequence, promotes laryngitis, bronchitis and asthma." Some time in November, John D. Williams and I, after a very wet dinner, resolved boozily to call upon Dreiser, but when we got to 165 West 10th Street, there was no response to our ring.

We were thus on more or less friendly terms again, but our old intimacy was pretty well over. It did not, however, blow up altogether until December, 1925.

CHAPTER XIV

I PRINTED TWO BOOKS in 1918—*Damn!: A Book of Calumny* and *In Defense of Women*—both done by Philip Goodman. He was a New York advertising man, hailing from Philadelphia, who had an itch to escape the advertising business, and was destined, after failing as a publisher, to make a considerable success as a theatrical producer. It must have been early in 1917 that I first met him through John D. Williams, probably soon after my return from the war. I was in treaty with Alfred A. Knopf, by the summer, for the publication of *A Book of Prefaces*, but meanwhile Goodman had asked me to give him a MS. and I had promised to do so.

He knew a great deal about printing and appeared to have ample capital; better still, he had a new idea, to wit, that it should be easily possible to develop a better market for books than the usual bookstores, which were predominantly run by idiots, most of whom barely made livings. In particular, he had his eye on the drugstores of the country, which were then beginning to handle miscellaneous merchandise on a large scale. I agreed with him thoroughly that the orthodox booksellers were hopeless, and was quite willing to join him in tackling the druggists, which he proposed to do by mail. Unfortunately, he was a bit ahead of his time, and so failed. Twenty years later the sale of books by drugstores had grown into big business, but in 1918 a great many difficulties remained to be surmounted, and Goodman gave up before he had really given his idea a fair chance.

But despite the fact that our joint venture was unprofitable to both of us, he and I remained good friends, and during the fifteen years following I saw more of him than of any other man in New York. We also met abroad, and on both sides of the water we put in many a gaudy evening drinking beer and laughing at the world. When we were separated we exchanged jocose letters, and before the end of 1918 we were toying with a plan to make a book of them. Most of his to me have been lost, but a large number of mine to him were lent to me by his widow after his death in 1940, and copies of them are bound in three volumes entitled *Letters to Philip Goodman, 1918– 1933*, to go to the Pratt Library, Baltimore, at my death. There is also a rough draft of the proposed book, made by Goodman, in a volume entitled *Extracts from Letters Between H. L. Mencken and Philip Goodman, c. 1918*, to go to the Pratt Library likewise. Nothing came of this project, though Goodman and I discussed it off and on for years, but just before his death he worked his share of some of the material into a book brought out by Knopf, in 1941, as *Franklin Street*. In the same way my share had something to do with the genesis of my *Happy Days*, published by Knopf early in 1940, though I used none of it directly.

Damn!: A Book of Calumny came a little ahead of *In Defense of Women*. At the start Goodman and I decided to call it *Forty-nine Little Essays*, and it was under that title that he announced it on February 2, 1918. On January 23 I wrote to him that I was at work on the MS. and that it was "no easy job," which was a fact, for though the book was made up almost entirely of stuff that I had already printed in either the *Smart Set* or the New York *Evening Mail*, I undertook a rather careful rewriting.

At the end of February Goodman began pleading for a change in the title: *Forty-nine Little Essays*, he argued, was colorless and would discourage buyers. He suggested *Damn!* as a substitute and I suggested *A Book of Calumny*, and in the end we decided to use the two in combination. There were no changes in the contents of the book, which consisted of the forty-nine pieces I had originally selected. The longest of them was less than six pages long and the shortest filled but five lines. Altogether, they made a little volume of one hundred and three pages, and Goodman bound it neatly in a greenish gray cloth, with gilt stamping. The retail price was set at ninety cents, and he offered it at the large discount of 50% to the druggists and other new retailers he hoped to round up. The same offer was made with respect to two other little books that he brought out at the same time—*A Book Without a Title*, by George Jean Nathan, and *How's Your Second Act?*, by Arthur Hopkins, a successful theatrical producer of the era, recruited by Nathan. In order to launch the three he prepared an inflammatory circular to the trade and potential trade, printed in orange and black, and sent out thousands of copies.

In order to encourage the idea that the book was full of bold, bad stuff Goodman devoted the slip-cover, not to the usual encomiums of the author, but to denunciations of me by various watchmen of the Puritan *Kultur*. This device, alas, failed to arouse either the druggists or their customers, but it at least helped to provoke some hostile reviews, and out of them I got a good deal of useful publicity. By this time, in fact, I was beginning to get a really large amount of notice, and that notice began to include editorials, news stories and cartoons as well as book reviews and reprints. But all this notice did not make a success of Goodman's new scheme to sell books, and *Damn!* was a commercial failure, along with its two running-mates, *A Book Without a Title* and *How's Your Second Act?*.

His promise to the druggists that all three would be "liberally publicized in your city" was not made good, and the only actual advertisements of *Damn!* were a few inconspicuous one-inchers. The sales were very poor—in fact, downright miserable. Reluctant to admit that his revolution had been a flop, Goodman put the blame on the format of the book, which had been set in rather small type, and in July he had it reset in larger type and reissued it. It now extended to one hundred thirty-nine pages, and the price was raised to $1.25. I contributed a preface to the new edition and Goodman gave it a new binding (brown cloth, with black stamping) and called it the fourth, though it was really only the second. Simultaneously he sent out press notices that "a prominent New York bookstore refused to stock it because of its 'shocking content,' " but all that, of course, was only selling talk, and it failed to stimulate sales.

Later in 1918 Knopf took over such sheets as Goodman still had in stock, changed the title to *A Book of Calumny*, and reissued the book without the preface that I had written for Goodman's "fourth" edition but with his (Goodman's) advertising page at the end. This Knopf edition, the price of which was raised to $1.35, was much sightlier than either Goodman printing, but it failed again and was soon scrapped.

In Defense of Women got under way as soon as *Damn!* was off my hands. On February 6, 1918, I wrote to Goodman that the MS. would be delivered to him by March 15, and by May I was busy with the proofs. At the start there seems to have been some uncertainty about the title, and at one stage I was referring to the book as *The Eternal Feminine*, but in a little while I thought of the ironic *In Defense of Women*, and so it was.

The book was set up and corrected by this time, and ready for the press, but Goodman seems to have had some difficulty in getting paper for it, and the first copies were not ready until the middle of September. The sales remained small, and Goodman, characteristically, searched for reasons lying outside his unfortunate selling scheme. He seems to have embraced the theory, among others, that the failure of various important papers to print reviews was responsible, for on November 13, 1918, I wrote to him satirically: "The paucity of reviews is easily explained. William Dean Howells and Dr. Henry Van Dyke are conspiring against it." How many copies he sold during the first few months I do not know, for he sent me no royalty statement until May 1, 1918, and the period it covered apparently ran only from January 1 to April 1. It showed sales of but one hundred forty-five copies. On June 25 he sent me a second statement, running from April 1 to date: it showed sales of one hundred forty additional copies. His first print-order must have been very small, for there was a second printing, marked "Second Edition" on the title page, before the end of 1918, and on February 8, 1919, he announced a "fourth edition" that never actually appeared.

By this time it was obvious that he could not sell the book—indeed, it was obvious that his publishing venture was a complete failure and he was already preparing to try theatrical management. Early in June, 1919, I proposed that he turn over *In Defense of Women* to Knopf, who had already taken over *Damn!*, and they entered into negotiations at once. These negotiations were carried on in the best Jewish manner, and on June 20 I was writing to Goodman:

> Knopf's bookkeeper, Miss Rabinowitz, who listened in on your palaver, tells me that there were many dramatic episodes. She says that when Knopf bared his breast and invited you, with his voice full of sobs, to cut out his heart and have done, she was deceived by the realism of it and came damn nigh fainting. Miss Rabinowitz inclines to think that you might have got 1⅛ cents more a copy if you had not drunk that doped raisin wine. She carried off a high appreciation of your forensic talent, and has

mentioned you to her sister, Miss Birdie, who is stenographer to Morty Schiff.

On July 2 I wrote to him: "Knopf has been awarded the Ordre Pour le Mérite, with palms, by the Oheb Shalom Congregation for horning you. A case of Rhine wine goes with the award." And on July 8: "Knopf is examining every book separately and personally. When he bought out the Torah Publishing Company and took over the sex hygiene books of Dr. Maurice Hutzler they worked off half a bale of toilet-paper on him."

When they came to terms—just what those terms were I do not recall—Knopf bound Goodman's remaining sheets in the neat blue binding, with gilt stamping, that he had adopted for my books, and by the end of 1919 he had worked off the whole stock in hand and *In Defense of Women* went out of print. It needed, as it stood, a considerable revision, for a large and important part of it dealt with the extension of the suffrage to women, and that extension, since the date of its first publication, had been converted from a mere threat or prospect into a reality.

Unhappily, I was so heavily beset by other jobs in 1920 that I could not undertake the business until 1921. In May of that year I was stimulated to fall to by the fact that a request for the German rights came in from Dr. Franz Blei, an important German author. By July I was hard at work on the revision and by September it was in Knopf's hands. He decided to make it Volume VI in the series of Free Lance Books that I had been editing for him and hoped to get it out in time for the Christmas trade, but this was made impossible by printing difficulties, and it did not actually come out until January, 1922.

As in the case of *A Book of Burlesques*, Knopf's superior publishing skill and energy succeeded where the efforts of another publisher failed, and it was apparent at once that the new edition of *In Defense of Women* was a considerable success. By June 30, 1922, he had sold 2,519 copies and by December 31 he had sold 1,463 more. Thereafter it remained in print for ten years, and was a steady source of income. When, in 1933, *In Defense of Women* went out of print at last and Knopf melted the plates, he and Goodman had reported sales of 21,509 copies and the Garden City Company had sold 20,915 more, making 42,424 in all.

WITH THE MS. OF *In Defense of Women* off my hands by July, 1918, I began at once to put in some heavy licks upon that of *The American Language*, which I had had in mind for a long while. I had been collecting materials for it, in fact, since 1910, when I wrote five articles on American speechways for the Baltimore *Evening Sun*. In August, 1913, I printed a first reworking of them in the *Smart Set* under the title of "The American: His Language," and in 1917 and the early part of 1918 I returned to the subject in the New York *Evening Mail*. I now unearthed this accumulation and sought to augment it by a study of previous writers.

The summer of 1918 was a very hot one, and I remember that I carried my books to my sleeping porch in Hollins Street on blazing afternoons, and there, with my shirt off, sweated through them, making notes. By the end of the autumn the manuscript was complete, and by the end of the year Knopf had set it up and I was at work on the index. But the history of the book belongs to 1919 and thereafter and will be reached in due course. Soon after it was launched I began to make plans for the first volume of my *Prejudices* books, and meanwhile I put in time and energy on various minor book-making enterprises. For Moffat, Yard & Company I did a preface for a new edition of Oscar Wilde's *A House of Pomegranates*, with illustrations by Ben Kutcher, and for Boni & Liveright I did another for a volume of three plays by Ibsen in their new Modern Library. I also, at the suggestion of Philip Goodman, wrote a preface for a new edition of Arthur Morrison's *Tales of Mean Streets*, but Goodman quit publishing before it was finished, and the new edition did not appear until 1920, when Boni & Liveright published it in the Modern Library.

By this time I was becoming known among publishers, and requests for such prefaces reached me rather often, but I seldom wrote them, for I soon learned by experience that they involved too much hard work and yielded too little profit. I was much more interested when requests began to come in for permission to include this or that writing of mine in an anthology. The first of these requests, so far as I can recall, reached me from Willard G. Bleyer, professor of journalism at the University of Wisconsin. He wanted to reprint my "Newspaper Morals," first published in the Atlantic Monthly for March, 1914. I gave him permission and it appeared in his *The Profession of Journalism*, published by the *Atlantic Monthly* Press in 1918. The next year Ludwig Lewisohn included three brief selections from discourses of mine in *A Modern Book of Criticism*, prepared by him for the Modern Library.

By the beginning of 1919 I was getting frequent notices, not only from newspaper reviewers and editorial writers, but also from writers of greater influence, *e.g.*, Frank Harris, James Huneker, William Marion Reedy, E. W. Howe, Vincent O'Sullivan, Carl Sandburg and Upton Sinclair. I was also being mentioned oftener and oftener in foreign papers and magazines, *e.g.*, the London *New Age*, then edited by A. R. Orage; *Everyman* (London); and the *Triad* of Sydney, Australia, on the staff of which last I had acquired a number of disciples; and by the early part of 1919 Knopf was able to boast, in a four-page leaflet brought out to advertise *A Book of Prefaces*, that I had been called "the best of the existing critics" of the United States by the *Mercure de France*.

On May 28, 1918, Abraham Cahan, editor of the New York *Daily Forward*, then an important newspaper among the Jews, printed a long article on me in Yiddish, and on December 7, 1917, Elias Lieberman, writing on "The Jew in American Letters" in the *American Hebrew*, put me in a list of Jewish members of the Authors' League of America and hinted that I was a glory to his race. I protested politely against this last in a letter to the editor, printed December 14, as follows:

Kind friends of Old Testament learning send me news that I am listed, in the current issue of the *American Hebrew*, among the Jewish authors of America. Thus an old piece of flattery gets on its legs again: for three or four years running I was listed annually in the Jewish Year-Book. Unluckily, I can't claim inclusion among the chosen, and so I hasten to present this renunciation of the advantages that go therewith. I am, in fact, a strict Presbyterian, and always have been. I belong to the Lord's Day Alliance and teach in a Sunday School. So much for the spiritual facts.

Seriously, I can produce an ancestral gallery of *Vorhaut* running back 400 years, and on both sides. This is something unusual. I think I am the only pure Christian left in the world. So don't credit me with seeking to steal a place on the bench with Louis Untermeyer and James Oppenheim; my place is among the

Goyim. But if you ever print a list of devoted partisans to *gefüllte Ganshals* and *Süss und Sauer*, then please put me down.

The editor printed this letter with a shirt-tail saying "the loss is ours" and "our grief is only slightly palliated by the fact that he is one of us gastronomically at least." As incredible as it may seem, he had not recognized *Vorhaut* as the German word for "foreskin." But all his Yiddish- or German-speaking readers recognized it instantly, and for weeks thereafter, as he wrote to me sadly, he was bombarded with protests from tender Jews (and Jewesses) who objected to the forthright printing of so indelicate a word in a periodical designed for reading at the domestic hearth. I also received some protests myself, for using it. To them I replied that I had no idea that the editor would print the letter.

My mail, in those days, began to take on the burdensome proportions that it has maintained ever since. In 1918 I had to get some secretarial help, and by 1920 I was claiming an expense of $250 for postage and stationery against my income tax. Some time toward the end of 1918 I got out a printed slip listing my books to date, and copies of it were inserted in my replies to letters from strangers. It showed eighteen volumes with my name attached, but this included three editions of *The Philosophy of Frederich Nietzsche*, separately listed, and also four books of which I was only the editor.

The war fever hobbled me seriously during 1918 and even into 1919 and 1920, and I was frequently attacked, as I have recorded, as a German. In particular, the patriotic watchmen objected to my frequent use of German words and phrases. A long and violent correspondence about me went on in the Toronto *Mail and Empire* during the summer of 1918, chiefly fomented by a 100% Canadian Hunhunter named Reginald Gourley, and on October 15 one A. W. Sweeney had at me with great ferocity in a letter to my old paper, the Baltimore *Evening Sun.* I never, of course, paid any attention to such attacks, but they did me no little injury, if only by alarming my various publishers.

In Baltimore I led a very retired life, and seldom went to the *Sun* office. I saw Paul Patterson, at his home or mine, pretty often, but not Harry C. Black, for Black was still in the Navy. My one recreation was the Saturday Night Club, which managed to survive the war, despite the fact that there was a sharp diversity of opinion among its members. My closest friend among them, Theodor Hemberger, was an unnaturalized German, and the plupatriots of the time badgered him constantly. Worse, his income was sorely depleted, for the German singing societies that he served as conductor had to suspend their sessions, and many of his violin pupils dropped off. Yet worse, he had an hysterical wife, American by birth but a German national through her marriage to him, who had at him day and night with extravagant fears and alarms. Altogether, his situation was so much worse than mine that I got a kind of consolation out of trying to cheer him, and to that end I saw him as often as possible.

Early in 1918 I suggested that he try to get rid of the pains and forebodings of the time by applying himself to some large work, and he accordingly began writing a symphony. Soon after the war it was completed, and later on it was played by the Baltimore Symphony Orchestra, and he made an arrangement of it for the Saturday Night Club. It was a charming work, as he was a charming man, but it lacked dramatic effectiveness, and thus made only an indifferent impression and has never been published. In 1921 or 1922 I tried to have it published in Vienna, but nothing came of this.

Hemberger was naturalized during the post-war period, and likewise his wife, who had lost her citizenship by marrying him. When World War II began she took to hysterics again, and he dropped out of the Saturday Night Club. On her death in 1942 he rejoined, and is still a member (1948). But he is now beyond seventy-five, and his beautiful playing and infectious enthusiasm of twenty-five or thirty years ago are no more.

I acquired a long blacklist of Baltimoreans who offended me in one way or another during World War I, and during the years since I have avoided them as much as possible. In New York I added a few, but they were not of any importance: most of them, in fact, were mere hangers-on. One such was the Harold Hersey who has been hitherto mentioned as the agent of the Authors' League in the matter of the Dreiser Protest. This Hersey hailed from Montana, but when I first heard from him he had a job in the copyright office of the Library of Congress at Washington and was publishing a small poetry magazine, the *Open Road,* in association with another library clerk named Herbert Bruncken. He sent me various contributions for the *Smart Set* and I accepted and published a few of them. He came to New York in 1916, bringing a young wife and a baby, and was presently established in Macdougal Alley, the heart of Greenwich Village. Once, I recall, he lured me to dinner there to meet his wife, and I found that the place was quite devoid of plumbing. In association with two other young men, Arthur Moss and Forest Mann, he set up a magazine called the *Quill*, and was presently a salient figure in the Village.

He professed to be violently pro-German, and in that character made up to Dreiser and me. But when the United States entered the war he signed up almost at once, and soon afterward he came to see Nathan and me at the *Smart Set* office in a lieutenant's uniform. We were so disgusted by his facile turning of his coat that we were extremely chilly to him, and in fact never saw him again. But Dreiser remained more tolerant of him, and was still seeing him in October, 1917. My attitude must have offended him greatly, for he was still cherishing a bitter hatred of me years afterward. When the war ended he got a job on the staff of W. M. Clayton, the bastard son of Colonel W. D. Mann, whose efforts to rival the *Smart Set* with *Snappy Stories* I have hitherto recorded. Soon he was launched upon a long career as editor and publisher of pulp magazines, and now and then he had a considerable success and made money. But in the long run he did badly, and at last accounts he was far from prosperous. He cherished his animosity to me through his years of glory, and once, when he had some cash in hand, he brought out one issue of a so-called quarterly, the *American Autopsy*, wholly written by himself and mainly devoted to denunciation of me.

In 1937 he published a biography, *Pulpwood Editor*, detailing his services to the national letters. It showed that he had been the editor or publisher, first and last, of no less than seventy-two pulps, among them, *Speakeasy Stories*, *Thrills of the Jungle*, the *Complete Gang Novel Magazine*, *Strange Suicides*, *Clues*, *Loving Hearts* and *Murder Stories*. At one time he was supervising editor for Bernarr Macfadden, but he did not last long. Another time he worked briefly for Street & Smith, the original begetters of the pulp magazine, but mostly he was in the service of Barabbases much further down the scale. On August 12, 1940, he wrote to me from Waterford, Connecticut, saying that he was at work on a history of American magazines, and asking me to recommend him to Knopf for one of the literary fellowships that Knopf was then offering. I did not answer this letter. A year or two later I received a notice from "the Connecticut State Employment Service, affiliated with the Social Security Board," saying that he had applied to it for a job and had given me as a reference. To this I likewise made no reply.

I have hitherto listed some of the other *Smart Set* contributors of the 1914–1918 era who, after showing promise, blew up and disappeared. They had plenty of company outside our fold—for example, Henry Sydnor Harrison, Winston Churchill (the American novelist, not the English savior of humanity), Rowland Thomas, Robert Cortes Holliday and Ernest Poole. Harrison was typical of that melancholy company. A Tennesseean, born in 1880, he made a huge popular success in 1911 with *Queed*, an imitation of the sentimental comedies of William J. Locke. When his *Andrew Bride of Paris* appeared in 1925 I had to describe it in the *American Mercury* for April, 1926, as only "pathetic hollowness." I went on: "His trade, I suspect, has now deserted to Christopher Morley. . . . The thing is childishly transparent—a moral tale that even schoolboys—nay, schoolmasters—must laugh at."

Morley had less talent than Harrison, but was a great deal smarter, and so he got on; in the end, indeed, he became one of the most successful of American literary racketeers. But he never quite managed to wriggle himself above the salt: even with such masterpieces as *Where the Blue Begins*, *Thunder on the Left* and *Kitty Foyle* behind him, he remained a denizen of the literary half-world, along with the outright quacks of the Alexander Woollcott variety. I gave the first of his books that I had encountered, *Songs for a Little House*, a brief but friendly notice in the *Smart Set* for June, 1918, and I gave his *Shandygaff* an even more friendly one the month following, but by the time *Mince Pie* appeared, in 1919, I was full of doubts, and my notice of it in May of that year was extremely sniffish. After that I never reviewed him at all. He was the inventor, or, at all events, the first abettor, of the scheme for authors to make tours of bookshops, autographing books and basking in the lubricious stares of the lady customers. He also cultivated the reviewers and was a frequent speaker at literary lyceums. By such devices he greatly increased his sales, but he never managed to convince any competent person that he was a sound and honest author. He resented my contempt for his books and sometimes had at me waspishly, but I refused to be annoyed, and remained, at least ostensibly, on good terms with him.

Holliday was of the same cut, but even worse. There was a time when he got an enormous amount of space in the literary columns of the newspapers, but his season did not last long and he was soon forgotten. When his *Walking-Stick Papers* came out in 1918 I described them as "rambling and inconsequential" but was otherwise polite to them, but when he followed with *Peeps at People* and *Broom Street Straws* in 1919 I fell upon both books with derision. "What could be more trivial and uninspired," I asked in the *Smart Set* for May, 1920, "than the short pieces in *Peeps at People?* . . . That sort of thing inevitably suggests the heavy whimsicality of *Life* and the other barber-shop weeklies. It is standing refutation of the notion that Americans have a sense of humor." Holliday died in 1946 or thereabout, quite forgettable.

The American Churchill stood far above such mountebanks as Morley and Holliday, if only because he was a profoundly serious man, but though he was a big success for a while he quickly blew up, and after 1917 he disappeared. In 1941 he published his first book in twenty-four years, and many readers of the reviews of it were astonished, I daresay, to discover that he was still alive. Most of his more popular novels—for example, *The Celebrity*, *Richard Carvel*, *The Crisis*, and *Coniston*—came out before I was writing for the *Smart Set*. The first of his major canon that reached me for review was *A Modern Chronicle*, published in 1910. I gave it a friendly but far from enthusiastic notice in the *Smart Set* for July of that year. When *The Inside of the Cup* followed in 1913 I made it the text for a long discourse on theology as a theme for fiction, and pointed out some of its more salient shortcomings as a study of human motive and action. When *A Far Country* appeared in 1915 I made it the text of another lengthy disquisition—this time on the impact of the uplift upon American politics—but had to be even more reserved about the story itself. That was the last time I had to deal with Churchill until *The Dwelling Place of Light* was published in 1917. All I could say of that dreadful book, in the *Smart Set* for December, was that I could not read it.

Another dud of the same melancholy sort was Ernest Poole. When his first really ambitious novel, *The Harbor*, came out in 1915 it was hailed by the newspapers and literary weeklies as a masterpiece of the first chop, but when I read it the most I could find in it, as I said in the *Smart Set* for June, was "the somewhat stilted and oratorical tale of a young magazine hack's grappling with various abysmal sociological problems, leading to conclusions as vague as they are highsounding." Poole wrote more books—indeed, at least eighteen—but though his partisans made hard efforts to whoop him up he gradually faded into oblivion. At last accounts (1943) he was engaged in some sort of war work. He had a certain slender talent, but it did not hold up.

The case of Thomas was even more lugubrious. He came into sudden and blinding fame with a short story, the name of which I unhappily forget. It won some sort of prize and for a year or two he got almost as much attention in the literary weeklies as Wells or Bennett. But then he began to fade out, and in a few years he was quite forgotten, though he continued to write.

I noted the collapse of Churchill and Poole with genuine regret, for they were earnest men and it would have been a pleasure to support them as I tried to support Conrad and Dreiser, Wells and Bennett, Cabell and Hergesheimer. Despite the general impression that I was a killer, seeking only literary skulls to smash, I actually printed a great many more favorable reviews than slatings. I was always eager to give a hand to newcomers of any merit—for example, Carl Sandburg, Montague Glass, Abraham Cahan, Sholom Asch, E. W. Howe and Sherwood Anderson—and I roved widely in search of striking and genuine novelties. I was quick at all times to applaud fellow critics who showed any sense—for example, Ernest Boyd, Francis Hackett, Huneker, John Macy, Ludwig Lewisohn and J. E. Spingarn. I had beat the drum for William Lyon Phelps so early as June, 1910, when he made American literary history by bringing out the first book in which a respectable college professor praised *Huckleberry Finn*, and I was sincerely sorry when, in 1916, he returned to the imbecility of his craft in *The Advance of the English Novel*, and I had to denounce him. I was very polite to Spingarn when he published his *Creative Criticism* in 1917, and returned to it in the first volume of my *Prejudices:* indeed, Spingarn and I remained on friendly terms until his death in 1939, though his general position and mine were always somewhat in conflict.

I even gave a welcome to Wilson Follett when his *Some Modern Novelists* appeared in 1918, though I found a good deal to cavil at in it, and not long afterward began to realize sadly that he was a jackass. Back in November, 1916, I had actually given a tolerant review to Fred Lewis Pattee's *History of American Literature Since 1870*, and out of that review flowed friendly exchanges with the old boy that went on until after he quit his job at the Pennsylvania State College in 1928 and took himself to Florida. Nor was I impolite to Paul Elmer More and Irving Babbitt, though the fundamentals of their doctrine seemed to me to be bosh. But I had at such frauds as Stuart P. Sherman, Edward J. O'Brien and William Stanley Braithwaite without tenderness, and I still think my condemnation was well deserved. Likewise I plastered the Greenwich Village critics and the apostles of Imagism.

So in music and in the field of general ideas. I gave a welcome to Carl Van Vechten and praised Huneker, but heaped scorn on Henry E. Krehbiel and Henry T. Finck. Among the psychoanalysts who flourished during the war years I chose Adler as against Freud, for the inferiority complex of the former seemed to me to be much more rational than the sex flubdub of the latter. As the opportunity offered I belabored spiritualism, Prohibition and the other manias of the time, always with special attention to the fundamental theories of Puritanism.

A number of the current literary sensations seemed to me to be vastly overpraised, and I said so. One was Logan Pearsall Smith's *Trivia*, which was greeted in 1918 in terms fit for a new *Essay on Man*, and another was the series of books by W. H. Hudson. Hudson's *Green Mansions* was a great success in the United States and set Knopf on his feet as a publisher, but I found it much inferior to the books of Joseph Conrad, and when *Tales of the Pampas* followed I could only report that it left me cold.

I made no attempt, in those days, to formulate a literary theory, nor did I undertake the usual laborious "revaluation" of the classics. I let it be known, plainly enough, where my tastes in the latter direction lay, but it seemed to me to be idiotic to discuss Dreiser and Huneker, in the customary pedagogic manner, in the light of Thackeray and Macaulay. My chief concern was always with the literature that was in being, to wit, the unrolling literature of a far from civilized, and even not altogether literate democracy. When the *Cambridge History of American Literature* came out in 1917 I used it as a text for a denunciation of the whole professorial point of view, and at other times I beat a loud drum for Mark Twain, who, in spite of Phelps, was still lingering outside the academic grove. No reasonably attentive reader of my monthly discourses, by the beginning of 1917, could be in any doubt about my fundamental ideas, which were, in the main, scientific rather than moral or aesthetic: I was in favor of the true long before I was in favor of either the good or the beautiful.

CHAPTER XV

ESPITE THE DIFFICULTIES of the *Smart Set* and the hobble put on us by the various censorships, official and unofficial, that raged during the war years, Nathan and I managed to enjoy ourselves pleasantly, and, what was better, to make steady progress professionally. My own situation, of course, was measurably more uncomfortable than his. In the theatre he was confronted by the war issue as I was, but it usually appeared in the form of very bad plays, and so he could denounce them as works of art without entering upon any serious consideration of their theses. That was not true of most of the war books that came to me for review: if I was to keep out of trouble I simply had to ignore them altogether, which deprived me of many a chance to shine.

Moreover, I had printed a great deal of anti-English stuff in the Baltimore *Evening Sun* during the first year of the war, and it was remembered by the Anglomaniacs of that time, and frequently thrown into my teeth. Some of them I annoyed excessively—for example, Robert W. Chambers. After 1914 I refused to print any formal reviews of his almost innumerable bad novels, but mentioned him frequently in my reviews of other books, always in the character of a literary prostitute. He took this very badly and thirsted for revenge. This took the form of circulating all sorts of defamatory stories about me, chiefly to the effect that I was a German spy. Sometimes he branched out into bolder libels. One day, Lilith Benda, who knew him, told me he had assured her that Nathan and I were homosexuals and engaged in mutual carnalities. When I passed this on to Nathan he said: "Tell Benda to tell him, 'Not yet, but we may some day follow his suggestion—and example.'" I never met him, for I always kept clear of the arty circles he frequented. He died in 1933 and is now completely forgotten, though he wrote and published in his time, at least thirty novels, beside plays and other things.

He was not the only well-known writer of the time who disliked me intensely: another was the once-celebrated Paul Elmer More. Later on the roster of them grew to large proportions, and included, *inter alia*, Edna St. Vincent Millay, Irvin Cobb, Ernest Hemingway and Heywood Broun. On lower levels the number of Menckeno-phobes was almost limitless—many of them members of what I used to call the *Smart Set* Rejection-Slip Association. This organization, in 1924, was converted into the *American Mercury* Rejection-Slip Association and became even larger. I had the power, for twenty years on end, to bar authors I held in contempt from two magazines that, each in its time, were considered very attractive platforms, and I exercised that power with great satisfaction. But for every enemy that I thus made, I made a friend in some other way, and the number of them went on increasing until I finally quit magazine editing at the end of 1933.

The most durable and agreeable friendship that grew out of the war years was that with Joseph Hergesheimer, but while they dragged on I made my first contact with a number of men who were to color and embroider my life thereafter. One of these was Fielding H. Garrison, the medical historian. He was then a lieutenant-colonel in the Army Medical Corps, attached to the surgeon-general's library at Washington, and I met him almost by accident. As I have hitherto recorded, I had begun to write medical articles in collaboration with Dr. L. K. Hirshberg back in 1907, and a series of them that I sold to Dreiser had appeared in the *Delineator* and then as a book. The experience thus gained made me familiar with medical terms and ideas, and some time later I wrote a number of circulars and leaflets for Dr. Joseph C. Bloodgood of Baltimore, who was then carrying on a so-called cancer education campaign. I used to see Bloodgood frequently during the early days of the war, and also spent a great deal of time with his office factotum, Herman Schapiro, a Russian Jew and a remarkable linguist, who was a non-playing member of the Saturday Night Club.

One day early in 1918 Schapiro told me that he and Bloodgood, seeking to get some light upon a surgical problem, had been searching *The Medical and Surgical History of the War of the Rebellion,* brought out by the federal government, in a long series of volumes, between 1870 and 1888, and that they had found it an almost impenetrable wilderness of unorganized material, some of it very useful but most of it mere trash. The record had been thrown together without proper planning, and as a result the work was almost unusable. A few days later I encountered Bloodgood, and he discoursed at length upon the same theme. He was by this time in uniform as an officer in the Medical Reserve of the Army, and his chronic itch to reform and instruct was beginning to afflict him again. This time what he had in mind was a more orderly and scientific record of medical and surgical experience in the World War than the one the Civil War had produced. He argued that what wrecked the latter was a lack of technical editorial competence in the editors, and then proceeded to say that I could supply that lack this time, if I would, and that it was my patriotic duty to volunteer for the service.

I was certainly not eager to serve my country in the current war—indeed, I was determined not to do it if it could be avoided—but when it appeared as the discussion went on that what he wanted me to do would not promote the actual conduct of the war, and that my labors, if any, would really not begin until the war was over, I said yes to get rid of his solicitations. The next day he was at me again, and again the next, and in the end, succumbing to his urging, I wrote a letter to the surgeon-general, setting forth my experience and offering to give him any editorial aid that he needed and wanted. At the same time Bloodgood sent along a strong recommendation, saying that my equipment was precisely what the official historians of the Army Medical Corps in the war would have use for, and that I was an author of the highest talents and dignity and would lend a kind of literary glamor to the whole enterprise.

My letter was turned over to Garrison, himself a literary man rather than a medical man, by the surgeon-general, and in a little while I had a brief, official note from him, asking me to come to see him at the surgeon-general's library, where he had been the assistant librarian since 1889. For years he had served as a civilian, but on the entrance of the United States into the war he had been commissioned a major in the Army Medical Reserve Corps and early in 1918 he had been promoted to lieutenant-colonel. A week or two later I dropped in on him at the quarters in the Army Medical Museum, and we had a brief but pleasant session, though one showing certain signs of suspicion on Garrison's part. He knew my writings, for he apparently read everything, and he professed to be greatly interested in them, but he was at bottom, for all his learning, a typical Washington functionary, and so he resented the intrusion of a stranger. There was, he explained to me at once, no need for any aid from outside: he himself was already designated to edit the medical history of the current war. This, of course, disposed of me, for I was familiar with the first edition of his excellent *Introduction to the History of Medicine*, and knew that he was quite competent to make an enormously better job of it than his predecessors had made of *The Medical History of the War of the Rebellion*.

It turned out, in the brief talk that followed, that he and I had many interests in common. For one thing, we were both amateur pianists, and for another thing we were both enthusiasts for Brahms. Also, we had a number of common friends, including especially some of the notables of the Johns Hopkins Medical School. By the time I left we were on amicable terms, despite his plain distrust for me, and he was inviting me to return to Washington for dinner with him. I went a little later and we had another, longer and even friendlier palaver, and soon afterward he came to Baltimore, at my invitation, for dinner with the Sunday Dinner Club.

After that we exchanged visits with some frequency, and in the end we became warm friends, but it took Garrison some time to get rid of a certain uneasiness in my company. In part this was born of his knowledge that I was pro-German and a derider of the whole American scheme of things, but in even larger part, I believe, it flowed out of a lingering suspicion that I was bent on invading his prerogative and maybe even stealing his job. He was a highly intelligent man, but he had been a minor bureaucrat for twenty-nine years, and he could not throw off the qualms and fears of his craft. On August 19, 1918, after we had had several very pleasant meetings, he was still suspicious that I wanted a post on the staff of the surgeon-general, and sought to throw me off by warning me that I would have to take an examination and that my starting salary would be $1,100 a year. "We are stocked up with helpful people now," he went on, "in all departments." It took me some time longer to convince him that I was not looking for a job, that I did not need one, and that if one were thrust upon me I'd not expect any pay for my services.

After the summer of 1918 the imminent end of the war threw a heavy burden of work upon him, and our exchange of letters fell off, but it was resumed in December and went on for years. I saw him off and on, and we often discussed the medical history that he was to edit, but mostly our talk was of things remote from the war. In the end he was ordered to duty in the Philippines. This was in 1922. He was as unfit for medical service in the field as any M.D. on earth, for he had not practiced for years and he was always restless under military formalities, but he took his assignment docilely and was on his way to Manila by the end of August. He was supposed to stay there for three years, but after two had come and gone he was on his way back to the United States. It didn't take his superiors long to discover that he was a poor administrator and that the morning *Schwanzparade* of the soldiers filled him with disgust, so after the first few weeks he was left pretty much to his own devices. He devoted six or eight months to training groups of Filipinos for a performance of Schubert's octette, which he put at the head of all chamber music, and though the climate was unfavorable to hard study, he put in a good many licks on a revision of his *History of Medicine*.

After his return from Manila he resumed his duties in the surgeon-general's office. Most of his time was devoted to the *Index Medicus*, of which he was the editor, and the quarterly *Cumulative Index Medicus*, of which he was the associate editor. Early in 1930 he was offered the librarianship of the new Welch Medical Library at the Johns Hopkins, and in May he retired from the Army in order to accept it. There was a farewell dinner to him in Washington before he moved to Baltimore and I went to it and was one of the very few lay guests.

When he got to Baltimore our correspondence naturally fell off, for I saw him pretty often, but, despite an occasional difference, our friendship continued until his death in 1935. The nearest it ever came to blowing up altogether was in 1926, when the Boston Comstocks undertook to suppress the April issue of the *American Mercury*, containing Herbert Asbury's "Hatrack," and I went to Boston to challenge them. Garrison had an article on William S. Halsted, the famous Johns Hopkins surgeon, in the same issue of the magazine, and was considerably upset when the Post Office, in order to help the Comstocks, barred it from the mails. This, I suppose, was mainly because he got some ribbing from his colleagues in the surgeon-general's library, but there was also something else: he remained a

Puritan under his skin. But he soon cooled off, and our friendly exchanges were resumed.

Another interesting acquaintance I picked up in 1918 was Abraham Cahan, editor of the *Jewish Daily Forward*, the principal daily newspaper of the New York East Side, and the author of a really remarkable novel, *The Rise of David Levinsky*. My relations with him were always more or less formal, and I seldom saw him or heard from him, but nevertheless we continued on good terms, and have remained so to this day (1943). My attention was first directed toward him by the woman called Bert in Dreiser's diary, a diligent reader of all fiction originating in Russia, whether in Russian or Yiddish. This must have been some time in 1917, just after the appearance of *David Levinsky*. I read it at once and was greatly impressed by it, and I reviewed it at length in the *Smart Set* for May, 1918.

I really liked the Cahan book immensely, and I must have written to the author to say so, for the first letter from him in my letter-file is dated April 5, 1918, before the May *Smart Set* was out. We met soon afterward, and I found him to be as civilized face to face as he was pen in hand. He was at that time approaching fifty-eight, and was a notably handsome man, with an erect bearing, Jewish features that were without grossness, and a mop of wavy hair that gave him, somehow, a very dignified appearance. I was at that time beginning work on *The American Language* and I naturally asked him for information about the Yiddish spoken in America—especially its use of loan-words from American English.

Soon after our first contact Cahan went abroad to visit his Russian homeland, and I did not hear from him again until 1921, when he wrote on March 7 that the copy of *The American Language* that I had sent to him had never reached him. In this letter he sent me some notes on Yiddish in America, and also told me of the battle then going on in the New York ghetto between the so-called Yiddishists, who were trying to preserve Yiddish in America, and the anti-Yiddishists, who were glad to see it dying out. Cahan's own sympathies, it appeared, were with the latter party, though its triumph would ruin his newspaper.

I saw him off and on after that, but not often. On March 16, 1926, he asked me to write an article for a new and enlarged English supplement to the *Daily Forward* that he had in preparation. I did so and it appeared in the first issue of the supplement, on April 4. Meanwhile, he had long ago paid me back for my encomiastic review of *The Rise of David Levinsky* by writing an article on me, with a portrait, and printing it in the *Daily Forward* on May 26, 1918. Under date of April 26, 1930, I received a note from him saying that he wanted to have a chat with me "as an old friend," and I invited him to lunch at the Algonquin. When he arrived it appeared that he was greatly troubled by a characterization of the Jews that I had printed in my *Treatise on the Gods*. The book had come out only a month before, but already, so Cahan told me, the Yiddish papers were ringing with denunciations of me and various blood-sweating rabbis were preaching against me as a violent anti-Semite.

But Cahan himself was too civilized to be upset; he had noted and now admitted freely that my characterization of the Jews as "the most unpleasant race ever heard of," showing "vanity without pride, voluptuousness without taste, and learning without wisdom," was only a small part of a discussion that was generally favorable to them; moreover, he was ready to grant that, in the case of large numbers of them, it was well justified by the facts. But inasmuch as most of the other Jewish literati knew that he and I were friendly, he wanted to have it out with me in the frankest way, and so be in a position to write an article testifying that I was not actually an enemy of the Chosen. We came to terms without difficulty and soon afterward he printed a defense of me in the *Daily Forward*.

Meanwhile, some of the blood-sweating rabbis aforesaid had tackled the Knopfs, upbraiding them as Jews for printing my characterization of their race, and old Samuel Knopf was considerably upset. But when he came to me with a suggestion that the passage complained of be modified I refused flatly to consent, on the ground that I could not yield under fire. Thus it remained unchanged through the ten printings that came out from 1930 to 1933.

In July, 1930, Cahan celebrated his seventieth birthday, and I sent him a telegram of felicitations and got a pleasant reply. I heard no more from him after that until 1933, when, under date of February 1, he wrote to me at length to approve a review of two books on Russia, *Russia in Transition*, by Elisha M. Friedman, and *Soviet Russia as I Saw It*, by William J. Robinson, that I had published in the *American Mercury* for February. The great majority of American Jews, in 1933 as today, were violent partisans of the Bolsheviks, but not Cahan. He was too intelligent to be deceived by their blather, and too courageous to keep his views to himself. His denunciations of them cost the *Daily Forward* a great many readers, and brought down upon him the bitter reviling of the Jewish radicals, but he stuck to his guns.

Early in 1940 Cahan's colleagues of the *Daily Forward* began to make plans for the celebration of his eightieth birthday, and I was asked to do an article on him in his character of novelist for a special issue of the paper. I wrote it and sent it in, but got no acknowledgment of it. In January, 1941, I wrote to Cahan himself, asking him when it had been printed, and received from him a reply saying that the special edition had been delayed at his order. It was finally printed, in Yiddish and English, on June 7, 1942.

On July 6, 1941, the sixtieth anniversary of his arrival in America, the *Daily Forward* brethren surprised the old man with a gala luncheon at the Commodore Hotel and I was invited to join them, but other business got in the way and I had to decline. I saw little of him in those later years, and heard from him only seldom. He had published nothing of any significance after *The Rise of David Levinsky* save an autobiography in five volumes, *Bleter fun Meinen Lebn*, and that appeared only in Yiddish. His name disappeared from *Who's Who in America* after the 1938–39 volume.

The *Daily Forward* was losing ground steadily, and for two reasons. The first was that the tide of Jewish immigration from the Yiddish-speaking areas of Eastern Europe, once a mighty flood, had declined to a trickle, and the second was that Cahan's animosity to the Russian Communists (though he remained a Socialist) had alienated a good many of his readers. In 1925 the *Daily Forward* had a circulation of 156,812 for its daily edition, 159,543 on Sunday and 172,245 on Saturday, then its main day, but by 1945 these figures had fallen to 98,969, 117,242 and 115,603 respectively.

In 1944 I encountered Cahan one day in the elevator of the Algonquin, and learned to my surprise that he and his wife were quartered in the hotel. After that I saw him off and on, and we had some pleasant palavers. But by 1945 he was eighty-five years old, and both he and his wife, to whom he presented me, were sadly enfeebled. Soon afterward she died.

CHAPTER XVI

As I have recorded, the *Smart Set* that I came back to from the war in 1917 was anything but exhilarating. There was not much improvement during 1918, but in 1919 some rays of light began to appear upon the horizon. In April of that year Nathan and I printed the first instalment of "Repetition Generale," a joint department that was to go on until we quit the magazine at the end of 1923. In October we changed to a new type in headings and by-lines, though not to a new body type, and toward the end of the year we began to make plans for the *Black Mask*, our third device to keep the pot boiling.

"Repetition Generale" was my idea, and I gave it its name. I had already acquired, in those days, the habit of making a note whenever anything interesting occurred to me, and these notes, in the years to come, were destined to run to immense numbers. Many of them, of course, were consumed by my newspaper and magazine articles and my books, but there was always a surplus, and early in 1945 I resolved to go through it critically, throw away all the useless stuff, and reduce the rest to coherent terms, for not a few of the notes were confined to reminders of a few words, unintelligible to anyone save myself. Indeed, when I settled down to work upon them I found that some were baffling to me as well. When I finished the job I had enough material to fill four letter-files.

My first contributions to "Repetition Generale" included some by-products of *In Defense of Women*, but there were also notes on romanticism and realism, actors, the American hustler, sex hygiene, agnostics, posthumous fame, telephone bells, snobbery, and dogs. I always wrote more for the department than Nathan, but he adorned

No. 1 with a memorable definition of a chorus-man: "one whose father and mother had prayed for a boy." He had always followed the somewhat childish vanity of running his name ahead of mine on the flagstaff of the magazine, but when I suggested that the two alternate in first place in the by-line of "Repetition Generale" he agreed with good grace. In the third instalment, in June, 1919, we began to print the idiotic folk-lore that was to enter, a year later, into the book called *The American Credo*. This first crop consisted of eleven articles, as follows:

1. The doctrine that a man like Charley Schwab, who has made a great success of the steel business, could in the same way easily have become a great composer like Bach or Beethoven had he been minded thus to devote his talents.

2. The doctrine that the man who doesn't hop promptly to his feet when the orchestra plays "The Star-Spangled Banner" as an overture to Hurtig and Seamon's "Hurly Burly Girlies" must have either rheumatism or pro-German sympathies.

3. The doctrine that something mysterious goes on in the rooms back of chop suey restaurants.

4. The doctrine that every workman in Henry Ford's factory is the owner of a suburban mansion and a rose garden.

5. The doctrine that all sailors are gifted with an extraordinary propensity for amour, but that on their first night of shore leave they hang around the water-front saloons and are given knock-out drops.

6. The doctrine that a napkin is always wrapped around a champagne bottle for the purpose of hiding the label, and that the quality of the champagne may be judged by the amount of noise the cork makes when it is popped.

7. The theory that because a married woman remains loyal to her husband she loves him.

8. The doctrine that a man's stability in the community and reliability in business may be measured by the number of children he has.

9. The feminine social theory that going to a fancy dress ball rigged up as a Peruvian street-sweeper makes a man feel vastly Parisian.

10. The doctrine that it is inconceivable that a man and woman entering a hotel without baggage after 10 p.m. may be married.

11. The theory that all country girls have clear, fresh, rosy complexions.

All these, as I recall it, were genuine collaborations. Nathan and I met one evening at our favorite *Biertisch* in Rogers' restaurant in Sixth Avenue, and concocted them together. But after that we usually did our contributions separately, and Nathan put them together. We were a little uneasy about Repetition Generale at the start, for there were some things in it that grossly violated the pruderies, and especially the patriotic pruderies, of the first post-Armistice year, but in a little while so many encouraging letters began to come in from readers, and the new department got so much notice in the newspapers that we were reassured. Many of my contributions during the remainder of 1919 went into *Prejudices: First Series*, which Knopf brought out in September.

Toward the end of 1918 Nathan had permitted some agent to sell him a banal serial called "Enchanters of Men," signed Thornton Hall and made up of steals from the French memoir literature. I did not like it, but we were very short of printable stuff at the time, so I waived my veto and let him buy it. It ran to twelve instalments, and was not finished until the November, 1919, issue. For the rest, we depended mainly, during the year, upon our tried and true stand-bys—Thyra Samter Winslow, Ben Hecht, L. M. Hussey, John McClure *et al*. Our novelettes, as usual, constituted our weakest feature: indeed, there was only one of any merit whatsoever, to wit, La Winslow's "A Cycle of Manhattan," printed in the March issue. Our one-act plays were also inferior, though there were two by George Sterling, two by Harlan Thompson and one each by F. Scott Fitzgerald and Leonora Speyer.

La Speyer, who was both a musician and a writer, had a German father (a Count von Stosch) and an American mother, and was born in Washington in 1872. In early youth she developed a talent for the violin, and was sent to Europe for training under the celebrated pedagogue, Leopold Auer. At eighteen she made her debut with the Boston Symphony Orchestra, and a successful career seemed to be ahead of her, but soon afterward she married and thereafter her fiddling was neglected. This first marriage soon blew up, and in 1902 she married Edgar Speyer, a member of the famous family of Jewish bankers, long denizened at Frankfort. Edgar was himself in charge of the London branch of the business, and for some years was conspicuous in English life, especially as a patron of music. He was knighted for these services, and Leonora became Lady Speyer. But when World War I began Edgar remained loyal to Germany, and so his knighthood was taken from him and he had to move to New York, where his brother James was in charge of the American house of Speyer.

I met Edgar through Frank Harris in 1916 or thereabout, and he soon afterward invited me to his house in Washington Square. There, of course, I met his wife and also her three daughters by her first marriage, then small girls. I never heard her play the violin, but more than once she and I did piano duets after dinner, with her husband as our whole audience. On the two grounds of our common love of music and our common disbelief in the English buncombe as to the origin and purposes of the war we got on very well, and frequently exchanged ideas.

Edgar was a small, swarthy fellow with coal-black hair and a bushy black moustache. Leonora, on the contrary, was blonde and tall—at least a head and a half taller than her husband. She was at that time beginning to try her wings as a writer, and she naturally showed me what she had done. It must have been toward the end of 1918 that I thus saw her one-act play, *Love Me, Love My Dog*. It seemed to me to be fit to print in the *Smart Set* and I took it to Nathan, who agreed. It was printed in the issue for January, 1919, and Nathan signed it *Lady* Speyer, though Edgar had already lost his knighthood. She followed it with a short story in the May issue, and another in the June issue, and after that she appeared in it a number of times as a poet. These later contributions, at Edgar's earnest request, were not signed *Lady* Speyer, but simply Leonora Speyer. She devoted more and more of her writing to verse, and in 1921, at my suggestion, Knopf brought out her first volume, *Canopic Jar*. I did not review it in the *Smart Set*, but five years later, when her second volume followed, I gave it a brief but friendly notice in the *American Mercury*.

This second volume, *Fiddler's Farewell* by title, made a considerable success, and was awarded the Pulitzer Prize as the best book of verse of the year. After this Leonora became a prominent figure in the poetical circles of New York, and was a leading spirit in the Poetry Society of America. Her wealth, of course, made her conspicuous, for most of her fellow poets were poor. Not a few of them, I suspect, got money from her. Without positively disliking her, I found her rather hard to take, so I saw nothing of her after her husband's death.

In January, 1930, on my return from the Naval Conference at London, I crossed the ocean with the two Speyers. We traveled in a German ship—I think it was the *Bremen*—and accompanying the Speyers was Leopold Auer. The old master—he was then eighty-five—had fallen upon difficult days, and I suspect that Edgar was financing him. Born in Hungary in 1845, he had spent nearly all his years in St. Petersburg, where he was an eminent figure in the musical life of the Czar's capital. The Tschaikowsky violin concerto was written for him and among his pupils were such famous virtuosi as Heifetz, Elman and Zimbalist. After World War I he was barred from Russia, and in 1918 he came to New York, seeking to begin a new life. He obtained some pupils, but advancing years diminished his earnings, and when I saw him in 1930 he was only a shadow of the Auer of *c.* 1910. But he was still full of plans, and one day he showed me some sheets of music MS. that he said were part of what was to be a revolutionary contribution to violin pedagogy. The usual texts, he explained, laid too much stress on mere technique, and thus neglected aesthetic values. The one he was doing would offer exercises that were not only instructive but also beautiful. What became of it I do not know.

Auer, the Speyers and I took our meals together on the ship. One day, inspired by the usual suggestion of the chief steward, I gave the others a gala dinner, with plenty of German wine to wash it down. Speyer enjoyed it so much that he announced that he would get revenge on me the next day with a *kosher* dinner, for he had found that there was a Jewish chef below decks. This *kosher* dinner turned out to be a gaudy affair indeed, with enough food on every plate to feed a squad of policemen. Old Auer was delighted with it, and so was I.

The next morning, as I was walking the deck with Speyer, he was approached by a deck steward who said that the *kosher* cook wanted to see him. Presently the cook himself appeared—a formidable figure in a white chef's cap, a long white apron, and a rabbinical beard. He announced forthwith that he had come to collect his tip. This brusque announcement irritated Speyer, and he proceeded to bargain. How much? The cook said $20. This large demand filled Speyer with indignation, and he declared that he would not pay a cent.

Rather than do so he would send a wireless to the head of the North-German Lloyd at Bremen, and meanwhile he demanded to see the chief steward and the captain. But the *kosher* cook stood his ground, and in the end Speyer forked up the $20. He referred to this episode every time I met him afterward, and declared that he had never in all his life been the victim of another such bold and unconscionable hold-up.

Beside La Speyer the *Smart Set*'s recruits in 1919 included Willa Sibert Cather and F. Scott Fitzgerald. I had been reviewing Cather's books favorably since the appearance of *Alexander's Bridge* in 1912. It was a palpable imitation of Edith Wharton, but it was a very good imitation; indeed, it seemed to me to be better than anything La Wharton herself had done save *Ethan Frome*. I gave a brief but equally friendly notice to *O Pioneers!* in October, 1913, and said of *The Song of the Lark*, in January, 1916: "I have read no late novel with a greater sense of intellectual stimulation." In 1918 came *My Ántonia*, which I reviewed at length in the issue for March, 1919, saying of the author: "There is no other American author of her sex, now on view, whose future promises so much."

I must have had some communication with her after my review of *The Song of the Lark*, for I find a letter from her, dated May 12, 1916, in which she discusses the suggestion (apparently made by me, though not in my review) that the heroine of the story was Lillian Nordica (1859–1914). I gather from this letter that she actually had Nordica in mind, but had been careful to conceal the fact as much as possible, for the singer's last husband, George Washington Young, was still alive, and he was known to be a bellicose and litigious fellow. Cather's associations, in those days as in her later years, were largely with musicians and music-lovers. She was one of the most assiduous concert-goers New York ever saw, and apparently had no social life save that connected with music.

Her publisher, in the 1912–1919 period, was the Houghton Mifflin Company of Boston, but she had been greatly taken by the sightly format of the books brought out by Knopf, and one day she walked into his office and proposed that he take over. This must have been in 1918. Unfortunately, it was difficult to get rid of her contract with Houghton, and the first of her books to appear with the Knopf imprint was *Youth and the Bright Medusa*, which came out in 1920 and was reviewed by me in the *Smart Set* for December of that year. I must have written to her in 1918, proposing that she do something for the magazine, for I find a letter from her, dated December 6, 1918, saying that she was projecting "several shorter things" and would let me see them when they were finished. On May 2, 1919, she sent in "Her Boss" and we printed it in the October issue. Dreiser and Lord Dunsany were also represented in that issue, but otherwise it was undistinguished. Some time a bit later she sent me another story, saying frankly that it had been declined by T. R. Smith, then managing editor of the *Century*, and offering it "at a bargain price— a hundred dollars."

I was always on friendly terms with Miss Cather, and had a high respect for her, but I saw her very seldom, and we exchanged only occasional letters. She lived in New York most of the time, but took long and frequent holidays, some of them abroad. There were periods of as much as a year when she seemed to be quite incapable of work; then she would fall to with energy, and stick to her desk with great diligence. But she was never what would be called a facile writer, and I heard from Knopf that she sometimes took as long as a week to perfect a few paragraphs. In the early days of their association he made some effort to increase her output, for her books were valuable properties and gave prestige to his list, but she refused to be hurried. Between *Youth and the Bright Medusa*, 1920, and *Sapphira and the Slave Girl*, 1940, the average spacing between them was two years—and the ten that she published included several short ones and a volume or two of short stories. She was inclined to be reticent and indeed almost secretive about both her work and herself, but in 1922, she tried rather artlessly to disarm my probably unfriendly view of her next novel, *One of Ours*, published by Knopf in 1922. She knew that I had a low and contemptuous opinion of the American part in World War I, and she suspected that I'd not care much for a soldier hero.

This interested me very much. I had, as I have indicated, a high opinion of La Cather's abilities, and I began to hope that she had done a war novel of a genuinely superior sort—something as honest and straightforward as John Dos Passos's *Three Soldiers*, but better organized and better written. What I found, alas, was a mixture of authentic Cather and the maudlin buncombe of the time—a story about a maladjusted young Nebraskan who found a solution for all his insoluble problems in a melodramatic death in battle. If the second half had been as good as the first it would have been work of the first quality—but the second half was dreadful stuff indeed. It was so bad, in fact, that it won for *One of Ours* the Pulitzer Prize of 1923.

I had no further communication from Miss Cather for more than a year. Toward the end of 1923, having learned from Knopf about our plans for the *American Mercury*, she wrote to me from Aix-les-Bains saying that she was "greatly excited" and promised to write something for it. But Knopf told me at once that she was offended because she had not been consulted about it in its first stages, nor asked to take a hand in its editing, and I never pressed her to make good on her promise. She did not, in fact, make good on it. So far as I can recall she never sent me anything for the magazine save a clipping in French from a Paris newspaper, with a suggestion that I reprint it. Inasmuch as I was trying to confine the magazine to the American scene I paid no attention to this suggestion. During the years following I saw her only occasionally, always at parties given by Knopf. I was never in her house, and she was never in mine.

I MET Francis Scott Key Fitzgerald in June or thereabout, 1919, and his first contribution to the *Smart Set*, a short story called "Babes in the Wood," was printed in the issue for September of that year, to be followed in November with a one-act play, *The Debutante*. It is my recollection that I first saw him in George Nathan's apartment in the Royalton, and that George had picked him up somewhere or other a little while before. He was then a slim, blond young fellow, tall and straight in build and so handsome that he might even have been called beautiful. There was something milky about his complexion and cerulean in his blue eyes, and he looked much more the boy than the man. He was, in fact, less than twenty-three years old.

A native of St. Paul, Minnesota, he was related to the Key family of Maryland and hence had in him the blood of the author of "The Star-Spangled Banner." He was a student at Princeton when the United States entered World War I, and he left college to join the Army. He got a commission as a lieutenant of infantry in November, 1917, and by the time he returned to civilian life in February, 1919, he had become an aide-de-camp to Brigadier General James Augustine Ryan, commander of the First Cavalry Brigade, Fifteenth Cavalry Division. I well recall that he was still so full of Army ways when we first met, and so shy a young fellow by nature, that he not only mistered Nathan and me, but also sirred us.

Fitz had begun to write as a schoolboy in St. Paul, where he was born on September 24, 1896, and his first efforts seem to have been directed toward musical comedy libretti. When he got to Princeton in 1913, he offered himself as librettist for the annual Triangle Club piece, and was accepted. He worked so hard at this job that he failed in most of his examinations, and suffered a breakdown in health, but after a couple of months out for recuperation at home he was back in college, and again writing furiously—this time, poetry. His first attempts at prose were made while he was in training at Fort Leavenworth, Kansas, in 1917. The result, after much struggle, was an autobiographical novel called *The Romantic Egotist*, which was promptly rejected by the first publisher to whom it was sent, and went on the shelf.

There was no more writing after that until his return from the war early in 1919. He then tried to get a job on a New York newspaper, but had to be content with one in an advertising agency, at $90 a month. Between March and June, 1919, he wrote nineteen short stories, and they were sent the round of the magazines. The only one of them to be accepted was "Babes in the Wood," for which Nathan, who was in charge of our money-box, paid Fitz $30. The failure of the others discouraged him so much that he returned to St. Paul, and there applied himself to a second novel. It was *This Side of Paradise*. He also wrote more short stories, and in November one of them was taken by the *Saturday Evening Post*. After that the *Post* took many others, and by the time *This Side of Paradise* was published by Scribner, early in 1920, Fitz was in easy waters.

Nathan and I, in those first days of our acquaintance with him, heard a great deal about *This Side of Paradise* and his plans for other stories. This was the first year of the attempt to enforce Prohibition, and we gave frequent late-afternoon parties in Nathan's apartment: he would provide the cocktails one day, and I would bring a bottle of them, mixed in Baltimore, the next. We had both laid in heavy stocks against the Eighteenth Amendment, and had, in particular, a great deal of gin and a great deal of Italian vermouth, so it was easy for us to be hospitable. Some time before the Thirteen Awful Years began, we had acquired in Del Pezzo's restaurant, then in 33rd Street opposite the Pennsylvania Station, the formula of a cocktail that we called the Coffin Varnish—one-third vermouth, two-thirds gin, and a dash of the Italian bitters, Fernet Branca—and this we served to our guests, who were mainly literati, with an occasional sprinkling of Nathan's female friends of the stage.

Fitzgerald was a steady customer, and made heavy practice with the drinks. He was already, in fact, a considerable boozer, and during the twenty-two years that he was destined to live he drank more and more. He was, at this time, still a bachelor, but on April 3, 1920 he married Zelda Sayre, of Montgomery, Alabama, herself a bold patron of the jugs. I recall an evening soon after their marriage when they were guests of Nathan and me at dinner at the Plaza Hotel. They were then living somewhere on Long Island, and had come in in a roadster that they had lately bought. By the end of the evening both were far too drunk to drive a car, and Nathan and I tried to induce them to go to bed in the hotel. But Scott insisted on setting forth, and when we saw him start from the hotel and dash across Fifth Avenue we concluded sadly that he and his bride would never reach home alive. It was, in fact, a genuine surprise when he called up the *Smart Set* office the next day, and reported both of them recovered and whole.

This Side of Paradise, which came out just before his marriage to Zelda, was an immediate and resounding success, and Scott was soon in great demand among the magazines, and also beginning to taste the profits of movie rights. As money started to roll in he decided to take his bride to Europe to see the sights, and on their departure he confided to Nathan and me that there was another motive: Zelda was pregnant, and they had decided that the coming child deserved to be born in some historic and romantic place. Paris seemed a likely choice, but when they got there they found it dull and shabby, so they bought tickets for a Cook's tour of Northern Africa. But Algiers and Tunis turned out to be even worse than Paris, and they moved into Spain and Italy. Finding Spain and Italy also disappointing, they began a frantic chase over Europe, looking for an ideal place for the nativity. In the end Zelda approached her time without any such ideal place being found, and in a sudden panic they sailed for home. The poor baby was actually born (1922) in St. Paul, Minnesota!

I reviewed *This Side of Paradise* in the *Smart Set* for August, 1920, and treated it very politely indeed. It was, I said, "the best American novel that I have seen of late, . . . original in structure, extremely sophisticated in manner, and adorned with a brilliancy that is as rare in American writing as honesty is in American statecraft." I later revised this estimate somewhat, but I am still of the opinion that *This Side of Paradise* was one of the best first novels ever done by an American. *Flappers and Philosophers*, the collection of short stories which followed before the end of 1920, seemed to me to be a great deal less promising. It included at least one good story, "Benediction," first published in the *Smart Set* for February, 1920, but also included a lot of trade-goods done for the *Saturday Evening Post*.

Fitzgerald's next book, *The Beautiful and Damned*, was under way before the end of 1920. He was seldom in New York at this period, but I remained in friendly contact with him, and he told me of his projects. They included not only plans for his own work, but also plans to promote the work of others. In September, 1920, for example, he was writing to me about a scheme for a collected edition of the novels of Frank Norris, with prefaces by Dreiser, Hergesheimer, Tarkington, Francis Hackett, myself and others. "Do you think," he asked, "it would be worth while? If you do I'll write Charles Norris for data and commence planning it." I must have given him encouragement and he must have written to Charles, but nothing came of the scheme at the moment, though Charles was to execute it himself, some years later. In February, 1921, he wrote to me announcing the discovery of an "exceptional but unfortunate novel MS. . . . by a man of my own age who is at present studying law at Cambridge." I asked him to send it to me and after I had read it forwarded it to Knopf, who declined it. Fitz tackled him in person in its behalf, but in vain. The name of the author was apparently Biggs. What became of his novel and of him I do not know.

Fitz also devoted himself in those days to promoting the interests of Edmund Wilson, who had been a fellow student at Princeton. It was, I think, at his suggestion that Nathan and I accepted for the *Smart Set* parts of *The Undertaker's Garland*, by Wilson and John Peale Bishop. It came out as a book in 1922 and I reviewed it favorably in the *Smart Set* for March, 1923. Fitz was himself no mean critic, and he saw clearly the hollowness of such notables of the time as Floyd Dell and Ernest Poole. Now and then he wrote book reviews, and when my *Prejudices: Second Series* appeared at the end of 1920 he reviewed it for the *Bookman*.

When *Tales of the Jazz Age*, a second collection of short stories, was published in 1922, I gave it only a brief notice in the *Smart Set* (July, 1923), and that brief notice was not very favorable. Fitz was being considerably injured, it seemed to me, by his great popular success, and the influence of the *Saturday Evening Post* was beginning to leave unpleasant marks upon him. "The spread between his best work and his worst," I wrote in my review, "is extraordinarily wide. Even within the bounds of a single volume, say, *This Side of Paradise*, he manages to range from satirical writing of the first order to the cheapest sort of Robert W. Chambersism. That dangerous versatility lies over *Tales of the Jazz Age*. It is a book that would have been far better if it had been more rigorously edited."

Fitz took such caveats and remonstrances in good part, and in fact accepted them as sound. Before the end of 1922 he began to make plans to go abroad with Zelda and the baby, and settle down for a hard tussle with a novel that should be better than anything he had previously published. He was deadly in earnest, and determined to shake off the *Saturday Evening Post* influence. The result was *The Great Gatsby*, a book full of faults, but still enormously better than anything he had done before. When it reached me I saw that it showed a really serious purpose, and I said so in the *American Mercury* for July, 1925. Thus:

> Most of the novelists who are obviously on solid ground today had heavy struggles at the start: Dreiser, Cabell, Hergesheimer, Miss Cather. Fitzgerald, though he had no such struggle, now tries to make it for himself. *The Great Gatsby* is full of evidences of hard sober toil. All the author's old slipshod facility is gone; he has set himself rigorously to the job of learning how to write. And he shows quick and excellent progress. *The Great Gatsby* is not merely better written than *This Side of Paradise;* it is written in a new way. Fitzgerald has learned economy of words and devices; he has begun to give thought to structure; his whole attitude has changed from that of a brilliant improvisateur to that of a painstaking and conscientious artist. I certainly don't think much of *The Great Gatsby* as a story. It is in part too well-made and in part incredible. But as a piece of writing it is sound and laudable work.

Fitz and Zelda remained in Paris, save for a brief trip to Brussels and a stay at Juan-les-Pins, through 1925 and most of 1926. I heard from him occasionally, but not often. Paris was then swarming with American émigrés, and Ezra Pound and Gertrude Stein were their chief mentors. Not one of these followers wrote anything worth reading, not even Fitz himself. "I have met most of the American literary world here (the crowd that centers about Pound)," he wrote to me in the autumn of 1925, "and find them mostly junk-dealers." But he seems to have been much impressed by Ernest Hemingway, whose first long story, "In Our Time," had come out in 1924, and who was to follow it with a resounding popular success, *A Farewell to Arms*, in 1929.

I never met Hemingway, and my view of his work was never exalted. He had a great hand for dialogue, and knew how to shock the women's clubs with dirty words, but his longer stories always struck me as melodramatic and obvious. He was at his best in the short story. Some of his most effective tricks, though his admirers never noted it, were borrowed from the dialogue of the drinkers in Rabelais. He was an excessively vain fellow—challenging, bellicose and not infrequently absurd. Anyone who refused to hail him as a towering genius was an evil doer, and probably in receipt of foreign money.

When Fitz got back to the United States in 1927 he spent some time traveling about the country and then settled down at Edgemoor, Delaware, a few miles from Wilmington, on the Delaware river. How this town came to be chosen I do not know: probably he and Zelda happened upon it on their rovings. I never visited them there, for soon after they went into residence I began to hear that both were drinking excessively, and that the place was a madhouse. Even Ernest Boyd, himself one of the heaviest drinkers of modern times, came back from a visit with the report that the pace was too hot for him. Zelda was the worst housekeeper ever heard of, and as a result all the household arrangements were in chaos. To summon the maid at meals she affixed an old Ford horn to the edge of the dinner-table, and frequently gave it a squeeze. Once Joseph Hergesheimer, who lived at West Chester, Pennsylvania, not far away, invited the two to spend a weekend there. What happened at the party he never told me precisely, but I gathered from him that Fitz got violently drunk, made a great deal of uproar, and went about the house naked, or nearly so. The Fitzgeralds were never asked to West Chester again.

Fitz published no book after 1926 until 1934, a period of eight years. It was a time of steady deterioration for him, and he never recovered from it. He was drunk four-fifths of the time, and Zelda was but little more sober. By 1930 it began to be apparent that her mind was affected. There was a good deal of insanity in her family, the Sayres of Montgomery, Alabama, and she showed increasing symptoms of having inherited it. On February 15, 1931, when she and he were visiting in Montgomery, I received the following telegram from him:

> Will you kindly wire me the name of the biggest psychiatrist at Johns Hopkins for non-organic nervous troubles? Address 2400 16th Street, Washington, D.C.

I assumed at once that Zelda was the patient, and recommended Dr. Esther Richards, of the staff of the Phipps Clinic, the psychiatrical pavilion at the Johns Hopkins Hospital. Fitz came to see Dr. Richards in Baltimore, and she recommended that Zelda be kept in Montgomery. But soon afterward she had to be confined, and thereafter, for a dozen years, she was in and out of lunatic asylums. In 1932 she moved from the Phipps Clinic to the Sheppard-Pratt Hospital near Towson, Maryland, and Fitz took a house at nearby Rodgers Forge.

Their house was a ramshackle old barn in a deep woods, and the whole place had a spookish air. One evening during the spring of 1934 Sara and I went there for dinner. (Sara, who was a little older than Zelda, had known her in Montgomery in childhood, and also knew her family.) Zelda took the hostess's place at table, but it was plain at once that she was not herself. Whatever superintendence the dinner got came from Scotty, then a child of twelve or so, and it was not much. The courses came on in the wrong order, with the soup last, and the only servant visible was a decrepit old colored woman who now and then appeared from the kitchen. Fitz was too drunk to notice, but to Sara and me the meal was painful indeed, for Zelda did all the talking, and what she had to say was only half rational. As soon as dinner was over we prepared to go home, but Zelda insisted that we stay to see her drawings. She had, a few years back, set up shop as a writer, and had actually found a publisher (no doubt through Fitz's influence) for a weird novel called *Save Me the Waltz*, and at another time she had undertaken the Russian ballet, but now she had turned to drawing and painting.

She ran upstairs for the drawings and came down with a large armful. Laying them on the floor of the living-room she sprawled on her belly to show them to us, and we had to sprawl too. They were mainly in color, and most of them were only too painfully psycho-pathic. But we had to linger over them for an hour or two, and when we escaped at last we were shivering. Fitz, meanwhile, had kept on drinking, and was by now so drunk that he could hardly stand up. A little while after this we had to invite them to a return dinner in Cathedral Street, and it was almost as bad. Zelda had little to say, but every few minutes she would drop her knife and fork and grab and squeeze the arms of her chair. Obviously, she was trying desper-ately to hold herself together, and equally obviously she was finding it difficult.

On June 16, 1933, the house at Rodgers Forge had a fire, and by the time the Towson firemen put it out the whole top floor was wrecked. The Baltimore *Evening Sun* reported that "apparently the blaze was caused by a short-circuit in the wiring in the attic," but about this I had some doubt. In a little while Zelda was back at the Sheppard-Pratt Hospital, and Fitz was carrying on at Rodgers Forge with Scotty. During the autumn of 1933 Zelda was sent to an asylum at Asheville, North Carolina, and Fitz and Scotty moved to 1307 Park Avenue, Baltimore.

I never saw him there, for I heard at once that he was drinking on a grand scale, and that the house was an almost incredible mess. Most of my news of him came from the young Johns Hopkins doctors who attended him in succession. They took him in relays simply because he was a very vexatious patient. He was constantly on the verge of delirium tremens, and would often call up his current doctor in the middle of the night, demanding immediate help. Before the repeal of the Eighteenth Amendment went into effect he always accompanied these demands with suggestions—added as apparent afterthoughts—that the doctor bring him a bottle of gin. The poor medicos quickly got tired of these disturbances to their sleep, and so refused, one by one, to answer his calls.

Finally, he fell into the hands of my own physician, Dr. Benjamin M. Baker, a kindly fellow and a very competent practitioner. Baker refused flatly to answer night calls, but decided instead to send him to the Johns Hopkins for a thorough investigation. This revealed that he was suffering from cirrhosis of the liver, and that the disease was greatly exacerbated by his heavy drinking. Baker kept him in hospital, without alcohol, for three weeks, and then turned him out much improved. But in a little while he was back at the jugs, and not long afterward he was back in hospital. This alternation kept on into 1936. He always promised faithfully to remain on the water-wagon, but he never did so.

During one of his sober intervals Sara invited him to Cathedral Street to lunch, and the party passed off very well. When it was over he said that his car was parked in front of the house, and asked Sara to join him in a little automobile ride. When she got back she reported that he had managed his car very well. A few weeks later she invited him to lunch again, and again he took her for a ride afterward. But this time he was beginning the process of leaving the wagon, and on her return she had a disquieting tale to tell. His driving had been very eccentric, and in getting around the Washington Monument he had mounted the curbing. She had been alarmed and urged him to bring her home at once, but he had insisted on a longish tour of the suburbs. I advised her to go with him no more, and the next time he appeared she made an excuse. The fourth time he was plainly drunk, and I decided that he had better be barred from the house thereafter.

Sara was fond of him and so was I, but we simply could not endure him. He called up half a dozen times afterward, fishing for more invitations to lunch, but Sara managed to get rid of him. After her death in May, 1935, I saw little of him, but I encountered him at the Johns Hopkins at Christmas, 1936, when I was myself a patient there. He was then undergoing one of his regular cures under the care of Baker. He was in a very dilapidated state, and looked wretched indeed. This time he seems to have become alarmed, for when he was patched up he promised Baker to go on the water-wagon for good. Soon afterward he moved to Asheville, to be near Zelda. On July 1, 1937, Baker told me that he was still on the water-wagon, but I doubted it. What had become of poor Scotty I do not know: apparently she had been sent to a boarding-school. Her life with her father in Park Avenue must have been a dreadful experience for a child of her years. I heard from his doctors and his occasional visitors that he spent weeks on end in a dirty dressing-gown, seldom getting out of bed. He reached for the bottle when he awoke in the morning and it was by his side until he fell asleep again. The whole house was filthy.

How he made a living in those days I do not know. His market was still good, but he was seldom in a condition to serve it. He had some revenue, to be sure, from the books of his earlier years, and he occasionally sold a short story to one of the popular magazines, or maybe movie-rights in Hollywood, but, with Zelda needing constant and costly care, his expenses must have been heavy. Now and then he sent me a short story for the *American Mercury*, but I never took any of them, and his only appearance in the magazine, in fact, was with a story called "Absolution," in June, 1924. He put in the better part of the eight years from 1926 to 1934 playing with *Tender Is the Night*, but when it was finished at last it turned out to be poor stuff indeed. I was done with book reviewing by that time, and did not even read it.

I did not hear from him again until June, 1936, when I received a postcard from Washington, saying that he was reading the fourth edition of *The American Language* and "appreciating it more than ever." When he went to Hollywood I do not know, but it must have been in 1937. His first job there was to make a movie of Erich Maria Remarque's *Three Comrades*, and he apparently did well with it. But it had no successor, and according to Frank Scully, a Hollywood historian, he was presently "assigned to doctoring scripts on what turned out to be a life sentence." Scully added that he had "got over wanting to drink himself to death before life could begin at forty," but this may have been only a polite gesture to *de mortuis nil nisi bonum*, for in another place in the same article he said that "F. *Scotch* Fitzgerald was one of the names he was known by."

His physical deterioration had gone so far by the time he got to Hollywood that there was no hope of amelioration, even by the most rigorous abstention. The liver disease that beset him was completely incurable, and his heavy drinking for so many years hurried it on. He had brought out a book called *Taps at Reveille* in 1935, but after the movies had swallowed him he did no serious work save a few licks at a story that was to have been called *The Last Tycoon*. He died on December 21, 1940, leaving it unfinished. His body was brought to Washington, and after services in a funeral parlor there, conducted by the Rev. Raymond P. Black, of Christ Episcopal Church, it was buried at Rockville, Maryland, beside the graves of some of his Key relatives. This was on December 27.

Whether or not Zelda was present at the funeral I do not know.

The newspapers reported that, at the time of his death, she was "visiting her family in Montgomery, Alabama." Little Scotty, now nineteen, came down from Poughkeepsie, where she was a student at Vassar College. I often think of this poor girl's unhappy youth with an insane mother and a dipsomanic father, and of her baleful heritage. I don't recall seeing her since she was in her early teens, nor have I ever heard from her.

CHAPTER XVII

I T MUST HAVE BEEN in 1917 or 1918 that Zoë Akins moved to New York from St. Louis: I am uncertain because there is a gap in my file of letters from her, stretching from 1917 to 1921. That gap, perhaps, is to be explained on the ground that I saw her often during most of the period, and there was no need for correspondence. Nathan and I had both been greatly impressed by her fantastic play, *Papa*, published by Mitchell Kennerley in 1914, but not put upon the stage until 1919. When she marched on the great theatrical center she had a couple of other plays in her knapsack, but it was a year or more before she could induce any manager to look at them. How she got her hearing at last I don't know, but in all probability Nathan had something to do with it. She was then still somewhat arty, and I well recall that the first time he and I waited on her at her small apartment she entertained the company by reading a couple of her poems. They were anything but bad, but we had only small taste for such divertissements at 9:30 p.m.

Zoë was then slim and graceful, and dressed predominantly in dark clothes. She seemed to be in sufficient funds to keep her going, but it was plain that she had no surplus. Then one morning in 1919, New York heard of the great success of her *Déclassée* the evening before. It was, in fact, something of a sensation, and her days of waiting were over. A few nights later Nathan and I, returning from our evening revels at 1 a.m. or thereabout, encountered her and her friend Jobyna Howland in the lobby of the Algonquin Hotel. Zoë was dressed up in a manner downright overwhelming. She had on an expensive-looking evening gown showing half a dozen colors and an even more expensive opera cape, and hanging from her, like balls from a Christmas tree, were at least a dozen pendants of one sort or another, all of them glittering. It appeared at a glance that both she and Jobyna were a bit in their cups. When we exclaimed at her magnificence Zoë drew herself up in the best manner of a stock company leading-woman, and demanded: "Why shouldn't one wear beautiful clothes when one is affluent?" We could think of no reason against it.

Soon after this she abandoned her small apartment, took one that was much larger, and proceeded to give a series of lavish parties. The decorations of the new place were in the most advanced style of 1919. I recall especially a greenish valance strung along the walls just under the ceiling: it was always fetching loose from its moorings and hanging in loops. The dining-room was pitch dark save for a couple of altar candles three or four feet high, and the couch in front of the fireplace in the sitting-room was eight feet long, with stuffing more than a foot thick. One night Nathan and I were summoned there to dinner, and found that the other guests were Jobyna Howland and Ethel Barrymore. Jobyna and Ethel, in those days, were the champion lady boozers of Broadway, and Zoë herself was no dilettante at the bottle, though her main delight was eating. The dinner was long and elegant, and there was a large flow of wines and liquors. By the time we got to the dessert all hands were somewhat over-surfeited, and Nathan and I retired to the couch in the living-room to smoke and recuperate. There we presently fell asleep, and when we awoke it was 3 a.m. But Zoë, Jobyna and Ethel were still at table in the dining-room, and still patronizing the refreshments. Their talk was so loud that we couldn't help hearing it. It consisted mainly of an exchange of objurgations—amiable enough, but all the epithets they were hurling at each other were anatomically unsuited for use against females. Fearing that if they recalled us they might open on us with billingsgate in compensatory contempt of our maleness we made a quiet sneak.

Jobyna came originally, I think, from Denver, and was the first model for Charles Dana Gibson's famous Gibson Girl. She was extraordinarily tall and in her day had been considered a great beauty, but by 1919 she was showing signs of oxidation, and in the theatre she commonly played middle-aged parts—retired opera singers and the like. Some of these parts were in plays written for her by Zoë. She had been married, back in 1900, to Arthur Stringer, the Canadian poet and novelist, but they had separated in 1914 or thereabout.

Years later she came to Baltimore as the star of a play, and I dropped into her dressing-room one evening to greet her. This was in Prohibition days, and she had a large supply of drinkables in a special trunk, including some excellent ale, of which she insisted on giving me several bottles. In the course of our talk I said, jestingly, that I marvelled that so handsome a young girl should remain unmarried. Instead of giggling Jobyna burst into tears. It was simply impossible, she sobbed, for her to forget Stringer. She still loved him as she had always loved him, and she would never love another. The quarrel that caused their divorce was a trivial one, and should have been patched up. Unhappily, Stringer married another woman immediately after the decree was issued, leaving poor Jobyna in desolation. The common report in New York was that she had had a long affair with Andrew Freedman, the baseball magnate, but she seemed so earnest that I believed her story, and was touched by it. The love agonies of a woman six feet in height are always extra poignant.

After a year or two in her heavily decorated apartment, which, as I recall it, was somewhere in the East Forties, Zoë moved to 20 Fifth Avenue, then a favorite neighborhood among the more opulent literati. She took most of her decorations with her, and the new apartment was almost as oppressive as the old. She was, in those days, a big success in the theatre, and her income must have been large. She spent it liberally, but still managed to accumulate a surplus, and this was invested for her by Otto H. Kahn, who loved literary society and was financial adviser to a long string of authors, including Mike Gold. Unhappily, his advice was anything but sound, and when the Depression came on with the 30's Zoë suffered a substantial loss. Simultaneously she had several successive failures in the theatre, and presently she was hard up.

Nathan always ascribed these failures to her great fancy for fashionable life, which was unaccompanied by any acquaintance with it. Her swells, in consequence, talked and acted in a way that was often far more ridiculous than impressive. When she went to Hollywood I do not recall, but it must have been in 1930 or 1931. On March 12, 1932, she astonished her New York friends by announcing her marriage to Captain Hugo Cecil Levinge Rumbold, an elderly Englishman. Who he was no one seemed to know, but soon New York was full of fantastic rumors about him, including one to the effect that he was a homosexual.

I heard from her only occasionally during those years. Her husband died some time before 1940, but she went on living in a large house that they had taken in Pasadena. Once, when she was on a visit to New York, she showed me some photographs of it. It was a really palatial place, and it was surrounded by wide grounds. On these grounds she grew supplies for her table, which was always well served. One of its prize exhibits was a lime tree that furnished her with limes for drinks all the year round. Once she sent me a large box of its fruit, and it turned out to be superb. She was very fond of turkey, and told me on one of her visits to New York that she raised fifty-two turkeys a year for her own table—one a week. In May, 1943, she sent me her favorite recipe for preparing it—a formidable formula indeed.

On her trips eastward she usually stayed at the Algonquin, which was my own hotel in New York. One morning, as I left it to go to the *American Mercury* office at 730 Fifth Avenue, I encountered her on the sidewalk, about to climb into a car with Jobyna Howland. I asked them where they were going, and Zoë replied that they were off for a week-end at a place Jobyna owned somewhere in Connecticut. Jobyna invited me hospitably to join them, and when I replied that I had to get back to Baltimore that afternoon, she insisted that I let her haul me as far as the *American Mercury* office. She and Zoë took the front seat, and I was waved to the back of the car. When I opened the door I found that it was packed to the ceiling with cases of liquor. "What are you up to?" I asked. "Are you opening a roadhouse?" "We are not," replied Zoë primly. "We expect a few guests for the weekend." It seemed impossible for me to squeeze in but I finally managed to do so, and in a minute I was being whirled up Fifth Avenue, trembling lest that monument of gins and whiskeys fall over and crush me.

Zoë's main business in Hollywood was naturally with the movies, and she had an apparently lucrative job with the Metro-Goldwyn-Mayer company, but she also wrote a few plays, and in 1940 she did a novel. This novel, *Forever Young*, was published by Scribner early in 1941. I read it at her request, but did not like it: by that time, in truth, it was hard for me to read a new novel, for I had got a massive overdose of them during my twenty-five years as a book reviewer. She also did an occasional poem, and in 1943, when Mme. Chiang Kai-shek was on a tour of the United States, and was feted in Hollywood, Zoë wrote three sonnets in honor of the visitor, and sent me copies of them.

Soon after this she was in New York with a new play—a satirical piece with Calvin Coolidge (retired from the White House) as its hero (so to speak) and a much-married woman, with children by three husbands, as its heroine. I read it at her request, and found the idea amusing and some of the writing excellent, but there was a letting down toward the close. When I saw her she told me that she was undecided whether to let Coolidge (depicted as a widower) marry the woman, or have him recover his senses and kick her out. I voted for kicking her out, but the Jews who put on the play demanded wedding bells, and as a result the play became incredible and was a failure.

At the time of this visit to New York Anita Loos was also there, and one night in October, 1943, Nathan and I took the two to dinner at Lüchow's. Zoë had grown noticeably bulky, and looked her years, which were then fifty-seven. But her old Missouri appetite was unabated, and she got down a really appalling meal, with a bottle of Rhine wine to ease its way. During the summer of 1945 Anita wrote to me from Hollywood that Zoë had sold her place in Pasadena.

Nathan and I saw La Loos and her husband, John Emerson, very often in the 1919–1925 period. She and John, at that time, had been but lately married, and spent most of their time in New York. Anita was a very small and slight woman, with coal-black eyes and black hair cut in a boyish bob. She was the daughter of show people, and had got into the movies, as a writer of scenarios, in her early youth. She worked for D. W. Griffith for five years, and afterward for Douglas Fairbanks, Constance Talmadge and other stars. First and last, she probably wrote more movie scripts than any other writer in Hollywood history. What was in those scripts I do not know, for I never saw any of the ensuing pictures, but I have no doubt that they were mainly bilge.

But Anita herself was by no means a female Robert W. Chambers. On the contrary, she was an extremely intelligent woman, and full of a kind of wit that was often malicious, and indeed downright cruel. I well recall her bitter characterizations of some of the Hollywood eminentissimos of the time. She and John would often sit of an evening with Nathan and me, sometimes with John D. Williams joining us, and Nathan and I were always delighted, if sometimes misled, by her acidulous chatter. One of the misleadings had to do with Lillian Gish. As depicted by Anita, Lillian was next door to an idiot: indeed, Anita declared that she was the original asker of the famous question, "What was the name of the Unknown Soldier?" Neither Nathan nor I had yet met her at that time, so we swallowed these libels innocently. It was 1924 before we discovered that she was really a shrewd, well-informed and amusing woman. Nathan then crowned and glorified our new respect for her by falling in love with her.

One of Anita's favorite butts was Margaret (Peg) Talmadge, the mother of the three Talmadge sisters, Constance, Norma and Natalie. My first introduction to this interesting family group had not come through her, but through Zoë Akins. One evening Zoë told me that she was in treaty to do a movie for three Brooklyn girls who hoped to make careers in Hollywood, and invited me to join her on a visit to them. This must have been in 1915 or thereabout. The trio and their mother were then living in a small ground-floor flat in a converted brownstone house somewhere on the mid-town East Side. They had emerged from the wilds of Brooklyn only a few years before, and were still almost unknown to Broadway. What their actual names were I do not know, but it was plain at a glance that their mother was Jewish. She did all of the talking, and it was aplenty. When we left I suggested to Zoë that her manner and vocabulary strongly suggested those of an up-and-coming whore madam on a busy Saturday night, with a gang of Elks in the parlor, and Zoë replied that there were reports that this had been her actual former profession in Brooklyn. She was short and squat, had a raucous voice, and wore a florid, sloppy dress on the order of a Mother Hubbard. The three girls, who were all still young, had next to nothing to say.

The next time I saw them was in 1921, after they had made great successes in the movies. This time I was taken by Anita and John. By now the converted flat on the edge of the slums had been forsaken, and they were living at the Ambassador Hotel in Park Avenue, opened on April 26. Anita warned me in advance that their apartment was a masterpiece of hotel decoration at its worst, but I was hardly prepared for the gaudiness I encountered. When Peg opened the door for us I was almost blinded by a blaze of pink—pink carpet, pink hangings, pink upholstery, and a pink Mother Hubbard on Peg herself. "What does it remind you of?" asked John. I replied discreetly, but Peg laughed understandingly and loud.

It appeared that the second daughter, Constance, was ill, and we were presently ushered into her bedroom, where she languished in a pink dressing-gown under a pink coverlet. She was already married by this time to a mysterious Greek named John Pialogiou, but her marriage had gone to pot and she was attended in her illness by a new beau, one Willie Rhinelander, a fashionable nonentity of the time. He sat by her bedside radiating sympathy, and we lingered with her for only a few minutes. Soon afterward he was given his congé and she married Allaster McIntosh: in 1929 she followed him with a third husband, Townsend Netcher.

The rest of our visit was spent listening to Peg, who talked out of the corner of her mouth and gave many other indications that the rumors about her former vocation were far from incredible, if not exactly proved. The Talmadge girls, at least in those days, were slight and sightly youngsters, and showed only the faintest traces of Jewishness. It was hard to believe that such loveliness had issued from so gross a mother. In truth, there were plenty of Broadway wiseacres who openly doubted it. To these cynics it seemed far more likely that Peg was the padrone of the establishment, not the mamma.

I did not see any of the Talmadges again until 1926, when I was in Hollywood with Joseph Hergesheimer. One day Anita Loos asked me to go with her and John to an afternoon party at the home of Norma, who had been married to Joseph M. Schenck, the movie magnate, in 1917, but was now separated from him. Her house, unlike most of the establishments of movie stars, was not a Byzantine villa set in a baronial park, but an old-fashioned frame building in one of the nearer suburbs of Los Angeles, with a wide porch. The hostess, of course, did not recall me, and I passed as a newspaper friend of John and Anita. At least forty other guests were already on hand when we arrived, and Constance Talmadge was behind a bar, mixing drinks. I was presented to a number of the Hollywood notables of the time, including Jack Dempsey and Mrs. Leslie Carter, but none of them had ever heard of me.

After a while Anita went into a huddle with Norma, and returned with the news that a dinner party was to follow, but that Norma wanted to first get rid of most of her visitors. When this was accomplished we sat down to a long and lavish but badly cooked meal of the sort that movie stars then always served, and the drinks kept passing round and round. I had La Carter to one side of me, and Mabel Normand, a favorite star of the day, to the other. La Normand was already half seas over.

At 9 p.m. I had to leave to keep an appointment downtown, but

John and Anita remained. The next day Anita told me that I had missed the show of the evening. Along toward midnight La Normand, by this time dead drunk, staggered out to the porch, and there squatted down and let go her bladder. Norma, who pretended to elegance, as elegance was then understood in Hollywood, denounced this as a vile and anti-social act, and there was a considerable uproar, with La Normand defending her right to void wherever she pleased. Anita and John greatly enjoyed the performance, and spread the news of it all over the movie Jerusalem. Not long afterward La Normand succeeded in drinking herself to death. Her funeral was a festive event in Hollywood history.

John was nineteen years older than Anita, who was born in 1893, but they seemed, in those days, to get on very well. He was almost as adept a wit as she was, and sitting with them at the *Biertisch* of an evening was always a pleasant event of my visits to New York. John had started out as an actor, and remained one officially: from 1920 to 1928 he was president of the Actors' Equity Association, the trade union of the profession. But he had moved on to management, and at one time he had been general stage director for Charles Frohman. Before his marriage to Anita he had had a hand in many of her movie scripts, and afterward the two worked together. In 1932 they had themselves incorporated as the Emerson-Loos Company, "writers and producers of motion pictures." John was eager for money, and squeezed a great deal of it out of the Jews, so that he and Anita eventually became very rich.

One day in New York, as Anita was walking down Fifth Avenue, a board fetched loose from a building under erection and struck her, inflicting a slight bruise. John had a lawyer after the builders the next morning, and made them pay $500 damages. This led John D. Williams to spread the story that John set Anita to perambulating the streets every morning before all the new buildings under way, hoping for a better haul next time.

In 1937 poor John lost his mind. He recovered in 1938, but in 1940 broke down again and had to be put away. His chief hallucination was to the effect that he was charged by God to dissuade Anita from sin by killing her. This made life somewhat uncomfortable for her, for she feared that he might escape from the asylum and undertake to carry out his mission. But he never did so, and on April 17, 1945, she wrote to me that he had recovered again and was once more at large. But I doubt that they resumed living together, for about this time news spread in New York that Anita was about to divorce him and marry one of the higher functionaries of the Associated Press, whose name I forget. The announcement greatly upset the bridegroom-elect's colleagues of the A.P. staff, for he already had a wife and three children, and there was no apparent reason why he should abandon them. In the end he lost his position, and simultaneously the projected marriage blew up.

Anita made a great success in 1925 with a little book called *Gentlemen Prefer Blondes*, a masterpiece of malicious humor. It was, indeed, one of the most diverting pieces of humor of its era, and it well deserved its huge sales. Three years later Anita followed it with a sequel called *But Gentlemen Marry Brunettes* that was quite as good, though it did not sell quite so well. John helped Anita to make a stage version of *Gentlemen Prefer Blondes* and it had some success, but it was not the resounding hit that the book had been. I myself gave her a few odds and ends of material, for example, the idea of the Jew who changed his name from Ginsberg to Mount Gins. This, of course, was suggested by the Battenbergs, the poor relations of the British royal family who had changed their German name, during World War I, to Mountbatten. In 1943, when I was beginning work on the two supplements to *The American Language*, Anita repaid me royally by revising, at considerable trouble, the section on movie argot, planned for Supplement II.

My friendship with Joseph Hergesheimer made progress in the 1919–20 period, I managed to keep on fairly peaceful terms with Dreiser, and I picked up a great many other literary acquaintances, some of them enduring—for example, with Paul de Kruif, James M. Cain, Ludwig Lewisohn, Hendrik Willem Van Loon, Louise Pound, E. W. Howe, George Sterling, Benjamin De Casseres and Carl Van Doren.

I first heard from de Kruif toward the end of 1919, when he was twenty-nine years old. Born in the Dutch colony of Michigan in 1890, he had taken his B.S. degree at the University of Michigan in 1912, and his Ph.D. (in bacteriology) in 1916. Between these two events he had married a woman medical student named Mary Fisher, and in 1917 and 1919 she had presented him with two sons. He was an instructor in bacteriology on the staff of the Michigan State University from 1912 to 1917, but when he wrote to me in 1919 he was out of a job and at loose ends. Soon afterward he was given an appointment on the staff of the Rockefeller Institute in New York, and there he remained until 1922.

His early letters to me have been unhappily lost, but it is my recollection that I did not meet him until he came to New York in 1920. His marriage was already on the rocks and in 1922 it was terminated at Reno, but his wife accompanied him to New York, and I well recall a most unpleasant visit from her at the *Smart Set* office early in 1920. She was a solemn woman, and apparently somewhat older than Paul. She came, she said, to beg me to cease leading him into the abhorrent wilderness of Nietzscheism, peopled with everything immoral and subversive. I replied that I had led him nowhere, had no desire to be an evangelist, and, to the best of my knowledge and belief, had no influence over him whatsoever. But it was hard to convince her of this, for it appeared from her talk that Nietzsche had been a bitter subject of debate at their fireside, and that all either of them knew about him came out of my *Philosophy of Friedrich Nietzsche*, published more than ten years before.

It is my recollection that I had not yet met de Kruif himself at this time. But soon afterward he turned up, and I took a liking to him at once, for he was a very attractive fellow. Typically Dutch in his general aspect, he was tall, heavily-built and rosy-cheeked, with a neck that must have needed a No. 20 collar, a small but bristling moustache, and a highly cordial and even somewhat exuberant manner. There was something unmistakably boyish about him, and this air he kept into his middle years. He was a natural enthusiast and embraced every new idea with roars. He had done well as a bacteriologist at Michigan, and had a good career ahead of him at the Rockefeller Institute, but he was too impatient to endure the tedious routine of a junior member of the staff.

The first job set before him when he joined up was the tracking down of a mysterious organism that was killing large numbers of the laboratory animals. He fell upon it with high confidence and violent industry, but as the organism continued to elude him he lost interest, and was presently full of complaints about the management of the laboratory. Its chief, in those days, was Simon Flexner, a product of the Johns Hopkins who had come to the Rockefeller by way of the University of Pennsylvania Medical School. Flexner was competent, but he was a precise and somewhat pompous fellow, and de Kruif took a dislike to him, and, with characteristic exaggeration, denied that his scientific work was of any value. On the contrary, he greatly admired Jacques Loeb, head of the division of general physiology at the Rockefeller, and insisted that he was a really first-rate man and worth five Flexners. This was probably a sound judgment, but it made for unpleasantness when de Kruif expressed it loudly, and in 1922 Flexner seized a flimsy excuse to get him out of the Rockefeller.

I had advised him against antagonizing Flexner too openly, for it seemed to me that, with Loeb to train him, he had an excellent future in the laboratory. But there was a missionary hidden in him, a heritage from his Dutch Calvinist ancestors, and he longed to take the gospel of science to the plain people. He was, in fact, already writing busily, and he brought me frequent specimens of his work. Did I think he had any chance of success if he abandoned laboratory work and devoted himself wholly to writing? I replied that I thought he had, though I was still against his desertion of his profession.

This was enough to set him off in earnest, and at the end of 1922 he brought out his first book, *Our Medicine Men*. It was iconoclastic and amusing, and though very far from profound, it showed a considerable shrewdness. Its attack upon the rising tendency of the clinician to depend too much upon laboratory aids, upon the defective organization of the then novel group system of practice, and upon the hocus-pocus of public hygiene, by quackery out of the uplift, was especially effective.

The angry attack duly followed, but despite some extravagances in its manner, the book had a generally friendly reception, and de Kruif got some invitations to do magazine articles. His chief customer was Loring A. Schuler, then managing editor of the *Ladies' Home Journal*, after 1924 editor of the *Country Gentlemen*, and from 1927 to 1935 editor of the former, but he also wrote for *Harper's Magazine*, *Harper's Weekly*, the *Century* and other magazines. This work kept him busy, and it was four years before his second book, *Microbe Hunters*, came out. I saw him frequently in those days, and it was at my suggestion that Harold E. Stearns chose him to do the chapter on medicine in *Civilization in the United States*, published in the spring of 1922. It had been his first plan to print *Our Medicine Men* anonymously, but when Flexner had him on the mat for writing the Stearns chapter he decided to sign the book, and as a result he had to quit the Rockefeller.

His marriage, which, as I have said, had gone on the rocks before I met him, came to its final catastrophe in 1922, and in June of that year he went to Reno to get a divorce. He got his divorce toward the end of 1922, and on December 11 he was married to Rhea Barbarin, of Freeland, Michigan. This marriage was an immediate and enduring success. Rhea was a small and pretty woman, and extremely amiable. I got to know her well, and was very fond of her. Once I asked de Kruif, in her presence, where and when they had met. He replied that it was while he was teaching bacteriology at Michigan. "One day," he said, "I looked over my class, and found those lovely blue eyes fixed on me admiringly, and after that it was all over." This must have been about 1917.

Early in 1923 Sinclair Lewis was seized with a yearning to do a novel about a scientific man, and with his usual painstaking (at least in those days) looked about him for someone who could supply him with facts and keep him on the track. Whether or not I introduced de Kruif to him I don't remember, but it seems likely. During the winter the two started off on a tour of the West Indies to gather material, leaving Rhea behind. I received a number of notes from de Kruif during this expedition, all of them recording tremendous adventures with the native stimulants. One of them, countersigned by Lewis, bears a notation by de Kruif: "Lewis is skished again." Another, dated February 9, says: "Panama nearly killed me and I have climbed upon the wagon, leaving Lewis on his way to a drunkard's grave. . . . We have a good start on the book. If Lewis sobers up we may finish it." Poor Red, an habitual drunkard, was no match for de Kruif, who had an enormous alcoholic capacity, and could drink any ordinary man under the table. The two started for England in February by the way of Trinidad and Barbados, and by the end of March were in London, where Rhea joined her husband.

I had naturally written to de Kruif about my plans for the *American Mercury*, and on his arrival home in November, 1923, he sent me an article for it. Unhappily, I had to refuse it. He took my refusal in good part, and presently submitted another, this time a small piece called "What Is Disease?" which I printed in our department of the Arts and Sciences in September, 1924. A little while later he wrote, at my suggestion, an article on his idol, Jacques Loeb, and I printed it in July, 1925. After that he did no more for the *American Mercury*, for before the end of 1925 he joined the regular staff of the Curtis

Publishing Company, and was kept busy by the *Saturday Evening Post*, the *Ladies' Home Journal* and the *Country Gentlemen*, and by his books. He went to Rhea's home at Freeland, Michigan, after his return, but was hauled back to New York before Christmas by a libel suit and after that, for five years, he spent a large part of his time there. He lived first at Mt. Vernon, then at Pelham Manor, and finally in Bronxville.

I saw him often on my visits to New York, and we had some merry parties, not only at his suburban retreats, but also in town and at Union Hill, New Jersey, then my favorite resort. He also came to Baltimore now and then, to foregather with the Saturday Night Club, and to test the home-brews of its members, including the two Johns Hopkins members, Max Broedel and Raymond Pearl. He was hard at work, in 1924 and 1925, on *Microbe Hunters*, and we discussed its contents at great length. He tackled this task in his usual gay spirits, and his off-record comments on the immortals he was dealing with were often very pungent.

I apparently made my first evening visit to Paul and Rhea in Mt. Vernon during the winter of 1924–25. He insisted on coming in to New York to haul me out to their apartment, and when the party was over he hauled me in again. As I have said, he was an extremely hearty drinker, and that night he got down the rations of a police lieutenant, but he stood it like a man of iron, and our return trip in his car was made safely. There were many other such trips. Rhea was the cook, and a good one she was, and in addition she was an adept home-brewer. As for Paul, he always accumulated half a dozen bottles of French and German wine against my coming. There were never any other guests, and I always enjoyed these evenings immensely.

I remember making the trip one night in a blizzard. When Paul picked me up at the Algonquin the streets were swirling with snow, and by the time we got half way to Bronxville the windshield-wiper of his car became jammed, and he couldn't see to steer. I therefore had to lean out of the car to call directions to him, and in consequence our progress was slow, but we arrived at last, and found Rhea ready for us with a whole pitcher of cocktails and a gargantuan meal on the fire. When I was ready to return to the Algonquin the snow was still coming down, but the wind was from the north and would now be behind us, so Paul insisted upon bringing me in. No doubt my willingness to let him attempt it was promoted by the refreshments both of us had got down. At all events, I recall nothing of the return journey, though I remember the trip to Bronxville very vividly.

Arrowsmith, which came out early in 1925, did not sell nearly so well as *Main Street* and *Babbitt*, and in consequence Paul got a great deal less revenue from it than he had counted on. This fact prompted him to push *Microbe Hunters* to a finish, and it was published in 1926. *Our Medicine Men* had been brought out by the Century Company, then in an advanced state of decay, but *Microbe Hunters* had the imprint of Harcourt Brace & Company, a young and enterprising firm, organized in 1919 by Alfred Harcourt. Harcourt and Paul became close friends, and their business connection worked out profitably for both. The book made a big success, and deserved it. There was nothing profound about it, but it was well informed, full of shrewd judgments, and immensely amusing. Paul got into it something of his own boyish exuberance. He made the story of bacteriology seem dramatic, and important, and even a bit raffish. It was one of the best jobs of popularization ever done.

The de Kruifs moved back to Michigan in 1929. They bought a small place at Holland, on the shore of Lake Michigan about thirty miles from Grand Rapids, and this has been their home ever since. I naturally saw them less after that, but they occasionally returned to Bronxville and more than once they visited Baltimore. In July, 1930, they went abroad, planning to stay six or eight months, but they had hardly landed before Paul began to grow homesick and by October they were back in Michigan. After my marriage in 1930 they came to Baltimore to meet Sara, and she and I saw them later both there and in New York. They pressed us to visit them in Michigan, but though we made frequent plans to do so the journey was never undertaken.

Just when his interest began to turn for what *had* been done in science to what *might* be done I don't know precisely, but it must have been early in 1931. There was, of course, nothing surprising about this shift. He had started out as a research man, and despite his efforts to convince himself that the Rockefeller Institute was a den of quacks (all, that is, save Loeb and one or two others), I could see plainly that he missed and mourned the professional opportunities that it had opened to him. Writing about scientists, to be sure, was an exhilarating job and it brought him a good living, but he was uneasily conscious that it was a cut below scientific work itself.

I was thus far from astonished when he told me, under date of November 25, 1931, that he proposed to take a hand in a research into the fever treatment for syphilis, then under way in Dayton, Ohio. The head of this project seems to have been a medical man named Fred Kisling, who was to die in 1933, but another associated with it was much more stimulating, to wit, Charles F. Kettering, manager of the research laboratories of the General Motors Corporation and inventor of the Delco light. Paul was greatly taken by Kettering, and began a series of articles on him for the *Saturday Evening Post*. Meanwhile, he worked with Kisling on a heat machine for raising the temperature of syphilitics without resorting to malaria germs or other fever-producing organisms, most of them dangerous. But the heat machine turned out to be dangerous too, and unfavorable reports about its performance began to circulate in medical circles.

To Paul, always full of a boyish enthusiasm, these reports were no more than fresh evidences that the Medical Trust was up to its old tricks. So bemused, he developed a violent hate for the chief spokesman of organized medicine, Morris Fishbein, editor of the *Journal of the American Medical Association*, and gradually formulated the doctrine that Fishbein was at the head of an organized conspiracy to keep the boons of scientific medicine, whether demonstrated or only projected, from the plain people.

This, I suppose, was the origin of his flirtation with Communism between 1934 and 1939. I first heard of it from Raymond Pearl, and must have sent Paul himself some jeering comment, for under date of February 14, 1935, I received from him a defensive letter in which he denied that he was "kissing the masses' asses," alleged seriously that "a curious lot of the inspiration" for "the new trend" of his work came from the last section of my *Treatise on the Gods*, and ended with "would like to talk to you about it." This palaver never took place, and during the next five years what little news I got of him came mainly through Pearl.

The first fruit of his new obsession was a book that was at first called *Men Without Greed*, but eventually came out in 1936 as *Why Keep Them Alive?* It was a florid plea for state medicine, embodying all the familiar arguments of the quacks who were promoting it, and it had a generally hostile reception from the reviewers. I never read it, and so do not know precisely what was in it, but I gather that it went the whole hog. Another similar book, *The Fight for Life*, followed in 1938, and there was a third, *Health Is Wealth*, in 1940.

Having proceeded so far into the swamps of the uplift, it was easy for poor Paul to go over his head, and presently the Red brethren were hauling him ashore with loud hosannahs. Years later he assured me solemnly that he had never become an actual Communist, but that is what they all say after the pains of disillusionment have begun to seize them. Certainly it is a fact that the comrades regarded him as a convert, and announced him to be one, and that his name was signed, so late as April 15, 1939, to a circular cadging funds for the *New Masses*, and arguing idiotically that "America cannot afford to let it die."

During this period he was whooping up the heat machine for roasting luetics in a number of magazine articles, all of them extravagantly optimistic in tone, and following them he printed articles on various other new sure-cures, including testosterone. These manifestoes often went considerably beyond the established facts, and were consequently denounced in the medical journals, especially the *Journal of the American Medical Association*. As a result, de Kruif became more and more convinced that there was a conspiracy of prehensile doctors to keep the boons of research from the proletariat, and though he had ostensibly said good-bye to Communism he continued among the more ardent fellow-travelers.

It was a sad finish for a man who started out with such high promise, but there was nothing to be done about it and I did not attempt to dissuade him from his follies. He was a charming fellow, and one of the best booze-companions ever heard of, but we were so widely separated in space and ideas that I naturally saw less and less of him and heard from him only occasionally. His chief medium, after 1940, was the *Reader's Digest*. In it he announced a series of new medical marvels that greatly upset the medical men.

CHAPTER XVIII

I HAD TAKEN THINGS somewhat easy during the war years, and kept rather much to myself. In Baltimore I saw the brethren of the Saturday Night Club regularly and those of the Sunday Dinner Club until it blew up, but I seldom went to the *Sun* office, and my contacts there were only through Paul Patterson, who was then full of plans for the rehabilitation of the *Sunpapers*. Most of the *Sun* men of the time were abject Anglomaniacs, and I simply could not endure them. Patterson himself, in the years to come, was to become the most ardent and humorless of them all, but in 1918 and 1919 he harbored some healthy doubts, so I got on with him well enough. In New York I saw regularly only Nathan and a small circle of common friends—for example, Dreiser, John D. Williams, Edgar Selwyn, T. R. Smith and Alfred Knopf, and a few women—though even while the war was actually going on my circle of acquaintances was widening.

It must have been in 1914 that I began those reconstructions and rehabilitations in Hollins Street, which provided me with welcome exercise during the sixteen years following, and resulted in the complete transmogrification of the old house. My first operations were directed against the late Victorian furnishings which bedizened it: I made a bargain with my mother that, whenever I bought something new and better, I was to have what was displaced, and nine-tenths of the things thus displaced I knocked to pieces in the backyard. There had been a carpenter's bench in the cellar since my boyhood, and presently I began to buy good tools for it, and after a while I supplanted it with another and better of my own construction.

The first considerable operation that I undertook in the backyard was the underpinning of the pony-stable, which had begun to sag. I dug out the lower sections of the wooden posts, by now pretty well rotted, and put in foundation pillars of concrete, and I covered the old dirt floor with a mosaic of brick and stone set in cement. This new floor looked a good deal like a magnified section of what Baltimore called hog's-head cheese, the German name for which (well known to all Baltimore market-people and to most of their patrons) was *Schwartenmagen*. My first masterpiece thus came to be known in the house as the *Schwartenmagen* floor. Part of the material for it was flat strips of marble that had been parts of mantles in the parlor and in my mother's bed-room. These mantles were of bad design, and there was thus no profanation in using them to pave a stable.

My second job was the underpinning of the old summer-house in the yard. Its wooden floor had rotted and its foundations were growing shaky. During the summer of 1916 I built a sort of crib around its posts, and then hoisted the whole, inch by inch, with my automobile jack. I had no help in this feat of engineering, and was very proud of it when the summer-house was at last in air, and I could tear out the old flooring and replace it with a brick platform, set in herring-bone pattern. The frost-bed that I laid was not as deep as it should have been, but the platform nevertheless held up pretty well, and had shown only a few cracks in thirty years—all of them small, and easily repaired. I used some tiles made at Doylestown, Pennsylvania, to relieve the monotony of the brick, and they, too, have survived the years. After my return to Hollins Street in 1936 I had the super-structure of the old summer-house pulled down by wreckers—it was too heavy and hazardous a job for one man—and since then the platform has been a platform and nothing more. When it was finished I undertook to design and cast a concrete covering for the hydrant in the yard. This hydrant was simply an iron pipe coming up from the ground, with a brass spigot at its upper end. In order to enclose it I had to build my concrete forms about it—a somewhat ticklish operation. But I managed it successfully, and the result was a simple and graceful fountain that still stands.

When I began work on the brick fence now in the backyard I do not recall precisely, but it must have been some time in 1918. The design was drawn by my brother August, and I did all the work myself—making the concrete forms, mixing and laying concrete, laying the bricks and mixing and hauling the mortar. It was heavy labor, and sometimes, after two hours of it of an afternoon, I'd be pretty well exhausted. But a shower bath and a nap always restored me, and I felt the better for the exercise. All the common forms of physical exertion save walking—for example, such games as golf and tennis—bored me beyond endurance, but I enjoyed solving the problems that my brick-laying and concrete-mixing presented, and did not mind the heavy lifting.

I would commonly devote my mornings to my mail and to the reading of MSS., and then, after lunch at home, begin work in the yard. Nearly all my writing was done in the evening—a habit established in my early newspaper days, and only partly broken even today (1948). I got the bricks for the wall from my old friend, L. H. Spelshouse, who had opened a hay, feed, lime and brick warehouse at 1621 Frederick Avenue, at the corner of the alley west of Baltimore Street, just after the Civil War. Many of them came from old brick sidewalks of West Baltimore, then being supplanted by concrete. Many were worn thin, but they were well made to begin with, and some of them showed beautiful colors.

Work on the fence moved slowly, and it was 1919 before I finished the first unit. I then tackled the others in order, but finished only five in all, for our neighbor to the westward, Lillie Fortenbaugh, began to complain bitterly about the slow progress of the work, and I soon found that she objected even to the fence itself. She preferred, it appeared, the decrepit old wooden fence that I was gradually displacing, and after my five units were finished, and I annoyed her no more, she had her side of the fence painted—including the tiles that I had set into the brick! These tiles came out of a collection that I had been assembling for five or six years, and included some very good pieces. But Lillie preferred wooden boards, and, with the boards gone, tried to hide the new eyesore with paint. On our side the brick pillars and panels and narrow concrete frame and caps quickly mellowed, and the fence became very beautiful, especially after runners of ivy began to make their way up its surface.

What remained of the old wooden fence became correspondingly more unsightly, and after a little while I called in bricklayers and carpenters and had it extended to the alley—not on the elaborate plan of my own section, but in a simpler design, with brick pillars and wooden panels. It pleased me to note that the professionals who erected those pillars, which were identical to my own, made much less sightly jobs of them, and failed to get them precisely in line, as I had done with mine. In 1929 August had in another gang of experts, and the fence along the east side of the yard, separating it from the yard of William F. Stricker, was replaced according to the same design. Stricker was delighted, and took good care of his side.

Soon after my own operations on the Fortenbaugh fence had to be suspended I undertook a pergola over the sidewalk in the yard, to replace the old grape-arbor, by now falling to pieces. It was planned like the fence by my brother, and turned out very well. Into one of the pillars I sank a gorgeous multichrome tile designed by Ignacio Zuloaga, the Spanish artist, and made by his brother. I cast and put in place the concrete caps for the whole of the fence, including the parts erected by professionals. Making the casting-boxes was not easy, for the tops of the caps were flat pyramids, but I managed it by trial and error. Beside the Zuloaga tile, I sank twenty-five or thirty others into the brickwork of the fence, pergola and kitchen, and also a bronze cast of the family coat-of-arms, modelled by my brother, and another of a marker once used on the Maryland state roads, designed and modelled by him. Many of these tiles were presents from friends.

Work in the yard, of course, was possible only in fair and warm weather. On rainy days and during the winter I tackled various jobs in the house. My first was the conversion of my father's old wine-room, built of strips of wood in 1883, with wide spaces for ventilation, into a tight stucco vault, designed to be proof against prowlers. This was done in 1918, and I had the approach of Prohibition in mind. The job was finished some time before the last wine-merchant closed his doors, and I proceeded at once to lay in stock. To that end I sold my first and only car, a Studebaker four, 1915, at Christmas, 1918, and invested all the money I got for it in the best wines and liquors I could find. The vault, in fact, was packed to the ceiling, and by the time I began to notice a shortage the severe drought that followed Prohibition was over, and the bootleggers were offering plenty of replenishments. In order to safeguard my stock further I had a sign-painter make a sign showing a skull and crossbones and reading:

> This Vault is protected
> By a device releasing Chlorine

Gas under 200 pounds pressure.
Enter it at your own Risk.

The capitalization was supplied by the sign-painter. I nailed the sign to the door, and it worked very well, for the vault was not once tampered with during the Thirteen Years, though many strange workmen, deliverymen and so on, both white and black, were in and out of the cellar. This wine-vault, which is still in use (1948) is ten feet six inches long by six feet deep, and has shelf-space for many hundreds of bottles. Next to it I built a concrete strong-room for the storage of papers, four feet six inches wide and six feet deep, and next to the strong-room a storage-room for my mother, made entirely of aromatic cedar-wood. This cedar room has been in use for more than twenty years, and so far as I know no moth has ever ventured into it.

I also put in a lot of my play-time building bookcases in various parts of the house, and eventually had enough space for about five thousand books. For the cases in my bedroom I had a cabinet-maker make mahogany fronts, and meanwhile I had all of the worn old floors in the house covered with parquetry, and replaced the old vestibule and front doors with better ones designed by Edward L. Palmer, and put in new doors and frames in all the downstairs rooms, and had a contractor build a new brick kitchen and pantry. My operations in the yard produced a large amount of old wood, and this wood I sawed into fire lengths for an open fire-place that I had put into the downstairs sitting-room, c. 1921.

In the intervals of these tasks and enterprises I undertook all of the minor house repairs. August, in those days, was out of town on engineering jobs most of the time, so I was the family handy-man. This kept on until my marriage in 1930. When I returned to Hollins Street in 1935 I found that I had lost my wind and some of my former skill with tools, and so gradually resigned my offices to my brother. But I still do my full share of work in the garden, and occasionally mix a bucket of cement and undertake minor repairs in the brickwork.

But such activities, though pleasant and also, I suppose, salubrious, were never allowed to interfere with my work, and from 1919 onward I carried a burden of it that was to increase steadily until the middle of the 20's, which were destined to be the busiest of all my years. Two of the principal enterprises of my whole life, the publication of the first edition of *The American Language* and the launching of the *Prejudices* series, both belong to 1919, and in addition I undertook the editing of various books not my own and began my long service to Knopf as a volunteer manuscript scout. Also, I began a venture into play-writing, taking Nathan with me, and had a brief brush with the movies.

The play-writing experiment had its origin in 1917, when Knopf started a series of translations of contemporary foreign dramas under the title of the Borzoi Plays, the third volume of which was a translation of Ludwig Thoma's *Moral* by Charles Recht. I had been introduced to the work of Thoma by Percival Pollard, and was greatly taken by it. I thus reviewed his version of *Moral* at some length in the *Smart Set* for May, 1917, and added an account of Thoma himself. This review was read by a New York theatrical manager of the time named Lee Kugel, and it set him to reading the Recht translation. He found the play very interesting, but the translation crude and ineffective, and presently he proposed to Nathan and me that we attempt a better. It was impossible at that time to enter upon direct negotiations with Thoma, for the peace treaty with Germany did not go into effect until July 2, 1921, but Nathan and I nevertheless undertook the job, hoping to come to terms with the author later.

Unhappily, we quickly found that the play needed a new first act, for that of the original was grounded upon German ways and conditions that would have been unintelligible to a Broadway audience. Writing this new first act was comparable to putting a new foundation under a building, but after some effort we managed to get it designed and executed. Kugel professed to like the result, but by this time he had made enough money to content him and was planning to retire from management, so he never put the play on.

This threw it upon Nathan's hands and mine, and we offered it to several other managers, including John D. Williams, but they were all afraid to present a German play so soon after the war; moreover, the question of our rights was still in doubt. One manager—I forget who he was—hinted that he would be inclined to risk a production if we could get the imprimatur of the Alien Property Custodian, then Francis P. Garvan, and we accordingly tackled him. This Garvan was an Irish lawyer of New York who had made a fortune during the war by collaring the patents of various German chemical manufacturers, and was naturally violently anti-German. I remember well our call upon him at his office in New York, for I was suffering from hay-fever and uncomfortably photophobic. He treated us with scant politeness and we gave up the project.

As soon as communications with Germany were opened I communicated with Thoma through my friend Dr. Wilhelm Schler of Munich, and under date of January 22, 1921, he sent me a friendly letter, pointing out that *Moral* had been translated in 1916 by Recht but offering us the American rights to some of his other works. We had already come to terms with Recht, but did not return to *Moral*, and before the end of 1921 Thoma was dead. The typescript of our translation is in a book entitled *Attempts at Plays, 1909–1920*, to go to the Pratt Library, Baltimore, at my death. It is signed "by Wilbur Abbott." Who proposed this pseudonym I forget.

Nine-tenths of the play was my work, but Nathan offered some good suggestions on the final revision, and after we had finished it I proposed to him that we do a play of our own. I remember that this suggestion was made during one of our beer-evenings at Rogers' restaurant in Sixth Avenue. My experience with *Moral* had somehow convinced me that writing a play was easy, and I offered to wager Nathan we could turn out one in a couple of months. He was doubtful of this, but I managed to convince him, and we started making plans at once.

I suggested that it might be a good idea to pick a hero from history, and that it might help to choose a very despicable one, and then devote the play to proving ironically that he really had a heart of gold. We quickly decided on the Roman emperor Heliogabalus, who, by the agreement of all historians, was the most vicious of his line. It was an easy thought to contrast him with the Christians who badgered him, and before the evening was over we had the play pretty well outlined. We agreed that in the writing we were to stick close to the traditional hokum of the theatre. Nothing was to be admitted that was in the faintest sense intellectual: what we had in mind was a burlesque of the current trade goods, and nothing else. The result was *Heliogabalus: A Buffoonery*, brought out by Knopf in 1920. I actually wrote the first draft of it in the leisure of six weeks. The idea of the play was mine and so was most of the writing, but Nathan, as in the case of *Moral*, made some good suggestions when the time came for the final revision.

I used to argue with him in those days that he was wasting his time by devoting all of it to play-reviewing. "Soon or late," I said, "you will be the oldest dramatic critic in New York—and I can imagine nothing more horrible than that." Nathan knew a great deal about the stage, and was privy to all of the tricks of the current dramatists, but I gradually became convinced that he really had no capacity for dramatic writing. He was, in fact, a dramatic reviewer and nothing else, and that is what he remains to this day. He has tried other forms of writing at different times, usually under my urging—once he actually attempted a book for children—but he has failed at all of them.

It was obvious that, in the then state of comstockery in New York, *Heliogabalus* could not be done on the stage, so we made a virtue of necessity by bringing it out in a limited edition of two thousand copies and announcing that we'd never permit its presentation in New York until the United States became a civilized country. This *blague* naturally attracted attention, and soon the late Will A. Page came to us with an offer of $10,000 for the American rights. Nathan was in favor of accepting, but I vetoed the proposal, and *Heliogabalus*, in fact, has never had a production. In later years, William Gillette and John Barrymore were interested in it, especially Gillette, but by that time he was approaching eighty and nothing came of his interest. He once told John D. Williams that he thought the title role would have offered him the fattest part of his career. I marvelled at the time that some composer did not try to get the play for a libretto, for it would have made a capital *opera comique* in the grand manner, but none ever did.

When Charles Feleky asked us for the German rights we gave them to him, and he had the play translated by a German using the pseudonym of Peter Perpentikel, and published by the Theatralia Verlag of Berlin. It was described on the title-page as a "Schwank in drei Akten aus dem Amerikanishen" and was presently going the round of the German theatrical managers. Several of them showed interest in it, and one began plans to present it, but it required an expensive set of scenery, and in a little while the inflation had made any heavy expenditure impossible in Germany. By the time the inflation was over and forgotten, the play was also forgotten.

The limited American edition of two thousand copies was sold out before publication, and the Comstocks were thereby baffled. The play yielded me but $343 altogether, for I had to share the royalties with Nathan, and we had given Knopf a contract, dated October 29, 1919, whereby he paid us nothing on the first five hundred copies. He brought it out in two forms. The first, on paper, was bound in black cloth with gilt stamping. The second, on imperial Japan vellum, bound in mottled boards with a white vellum back, was of sixty numbered copies. In addition Knopf gave us one hundred and fifty copies bound in tan paper with brown stamping. These one hundred and fifty copies cost us nothing, but we got, of course, no royalty on them. The play was soon in heavy demand among the antique book-dealers, and sound copies still bring good prices (1945).

Another of my enterprises in 1919 was a translation of Nietzsche's *Der Antichrist*. It was suggested by the fact that the translations in the complete works of Nietzsche in English, brought out by Dr. Oscar Levy in the 1909–1911 era, were all very bad, and that that of *The Antichrist*, by Anthony Ludovici, was one of the worst. I well recall plugging away at my translation during the unhappy months spanning the Treaty of Versailles and wondering what was happening to some of my friends in Germany. I used the Ludovici version as a crib, but it was of small use, for its academic stiffness libelled the extraordinarily fluent and colorful German of the original.

I had been in contact with Levy since 1911, and had met him in 1912 in London, where he was practicing as a physician but devoting most of his time and means—he appeared to be well-to-do and had a house at 54 Russell Square—to promoting Nietzsche. In 1915 the English expelled him from England as an enemy alien, for he was a German citizen, and he went to live at Geneva. Early in 1917, when I came out of Germany from the war and started home by way of Switzerland, France, Spain and Cuba, he ran up from Geneva to see me, and we had a palaver in Basle. That palaver attracted the attention of the English spies who swarmed in the town, and afterward some of his letters to me opened with "Dear Mr. Mayfield," to avoid the suspicion engendered by my German name. On February 22, 1918, he wrote to me from Geneva saying that he was thinking of bringing out a six-volume edition of Nietzsche in New York and asking me if I cared to "help in the matter directly or indirectly." I do not know what I replied, though I judge by a letter from him dated May 5, 1918, that I must have shown some interest. But nothing came of this, and before the end of 1918 we were discussing, not the projected six-volume edition, but a new translation of *Der Antichrist*.

Levy claimed all American rights to Nietzsche. I found that this claim was invalid, but I decided not to proceed without his formal permission, and on December 18 he was reporting that he had gone to the American consul at Geneva to execute it, but had been told that it would have to wait until peace between Germany and the United States was proclaimed. In January, 1919, he wrote to me that a simple letter from him would be sufficient, so I went on with the translation. On April 5, 1919, he sent me a copy of a letter that he had written to Foulis the publisher, notifying him of my plans, and by the end of the year I finished the job. A carbon of my preface to *The Antichrist* reached him on December 16, and he suggested a few changes in it. A copy of the book must have reached him soon afterward.

The Antichrist was published as Volume III of the series called "The Free Lance Books." This series was my idea, and my original plan for it was to devote it to reprinted essays. But Knopf suggested the title for it, which was borrowed, of course, from that of my "Free Lance" column in the Baltimore *Evening Sun,* and the first volume, a translation from the Spanish of Pío Baroja by Jacob S. Fassett, Jr., entitled *Youth and Egolatry,* was not my find but turned up in his office. It was dated 1920, and seems to have been preceded by the second volume, *Ventures in Common Sense,* by E. W. Howe, which was dated 1919. The third volume was *The Antichrist,* 1920; the fourth was *We Moderns,* by Edwin Muir, 1920; the fifth was *Democracy and the Will to Power,* by James N. Wood, 1920; and the sixth and last was a revision of my *In Defense of Women,* 1922.

Though three of the six books—*The Antichrist, Ventures in Common Sense* and the reprint of *In Defense of Women*—sold pretty well, the others were complete failures, and the series was soon abandoned. Knopf turned it out beautifully, with board covers in various colors and black cloth backs with paper labels, and I put in some hard work on my introductions and on the editing of the texts, but all of this labor was in vain.

This experience taught me that editing the books of other men was an unprofitable business, and I kept away from it as much as possible. But it was not always easy to do so, for sometimes the requests and suggestions that came to me were reinforced by considerations of friendship or common interest. It was for such reasons that I edited three plays of Ibsen for the Modern Library in 1918 and a volume of Oscar Wilde's short stories during the same year. Both projects, if I recall correctly, were brought to me by T. R. Smith, then managing editor of the *Century Magazine* and one of my frequent companions in New York. The edition of Arthur Morrison's *Tales of Mean Streets* which I did for the Modern Library in 1920 was also probably promoted by Smith, though I seem to remember that it was first projected by Philip Goodman, probably in 1918. Smith likewise had some hand in the volume of Nietzsche-Wagner correspondence, brought out in 1921 with an introduction by me.

So far as I can recall, the first anthology in which anything of mine appeared was *The Profession of Journalism*, by Willard Grosvenor Bleyer, Ph.D., professor of that science in the University of Wisconsin. This book was made up of articles that had been published in the *Atlantic Monthly*, and my contribution was "Newspaper Morals," printed in March, 1914. After 1919 requests for permission to reprint articles of mine began to come in with increasing frequency. I usually granted them, but not always, for some of the requests came from persons I knew to be only racketeers. In some cases permissions were granted by magazines or newspapers which owned copyrights on my material, and I knew nothing of it. It was in those days, also, that I began to be discussed, not only in articles but also in books. The first mention of me in a book that I can trace was in W. L. Courtney's *Rosemary's Letter-Book*, published in London in 1909. Thereafter came a ten-year hiatus, but from 1919 onward I began to be mentioned frequently, and often very tartly.

CHAPTER XIX

IN THE PREFACE to Supplement I to *The American Language*, I have described briefly the origin of my interest in American speechways. My first article on the subject was printed on the editorial page of the Baltimore *Evening Sun* on October 10, 1910, and they continued intermittently after that until May, 1911, when my daily miscellaneous article was displaced by a column entitled the "Free Lance." The "Free Lance" was mainly given over to excoriating the politicians, reformers and other frauds of the time, and there was not much space left in it for discussing language, but now and then I managed to return to the subject.

When I abandoned this column in October, 1915, I continued to write an occasional article for the *Evening Sun*, and one of these, headed "Notes on the American Language," was printed on September 7, 1916. When, in 1917, I left the *Sunpapers* and began writing for the New York *Evening Mail*, I made language a frequent theme, for I was bound by my contract to avoid all subjects likely to outrage the plupatriots of the time. Meanwhile, I had reworked some of my early *Evening Sun* material in an article for the *Smart Set*, entitled "The American: His Language" and published in the issue for August, 1913. This article was planned as a chapter in a book to be called *The American* but that book never got beyond six chapters and was then abandoned. By the beginning of 1918 I was playing with the idea of giving over a whole volume to the national speech, and by the spring I was at work upon it in earnest. Preparing for it involved a great deal of dull reading, and I recall that I did much of that reading, in the hot summer weather, lying in my sleeping-porch in Hollins Street. I made quick progress, and by October the MS. was in Knopf's hands.

No book on the subject had appeared for forty-seven years, and there had been no apparent demand for one. To be sure, I had received a good many letters from interested readers of my newspaper and magazine articles, but I was well aware that the American Dialect Society, founded in 1889, had been very poorly supported, and its organ, *Dialect Notes*, had only the most meagre circulation. We were, however, wrong about *The American Language*. Published in March, 1919, it had sold 1373 of its 1500 copies by June 30, and within the next year the small remainder followed. My royalties from it, to June 30, 1920, amounted to $609.20, and it was the first of my books to earn me more than $500.

The reviews, in the main, were very favorable. The Chicago *Tribune* led off on March 29 by describing the book as "monumental," and on March 30 the New York *Times* printed a three-column review by Brander Matthews (who was politely treated in my text), in which it was called "interesting and useful, well planned, well proportioned, well documented and well written." Matthews naturally added some reservations, and did not fail to note with pain my flings at the American Academy of Arts and Letters, of which he was a principal ornament, but on the whole he dealt with the book generously, and gave a fair summary of its contents and thesis.

There were caveats, too, from other quarters, mainly grounded on the proposition that any attempt to separate American from English was a Hunnish attack upon the Motherland. But the great majority of notices were very friendly—indeed, so friendly that they gave me some uneasiness, and even inclined me to cry down the book in my own mind. Early in June, 1919, I wrote to a correspondent in New York: "Now even the *New Republic* greases *The American Language*. What a farce! Every idiot slobbers over this bad book. The good ones get the hook."

But there was more in this than mere challenge and defiance, for I was acutely aware of some of the deficiencies of my first attempt, and on June 2 I was writing to Fielding H. Garrison: "The book needs a thorough overhauling, but it will have to wait at least a year. The first edition is almost sold out. It is getting good notices, and making me respectable." The need for that overhauling was impressed upon me by the letters that flowed in from readers. I had asked for corrections and additions in my preface, and now they were coming in in large number. "My *American Language* correspondence," I wrote to Garrison on October 16, "becomes enormous. Today I received from a man in Philadelphia the longest letter ever written—actually 10,000 words, and every page full of interesting observations."

This correspondence kept up through 1920; indeed, it has kept up to the present day. In all those years I can recall only a few days on which I have not received at least one letter about the book, and on many days I have received four or five. They have come from all sorts of persons, running from college presidents and United States senators to newspaper reporters, business men, bartenders and soldiers in the field, and from every state in the Union and scores of places abroad, including Finland, Turkey, India, South Africa, Australia, China and Japan. This correspondence brought me a large number of interesting acquaintances in far places, and some of them—notably H. W. Seaman and P. E. Cleator in England, and the late F. H. Tyson of Hong Kong—greatly enriched my collection of materials.

That collection at the time I write (1945), with Supplement I off my hands, fills thirty-four Globe Wernicke No. 591 transfer cases in my office, and flanking them and extending into two other rooms of the house is a library that includes virtually every book and pamphlet on the subject ever printed, in whatever language. How many items are in this library I do not know precisely, but the number must run well beyond fifteen hundred. It includes not a few unique items, and a dozen or more unpublished manuscripts. I have left orders that the whole collection, which grows constantly, shall go at my death to Dr. M. M. Mathews, of the University of Chicago, who is engaged upon a revision of *A Dictionary of American English* and apparently proposes to devote the rest of his life to the subject.

The first printing of *The American Language* was from type. This type was still standing at the end of 1919, for the quick success of the first edition had suggested to Knopf that a second would be needed, and I wanted to add to it some of the new material that was coming in. Philip Goodman, who was proud of his talents as a proofreader, volunteered to go through the book in search of errors, and I welcomed his aid. But he turned out, like most proofreaders, to be excessively pedantic, and I had to reject at least nine-tenths of his suggestions. I must have put in some licks on the revision all through 1920, but it was not until the end of the year that I settled down to it in earnest, and not until July 25, 1921, that the MS. was completed.

The first edition had made a sightly book, as Knopf's books always were, but it had seemed to me that it had been a shade too slim to be impressive, and I therefore urged Knopf to make the second one bulkier and heftier. "All I ask," I wrote to him on September 7, 1921, "is that you make *The American Language* good and thick. It is my secret ambition to be the author of a book weighing at least five pounds."

He missed this mark by one pound and thirteen ounces, but the volume that he produced was certainly sufficiently obese to look important, for it was two and one-quarter inches thick. In part, this increase in size was produced by the fact that the new edition had four hundred ninety-two pages, whereas the first had had but three hundred seventy-four, but something must also be laid to the extraordinarily heavy paper that Knopf had dug up.

The new edition showed a thorough reworking, with many considerable additions. The first four chapters, though they followed the lines of those in the first edition, were expanded from one hundred thirty pages to one hundred fifty-six, and from that point onward there was even heavier admixture of new matter, with the original nine chapters increased to twelve, and three appendices added. One of these appendices was devoted to American proverbs and popular phrases, another dealt with eleven of the non-English languages spoken in the United States, and the third was made up of four specimens of the American vulgate. Of the last-named one was a colloquy between baseball players, done for me by Ring W. Lardner, the second was a dialogue between two vaudeville actors from the same hand, the third was John V. A. Weaver's "Elegie Americain," and the fourth was my burlesque translation of the Declaration of Independence, later to be taken with complete seriousness by various American and English pedants.

The second *American Language*, marked *Second Edition; Revised and Enlarged*, came out in December, 1921, delayed a bit by my dreadful struggles with the Index and the List of Words and Phrases. I had done those of the first edition single-handed, but this time, remembering what an onerous job it had been, I resolved to get help. I had no regular secretary at the time, but the young woman who did my occasional copying volunteered to aid me, and presently we were hard at work. I would mark on the page-proofs the words and phrases to be indexed, and she would then make cards for them. After a few days I was doing the marking so much faster than she could do the cards that she brought in a couple of helpers. These turned out to be young girls with no capacity for the business, and presently they were bogged, and one of them departed in hysterics. In the end I took over the whole tedious task myself, and on October 26 I wrote to Blanche Knopf that I was working at it sixteen hours a day.

It was not my intention, when I began to make plans for a third edition in the spring of 1922, to undertake any extensive rewriting: the type of the second edition was still standing, and both Knopf and I thought that it would be sufficient to correct the errors that had been found in it—mainly by alert readers, for I was myself a very bad proofreader—and to make room for the accumulated new material by cutting out some of the old. But when I got to work it turned out that there would have to be changes on almost every page, and though I was able, here and there, to pick up some longish paragraphs my revisions necessitated a remaking-up of the whole book. Thus its size was increased, with the bibliography and indices omitted, from four hundred twenty-five pages to four hundred thirty-five, and the printer's bill ran to $500, with another $500 added for the plates that we now resolved to make.

I settled down to work in the spring, and by July 7 I had delivered the whole book. Unhappily, it had become apparent by that time that it would be impossible for me to undertake the two indices, for I was planning to go abroad about August 1, and, save by paying the printers overtime, the page-proofs could hardly be delivered before then. In this emergency Knopf suggested that I employ Wilson Follett to read these page-proofs and do the indices, and an arrangement with him was soon made. I thus went off on my holiday assuming that the whole book would be ready for a last looking-over on my return, but when I got back in October I found that Follett had done next to nothing. This was extremely irritating, but there was no help for it, and in October I had to tackle the indices myself. Follett was out of a job at the time, and had plenty of time on his hands, but he was simply too lazy to do what he had promised to do. On November 1 I wrote to Knopf: "Moral: never have anything to do with a man who is hard up." And on November 4: "One more proof that it is insane to do business with paupers. They are not poor without reason." Follett wrote to me on November 16, offering a feeble and unpersuasive excuse for his neglect and offering grandly to charge nothing for the little work he had done, but I insisted on paying him $25 to get rid of him.

My second large enterprise of 1919 was the launching of my *Prejudices* series, the first volume of which came out in September. The idea of this series was rather obvious, for my periodical writings, and especially my *Smart Set* reviews, were getting more and more notice, but rather strangely it did not occur to either Knopf or me. Knopf, indeed, was against it when he first heard it proposed. Its originator was a bookseller in Cleveland named Richard Laukhuff, and in a letter of April 23, 1943, he told me the story, which Knopf corroborated. Thus:

> During the days of the *Smart Set* I collected your book reviews and placed them in folders for easy reference by people coming to the shop. I found them much to the point, and thought others might, so I kept them lying around. People did pick them up and read them, and most lively discussions were started and people discovered books. One day Mr. Knopf, who in those days was his own salesman, came to the store. He invited suggestions. Among other ideas, I suggested publication of some of your reviews.
>
> Mr. Knopf: Nobody would buy them.
> Laukhuff: Many people will buy them.
> The next Knopf catalog had the announcement of *Prejudices*.

I was myself rather dubious about the project, for it was common publishing experience that reprinted reviews did not sell. Moreover, I was full of plans in those days for editing a history of the American share in World War I—not the military history, but the record of the spy-hunting, profiteering and patrioteering at home—and was eager to get to work on it. I had conceived it on a large scale, and figured that it would run to twenty-five or thirty volumes, and perhaps more—one, for example, to be devoted to the record of the American clergy in the war, another to the war-mongering in the colleges, a fourth to the Liberty loan campaigns, a fifth to the part played by the newspapers and so on and so on.

Such an enterprise, of course, was beyond the capacity of one man, so I counted on getting together a committee of like-minded persons, raising a fund to finance the writing and printing, and perhaps setting a mob of nascent Ph.D.'s to work at the amassing of materials.

This amassing would involve an examination of all the principal American newspapers from 1914 to date, and many of the minor ones, and it would also take a great deal of travelling. Unhappily, I soon found that executing the scheme on anything approaching an adequate scale would cost at least $1,000,000, and inasmuch as I could find no one willing to put up so much money I had to abandon it. But while I cherished it it entertained me pleasantly, and I accumulated myself a great mass of newspaper clippings and other documents. They nearly filled the loft of the little pony-stable in Hollins Street, and there they remained until I returned to the old house in 1936, when I called in a colored trash man and presented the whole lot to him as waste-paper.

The history of the American share in World War I has not been written to this day, and I doubt that it ever will be. The academic historians adopted the official view of it, and only a few of them have ever made any effort, however slight, to unearth and print the extremely discreditable facts. The same thing is now happening (1945) in the case of World War II, and I suppose the American people will continue to be fed balderdash until the end of the chapter. It is always possible, however, that some foreigner—say an Englishman— will attempt some day to tell the truth, but I should add at once that it is not likely. I often wonder whether the history of the remoter past is any more reliable. It has been investigated at enormous length by earnest and diligent men, and some of the delusions that once prevailed have been exploded, but in the main what we believe about it is probably quite as dubious as what Americans believe about World War I.

Following Laukhuff's plan, *Prejudices: First Series* was mainly made up of things that had been printed in the *Smart Set*, but I did some painstaking rewriting, and also added material from my articles in other magazines and in newspapers, and some stuff written especially for the book. On September 6, 1919, I wrote to Fielding H. Garrison: "It is full of rough stuff, perhaps too cruel—but, after all, it is foolish to be polite to frauds." And on September 28: "It is light stuff, chiefly rewritten from the *Smart Set*, but with now and then a blast from the lower woodwind. It will outrage the umbilicari, if that is the way to spell it. Such books are mere stinkpots, heaved occasionally to keep the animals perturbed. The real artillery fire will begin a bit later."

How many copies of the first edition Knopf printed I do not recall, but he had sold 1678 by December 31—a very pleasant surprise to both of us. It kept on selling steadily until 1931, eleven years after its first publication, when there was a drop, and Knopf and I began to discuss letting it go out of print. When the plates were melted in 1933 about 300 copies remained in stock. They were finally disposed of by 1942, and *Prejudices: First Series* perished from this earth. The total sales by that time, if I calculate correctly, were 15,712, and counting in the small fees paid for the English rights and the sums received from reprint rights, my receipts from it amounted altogether to $3222.33. This was certainly good pay for a book that I had compounded out of clippings in no more than a few weeks of intermittent labor. Requests for reprint rights still occasionally come in. After the first edition was published Knopf told me that he thought he should adopt a standard format for all of my books, and we decided upon dark blue cloth with gilt stamping, and my coat-of-arms in blind stamping on the front cover. This was first used for the second printing, and was retained for my books thereafter, though not invariably.

My description of *Prejudices: First Series* as a stinkpot designed "to keep the animals perturbed" was not altogether inept, for if that was not the fundamental purpose of the book, then it was certainly its effect. Most of the contents were not new, for they had been printed before in the *Smart Set*, but their impact, coming out in small installments, had been much less than their impact in one blast. I made a deliberate effort to lay as many quacks as possible, and chose my targets, not only from the great names of the past, but also from the current company of favorites. Thus butcheries of some of the elder demigods were accompanied by onslaughts upon some of the reigning favorites of 1919, ranging from H. G. Wells, William Dean Howells and George Bernard Shaw down to Henry Van Dyke, William Allen White, Irvin Cobb, Henry Sydnor Harrison, Hamlin Garland, Amy Lowell, Ernest Poole, Thorstein Veblen, Will Levington Comfort and Joyce Kilmer. Some of these attacks drew blood, and their victims never recovered afterward, notably Veblen, Poole, Garland, Comfort, Harrison and Cobb.

Nor did I spare, in my laying about, men with whom I was on good terms personally, and in whom I saw, mixed with fustian, some sound merit—for example, Edgar Lee Masters, Vachel Lindsay, Ezra Pound and Robert Frost. My book, of course, was not all abuse, for

I had friendly words in it for all these men, and also for Arnold Bennett, Jack London, George Ade, Elsie Clews Parsons, Hermann Sudermann, George Jean Nathan and many others. Also, I gave over several chapters to less personal themes—for example, the uproar over sex, then in full blast; the psychology of Puritanism; and the general state of civilization in the United States.

This sort of thing naturally alarmed many of the book reviewers, so they dealt with *Prejudices: First Series* in a rather gingerly fashion, avoiding too particular an account of its contents and tempering their approval with caution. The book puzzled and disquieted these poor dolts. They saw that it was far more than a collection of book reviews, and were inclined to treat it seriously, but they shied at its fundamental doctrine, not only as aesthetes of the current model but also as patriotic Americans. A common way out for them was to allege that I was not in earnest—that the whole thing was only a buffoonish play to the galleries, full of exaggerations and conscious falsifications. But just what galleries I was playing to they did not explain.

The downright excoriations were rather more amusing. The most violent of them was Stuart Pratt Sherman's, printed in the New York *Times* for December 7, 1919, under the title of "Mr. Mencken and the Jeune Fille." I had used Sherman harshly in the first chapter of my book, and on sundry other occasions, and he came back, characteristically, with the hint that I was somehow connected with the German spy system. Another appeal to the prevailing fears was made by the reviewer of the Los Angeles *Times* (shades of Willard Wright!) on November 30. He spoke of me as *Herr* Mencken, and declared that I had "a complete *Kultur*, but no culture whatever."

The discussion of *Prejudices: First Series* went far beyond the reviews. It continued, in fact, for months after the book came out, and was participated in by columnists, editorial writers and a miscellany of other sages. Indeed, it launched that debate over my ideas—and, by an easy transition, my objects and motives—which roared on for years afterward, and produced so vast a crop of invective that in 1928 I was moved to gather some of its pearls in *Menckeniana: A Schimpflexikon*. All of the discussion of me printed before the end of 1917 found room in little more than a single volume of the three-hundred-odd-page scrapbooks that I set up in that year, but 1918 needed more than one hundred fifty pages and 1919 more than two hundred, and after that there were many years that filled two or three whole volumes. I am now (August, 1945) in volume eighty-nine, and the flood still continues.

The close of 1919 thus saw me in the midst of a kind of whirlpool, and it goes without saying that the experience was exhilarating. My interest in the *Smart Set* was abating, but I still found it a good sounding-board, and concluded that I had better stick to it until a better offered. Despite the fast increasing notice that I was getting, the magazine itself was apparently stuck at a circulation of 30,000-odd—scarcely enough to content me. Moreover, though I left more and more of the details of administration to Nathan, it put a considerable burden of work upon me, and I had to listen constantly to the schemes and excuses of the imbecile Warner.

In the autumn of 1919 there was a pressmen's strike in New York, and it looked for a while as if we might have to miss an issue. This involved endless conferences, all of them dreadful bores. "My own belief," I wrote to my brother August on October 9, "is that it would be cheaper to pay the pressmen what they want, but the publishers have agreed to stick it out. I incline to think that the men will win." Whether they did or they didn't I forget, but I remember well that the printing of the December issue had to be moved to Albany and that it came out on paper even worse than usual and was altogether a bad job.

We had, fortunately, raised the subscription price from $3 to $4 and the news-stand price from 25 to 35 cents with the October issue, but this measure, which came only after endless palavers with Warner, did not bring in enough extra money to assure Nathan and me of our salaries, and we consequently began to hatch new schemes for replenishing the skinny treasury.

One was a plan to sweat some money out of the movies, which were then just beginning to become Big Business. There was at that time a fashion among their nascent master-minds for producing very short features, usually run in series, and we proposed that one of the companies, headed by the Sam Goldfish who had become Goldwyn, do a series based on the epigrams printed in the *Smart Set*. Goldfish thought it was a good idea, and agreed to make the experiment, but Warner had a hard time inducing him to sign a contract. Finally he did so—and then sent it to the *Smart Set* office by a slave bearing the verbal message that he had concluded, after signing, to drop the enterprise!

It was thus that movie magnates did business in those cradle days.

Warner was all for suing him for damages, but Nathan and I thought that it would be cheaper and more prudent to try to find another victim. We soon found him in Whitman Bennett, who was the literary adviser and general factotum to Ben B. Hampton, a magazine owner who had launched into the movies in 1916, and lasted precariously until 1922, when he succumbed to the purge of Christians, and Bennett with him.

This Bennett was an intelligent and pleasant fellow who had been a Shubert press-agent and had some literary taste. We arranged with him that we were to supply him with twelve *Smart Set* epigrams a week, and that he was to devise some means of putting them on the screen. I do not know what his scheme was, for I never saw the result, but it was certainly not a success. So far as I know, only one movie-parlor in the whole country ever actually exhibited these illustrated epigrams, and it abandoned them after a few weeks. It was, as I recall it, a second-rate house in Broadway. Its customers, fed upon the art of Theda Bara, could make nothing of them, and neither could the manager. But we continued to turn in our weekly dozen under our contract with Bennett, and he paid for them manfully. Altogether, we got $6,000 for the *Smart Set* by this transaction, and it tided the magazine over a time of very serious difficulty. Most of the epigrams were my own, but I got nothing personally. When I ran out of stock I began levying on the epigrams of all ages, and soon had three or four volunteers digging them up for me.

Whitman was a pleasant fellow, and Nathan and I saw a good deal of him while the epigram affair was on. Dreiser, at that time, was desperately hard up, and we adumbrated various schemes to get him money from the movies. One was to sell the movie rights to *Jennie Gerhardt* to Bennett. Bennett, who had read it, was greatly interested, but after a while he told us that the story was impossible. "Consider," he said, "the last scene, with Jennie looking through the bars at the railway station, watching them load Lester's body on a baggage-car. And consider the people who will see it—largely women who have stopped in at a movie-parlor on their way home from shopping, probably with babies in their arms. Think of the effect on such poor simpletons! Once one of them has been floored by that scene she won't come back to a movie-parlor for weeks."

This was sound psychology, and we had no answer to it. Unhappily for Dreiser, the Jews and their minions had not yet taken over the movies, and developed schemes for disposing of such difficulties. To-day (1945) it would be childsplay to get rid of that shocking last scene—and substitute one showing Jennie and Lester standing before the pastor. In 1944, in fact, I heard that the rights to *Jennie Gerhardt* had actually been bought by one of the Hollywood companies. But I doubt that it will ever be shown, for when Dreiser sees that new last scene he will raise an uproar that will shake even Hollywood.

Another plan that entertained Nathan and me during 1919 was one for a book of unprintable stuff. It was suggested by a short piece called "The Literary Approach," sent to us for the *Smart Set* by a New Orleans man named Moise. Superficially, it was simply a con-versation about books between a man and a woman, but underneath it was full of racy suggestions. In the then state of comstockery in New York publishing it was out of the question, but we liked it so much that we had Moise send it in two or three times, hoping to be able to devise a plan to make it printable. But every attempt to get it past the Comstocks destroyed some of its wit and ingenuity, and we had to give it up.

Other such things came in from time to time, so the idea of a book of them, privately printed, naturally suggested itself. I myself pro-posed to contribute a one-act play to be called "The Lady Em-balmer," showing such an artist getting stuck in the midst of embalming an elderly female client, and calling in a male expert by telephone to rescue her, and the male expert demanding a dreadful price for his aid. The curtain was to have fallen with the lady em-balmer stretched out resignedly on a sofa beside the corpse, and the he one taking off his coat and waistcoat.

Another candidate for the book was a one-act burlesque of Maurice Maeterlinck by Frederic Arnold Kummer of Baltimore, entitled "The Two Gonococci." Scene: the pudendum of an ancient harlot. Her-gesheimer promised to do a story for the book, Nathan proposed to contribute a realistic review of a musical comedy, with special atten-tion to the private lives of the chorus girls, and I tried to induce Fielding H. Garrison to let us include some of his college-day verse, which was highly Rabelaisian. But the project never got beyond talk, though Nathan and I played with it for half a dozen years.

It must have been in 1918 or 1919 that I took up my permanent New York headquarters at the Algonquin Hotel, where I have stayed ever since. Before that I had used a dozen or more different hotels in the Times Square region, but after trying the Algonquin a few times I found it the most comfortable and convenient, and so settled down in it. In those days it was the favorite New York hotel of many movie stars, including Douglas Fairbanks, Sr., and hence attracted girls aspiring to crash the movies. The elevator and lobby swarmed with them, and many of them were very sightly.

But the Algonquin was by no means only, or even mainly, a theatrical house. It also entertained many of the literati, and had curious groups of other guests, for example, the higher functionaries of the Salvation Army and a number of well-to-do East Indians, some of them in turbans. Most of the Hollywood luminaries moved away when the Ambassador was opened on April 26, 1921, for they were growing opulent by now and felt that the gaudy splendors of the new hotel better befitted their new and glittering station in life than the somewhat dingy comforts of the Algonquin.

Thereafter the Algonquin's chief glory was its Round Table, first set up in 1919. The members of this Round Table were all literati of the third, fourth and fifth rate—for example, Alexander Woollcott, Frank Sullivan, Howard Dietz, Heywood Broun, Donald Ogden Stewart, Robert Benchley, George S. Kaufman, Robert Sherwood, John V. A. Weaver, Franklin P. Adams and Deems Taylor—but they whooped each other up so diligently that they got a great deal of attention in the newspapers, and so passed among the innocent as the stars of a new Mermaid Tavern or Kit Kat Club. Sara once told me that when she was an undergraduate at Goucher College, early in 1920, she and several other girls saved their money, went to New York and put up at the Algonquin for a few days simply to feast their eyes upon the Round Table celebrities. Nathan and I knew these brethren and were on amicable terms with them, but we regarded all save a few as hollow frauds, and so avoided them as much as possible. Many a time have I seen the old head waiter, George, earn half a dollar by pointing them out to visitors peering at them from the lobby. They greatly enjoyed this notice, and carried on their combats of persiflage in tones loud enough to be heard by other guests in the dining-room.

I am now one of the oldest, if not the very oldest of the regular guests of the Algonquin, and have for many years enjoyed a sort of inside rate on the suite I always occupy. This rate started out at $6 a day, but was later raised to $7 and then to $8: other guests pay $10 for the same accommodation. When, in 1938, Frank Case, the proprietor of the hotel, made plans to publish a volume of reminiscences under the title of *Tales of a Wayward Inn*, and asked me to write a chapter for it, I did so very gladly, and so did some of the survivors of the Round Table, which had disbanded a few years before. But Case told me that when Woollcott was applied to he demanded $1000 cash for a contribution. The success of this book was probably due largely to the chapters by Case's old friends and patrons, for when he followed with two books all his own, *Do Not Disturb* in 1940 and *Feeding the Lions* in 1942, he scored complete failures.

His daughter, Margaret, is a writer of respectable skill, and has done a number of excellent profiles for the *New Yorker*, some of them later collected in books. She was married first to a Jew sporting the fantastic name of Morgan Morgan, and by him had a son; divorced, she married a nonentity named Harriman, and was again divorced. In her writing she uses the name of Margaret Case Harriman. Unhappily, she is given to the bottle, and when in her cups is inclined to be rowdy and even bellicose.

Her father is a somewhat dressy and vain fellow, and as he advanced in years tried to conceal his age. When he appeared in the Monthly Supplement to *Who's Who in America* for June, 1942, he gave the date of his birth as November 27, 1880: he was actually, at that time, close to 70. His second wife, Bertha Walden, is a pleasant woman but became a convert to Christian Science, and found herself in difficulties when she fell seriously ill in 1943.

The Algonquin was gradually redecorated, room by room, under Bertha's supervision, and she made a very good job of it. She and Frank maintained a pleasant atmosphere in the hotel, and held many of their guests for years. In this they were adeptly aided by two of their principal assistants—Mitchell (*geb*. Michel, a Hoboken German), the chief clerk behind the desk, and Miss Bush, the chief telephone operator. Once Case promoted Miss Bush to a clerkship, but soon afterward she was returned to the telephone board. He told me that he had to take her from the desk because she lavished all her time and attention upon the older guests of the house and grossly neglected transients.

CHAPTER XX

As of January 1, 1920, I returned to the staff of the Baltimore *Evening Sun* at $50 a week, and thereafter for twenty years, the first ten of them with high hopes and the second ten with hopes steadily subsiding, I gave almost as much time to its business as to anything else. My writing for the paper was, in theory, confined to one article a week, printed on its editorial page, but I not infrequently took a hand in news reporting, and during the early summer of 1920 covered both of the national conventions, one in Chicago and the other in San Francisco. Also, I was an active participant in all plans for the improvement of the evening paper and the rehabilitation of the morning and Sunday *Suns*, and spent many an evening in palaver with Paul Patterson and Harry C. Black.

As my interest in the *Sunpapers* thus revived, my interest in the *Smart Set* went on declining, but I by no means lost it altogether, and there were times when it put on me a heavy burden of work. I had come to an arrangement with Nathan by this time whereby he was in full charge of the covers, and he carried on our negotiations with artists, but I usually saw a given cover before it was sent to the engraver. They all followed the traditional *Smart Set* formula, with the long red *S*'s in the title, and the cadet-gray background, and most of them showed full-length figures of a man and a woman. These cover designs were mainly atrocious, and the color-plates from which they were printed were even worse, but now and then we printed one that had a certain amount of charm. The best that I recall was done by Archie Gunn for our September, 1919, issue. It was a pretty portrait of the artist's young daughter, and I liked it so much that I collared the painting, which was in oils, had it framed, and hung it in my house in Hollins Street.

The *Smart Set* marked time in 1920, and we depended heavily upon stand-bys for its contents. Our novelettes, in the main, were only trade goods, and no less than six of the twelve were written by Hussey, not to mention two by L. M. Barrett. The other four, however, were much better, for one was by Willa Cather, one by Harvey Fergusson, one by Lilith Benda and one by F. Scott Fitzgerald. We did fairly well with one-act plays, for two were by Fitzgerald, one was by Dunsany and one was by Aldous Huxley. Huxley, in those days, was known only as the grandson of the famous Thomas Henry, one of my heroes. My first contact with him came in 1919, when he reviewed *Prejudices: First Series* in the London *Athenaeum*, of which J. Middleton Murry, the husband of Katherine Mansfield, was then the editor.

At that time I knew nothing of Huxley save that he was the grandson of Thomas Henry, but that was enough to give me double delight in his good opinion. I sent him some more of my books, and in return he sent me his *Limbo*, a collection of short stories, republished soon afterward in the United States. This book struck me as a mixed dish, but there was one story in it, "Happily Ever After," that was really first-rate, and I said so when I reviewed the American edition in the *Smart Set* for August, 1920. Under date of March 12 Huxley sent me a one-act play and a short story, and we printed the play, "Among the Nightingales," in our November issue. Why I refused the story I don't recall, but I gather from another letter from him that it was with thought of the Comstocks, then in violent inflammation in New York. When *Prejudices: Second Series* came out in October I sent him a copy of it, and he apparently liked it as well as the first series.

Toward the end of the year the *Athenaeum* was absorbed by the London *Nation*, and he was forced to go to work for the English edition of the American *House and Garden* to boil the pot. He had been married in 1919 to a young Belgian woman named Maria Nys. In the spring of 1920 the two moved to Florence, for living was cheap there, and Huxley was eager to settle down to a book. I remained in communication with him, and his letters were made gay with salacious characterizations of such bogus eminentissimos of the time as D. H. Lawrence and Clutton-Brock, the latter then the king of London critics. In 1926 he went to the Far East, and on his return home by way of the United States I saw him in New York. He turned out to be an immensely tall and spare fellow, looking startlingly like his distinguished grandfather. He had suffered some injury to his eyes and was forced to use glasses so powerful that they magnified his eyes to the unearthly diameter of those of Ring W. Lardner. Our meeting was at Moneta's restaurant in Mulberry Street, and we got down a hearty dinner and heavy rations of Moneta's excellent bootleg Italian wine.

That, unhappily, was my only meeting with him, though in the late 30's he moved to the United States. He settled in Southern California, and was presently showing one of the characteristic stigmata of the literati of that great state. That is to say, he was writing a book whooping up one of its innumerable resident quacks. This quack offered a method of curing damaged eyes by means of exercise, and Huxley not only professed to have been benefitted by it, but became an ardent propagandist for it. His book on the subject, *The Art of Seeing*, was published in 1942. I never read it, for the thought of a grandson of old Thomas Henry succumbing to a medical charlatan was too much to be borne. By that time I had lost contact with him; indeed, I never heard from him after the end of 1934, and reviewed none of his books after 1926.

Among the other yet remembered names that appeared on the table of contents of the *Smart Set* in 1920 were those of Carl Van Vechten, Vincent O'Sullivan, Elisabeth Sanxay Holding, Stephen Vincent Benét and Hugh Walpole. Two rather curious contributors were Agnes Boulton, then the wife of Eugene O'Neill, and Luis Muñoz Marin, the husband of Muna Lee. La Boulton, a tall, washed-out blonde with a somewhat authoritative air, had married O'Neill as his second wife in 1918 and became the mother of two of his three children. When they were divorced in 1929 she made off with most of his current assets and he was left very hard up. Soon afterward, however, he had a big success in *Mourning Becomes Electra*, and thereafter there were more frequent productions of his earlier plays, so that he was presently in easy waters again. Before the end of 1929 he married Carlotta Monterey.

Marin's contributions to the *Smart Set* consisted of several very short poems. He was then quite unknown. Later on he became a successful politician in his native Puerto Rico, and is now (1945) the political boss of the island. Muna, at last accounts, had a job in the State Department at Washington. Whether or not she and Marin have separated I do not know. She was always a mousy and secretive creature and I have not set eyes on her for years. La Holding, for some years after 1920, was hymned by the newspaper reviewers as a woman of high promise, but she quickly degenerated into a writer of trash. I never reviewed any of her books.

Van Vechten, for many years, was one of the recognized eccentrics of New York. He hailed from Cedar Rapids, Iowa, and was the son of a banker there. Born in 1880, he pursued the humanities at the University of Chicago, and took a Ph.D. degree from it in 1903. He appeared in New York three years later as second-string music critic of the New York *Times,* but I did not meet him until 1916, when he sent me a brief note of thanks for my review in the *Smart Set* for July of his first book, *Music After the Great War.*

He was forever immersing himself in fads. When I first knew him he was not only the chief local fugleman of the more extravagant varieties of exotic music; he was also a proponent of the wildest sort of Greenwich Village *heliogabalisme,* and even went to the length of issuing dark hints that he had taken to homosexuality. Nathan always insisted that these hints had some substance in them, but I presumed to doubt it, for Van Vechten had married an extremely lively and even peppery Russian Jewess, Fania Marinoff, in 1914, and it was hardly believable that she left him any energy for extra-mural activities. His aspect, in some ways, supported the Nathan theory, for he was massive, loose-lipped and flabby, and so showed a considerable resemblance to Oscar Wilde. Also like Wilde, he liked gaudy surroundings, and the small flat that he then occupied, at 151 East 19th Street, was decorated in all the colors of the rainbow. Even many of his books were rebound in staring primary colors, and he had painted the walls behind his bookcases in the sort of red used for steel bridges and box-cars. But unlike Wilde, he did not go in for personal adornment, and his clothes, which commonly fitted him badly, looked as if they were ready-made.

In 1925 or thereabout he announced suddenly that he was an earnest partisan of the suffering Negroes of the country, and after that, for four or five years his apartment—he had moved to 150 West 55th Street—swarmed with the more raffish intellectuals of the race, chiefly writers and musicians. When, after my marriage to Sara in 1930, he and Fania invited us to dine with them, I had to make him promise solemnly that there would be no blackamoors at table, for though Sara had shaken off most of her native Alabama *Kultur,* she still declared that dining with them would make her uneasy. Van Vechten promised, and kept his promise.

The meal, as always at his house, was long and elaborate, and, also as usual, he and Fania embellished it by staging a quarrel that almost amounted to a riot. They were constantly at loggerheads, though they never, so far as I know, separated. Fania, who was an odd fish and very amusing, once confided to Sara that Carl sometimes got drunk and chased her about the apartment with edged tools. He was, in fact, a heavy drinker in those days, and I once saw him, at Alfred Knopf's apartment, drink the better part of a bottle of gin in an evening. He and Fania finally resolved their difficulties by taking two apartments instead of one. These were at 101 Central Park West, and were side by side. Carl occupied one and Fania the other, and from her side she could lock him out at need. After that they got on peacefully, if not exactly amicably. In 1940 or thereabout Carl went on the water-wagon, but how long he remained there I do not know, for I seldom saw either him or Fania after Sara's death in 1935.

He had a brother named Ralph who was a rich Chicago banker, and very proud of Carl. This Ralph was a frequent visitor to both New York and Baltimore, where he was a director of the Fidelity and Deposit Company. In New York he stayed at the Algonquin, and sometimes asked me to the parties he staged in his suite. These parties always consisted of Ralph, a male guest or two, and a swarm of chorus girls and minor actresses. He brought large supplies of whiskey from Chicago, and the proceedings sometimes became very gay. Once, as I recall, I passed out soon after one of his parties began, and was stored on a sofa. When I awoke after an hour or two the party was still in full blast—but with an entirely different set of girls. Ralph had thrown out the first gang and assembled another. He died in 1938 or thereabout, leaving a life estate in his property to his wife— they had no children—with reversion to Carl.

A year or so later the widow politely died, and Carl came in for a substantial amount of money—New York gossip put it at more than $1,000,000. Simultaneously, he announced that he was retiring altogether from the literary life and would devote his whole time thereafter to photography, which had been his dominant fad since 1932, when he retired from colored society. He laid in expensive equipment and built an elaborate dark-room in his half of the Central Park West quarters. Sara and I were among his first sitters. On July 12, 1932, a hot and muggy evening, we had dinner with him and Fania, and afterward sat to him for an hour or more. He made at least two dozen plates, but only a few of them turned out well.

His chosen specialty, it appeared, was portraiture, and during the years following he made many thousands of photographs of persons who, for one reason or another, interested him. He was always curiously reluctant to permit the reproduction of these photographs, though he commonly gave prints to his sitters. He simply hoarded them, apparently with some vague intention of producing a sort of National Portrait Gallery. He, of course, never took money for making them. He is still making photographs (1945), for the fad has lasted much longer than any of his others.

He took to writing novels in 1922, and his first was a fantastic piece called *Peter Whiffle*, which I noticed briefly but favorably in the *Smart Set* for July of that year. I passed over *Excavations* in 1926, and did not review Van Vechten again until late in the same year, when I noticed *Nigger Heaven* in the *American Mercury* for September, grouped with books by Aldous Huxley and Edna Ferber. This was the salient work of Van Vechten's time of enchantment with the darker races, and it seemed to me that he made a pretty good job of it. "His danger," I said, "as a Nordic blond of purest ray serene, was that he would make his hero simply another Nordic blond, perhaps somewhat sunburned; he has evaded that danger with great dexterity. The scenes of revelry in the book, to borrow a Confederatism, are genuinely niggerish. And the people, in the main, are very real."

Unhappily, this tragedy of Harlem did not please the denizens thereof, and its author presently found some of his colored friends looking at him askance. What they objected to principally, it appeared, was the title of the book, for the great crusade to put down that word *nigger* was then in full blast, and its use by even a notorious Negrophile was resented. Van Vechten was much surprised and not a little hurt by this resentment, for he hailed from the upper Middle West and really knew very little about colored folk. All his contact with them had been with a small class of sophisticates, most of them hoping to get something out of him.

But the uproar in the Negro papers was not the worst of the headaches that the book brought to him. Another and even more vexatious came in a claim for damages from a firm of Jewish music-publishers. These prehensile kikes, whose taste and talent for blackmail were well known in New York, though Van Vechten himself seems to have heard nothing of their operations, alleged that a quotation of a few snatches from a current jazz song had violated their copyright, and demanded that they be compensated for their loss, and that the quotations be expunged from the book. How much they asked for at the start I do not know, but Alfred Knopf finally compromised with them for $1,000. Van Vechten, of course, had to pay this money, for publishers' contracts provide that they are to be held harmless for infringements of copyright. Worse, he had to devise a new song to take the place of the one that could be quoted no longer, and this job gave him a hard strain.

After Sara's death I saw very little of him, though we remained in friendly if only occasional communication. He wrote four more books before he finally abandoned beautiful letters for photography, but I reviewed none of them, though they all came out before I ceased, at the end of 1933, to do book reviews. He and Fania sometimes invited me to dinner, but after 1934 I was in New York much less than formerly, and so seldom went.

Van Vechten's talent, at best, was rather slender. He wrote with some skill, and had a deft hand for humor, but his ideas in all departments were so extravagant that he seldom left a lasting impression. He was an amiable fellow, and got along well with Knopf and a large circle of friends. They ranged from fellow writers of the days before 1932 to opera singers, jazz composers, artists and newspaper columnists. He had a fine eye for the grotesque in art, and was the discoverer, I believe, of Miguel Covarrubias, the Mexican caricaturist. He also brought out Langston Hughes, the Negro writer, in 1925, and was of material aid to others of the African race, including especially James Weldon Johnson. His photography, as I have said, is far from first-rate, but inasmuch as he charges his sitters nothing he always has plenty of them.

His wife, Fania, was formerly an actress. She is small in stature, and set beside her tall and portly husband, looks like a tugboat towing an Atlantic liner. Her career on the stage was respectable, but not brilliant: the best role she ever had was that of Ariel in Shakespeare's *The Tempest*. She is given to extremely odd and gaudy dress, and has long been a figure in the upper circles of Broadway. I have often urged her to write her reminiscences, but she appears to be afraid to venture.

It was my custom in those days to print a round-up review of all the new poets once a year, sometimes oftener. These reviews, in the main, were devoted to a barbaric slaughter of newcomers to Parnassus, but now and then I did execution upon older and more pretentious fellows, for example, Alfred Noyes and Cale Young Rice. When Witter Bynner spoofed the critical faculty of the country in 1917 by bringing out a waggishly burlesque volume of the New Poetry under the names of Emanuel Morgan and Anne Knish I was not one of the reviewers who fell for it. Instead I described it as "nothing save a reboiling of the bones of Gertrude Stein, with music by the Greenwich Village *Stadtkapelle* of the cigar-box ukaleles."

One of the frequent *Smart Set* poets of the 1920 period was Jean Allen. This was the maiden name of the daughter of a wealthy New Yorker, then married to another man of wealth. She got rid of her husband and married a young man named Toby Balch, and they got on very well for some years, and had three children, all girls. Then, unexpectedly, Balch died, and she was so desolate that she took rather heavily to drink, which had been her consolation during her unhappy first marriage. She began to write for the *Smart Set* just after it ended—rather strange stuff in free verse, but always intelligent and well made. Nathan and I became acquainted with her, and one day she invited us to dinner at her apartment.

In those days of Prohibition we always took our own drinks with us when we made our first visits to new houses, and that night we toted a bottle of gin, another of Italian vermouth, and a third of absinthe, for our favorite cocktail of the time was concocted of the first two, with a shot of the third. Unhappily, we laid in a couple of drinks before we got to the Allen apartment, and when Nathan undertook to make the cocktails for dinner he made them of two-thirds gin, one third absinthe and a shot of vermouth. The result was that our hostess passed out, both Nathan and I fell down the stairway of her elegant duplex apartment, and Nathan lost his watch in a snowdrift outside the house.

I saw Jean at longish and irregular intervals for years afterward, during which time she married two more husbands. The last time I heard from her she was preparing to leave her fourth, for though he was a kind and generous fellow and very well heeled, he spent all his time fishing, and expected her to travel about with him on his odyssey. She was still a steady customer of the jug, but with her daughters growing up and marrying she had given up writing verse.

CHAPTER XXI

IT HAD BEEN MY PLAN to bring out a volume of *Prejudices* every two years, for they were to be made up largely of selections from my magazine stuff, and I wanted as wide a range of choice as possible, but the pother raised by Series I suggested to Knopf that we had better schedule Series II for 1920 instead of 1921. "I have discovered something," he said to me one day. "It is that H. L. Menchen has become a good property." *Prejudices: Second Series* was accordingly published in October, 1920.

It followed the plan of the first series closely. It opened with a 93-page blast entitled "The National Letters," mainly made up of reworkings of my *Smart Set* reviews and my contributions to "Repetition Generale," but it also included some surplus material left out of the 1922 revision of *In Defense of Women*, under way in 1921, and some revisions of newspaper articles, for example, "The Sahara of the Bozart," from the New York *Evening Mail*, and "The Divine Afflatus" from the same paper. "Exeunt Omnes" came from the *Smart Set* for December, 1919, and "Roosevelt: An Autopsy" was mainly lifted from my book article in the issue for March, 1920. "The National Letters" was based upon an article called "The National Literature" which I contributed to the *Yale Review* for June, 1920, but there was material in it from "Observations Upon the National Letters" in the *Smart Set* for July of the same year, "Notes and Queries" in the issue for September, and various other book articles.

From this time forward I kept the *Prejudices* books in mind in all my magazine and newspaper work, and not infrequently an idea that was first tried out in the Baltimore *Evening Sun* was later expanded and embellished in the *Smart Set* or some other magazine, and then finally polished for book form. This preparedness made the putting together of the successive *Prejudices* relatively easy. I did, of course, a good deal of rewriting but I also did a lot of mere pasting in, and my scissors and pot were worked almost as hard as my typewriter. From the first volume onward I provided each of the *Prejudices* books with an adequate index. Making it was tedious work, but I believed that that work was well expended.

The reviews of *Prejudices: Second Series* paid relatively little attention to the contents of the book, but were devoted mainly to discussions of the author. I had suddenly become, by the end of 1920, a sort of symbol of all the disillusionment following World War I, and was credited with a leadership in dissent that I did not want, and tried constantly to avoid. The messianic passion was simply not in me, then or afterward; indeed, it is probable that no articulate American ever lived who had less taste for the shroud of the evangelist. It was thus somewhat disconcerting for me to discover that I was becoming the text of all sorts of manifestos and homilies by propagandists of a score of warring sects, and the frequent theme of editorials by the dull idiots who write such things, and a favorite subject of debate in the colleges and women's clubs. The pedagogues of the land, of course, were against me almost to a man, and tried their best to stem the rising tide of interest in me among the youth they afflicted.

I found myself a champion of the students against their professors, and this unwilling role afflicted me for fifteen years afterward. I became, on the one hand, a constant point of reference in the campus revolts that then went on throughout the American colleges, and on the other hand I was besought with great frequency to come to this or that campus and harangue the rebels on the issues of the hour. Having, as I have said, no taste for saving humanity, and being, moreover, averse to making speeches, I refused all these invitations. In all my life, in fact, I talked to college boys but once, and that violation of my rules was forced on me in 1926, when the Harvard students staged a demonstration in my support when I tackled the Boston wowsers on Boston Common. But the invitations came on pouring in, and sometimes they were underwritten by the sassier faction of young tutors. Unhappily, I preserved none of these invitations, for I have always made a practice to destroy mail of no permanent interest. But there have been times since when I have doubted that such letters were as little interesting as I thought they were when they came in. If I had them today they would throw an illuminating light upon the play of opinion on American campuses in the 1920's.

Of the things that went into *Prejudices: Second Series*, as opposed to my current *Smart Set* stuff, the one that made the greatest uproar was my revision and expansion of "The Sahara of the Bozart." When it appeared originally in the New York *Evening Mail*, which had only a small circulation outside New York City, it seems to have been missed by the sub-Potomac editorial writers, but now they all became suddenly and painfully aware of it, and many of them had at me with great ferocity. The stuff these heroes printed was so amusing that I decided to throw some gasoline upon their flames, and in the *Smart Set* for August, 1921, I printed "The South Begins to Mutter." In this article, under cover of praising three Southern magazines that showed some impatience with the circumambient imbecility—*All's Well*, published by Charles J. Finger at Fayetteville, Arkansas; the *Double-Dealer*, published at New Orleans by a small group of young intellectuals, nearly all of them Jews; and the *Reviewer*, set up at Richmond, Virginia, in February, 1921, by a rebellious young woman named Emily Clark, with the imprimatur of James Branch Cabell— I piled insult on insult. Save for a few walled towns, I declared, the South was so far steeped in savagery that civilized men not only refused to live in it, but even avoided visiting it. "I know New Yorkers," I said, "who have been in Cochin China, Kafiristan, Paraguay, Somaliland and West Virginia, but not one who has ever penetrated the miasmatic jungles of Arkansas." This device worked very effectively, and the second wave of denunciation was ten times as violent as the first.

Meanwhile, a number of the more intelligent Southern newspapers took to discussing my allegations with some rationality and tolerance, and even with mild approval. This heretical party gradually gained recruits, and in the course of time the theory began to be heard that "The Sahara of the Bozart" had really done the South a valuable service, and was responsible for the resuscitation of its literature. I have since read many an article, written by a Southerner and printed in the South, which credited me formally with having set off such Southern authors of the new generation as Erskine Caldwell, William Faulkner, Frances Newman and even Thomas Wolfe. Thus I became once more a prophet in spite of myself.

In the North the reviews of *Prejudices: Second Series* were evenly divided between praise and denunciation, and most of them were discussions of me rather than of the book. A good many of the reviewers tried to account for and dispose of me by labelling me, and I was likened variously to George Bernard Shaw, Nietzsche, Brann the iconoclast and Elbert Hubbard! A few papers—for example, the Chicago *Tribune*—came out for me without qualification, but the majority were more cautious, and not a few expressed the opinion, plainly born of a hope, that Stuart P. Sherman had finished me, once and for all time. The debate over my ideas throughout the country had curious repercussions in Baltimore, where the notion that a local newspaper man could become a national figure caused astonishment, and even a kind of resentment.

In 1920 I saw books of mine listed, for the first time, in an antiquarian bookseller's catalogue. The bookseller was Meredith Janvier of Baltimore, and he asked $6 for *Pistols for Two* and $20 for an autographed first edition of *The American Language*, then only a year old. I was so delighted that I gave him the typescripts of two chapters, "Roosevelt: An Autopsy" and "The Sahara of the Bozart," in *Prejudices: Second Series*. Soon afterward he was offering the first for $25 and the second for $15. In September, 1921, the booksellers' trade-journal, *Biblio*, reported that, during the three months ending August 30, my books ranked eighth among the American first editions advertised for. In October they went up to third place, and that place they also held in November. On June 11, 1921, the New York *Evening Mail* listed Nathan and me among persons who "need no press-agents," along with Margot Asquith, Lloyd George, William J. Bryan, Andrew Volstead and Babe Ruth.

Knopf, in the 1920s era, was young, energetic and full of enterprise, and the rising sales of my books owed a good deal to his merchandising. Remembering the extraordinary success of *Pistols for Two* in 1917, he decided in 1920 to bring out a similar pamphlet devoted to my books to date, and the result was *H. L. Mencken*, bound in the same old-rose laid paper that had been used for *Pistols for Two*. Its contents were "Fanfare" by Burton Rascoe, then literary editor of the Chicago *Tribune;* a reprint of Vincent O'Sullivan's article, "The American Critic," in the London *New Witness* for November 28, 1919; a bibliography of my books down to and including *Prejudices: Second Series;* and a short list of articles about me in various American and foreign publications. The bibliography was signed by F. C. Henderson, an imaginary person: I actually did it myself. The pamphlet included a photograph of me by Meredith Janvier of Baltimore, a reproduction of a pencil drawing by Willem Wirtz, one of an imaginary portrait called "The Subconscious Mencken," by McKee Barclay, and one of the title pages of *Ventures into Verse*. The Rascoe contribution was destined to plague me for years. It actually gave Rascoe himself a great lift in credit, if only by coupling his name with mine, but he lived to claim (and probably believe) that it had made me, and to make various unpleasant attempts to cash in on that illusion. How many copies of the pamphlet were circulated I do not know, but it must have been a large number. Not a few newspapers reviewed it as if it were a book, just as *Pistols for Two* had been reviewed. I also undertook some discreet propaganda of my own, either alone or with Nathan.

When, on June 24, 1920, the Rev. A. C. Dieffenbach, editor of the *Christian Register*, printed a complimentary editorial on me, I had it reprinted in a small eight-page brochure bearing a cross on the cover, and got a lot of fun out of slipping it into letters. This Dieffenbach was a Marylander and had started out in life as a pastor in the Reformed church of his German forebears. In 1914 he flopped to Unitarianism and was called to a church in Hartford, Connecticut, and in 1918 he quit the pulpit to become editor of the *Christian Register* of Boston, the chief organ of the Unitarians. He held this job until 1933, when he became religious editor of the Boston *Transcript*. When the *Transcript* suspended in 1941 he undertook a sort of jobbing business among the Unitarian churches in the Boston area, and at last accounts (1945) was still so engaged.

I knew him well and found him amiable but not too intelligent. Like any other theologian who sought to get rid of the magic and wonder in Christianity, he found himself involved in numerous logical dilemmas, and beset by doubts whether the game, in the last analysis, was worth the candle. On his occasional visits to Baltimore, going to and from his native *Dorf* in Carroll County, Maryland, I took him on for solemn debates, and had a lot of fun trying to convince him that he was really an atheist. But at a time when I was being belabored as one myself, and as an agent of the German immoralists to boot, it was amusing to circulate his pastoral certificate.

This plan of goading enemies into spreading my name was one that

I often practiced, as I have lately recorded in the case of "The Sahara of the Bozart." It put the labor of *reclaim* upon them, and testified to my contempt for their ill will. Moreover, it enabled me to avoid all the kinds of advertising more commonly practiced by authors and editors—for example, writing blurbs for books, sitting on public committees, going to public dinners, making speeches, giving readings before women's clubs, signing manifestos, belonging to clubs and coteries, and so on and so on.

In my early days as a literary critic I was inveigled into doing blurbs for a number of books that I admired, but I soon concluded that it was a foolish practice, for one such complaisance led to another, and it was often almost impossible to avoid doing for B what one had already done for A. All publishers, of course, sought such helps to their selling technique with shameless persistence; what surprised me was the discovery that many authors, and some of them of considerable position, were quite as brazen. I soon made the rule that nothing of mine could be used in the promotion of a book until after it had appeared in print as part of a review, and to that rule I have stuck with very few deviations. In my day as an active reviewer it kept my name off slip-covers pretty effectively, for I made no effort to print my reviews promptly: they never came out in advance of publication, and very often they were delayed for six months or more afterward.

I was content to leave the blurb industry to men who appeared to delight in it: for example, William Lyon Phelps and, later on, Alexander Woollcott. There were times, in the later 1920's, when a dozen books were simultaneously current, each adorned with eloquent praise by both Phelps and Woollcott, but it was seldom indeed that one appeared bearing an encomium from me. I knew better ways of getting publicity than that, and they all had the advantages of separating me sharply from the other reviewers of the time. That was always my principal aim—to stand aloof from the general, and to make plain as dramatically as possible my differences from and contempt for the general. It was thus to my interest to be denounced more than to be praised, and I sometimes went to great efforts, not always ingenuous, to bring that about.

It was for the same reason that I refused to join literary coteries, or to take part in public shindigs as a literary character. I joined the Authors' League in 1916 or 1917 in order to get some help for my defense of Dreiser against the Comstocks, but as soon as the business was over I resigned, and never went back. The league was a useful agency to writers attempting the conventional things, but there was nothing in this programme that would have benefitted me: on the contrary, it would have done me harm, if only by bringing me into more or less intimate contact with a huge swarm of what Huneker used to call tripe-sellers.

In the same way I refused, save in the case of Dreiser, to sign public manifestos, or to go to public dinners: the only one of the latter that I ever attended, so far as I can recall, was one given in tribute to Jimmie Walker, then a state senator, for his success in killing a new and worse Comstock act projected by the Society for the Prevention of Vice. A magazine editor in New York receives invitations to such affairs in great numbers; indeed, no publisher ever gives a dinner, a luncheon or a cocktail party to one of his authors without inviting all the editors likely to be of use of him. Nor are they ever overlooked when the executive secretaries of ostensibly altruistic organizations go seeking whom they may feed, flatter and devour. I refuse all such invitations, though not infrequently they came from men who had, in one way or another, been of service to me.

I was interested for many years in the work of the American Civil Liberties Union, and made more than one contribution to its special fund for defending free speech, but I always refused to join it. As I have already said, I also refused all the numerous invitations that reached me to harangue college students, women's clubs and other groups and organizations, and whenever I made a speech, which was seldom indeed, it was always because of circumstances that vitiated all my usual excuses. On such rare occasions I usually left my audience far from satisfied, and was never bothered again from that quarter.

CHAPTER XXII

ATHAN GOT A FREE RIDE upon a lot of the publicity I began to get after 1919, but I did not begrudge it, for he was taking over more and more of the routine work of the *Smart Set*, and so giving me time for the labors that were thrown upon me by my new association with the Baltimore *Sunpapers* and my various other enterprises. His editorship was a great deal more useful to him than mine was to me, for it gave him an office in New York, and hence a place to see people without asking them to his small apartment in the Royalton at 44 West 44th Street. I cared nothing for seeing people, and had no desire to widen my circle of acquaintances in New York. Moreover, I aimed all my professional shots, not at New York, but at the country in general and the world beyond, whereas he was pretty well confined to the local theatre-going audience of Broadway, and in fact has nothing to offer any other.

I have related how I urged him to break away from play reviewing and attempt something on a larger scale, and how his somewhat feeble and timorous efforts in that direction always failed. One of these took visible form in *The American Credo*, begun in the *Smart Set* in June, 1919, and published by Knopf as a book in 1920. I contributed at least half of the four hundred eighty-eight articles included in the first edition, and wrote the whole of the long preface, which filled more than half the volume and gave me a capital chance to plaster the super-patriots of the war years. But Nathan did a fair share of the work of editing, and we agreed to divide the proceeds fifty-fifty. Knopf was somewhat dubious about the venture, for Nathan's own books seldom sold above two thousand copies, and their sales had an unpleasant habit of dropping to next to nothing before the end of the first year after publication. The size of the first edition I do not know, for all royalty statements were sent to Nathan and I received only an occasional carbon, but it must have been small, for it was soon exhausted, and at the end of 1921 we brought out a second.

In the latter the four hundred eighty-eight articles of popular belief in the first edition were increased to eight hundred sixty-nine and there was a "preface to the revised and enlarged edition" by Nathan, in which he gave profuse thanks to a number of imaginary authorities on folklore—for example, Mr. Aubrey Donaldson, M.A., Reader in Comparative Mythology at Oxford, and Prof. Dr. Gustav Simmelmeyer, of the University of Zurich—who had, so he pretended, given us learned aid and comfort. Most of the additions to the first printing actually came from readers in the United States, though Nathan himself provided us a good many. We had, when we finished the first edition, a surplus consisting of twenty-nine articles that we could not include in it because of the Comstocks, and these we put into a four-page leaflet, with the articles numbered from four hundred ninety-nine—an error for four hundred eighty-nine—to five hundred twenty-six, and the pagination running from one hundred ninety-three to one hundred ninety-six. Where we had this leaflet printed I do not recall, but I think it was in New York. The edition was limited to 100 copies for friends and was exhausted instantly. Within a few weeks, in fact, offers of $5 and even $10 were being made for it, and if a copy turned up today it would probably bring much more. I lost interest in *The American Credo* after the second edition, and in 1926 made over all my rights in it to Nathan. He then talked of bringing out a third edition, but whether or not he did so I do not remember.

The Knopf press department, in 1920, was very energetic and resourceful, and sent out many paragraphs that made long strings of paper. In April, 1920, it launched this one:

As a critic H. L. Mencken shows a certain bellicosity, but from the viewpoint of his publisher he is almost a perfect model of the tame author. He never accepts an advance on royalties; never offers any suggestions as to how his books ought to be printed and marketed; never complains about the way they are advertised, and always pays spot cash for the copies that he gives away. Moreover, whenever his publisher, Alfred A. Knopf, visits him in Baltimore he always has the cook prepare a special mess of Maryland delicacies for the visitor and gives him a couple bottles of 6% St. Louis beer, laid down in 1917.

Most of this was true enough. I had gone on with Knopf only a little way when I became convinced that he could be trusted to take care of his share of our joint enterprises without any suggestions from me. He was a diligent student of the new school of book design then rising in Germany, and he adapted its ideas to American conditions with great skill, and also reinforced them with excellent ideas of his own. If the history of the book in the United States is ever written, he must have credit in it for what amounted to a revolution.

Stone & Kimball and R. H. Russell had made some effort, before his time, to throw off the conventions that made American books generally flat and funereal in aspect, with formalized covers and ungraceful type pages, but nearly all the older publishers remained unaffected by these innovations. But when Knopf took the stage they had to heed him, for it not infrequently happened that the format of one of his books got as much attention in the reviews as its contents. By 1920 they were all imitating him, including even such ancient and hunkerous houses as Harper and Scribner, and all the newer publishers were his open disciples. He worked the same reform in magazine design with the *American Mercury* in 1924, and within a year *Harper's* and the *Atlantic* scrapped their old covers and took to following his lead.

In all my days I have never offered, or even harbored *in petto*, any criticism of his advertising of my books—a frequent theme of complaint among authors. In this field, as in manufacturing, he did his work wisely and well—at all events during his first ten years. After that the growth of his business, stimulated by the somewhat grandiose projects of his father, Samuel Knopf, forced him to farm out many of the details that he had hitherto looked to himself, and there was some letting down. But it was not much. To this day he makes books that, taking one with another, are more sightly than those of any other American publisher, and some of those that he has produced for me, notably the fourth edition of *The American Language* and Supplement I thereof, have been masterpieces of sound design. Since the 1930's the actual designer of my books has been W. A. Dwiggins, a man of the highest skill. More than once, on my first glimpse of Dwiggins' proofs, I have been considerably surprised and even perturbed, but in every case I have let him and Knopf have their way, and in every case I have been convinced later on that they were right.

It is usual for an author to receive ten free copies of his own book but from *A Book of Prefaces* onward Knopf has always given me twenty-five. These, and such other copies as I have bought, have mainly gone to private friends, for the copies sent to literati in the hope of attracting blurbs have been handled by Knopf. My private list, unhappily, has shown a steady tendency to expand, and even so early as *Prejudices: First Series*, there were, as an old account-book shows, fifty-two names on it. On the *Heliogabalus* list there were fifty, on the *Prejudices: Second Series* list sixty-six, and on the *Prejudices: Third Series* list no less than seventy-one—in the last case mainly because I sent copies to a dozen or more acquaintances made in Germany on my trip there in 1922. But after that I began to develop a prudent stinginess, so that my *Prejudices: Fourth Series* list was reduced to forty-six and my *Prejudices: Fifth Series* list was held at fifty-one. By 1945 I had got down the list for Supplement I to *The American Language* to thirty-five. I had hoped to bring it even lower, but the number of persons who *ask* for a new book is astonishing, and sometimes it is difficult to resist them.

I have always refused to take advances on my books, and I have urged Knopf, for many years, to cease giving them to other authors. More than once, sitting at the board table of Alfred A. Knopf, Inc., I have heard him report substantial payments to frauds who have made off without producing anything printable—payments that have swelled unpleasantly the profit-and-loss account of the company. He insists, however, that he must follow the trade practice, or lose good books. As for me, I'd rather lose them than pay tribute to a gang of swindlers. Very few really competent and worthwhile writers, I am convinced, would go away if advances were suspended—and the money now wasted upon them might be used to increase the royalties of men and women who produce profit for the house. But the publishing business, like every other American business, is burdened with many evil precedents and traditions, and such vain expenditures are among them. I have known authors, notably Ernest Boyd, who lived for years on publishers' advances without turning in a single profitable book. Boyd, in fact, got many such payments without turning in anything at all—and some of them came from Knopf.

The reference to my supply of pre-Prohibition beer in the communiqué of the Knopf press-bureau needed to be taken with more than a grain of salt, for the supply was not very large, and by the time Prohibition went into force officially, on January 16, 1920, it was pretty well exhausted. The alcohol content of all malt liquors was reduced in 1917, and as a result they did not keep. Some of the Trommer's *Dunkles* that I had laid in went bad on me, and so did some of the Anheuser-Busch "Faust." Early in 1919 I was told by my friend Harry Rickel of Detroit, a lawyer whose family had been in the malt business for years and who knew a lot about it, that home-brewing was quite feasible, and soon I was making experiments. The first were failures, but under Rickel's tutelage I soon acquired some skill, and by the spring my brother August and I were making quite potable brews. On April 5, 1919, I wrote to Philip Goodman: "I am experimenting with a light *Goldbrau* made of Czecho-Slovakian hops and running to 4.75% by volume." Goodman was inspired to tackle brewing himself, for he was an enormous beer-drinker, and soon we were busily exchanging ideas.

I saw Goodman frequently on my visits to New York, and as his skill as a brewer gradually developed often dined with him and his charming wife at their apartment. Lily Goodman, who had an excellent Hungarian cook, usually put on a roast goose, and her husband and I—he was a truly colossal eater—devoured it with loud grunts and gloats, and washed it down with home-brew. I also saw a good deal of Ernest Boyd, whom I had first met in Baltimore in 1914. After six years in the British consular service he resigned in 1920 and settled in New York, and thereafter, for ten years, I seldom made a trip there without having an evening with him.

Another of my constant companions was T. R. Smith. Smith, a native of New Jersey, had spent some time in England in his early youth, and had picked up certain English intonations and mannerisms, but he was otherwise an amiable and merry fellow, and I was very fond of him. He was doing a good job with the *Century*, despite the fact that he was afflicted with a publisher, M. Lincoln Shuster, whose training for literary enterprises had been got as a federal job-holder, and a titular editor, Glenn Frank, whose platitudinous editorials gave him the shivers. Smith had a wife hidden somewhere or other, and also a daughter, but I never met either of them, for in the days of our frequent foregatherings he kept bachelor's hall in an apartment house at 229 West 105th Street, bearing the strange name of the Esperanto. It was a housekeeping flat, but when Prohibition loomed into sight Tom cleared out the kitchen, which was quite large, and stacked it to the ceiling with cases of wines and liquors. Until this huge supply ran out he gave frequent tumultuous mixed parties, and Nathan and I often attended them.

He had a library that was curious. The major part of it consisted of decorous volumes of English modern history; the rest was pornographia. This pornographia was mainly illustrated, and I recall that its pearl was a portfolio of original drawings by Clara Tice, an artist of the time who was one of his friends. Every new woman guest was handed this portfolio to inspect, apparently on the theory that it would arouse her baser nature, but so far as I know it never worked, at least to Tom's profit. He was, in fact, not much of a wrecker of women: all his energies went into boozing. When, in 1921, he became literary adviser to Horace Liveright, the lines of his life ran precisely to his taste, for Liveright was also a considerable boozer and also a connoisseur of pornography. Tom never turned out for work until noon, but Liveright did not seem to object.

Two or three times a week they gave cocktail parties in their office, with gangs of chorus girls to make them gay. I never went to any of these parties, for I disliked Liveright, but I continued to see Tom at his apartment, and he, Nathan and I often had dinner together at the Brevoort, which was Tom's favorite downtown eating-house. In 1921 he compiled a *Poetica Erotica* in two large volumes, dedicated to "Henry L. Mencken and George Jean Nathan in friendship," and published by Liveright in fifteen hundred numbered sets "for subscribers only." The published price was $25 and Tom counted on getting a substantial revenue from the work, but it sold only slowly.

One evening in the latter part of 1920 Nathan and I went up to 105th Street to wait on Tom, and there found one of his usual parties assembled. There were two or three women and four or five men. We knew all save one of the guests, who was introduced as Sinclair Lewis. Lewis had published nothing, up to that time, save a few light novels that had been *Saturday Evening Post* serials, and I had never reviewed any of them, nor read them. He was, as always in society, far gone in liquor, and when he fastened upon me with a drunkard's zeal, declaring that he had lately finished a novel of vast and singular merits full worthy of my most careful critical attention, I tried hard to shake him off. But shaking off Lewis when he was in his cups was no easy task, and long before the usual time for departing I got hold of Nathan and proposed to him that we clear out. He agreed readily, and we were soon on Broadway, walking downtown.

"Can you imagine such a jackass," I said, "writing a book worth reading?"

Nathan couldn't imagine it.

"Never again!" he said. "If Tom Smith has taken to such nuisances, then I'll never go to his house again."

The next day I returned to Baltimore, and before leaving the *Smart Set* office gathered up an armful of review books to examine on the train. Among them was a set of proofs from Harcourt, Brace & Company. Ordinarily, I refused to read books in proof, for handling the loose sheets was an unpleasant chore, but this time, on a sudden and aberrant impulse, I took up the sheaf as soon as the train plunged into the Pennsylvania tunnel. By the time it got to Newark I was interested, and by the time it got to Trenton I was fascinated. At Philadelphia I called a Western Union boy and sent a telegram to Nathan. I forget the exact text, but it read substantially: "That idiot has written a masterpiece." The book was *Main Street*.

ALL THE WHILE I knew Sinclair Lewis he was either a drunkard or a teetotaler, so my relations with him never became what could be called intimate, for I am ill at ease with any man who is either. I saw most of him during the first eleven years of our acquaintance, from 1920 to 1931, and at times got a reasonable amount of pleasure out of his society, for he was an acute observer of types and an excellent mimic, and some of the imitations that he liked to give in company were really excellent. Moreover, the study of his psyche entertained me, for I learned at a very early stage that he was consumed by an inferiority complex, and it amused me to observe his innocent delight in the praise of persons far beneath him in intelligence and ability, and his abject subservience to his wife, Grace Hegger.

When Red (as all of his friends always called him) married Gracie in 1914 she was a very minor functionary in the office of *Vogue*, and no one paid any attention to her, but after *Main Street* and *Babbitt* made her husband a celebrity, she began to put on airs, and before long had converted herself into a fake English duchess, with a broad Oxford accent and a very haughty way with poor Red. She was, indeed, a poisonous woman, and I avoided her as much as possible. Our first meeting must have been early in 1921. Red called me up one day in New York, told me that he and Gracie were dining that evening with a rich pencil manufacturer named Faber at his house in Fifth Avenue, and asked me to drop in afterward—on the specious but not convincing plea that Faber was an ardent customer of mine. I agreed to come, for I was eager to hear more about *Babbitt*, which was already under way.

When I got to the place I found that Faber was a dull fellow who had barely heard of me, that Red was drunk and in a high state of animation, and that Gracie was fuming against him and the world in general. I took no notice of Gracie but confined myself to Red. When the party broke up I squired her and her husband home to their hotel, and in the taxi found myself the butt of one of her tirades. What I had done to offend her, save neglecting to pay her the attention she thought she rated, I do not know to this day. Nor do I recall the precise nature of her objurgations. All I can recall is that she had at me with great fury the moment the taxi started, and kept on until we reached the hotel. Taking my cue from her husband, I let her roar without answering. She was herself a little tight, and I myself was far from cold sober. The next time I saw her she was polite enough, but I had had a taste of her ring style, and kept away from her as much as possible.

Gracie led poor Red a rough dance, and all his friends were sorry for him. The aforesaid inferiority complex made it simply impossible for him to stand up to her. He lived in wonder that so ravishing and brilliant a female had ever condescended to marry him. She was, in fact, a good-looking and well-turned-out woman, but I could never discover any evidence that she was of superior mentality. On the contrary, she was vain and shallow. One evening in 1927 I was a guest of Walter Wanger, a rising man in movie production, and his wife at their apartment in New York, and found Red and Gracie there too. Red, as always, got drunk, and was presently engaged in reciting a long monologue that he had lately concocted, supposedly spoken by an imbecile Rotarian who claimed some sort of acquaintance with Calvin Coolidge, then President. I had heard it several times before, but urged Red to do it again, for the edification of the company. He was willing enough, but Gracie objected violently on the ground that it bored her, and when he began in spite of her—a rather unusual show of contumacy—she screamed in the manner of a stock-company actress, threw herself belly-down upon a couch, and kicked her legs. I thereupon led Red to another room, and there gave audience to him in peace. The recitation was longer every time I heard it, and showed new humors. After hard effort I finally induced him to put it on paper, and in January, 1928, I printed parts of it in the *American Mercury* under the title of "The Man Who Knew Coolidge." It had no title when I first heard it, and it is my recollection that I gave it the one under which it was printed.

It was the fashion in the Cocktail Age for married women of any pretensions to have followers, and Gracie soon acquired one in a man who alleged that his name was Telesforo Casanova and that he was a Spanish count. Nathan and I suspected that he was actually a Grand Street Jew, and diligently spread a tale to that effect, but Gracie took him at face value, and was vastly flattered by his attentions. Her flaunting of them caused a great deal of malicious snickering at Red, and he found that his inferiority complex was not enough to console him.

One day he came to lunch with me at my apartment in the Algonquin, told me at great length the tale of Gracie's *attentats* against his husbandly honor, and burst into hysterical tears at the table. Another time I invited him and Gracie to dinner at a restaurant in Hoboken, along with Philip and Lily Goodman, and Gracie insisted on bringing Casanova along. It was an unpleasant situation, and the Casanova made it worse by taking a seat beside Gracie, and stroking her bare arm throughout the dinner, the while she purred at him ecstatically. Red was white with rage and Lily Goodman was so scandalized that she would never meet Gracie afterward, but there was nothing to do about it at the time.

That Gracie and Casanova were taking frequent headers through the Seventh Commandment was believed by everyone who knew them, and certainly Red must have been aware of it, but it was not until early 1928 that he got up enough courage, obviously under the prodding of his second-wife-to-be, Dorothy Thompson, to insist upon a separation. Gracie then went to Reno—accompanied by Casanova!—and on April 16, 1928, got a divorce there. She naturally seized the opportunity to punish poor Red as hard as possible. She demanded and got the custody of their son, Wells, born in 1917, and she stood out for alimony of $1,000 a month.

Soon after the divorce she married Casanova and wrote a vituperative novel, *Half a Loaf*, which purportedly described the horror of her life with Red. It must have been anything but pleasant, for he was drunk three-fourths of the time during those years, and when he was drunk he was often noisy and a nuisance. Casanova, in the days when he was first heard of, had a small job in a brokerage house, but after he married Gracie and got command of her $12,000 a year he began to rise in the world, and at last accounts was the agent in Mexico City for a large firm of Wall Street brokers. Gracie, in the first days of Red's glory, subscribed herself Gracie *Sinclair* Lewis, but that did not last long.

In 1931, again under the prodding of Dorothy, Red asked the district court at Carson City to reduce his alimony payment to $200 a month, but with the provision that Gracie would get one-fourth of his annual income up to the amount of $12,000 a year, in case he should make $48,000 or more. The district court agreed, and on September 5 the Supreme Court of Nevada, on a hearing of an appeal from Gracie, affirmed the order. Gracie, in her appeal, did not mention Dorothy, but contented herself with alleging that he had undergone "a change of feeling and attitude" toward her, and that his application for a reduction in her alimony was suggested by his "hatred, resentment and antipathy for her rather than any falling off of his income."

Her affectation of elegance and consequence played sad tunes upon his inferiority complex, and he was always submissive under her tyrannies. She at least had the advantage of being presentable. Dressed up in her best finery, she was a very attractive woman, and it was not until she began to lose her pseudo-English accent and her Long Island society airs that the good impression she made began to fade.

The transition from her to Dorothy must have been a shock even to Red, though he made it in an alcoholic haze. Dorothy was the daughter of a one-horse Methodist preacher in a small town near Buffalo, and she looked it, talked it and acted it. Born in 1894, she got an A.B. from Syracuse University in 1914, and then took to so-called social work. Where she performed this work I do not know, but by 1920 she was a newspaper reporter, and had got a job with the Philadelphia *Public Ledger*, then owned by Cyrus H. K. Curtis, the enormously rich publisher of the *Ladies' Home Journal* and the *Saturday Evening Post*. Curtis was ambitious to build up a paper of high influence and authority, and to that end undertook to establish a comprehensive foreign service. But the correspondents he chose to man this service were all third-raters and it turned out a dismal failure, as did the *Ledger* itself.

Dorothy was sent to Vienna in 1920, there learned what passed sufficiently for German, and in 1924 was promoted to the Berlin post, and made chief of all the Curtis Central European correspondents. Meanwhile, in 1923, she had married a highly dubious Jew named Josef Bard, and thereafter he lived on her. The legend is that she met Red in an airship on the way from Berlin to Vienna, whither both were bound to have a look at one of the uprisings of the time, but this was denied by Red himself in London in 1928: they were actually introduced, he said, at the German Foreign Office.

Whatever the fact, he was no doubt in his cups at the time, for he was drunk during his whole stay in Europe that winter and spring. Now and then, to be sure, he melodramatically renounced whiskey, brandy and even wine, and went on an all-beer diet, but the amount of beer he got down was always enough to keep him in a haze. But despite this infirmity he was a distinguished novelist and in receipt of large revenues, and when Dorothy compared him to her parasitical lord and reflected on the fact that the *Ledger* was going downhill and she would soon be out of a job, he looked pretty good, and she resolved to corral him. He seems to have made some resistance, and there is even reason for believing that he undertook flight, but she was a resolute, two-fisted woman, and by May 14, 1928, she had him at bay in a London registry office, and they were made man and wife.

When they reached New York and put up at the Algonquin the infernal heat of August was in full blast, and it was hard upon both of them, especially upon Dorothy, who had lived in Europe for eight years. I well recall my first meeting with her. It was at breakfast the morning after their arrival, and we sat at table looking out on 44th Street, in a really dreadful glare of light. Poor Dorothy, who turned out to be on the plump side, with a distressing appearance of over-tight lacing, sweated like a colored bishop in fly-time. The perspiration, running down her forehead, continued along her nose, and then fell off in pink drops, colored by her make-up. Her cheeks, meanwhile, became sloughs of whitish, sticky mud. She appeared to suffer severely, and I was glad when the meal was over, and she could escape upstairs to renovate herself.

I gathered from this first meeting that she was far more intelligent than Gracie, but almost equally pretentious and cocksure. She was, I think, a little shy in my presence, for Red had apparently told her that he owed an enormous debt to my advocacy, but her shyness did not go far enough to make her conceal from me that she was familiar to the last detail with all the intricate politics of Europe, and full of secret knowledge of the progress of future events. I found her, alas, unattractive, and my congratulations to Red were so forced that even he must have detected their artificiality.

Soon afterward, at Dorothy's urging, Red began to look for a farm in New Hampshire. Hitherto, he had owned no place of his own, but had been a sort of nomad, living in no spot more than a few months. I believe that Dorothy had hopes that a rural life would reduce his excessive drinking, and that New Hampshire was chosen because it was far from big cities and in a region generally supposed to be almost dry.

When I heard from Red he wrote from Connett Farm, Woodstock, Vermont. It was thus Vermont, not New Hampshire, but they looked alike to me, and both seemed very remote. Red and Dorothy urged me to visit them, but I kept on putting it off from summer to summer, and it was not until that of 1931 that I made the trip. Meanwhile, Red had been awarded and accepted the Nobel Prize for 1930, greatly to my distress, for I believed and had often advised him that he should resolutely refuse all prizes, college degrees and other such empty honors, leaving them to the muckers who pulled wires for them. When, in 1922, he was elected a member of the National Institute of Arts and Letters, it was at my urging that he declined it with scorn, and when, in 1926, the Pulitzer Prize was awarded to him for *Arrowsmith*, it was again on my motion that he brushed it away.

But the ambitious and go-getting Dorothy was avid for honors and attention, no matter how cheap, and when, in 1930, they took the lordly form of the Nobel Prize she naturally grabbed for it with loud hosannahs. If I had heard of this award in time I'd certainly have made some effort to induce Red to decline it, for I had long been convinced that the Stockholm Academy, which chose the recipients of the prizes for literature, was a diligent player of politics. It would be impossible on any other ground to account for its choice of Carl Spitteler the Swiss in 1919, Wladyslaw Reymont the Pole in 1924, and the Italian woman writer, Deledda, in 1926. All of these were plainly third-raters, but Italy had not been honored since 1906 nor Poland since 1905, and Switzerland had never got a prize at all, though Belgium had got one, Denmark and Sweden had got two each, and Norway had got three, so the neglected had to have their turns. Hitler, I believe, was quite right when he denounced the whole Nobel Prize set-up as dubious and forbade any German to accept an award.

Red, who knew very well that, if any American deserved to be chosen, it was Dreiser, was in a prime position to strike a blow against this thimble-rigging, and at the same time to make himself immortal, for though George Bernard Shaw had pretended to refuse the award in 1925 he had nevertheless taken the money. Red himself didn't need it, for his royalties from *Dodsworth* were still flowing in, and he was getting large checks from the popular magazines. Unhappily, I was en route from Joe Hergesheimer's place at West Chester, Pennsylvania, when the news came out on November 30, and it was not until late in the afternoon that I reached the *American Mercury* office and found a telegram from the Swedish News Agency, asking for comment. I called up Philip Goodman and suggested that he and I tackle Red at once. The two saw each other much oftener than I saw Red, but Goodman could not tell me where the prize-winner was, save that he and Dorothy were somewhere out of town.

That evening I went to the Goodman apartment to discuss the business, and a little before eleven o'clock Phil got word that they had arrived at a hotel in 50th Street. He and his wife and I rushed there at once, for Goodman agreed with me fully, but it was by then too late to do anything. Red was still fairly sober, but he was applying himself to a bottle with great assiduity, and it was plain that he would be dead drunk in another hour. As for Dorothy, she was in the seventh heaven: indeed, she glowed almost as if she were phosphorescent. She was already full of plans for the trip to Sweden, and even consulted Lily Goodman about her clothes, so we saw that it would be useless to talk of refusing the prize.

In 1935, despite his scornful refusal in 1922, he accepted membership in the preposterous National Institute of Arts and Letters, and so put himself on all fours with such ornaments of the national literature as William Rose Benét, Struthers Burt, Louis Bromfield, Henry Seidel Canby, H. C. Chatfield-Taylor, Owen Davis, W. P. Eaton, Edna Ferber, Hamlin Garland, Ferris Greenslet, Hermann Hagedorn, Clayton Hamilton, Helen Keller and Lewis Mumford. On February 17, 1938, he was elevated to the American Academy of

Arts and Letters, thus rising to equality with Walter Lippmann, Deems Taylor, William Lyon Phelps and the recently departed Robert Underwood Johnson and Paul Elmer More. I have no doubt that Dorothy had a hand in this ignominious change of face. She was probably also responsible for Red's acceptance of an honorary Litt.D. from Yale on June 17, 1936.

But while basking in the first glory of the Nobel Prize he could still deliver a kick at all these pretenders, and he did so in his speech of acceptance in Stockholm, on December 10, 1930. He was irked at the time by the hostile reception the news of the award had got from the dignitaries of the academy—Henry Van Dyke had denounced it as "an insult to America"—and he had at them with some heat. But this heat diminished rather than increased the effectiveness of his argument, and his speech as a whole was pretty feeble stuff, with touches of the sophomoric. I suspect that Dorothy had more than a little to do with its composition, for it was full of her characteristic mixture of challenging cocksureness and moral indignation. The discussion of it at home was mainly stupid, with the Van Dykes arguing that strictures on the state of American literature, if they were ever allowable at all, ought to be delivered on American soil. I wrote nothing about it myself save a statement requested by the Associated Press and sent out on December 31, 1930. In this I rebuked Red gently for exaggerating the importance and influence of the academic critics, and for seeming to say that the young American writer had a hard time getting a hearing.

By this time, alas, I was beginning to suspect that Red's great days were over, and that he would never duplicate the magnificent reality and penetrating humor of *Main Street*, *Babbitt*, *Arrowsmith*, *Elmer Gantry* and *Dodsworth*. His next book, *Ann Vickers*, was in fact trash—and Dorothy appeared to be its heroine! Meanwhile, stories began to reach the United States of his carryings-on in Stockholm, and later in Berlin. He seems to have kept more or less sober at the great banquet which followed the prize-giving ceremony and at the ceremony itself, but after that he went on a drunk in the grand manner, and gave the Swedes a show that they did not soon forget. All those that he met, including even royal dignitaries, became Nils or Gustaf instantly, and he slapped many a back that had never been slapped before. More than once he had to be convoyed back to his hotel and put to bed. The Swedes themselves are hearty boozers, but this time they met their master—if not in holding it, then at least in getting it down.

The Lewises got home soon afterward, and in March Red got into a fracas with Dreiser that for some time entertained the newspapers. It had to do with a book by Dorothy entitled *The New Russia*, published in 1928. The Communists, when she went to Moscow to gather materials for it, took her for the dizzy ride always given to visiting American literati, and she returned home with her portfolio stuffed with highly optimistic press-matter, all of it turned into English for her, for she couldn't read Russian. She was led to believe, apparently, that this press-matter had been prepared for her individual use, for she slapped whole pages of it into her book as her own.

A little while later Dreiser also went to Russia and was taken for the same ride and loaded with the same material, and he used it likewise. The two books—Dreiser's was called *Dreiser Looks at Russia*—came out during the same year, but with Dorothy's six months ahead, and when their marked and inescapable resemblance was noted by reviewers she made the charge that Dreiser had stolen her stuff. This was absurd, for the stuff was not hers at all, but her clamor concealed the fact that the Russians had actually written a large part of her book, so she kept up with it.

On March 19, 1931, there was a dinner at the Metropolitan Club in New York given by Ray Long, then the general editor of the Hearst magazines, for Boris Pilnyak, a Russian writer whose things were appearing in the *Cosmopolitan*, to the great delight of all the American comrades. Red was among the guests, along with Dreiser, Rupert Hughes, Irvin Cobb, Laurence Stallings, James R. Quirk (editor of *Photoplay*), Arthur Brisbane, Will Lengel and various others, about thirty in all. Red, who got drunk as usual, was incensed to discover that among them were two men—they remain unidentified—who had sneered at the award of the Nobel Prize to him. Called upon to speak, he arose unsteadily and said:

I feel disinclined to say anything in the presence of the man who stole three thousand words from my wife's book, and before two sage critics who publicly lamented my receiving the Nobel Prize.

Everyone present knew that the man he had accused of filching from Dorothy's book was Dreiser, and there was an uneasy silence when Red sat down. Dreiser, however, said nothing, and presently the dinner broke up. But when the guests got to the cloakroom Red approached Dreiser and began to upbraid him, and Dreiser, much the larger man, slapped his face. They then parted, but a few months later they met again, and Red resumed his denunciation and Dreiser slapped him a second time.

My suspicion that Red's marriage to Dorothy marked the end of his great days, and that he would do nothing of the first chop thereafter, seems to have been shared by his publisher, Alfred Harcourt. He owed an immense debt to Harcourt, who encouraged him to do *Main Street* at a time when all the other New York publishers he approached laughed at his bombastic talk about it, just as Nathan and I had laughed. *Main Street* had been very adroitly and effectively handled, and so had *Babbitt*, and the books following had likewise got the aid of an extremely clever and resourceful publisher. It was probably Harcourt who pulled the wires that got Red the Nobel Prize, though when he hinted as much to Red, Red was indignant, and insisted that he had been nominated by a Swede. But who this Swede was he didn't seem to know, and there was nothing in his story to prevent one believing that Harcourt was at the Swede's elbow, whispering into his ear.

That, however, had been some time in the past, and by the end of 1930 Red and Harcourt were beginning to fall apart. Red, on his side, alleged that Harcourt was neglecting his books, and Harcourt was growing tired of Red's aberrations, and especially his almost constant drunkenness. After *Dodsworth* was published in 1929 Red set to work gathering material for a novel about a labor leader (this was undertaken at my suggestion), but he found it impossible to get enough of what he needed to start him at the actual writing, and by the end of 1930 he was playing with an idea for a story dealing with three generations of a radical American family—and boiling the pot by doing short stories for the *Cosmopolitan* and *Saturday Evening Post* at $3,000 apiece. Harcourt, meanwhile, was growing restive, for he believed that Red should produce a new book every two years, and so the difference between them grew.

After Dorothy recovered from an operation in Berlin she and Red went to London, and there Red encountered Alfred Knopf, who was on a business trip, and proposed out of hand that Knopf become his publisher. Knopf was naturally interested, but doubts at once began to consume him, for he knew about Red's heavy drinking, and feared that if he agreed he might be taking over a disintegrating author. He therefore cabled to his father, Samuel Knopf, in New York, asking him to call me up in Baltimore for my advice. When the old man told me that Red was asking for a $30,000 advance I objected strongly, for I had begun to doubt that he would ever write another big popular success. I also argued that Red, if taken on, would be a dreadful nuisance in the office, and that every time he and Knopf had a tiff, which would undoubtedly be often, he would come to me to settle it, and so bother and annoy me. The old man agreed with me, and Alfred was so advised by cable.

In a little while it was announced that Red had signed up with Doubleday, Doran & Company. He told me that he was to receive the $30,000 advance that he had demanded from Knopf. But his next book was not ready until 1933. It was *Ann Vickers*, which I had to describe in the *American Mercury* for March, 1933, as full of flubdub and "surely no great shakes." The influence of Dorothy was visible on almost every page of it, and that influence was uniformly deleterious. Red had made his great success by depicting realistically and with immense humor the quacks and frauds who raged in the United States, but now he was under the hoof of a woman who was completely of them, if not yet actually one of them, and she corrupted his whole point of view. At the same time she pumped a large part of his humor out of him, and he became something resembling an uplifter himself.

His deterioration was painfully visible in *Ann Vickers*, and it went on progressively. After 1933 I was happily free from my old chore of book reviewing, and hence did not have to write anything about the successors to *Ann Vickers*, but I read all of them, and found all bad. There were, to be sure, not infrequently flashes of the old Red, but they were no more than small raisins in a generally soggy and forbidding cake. It is possible, of course, that I put too much of the blame for this decade on Dorothy. Red, in all probability, would have gone down without her: alcohol had reduced him to a pitiable state by 1930, and when he went on the water-wagon in 1938 the damage was so deep that it was impossible for him to recover.

But Dorothy, though she may not have been the prime mover, certainly helped him down the hill. A vain, shallow and excessively cocksure woman, consumed during the early days of their marriage by an ill-concealed jealousy of his fame, she played assiduously and with great success upon his congenital inferiority complex, and left him in the end a sort of sorry *reductio ad absurdum* of his pristine self. I have never known another author who shifted his ground so radically, or who came to a more melancholy disaster.

I had an excellent chance to see Dorothy at work upon him in the summer of 1931, when Sara and I visited the two of them at their place in Vermont. It was in the high hills at South Pomfret, near Barnard, and getting to it from the railway involved a long automobile trip from Windsor. When news of my approaching marriage got out early in August 1930, Red and Dorothy sent me a jovial telegram of congratulation, and Red followed it with a letter proposing that Sara and I stop off at South Pomfret on our honeymoon. This invitation I evaded delicately, though our honeymoon journey to Canada took us nearby, but early in July, 1931, we actually made the trip, along with Philip and Lily Goodman.

Meanwhile, Red had come to see me in Baltimore, and met Sara for the first time. This was on March 23. He arrived from Washington with an Englishman—name forgotten—who was one of the directors of the Heinemann publishing firm in London, and both of them were more or less tight. Red, in addition, had a badly bunged nose, with blood still dripping from it. He said he had tripped and fallen in Washington, but offered no details. Sara, who had been ill, had gone to bed by the time he came in, but he insisted on going to her room to see her, and there he sat for twenty minutes or so, gabbling at his usual dizzy pace and dripping gore upon her coverlet. He and the Englishman drank a good deal more while they were in the house, and when they left at 12:15 a.m, proposing to drive back to Washington, both were very drunk.

The trip that the Goodmans, Sara and I made to South Pomfret was begun on July 3. Dorothy met us at Windsor with a car, and drove us up to the mountain road to the place. The plan was that we were to stay a week, but actually we left on the fifth day. The Goodmans, Sara and I discussed our unhappy adventures all the way back to New York, and all of us were inclined to sympathize with Dorothy. It was certainly no bed of roses that she had chosen to lie on—far away in those lonely Vermont hills with a baby to care for and a drunken and exasperating husband to police. She had done no complaining, but the two women had heard from her that Red was drunk nearly all the time. Sometimes drink reduced him to quick insensibility and he lay asleep for hours and even days, but more often it stimulated him to activity and he roved the fields and woods, getting into mischief. Dorothy tried to keep him within bounds by hiding the house liquor supply, but he had a ferret-like capacity for finding her hiding-places, and when he came upon a bottle he emptied it at once.

She would leave him of a morning to go shopping in Barnard, and return at noon to find him dead drunk. Every time he went to Woodstock he returned with several bottles of whiskey, gin or rum, and the better part of another one inside. She lived in terror that, driving drunk, he would roll his car down the mountainside or into a stream, or, worse still, crash into some other car. In addition to raiding her caches he established a number of his own—mainly behind books in the studio *geb.* carriage-house. He would get out of bed in the middle of the night and go to them, and before breakfast every morning he demanded—and usually got—a couple of stiff drinks.

Such was the man that Dorothy had to live with. It was impossible not to feel sorry for her, and the Goodmans, Sara and I duly mourned her woes. But the more we thought of the Lewis ménage the more we grasped the fact that Red also had his troubles, and in the end the preponderance of our sympathy went to him rather than to Dorothy. Our five days in the house had given us a full measure of her peculiar pestiferousness. She was the true daughter of her Methodist pa—a tinpot messiah with an inflamed egoism that was wholly unameliorated by humor. Her eight years abroad as the correspondent for a third-rate newspaper had filled her with the conviction that she knew all that was worth knowing about the political, social and economic problems of the world, and her views, stated freely, had all the confidence of divine revelation.

In brief, a sea lawyer, crackbox philosopher, and what the Germans call a *Biertisch* strategist of the most exaggerated sort, and in addition a bustling and aggressive woman. Add her obvious resentment of the fact that Red was a distinguished man and she was nothing—that people came to see him, not her—that life appeared to offer her little beyond a few beams of reflected glory—and you have some measure of her quality. Her years in Europe, to be sure, had smoothed her native rough edges more or less, and she had lost something of the crude tactlessness of the rustic evangelist, but she remained one nevertheless, and evidences of the fact were always showing through her surface. To Phil Goodman and me, who were married to women as unlike her as a lamb is unlike a lion, and much her superior culturally, she seemed intolerably forbidding and even alarming. We could not help ask ourselves how we'd like to be incarcerated with her on a remote Vermont hilltop, exposed all day and all night to her messianic frenzies.

She had, I should add, all the virtues that go with the evangelical character. She was relentlessly diligent and never forgot her mission to inform and save humanity. While Red loafed away at his bottles, she worked like a horse. She had projects for a thousand articles on the more unintelligible issues of the hour, and spent hours every day reading all the least interesting dispatches in the newspapers. Just before our visit she had sold the first of these articles to the *Saturday Evening Post*, and in the intervals of watching her husband, keeping house and entertaining her guests she labored at the translation of a book by a German Jew named Josef Roth. In winter she lectured before women's clubs and made her first appearances on the radio, and Red told us proudly that her income from all these activities, in 1931, would be at least $8,000. Her first book, *The New Russia*, had got no notice until Red accused Dreiser of plagiarizing it, but it was plain that she would not rest until she had made her mark. It took only half an eye to see that her marriage to Red was already on the rocks, but it was also manifest that in the impending battle between them he would have a hard time holding his own, and that she would not depart with her child until either she was far enough up or he was far enough down to satisfy her vanity.

In the end Yahweh, by a sort of miracle, delivered unto her both halves of this consummation, so improbable when she married Red. Red deteriorated steadily after he got the Nobel Prize, and meanwhile Dorothy fought her way up her somewhat creaky ladder. There were, of course, some missteps. Her naive and preposterous book on Russia has been mentioned; in 1934, just before Hitler became *Reichskanzler*, she printed one predicting that he'd soon be on his way out. But these were minor set-backs, and in 1936 she got her great chance at last, and within a year was, next to Eleanor Roosevelt, the most talked-of woman in America, and had thrown poor Red completely into the shade.

This chance was given to her by Helen Rogers Reid, the strange and unpredictable woman who operated the New York *Herald-Tribune* for her drunken husband, Ogden Mills Reid. Why La Reid chose her, a natural uplifter and liberal, to write for a paper so hunkerous as the *Herald-Tribune* I do not know. Dorothy had passed, in her day, for pro-German, as had Red himself, but after the Nazis invited her to leave Germany in August, 1934, apparently because of the before-mentioned bad guess about Hitler, she went over to the other side with a bang, and in all her days upon the *Herald-Tribune* she howled against the wicked Hun almost as violently as the editorial writers of the paper.

Whatever the fact about her beginnings as a female publicist, it is history that she was soon an extraordinary success—indeed, there is no record of any American woman journalist ever making one to match it. Nor did her column in the *Herald-Tribune* content her, for she was presently devoting a major part of her time to crooning *Weltpolitik* on the radio and unloading it upon the amazed and enchanted members of women's clubs, foreign policy associations and other such outfits.

No busier woman ever existed. When she was not making a speech she was issuing a pronunciamento to the newspapers. Her public honors, though of course they never included the Nobel Prize, were soon vastly more numerous than Red's. She was appointed to dozens of high-sounding committees, all of them devoted to saving the world, she was invited to the White House, and she began to be showered with academic dignities. Tufts College led off by making her an LL.D. before the end of 1936, and Syracuse (her *alma mater*), Saint Lawrence, Russell Sage, Columbia, Dartmouth and McGill followed. It quickly became impossible for her to get through her day's work unaided, so she built up a staff of secretaries, researchers, bookkeepers, traffic managers and other functionaries that took on the proportions of that of a lieutenant-general. Seldom a day passed that she was not mentioned in the newspapers, and seldom a week that did not see her favor the country with some new revelation, full of inside stuff.

When World War II duly began in 1939 she began hitting on fifty cylinders, and there were actually times when what she had to say was treated as first-page news. Before the end of that year some one in New York had the happy thought of proposing her as a candidate for president—on which ticket he did not say—and this proposal was discussed, sometimes spoofingly but more often seriously, for months. Red, asked what he thought of it, said: "If she is elected I'll have to begin writing 'My Day.' "[1]

There was, in this jocosity, a touch of something not far from tragedy. As Dorothy had gathered her rich and lush harvest of fame, his had gone on dwindling. His *It Can't Happen Here*, published October 21, 1935, had got a fair amount of attention, chiefly with the ardent aid of the Communists, but when *The Prodigal Parents* followed in 1938 it fell flat, and when he published *Bethel Merriday* in 1940 it got hardly any notice at all. Poor Red, by this time, seemed to be definitely done for. As Dorothy had gone up, he had gone down.

In July, 1938, when a strange version of *It Can't Happen Here* was presented by a summer stock company at Cohasset, Massachusetts, he appeared in the leading role, and after that, for several years, he was heard of, when he was heard of at all, mainly as an actor. During the winter of 1938–39 he actually went on the road with a company playing a piece called *Angela Is Twenty-Two* which he had written in collaboration with Fay Wray, an obscure stock company actress. It never reached New York. During the next two years he appeared in various other plays on the road, but I have been able to find records of but two of them—*There's Always Juliet*, played by the Spa Players at Saratoga, New York, in August, 1938, with the Fay Wray just mentioned heading the cast, and *Shadow and Substance*, put on in New Orleans in December, 1937, by Le Petit Théâtre du Vieux Carré, with Red playing the role of the Very Rev. Thomas Canon Skerritt. On January 26, 1941, he announced at Miami Beach, where he had been playing again in *Angela Is Twenty-Two*, that he was retiring from the stage to write a new novel. It was *Gideon Planish*, which came out in 1943 and fell dead. It bore the imprint of Random House, which is to say, of Bennett Cerf. Doubleday, Doran & Company had dropped him after the failure of *Bethel Merriday*.

Thus Dorothy had her double triumph, and in 1939 it became common gossip that she was through with Red and preparing to give him his congé. In 1928 she had emerged from nonentity as the wife of Sinclair Lewis, the distinguished novelist, but now Sinclair Lewis was only the husband of Dorothy Thompson, the eminent publicist.

1. A popular syndicated newspaper column by Eleanor Roosevelt.

I have no doubt that life with her was anything but restful in those days of her glory. In fact, Red told me in 1941 that she was completely unbearable, and that he had left her in 1940. He said that she was then spending all her time howling and ranting, and that her torrents of moral indignation finally drove him out of the house.

By this time her celebrity was beginning to fade a bit, and before the end of 1940 there was a sharp drop in the amount of notice she got in the newspapers. In 1941 Mrs. Reid let her go, and she transferred her flag to the New York *Evening Post*, which had come under the control, in 1939, of Dorothy Schiff Backer (later Thackrey), granddaughter of the enormously rich Jewish banker, Jacob Schiff. But the *Evening Post*, which was read chiefly by Jews, did not offer her the platform that she had had on the *Herald-Tribune*, which was the organ of the richer *Goyim*, and so she got less and less attention. She is still writing her column (1945), but she is no longer a public character of any size, and it is seldom that her name appears in other newspapers. But though she is in eclipse, she is hardly as far in the shadows as Red. Since *It Can't Happen Here*, nothing that he had done has got much serious attention. Meanwhile, he has fallen into the net of another Delilah, a Jewish girl calling herself Marcella Powers, and there is every promise that she will do him more damage than even Gracie and Dorothy.

Red apparently encountered Marcella some time in 1940 during his days as an actor. She was then an actress, though later she took to literary endeavor, or, at all events, to jobs on magazines. She came to Baltimore in October, 1941, as a member of a company presenting a preposterous play called *The Good Neighbor*, by Jack Levin, a Baltimore advertising agent, and Red came with her. The local critics handled it roughly, and it never reached New York. When I heard that Red was in town I invited him to Schellhase's restaurant for an evening session, and he asked me to pick him up at 10 p.m. at Ford's Theatre, where *The Good Neighbor* was playing.

I made off with him as soon as possible, and we sat at Schellhase's for an hour, the while he told me the sad tale of his troubles with Dorothy. He had been on the water-wagon since 1938, and drank nothing save iced coffee. At eleven o'clock or thereabout Marcella came in from the theatre, and I was presented to her. She turned out to be a faintly good-looking young Jewish girl, but vain and stupid. It amused me, but hardly surprised me, to observe Red's obvious admiration for her, and deference to her. His eyes were seldom off her, and when she spoke, though what she had to say was usually nothing, he listened with close attention. When I got to New York a little while afterward I heard that he had been carrying her about the country in the guise of his niece, and had been alarmed several times by hints that this laid him open to prosecution under the Mann Act. I also heard that he had put up the money for the production of *The Good Neighbor* in order to get a part for her, and that the venture had cost him $26,000. Broadway knew all about his infatuation, and was laughing at it.

It must have been plain to Red that I regarded La Powers as a piece of trash, and after that meeting in Baltimore I heard from him only a few times, and then very briefly. In November, 1944, I learned that Wells, his son by Gracie, had been killed in action in France on October 29, and sent him a note of condolence, proposing that we have a meeting at some time in the not too distant future. He replied cordially, but on my next two trips to New York I was too busy to see him, and it was not until April 18, 1945, that we met. I then invited him to dinner at a French restaurant in West 46th Street, and asked George Nathan to come along. He insisted, without any suggestion from me, on bringing Marcella, and Nathan and I put in an uncomfortable evening. She had by now grown very confident and possessive, and it was plain that she was trying to show Nathan and me that she had poor Red in her pocket.

He was leaving in a couple of days for Duluth, Minnesota, where he had rented a house. When I asked why he had chosen a mining and lumber town, with probably not more than a dozen civilized inhabitants, he replied that he had a yearning to return to the scenes of his youth. But his native Sauk Centre, I protested, was at least one hundred fifty miles from Duluth, and in a farming region differing as vastly from the Mesabi range country as the Kentucky Blue Grass differs from the environs of Pittsburgh. His only answer was the lame one that both, nevertheless, were in the same state. Later I learned that Marcella's mother was living in Duluth, and that it was she who had found and rented a house for him. It was a vast and dilapidated palace built by one of the early lumber kings, and had had no tenant for years. The news also filtered in that Marcella's ma was a female realtor. Obviously, Red was being taken again, and by a siren even worse than Gracie and Dorothy, for Gracie was at least a woman who made a good impression on the world, and Dorothy, for all her evangelical fervor, was at least more or less intelligent.

Red's appearance when he came to the Algonquin to meet Nathan and me before dinner was really shocking. He had suffered years before from a dermatitis which, on subsiding, left a great mass of scars behind it, and these scars were so numerous and so close together that they gave his skin a dead white look. They covered not only his face but his whole body, as I once discovered when I visited him in New York, and found him lying in bed drunk and naked. His friends gradually got used to his ghastly appearance, and for a long while he had apparently made no effort to improve it. But now there was unhappy evidence that some quack had been monkeying with him, for his dead white color had changed to a flaming red, his face was covered with a great mass of red scales, and up from them, at intervals, arose coal-black tumors. I am no pathologist, but I have seen the keratoses that are produced by X-ray burns, and I couldn't help suspecting that some quack had undertaken to treat him and that is what his tumors were.

His appearance when he walked into the lobby at the Algonquin was startling indeed. The black bumps were bad enough, but the red scales that surrounded them, covering his whole face, were even worse: they gave him the unearthly look of a scarlet lizard. Both Nathan and I surmised that he was retreating to that barn in Duluth to hide himself, though he seemed to be unconscious of his dreadful aspect, and Marcella did not appear to mind. When he reappeared in New York, six months later, all his scales and tumors had vanished, and Nathan wrote to me on October 6 that his face was "as smooth and white as, I presume, your own behind." Who had cured him, or how, he did not say.

It would certainly be an exaggeration to call Marcella attentive to him during our dinner in April; instead she basked complacently in his almost comic admiration, and, as I have said, tried to make it plain to Nathan and me that he was hers. We left the two of them very much depressed. Red had been a man of high achievement and even higher promise in his day, but now it was manifest that he was done for. His next novel, he told us, would tell the love story of a young girl and an aging man, and Marcella's smirks made it plain that she was to be its heroine. Drink and two bad wives had wrecked him, and now he was on his way to the bone-yard on the water-wagon, with an even worse wife preparing to climb up beside him.

Poor Red's troubles were all grounded upon the inferiority complex that he brought out of his native wilds. His early adventures as a writer accentuated it, for success was slow in coming to him, and he was thirty-five when he published *Main Street*. Before that, he had been looked upon disdainfully in New York, and, as I have recorded, I myself shared the prevailing view of him. He sought ease for his wounded ego in drink, but it only made him assertive, boastful and a nuisance. His unhappy marriages further exacerbated his congenital weakness, for both Gracie and Dorothy were frauds who treated him as an inferior, even at the height of his fame. Marcella, when she snared him in 1940 or thereabout, got only the wreck of a man. Physically, he had been brought down so far by drink that going on the water-wagon came too late to restore him altogether: indeed, it probably did him more damage than good. His heavy boozing alienated many of his most useful friends, and explains why I myself saw so little of him.

He was, in drink, noisy and hard to bear, and one quickly forgot the genius of the novelist in the spectacle of the man's degradation. By the time he tried to pull himself together alcohol and his two poisonous wives had so mauled him that it was impossible for him to reattain all of his old form. Moreover, he was so dull, sober, that many who had known him in his drunken days wished that they would return for though he was then a nuisance, he was also often amusing. Drinking soda pop and eating ice-cream, he was simply a bore.

That he had something properly describable as genius in the *Babbitt* era I fully believe. I knew all the principal novelists of that time, and a few of them, notably Dreiser, had genius too, but the overwhelming majority of them were much inferior to Red. His powers of observation were really amazing, and he knew how to present his material with great effectiveness. He was never a stylist comparable to Hergesheimer or Cabell, and he failed constantly when he tried to be touching or profound, but he could tell a story with really extraordinary skill, and his sense of character was greater than that of any of his contemporaries.

But he was an old and worn-out man before he was fifty, and after that he did nothing even half good until *Cass Timberlane*. I urged him over many years to stick to the broad national types that he knew so well how to depict, and made many concrete suggestions to that end, but once he began to break up he found it increasingly difficult to handle them, and from *Dodsworth* onward the people he dealt with became less and less interesting. In *Cass Timberlane*, despite its revival of something of his old skill, they were not interesting at all, and many of them were not even credible. All that remained of him was a melancholy reminder that he had once been a first-rate man.

CHAPTER XXIII

THE $6,000 that I earned for the *Smart Set* by the epigram-movie scheme tided the magazine over a bad place, but it did not earn anything directly for Nathan and me, so we toyed from time to time with other plans that would bring some money into our privy purses. Our success in launching the *Parisienne* and *Saucy Stories*, fattening them for sale to Crowe and Warner, and then going on their payrolls as "advisers," naturally suggested trying the same far from subtle device again, and by the end of 1919 we were busy with plans for the pulp that became the *Black Mask*.

The first issue was that for April, 1920. The cover, in full color, showed a man murdering another in a taxicab, with a third man dropping dead on the sidewalk. This picture had no bearing on anything printed inside, but it was gaudy and effective, and readers of such stuff are never too critical. The authors were all hacks of experience, and they produced stuff that seemed to please the murder fans, for the new magazine started off with an excellent sale and was quickly making money. In a little while we began to recruit authors of more skill, including S. Dashiell Hammett, a strange Marylander who had been a Pinkerton detective and was to develop into one of the most successful manufacturers of homicidal fiction ever heard of.

As in the cases of the *Parisienne* and *Saucy Stories* Nathan and I owned a third of the *Black Mask* between us. A woman named F. M. Osborne was put in as editor toward the end of 1920, and Nathan and I began to collect $50 a week for supervising her. Unhappily, she was incompetent, so the job failed as a means of collecting unearned increment, and involved us in a lot of hard work. The publisher of the new magazine was a small corporation called the Pro-Distributors Publishing Company: its name reflected Warner's current battle with the American News Company, and seemed to him to be a cunning device to get the good-will of the small independent wholesalers then struggling for places in the sun. The president was his bookkeeper, Arthur W. Sutton, and the secretary and treasurer was F. W. Westlake, Crowe's principal falseface. The circulation manager was Philip C. Cody, a mild and pleasant fellow who was almost stone deaf. He had been brought in when Warner had to fire Jack Glenister, formerly the circulation manager of the *Smart Set*, the two pulps and *Field & Stream*.

This Glenister hailed from Chicago and had been in his youth a champion swimmer; on one occasion he swam the Niagara rapids. When Warner hired him, in 1917 or thereabout, he had a reputation in magazine circles in New York as a live-wire circulation hustler, but Nathan and I soon put him down as a mere show-off, and were greatly amused by his bamboozling of Warner. In 1918 he was sent to England to try to open a market for returned copies of the two pulps, for word had reached us that the English unintelligentsia had come to know and love fifth-rate American fiction during the war. He made a deal with one of the English wholesale news-agents and returned triumphant, but when the contracts that he had signed were examined by Crowe's lawyers it appeared that he had made himself a party to them and was entitled to a substantial commission—how much, I forget.

This discovery greatly upset Warner, and he talked of firing Jack on the spot, but on second thought he decided to go on with the contracts for a while, to see how they panned out. When it developed that the profit under them was very small, he refused to deliver any more remainders under them, and Jack was duly dispatched. Jack thereupon set up a publishing business of his own under the name of Fiction House—a borrowing from his English experience—and soon had a string of profitable pulps. He was the first such publisher, I believe, to print a pulp devoted wholly to aviation stories. For a time he was a leader in the field, but strings of cheap magazines have their ups and downs, and in the end he seemed to have gotten into difficulties. I haven't heard from or of him for years (1945) and believe that he is now dead.

Nathan and I were credited with $2,840 each for our services to the *Black Mask* in 1920, but we drew only $450 apiece, and I so reported in my income-tax return for the year. Unfortunately, Sutton, the bookkeeper, turned me in to the Internal Revenue Bureau for the whole $2,840, and the result was a set-to with its agents. In the end I convinced them I had got but $450, and that inasmuch as I did business on a cash basis I was entitled to disregard the unpaid remainder. This negotiation even brought me a small profit, for in the course of their minute examination of my return for 1920 the agents found that I had made an overpayment of $1.90, and this sum was refunded.

Nathan and I had no desire to go on with the *Black Mask:* we had started it simply to sell it to Warner and Crowe, and we applied our lives to this business early in 1921. Crowe died on August 27 of that year, but the deal was completed before then. Just how much we got for our shares I forgot, but my recollection is that it was $20,000 apiece. Altogether, the *Black Mask* produced nearly $25,000 for me in little more than two years. Nathan and I, encouraged, hatched schemes for yet more magazines, but the death of Crowe forced their abandonment, and after 1922 we devoted ourselves mainly to efforts to sell our shares in the *Smart Set,* either to Warner or to some outsider.

The *Black Mask* is still in existence (1945), and still seems to be making money. Warner and the Crowe estate sold it in 1940 to Popular Publications, of which Harry Steeger (not a Jew) was and is the president. Steeger has an office at 205 East 42nd Street, New York, where he also operates various other magazines. His chief editor is Kenneth White, son of the Trumbull White who edited the *Red Book* in 1905 and bought from me a story called "The Bend in the Tube." I paid a visit to Steeger and White on April 23, 1943, and had a pleasant session with them. Steeger lent me copies of the first two issues of the *Black Mask,* but had no other of the early numbers, for when he bought the magazine from Warner in 1940 the files were incomplete. I found that there was no advertising in Vol. I No. I save two full-page ads on the back cover, inside or out. One advertised cheap imitation diamond rings and the other a preparation for making artificial eyelashes. The book notices at the end, signed Captain Frank Cunningham, were printed only because the Post Office made difficulties about granting second-class entry to magazines consisting wholly of fiction. There was no such provision in the law; the Post Office bureaucrats simply declared it to be their will. I remember going to Washington one day to wrestle with them, and failing to shake them. Who Captain Frank Cunningham was I forget—probably Miss Osborne, the editor.

Nathan and I continued to collect $100 a week apiece through 1921 for keeping our eyes upon the *Parisienne* and *Saucy Stories*, but when Warner merged the two magazines in July, 1922, this was reduced to $50, and at the end of the year we threw up the job and after that got nothing. The show had been amusing while it lasted, and when it was over we found ourselves pretty well heeled. My income from books was increasing steadily. In 1919 Knopf had paid me $655.18, but in 1920 his royalties came to $1007.57, in 1921 to $1351.55, and in 1922 to $2936.06.

CHAPTER XXIV

THE YEAR 1921 was a busy one for me, but I accomplished very little of any lasting significance. During the first half of the year I undertook a rewriting and enlargement of *The American Language* and it worked me very hard until the late summer, and all year long, whenever a few hours of opportunity appeared I put in some licks on *Notes on Democracy*. But *Notes on Democracy* turned out to be a vexatious enterprise, and I did not finish it until 1926. My trouble was that I had too many jobs, and that trouble I was not destined to throw off until 1934. On February 23, 1921 I wrote to Fielding H. Garrison:

I am rewriting *The American Language* (8 hours a day), helping to edit the *Smart Set* and the *Black Mask*, advising the editors of two other magazines, doing an article a week for the *Sun*, sitting in at least one long *Sun* conference a week, and doing casual stuff for the *Nation*, the *Post*, and the *Century*. In addition, I do a 6,000 word book article a month, write over half of Repetition Generale, and most of the "Conversations." Also, I am working upon *Prejudices III*, and editing a MS. for Dreiser. In brief, I am a damned fool.

The Dreiser book was *A Novel About Myself*, and was published in 1922. It was a dreadful specimen of Dreiser's writing at its worst, and I put in long hours trying to claw it into plausible English. Dreiser himself, at this time, was in Hollywood trying to sell movie scenarios to the Jews. He was also trying to finish a novel called *The Bulwark*, begun in 1914, but not actually brought to an end until September, 1945.

Before I finished the job of editing *A Novel About Myself*, I made various efforts, at Dreiser's request, to place parts of it with magazines, or all of it as a serial. One of the editors I approached was T. R. Smith of the *Century*, to whom I sent the MS. on March 10, 1921, with a long letter pointing out where there was material in it for eight possible articles. Tom Smith quit the *Century* in April, and Glenn Frank, who took over as editor-in-chief, declined the Dreiser chapters. They were also declined by George Horace Lorimer of the *Saturday Evening Post* and Carl Hovey of the *Metropolitan Magazine*. The more I plowed into the MS. the more I became convinced myself that it was not worth printing, so I finally resolved to wash my hands of the business. But I continued to be concerned with Dreiser's unhappy affairs through the year. What he was living on in Los Angeles, or with whom, I did not know, and he did not tell me. All I heard from him was that he was hard up and eager for money.

Meanwhile, a lawyer named Arthur C. Hume, with an office at 1 East 45th Street, New York, had taken over the moribund case against the John Lane Company for suppressing *The "Genius"*. In October Dreiser sent me a copy of a letter from Hume, dated October 17, which indicated that he was planning to use the "expert testimony of literary people." I got into touch with him in December, and advised him as well as I could. In May, 1922, I concocted with his aid and consent a scheme to induce John S. Sumner, the head of the Comstock Society, to abate his complaint against the book sufficiently to allow it to be reprinted.

All through the early part of 1921 I was greatly burdened by the care of my brother Charlie's wife, Mary, who had come to Baltimore for medical treatment. The two lived in Pittsburgh and my brother had to return there to look after his engineering duties with the Pennsylvania Railroad. This left Mary on my hands, and for two or three months on end I had to visit her at St. Agnes Hospital, at least two miles from Hollins Street. She suffered from a mysterious cyst in the region of the left kidney, apparently originating in the adjoining adrenal gland, and in March my old friend, Dr. Joseph C. Bloodgood, operated on her. Unhappily, it turned out that the cyst was so enmeshed in blood vessels that taking it out was impossible, and the best he could do was to sew her up and open a sinus for drainage. That sinus remained open for six or eight years, and during all that time she made frequent visits to Baltimore, and I had to take charge of her. She was an impatient patient, and during her first long stay at St. Agnes quarrelled constantly with her nurses, and was full of bitter criticism of Bloodgood, his assistant, Dr. George A. Stewart, and the house staff. Her uproars finally became so unpleasant that my poor mother, distracted, refused to visit her any more, and the whole load fell on me.

I made no less than twenty-three trips to New York during 1921, and sometimes remained there four or five days. I also made eighteen to Washington mainly on Baltimore *Sun* business, and one to Philadelphia. I got no vacation in the summer, and had to keep on working at full steam through the hay-fever season in the early autumn—a severe one. Also, I had several other illnesses, including a synovitis in my right wrist, produced by my bricklaying in the backyard in Hollins Street. The old house was very comfortable, and I could work there better than anywhere else, but its rehabilitation was still short of complete, and among other things it was yet lighted by gas. It must have been some time in 1921 that I had electricity substituted, but during the hot summer of the year, I believe, I was still working with my head two feet from an incandescent Welsbach gas-burner. I marvel that I stood it in a Baltimore July, but stood it I did.

The only break in my deadly routine during the year came late in November, when Joe Hergesheimer and I made a visit to James Branch Cabell in Richmond. It lasted only a few days, but it was very pleasant. I had been writing about Cabell since 1909 and had been in correspondence with him since 1916, but I had never seen him. All the arrangements for the trip were made by Hergesheimer, who had visited Cabell in Richmond during the preceding April, and had proposed that I join them then. I couldn't do so because of the illness of my sister-in-law, but she returned home during the summer, and we finally made the trip in November. The day Joe chose for our arrival in Richmond seemed to me to be unpropitious when I heard that in the evening Cabell and his wife were giving a coming-out party for one of her three young daughters by her first marriage, but it turned out very well.

We went from the station to the Jefferson Hotel, and there got into the evening clothes that Joe always loved to put on. Then we went to the home of Emily Clark, editor of the *Reviewer*, for dinner with her, her step-mother and her editorial associates, and afterward proceeded to the Cabell party at the hotel. Joe had sent me warning on two points: one was to the effect that Emily Clark was "the ugliest girl" he had ever seen "except for a very graceful, a very ingratiating coastline," and the other was notice that we had better take along a good supply of reliable drinkables, for those of Richmond were of the usual low Southern quality. The first point he reinforced on the train going down. "Don't look at her face," he cautioned me; "look at her legs: they are perfect." It turned out to be even so, and I enjoyed dinner at her house very much, though while it went on her legs were hidden by the table. Her step-mother, Alice, was almost as beautiful as she herself was homely, Emily had a lot of amusing chatter about her magazine venture, and her associates, male and female, were all agreeable youngsters.

When we got back to the hotel Joe and I brought out our supplies of wines and liquors, and were presently having a merry party in our rooms, auxiliary to the main party. I had brought, among other things, half a dozen bottles from my almost exhausted stock of "Faust" beer, and found an appreciative customer for it in Prince Pierre Troubetzkoy, the Russian painter who had married Amélie Rives in 1896. Amelie herself was not present, but the prince turned out to be a very pleasant fellow, and before the evening was over he had got down all of my beer, and was full of assurances of his eternal gratitude and undying friendship. When we parted I gave him a bottle of Burgundy and he pressed me to make an immediate visit to himself and his wife at Castle Hill, their place in Albemarle county, near Charlottesville, but I had to get back to Baltimore and my pressing chores. A week later I received notes from both of them. They had staged a little party with the Burgundy and drunk my health standing. "You've made the old South sit up often," wrote the princess, "but I don't believe it ever stood up unanimously for you before."

The next day Cabell gave us a party at his house in town, drove us out to his summer place at Dumbarton, and to a show-place called Tuckahoe on the upper James, and took us to visit various Richmond notables. One of the latter, I recall, was a judge who was supposed to have the best whiskey in town. When he produced it, it turned out to be corn, and of quality revolting to our refined esophagi. I managed somehow to get mine down, but at a moment when the judge's back was turned Joe discharged a large mouthful into the fireplace.

At Tuckahoe the chatelaine, a charming woman whose name I

forget, showed us the treasures of the house. Among them was a drawer full of letters from Thomas Jefferson. The drawer was in a magnificent old secretary, and the secretary was in the dining-room: there was no apparent thought of the dangers of fire, though Tuckahoe was in an isolated place on the river. When I remarked this, the lady replied that all the servants were instructed that at the first alarm they were to rush into the dining-room, pull the drawer out of the secretary, and run with it to the nearest neighbor's house. Such was fire protection in the Virginia of 1921.

On the morning after the Cabell coming-out party Joe tiptoed into my room at the hotel and beckoned to me to follow him. He led me to his bathroom, and there motioned to me to apply my ear to a door connecting with the bathroom of the adjoining bedroom. I could hear the voices of four or five young girls and it became immediately apparent from their talk that they had been guests at the party the night before. The conversation was really astonishing, for though I had read *This Side of Paradise* and had been hearing a lot about Flaming Youth, I was innocently unaware of the extent to which its revolt against all the ancient decorums had gone. The gabble of these fair flowers of Virginia almost made my hair stand on end. They seemed to know all the dirty words, and they used them with the freedom of Kipling's single men in barracks.

I BEGAN WRITING about Cabell in 1909 and have been in friendly correspondence with him since 1916, but I can recall meeting him face to face on but two occasions. The first was when Joe Hergesheimer and I visited him in Richmond in 1921, and the second in 1926. In 1940, when Louis Cheslock's setting of his *The Jewel Merchants* had its first (and only) performance at the Peabody Conservatory, Baltimore, he promised to appear for the debut, but at the last minute he sent his regrets. On our 1926 visit he entertained Patterson and me very pleasantly at a buffet supper at his home in Richmond, but the evening was spoiled and indeed made horrible by the presence of his son Ballard.

This Ballard was either a cretin or a Mongolian idiot: I could not make out which, but whatever he was he was surely a dreadful spectacle. His features were coarse and repulsive, his speech was muddled and unintelligible, and he walked with the shambling gait of a gorilla. I had heard of him from Hergesheimer, and had warned Patterson, but we were both shocked when he was introduced to us as if he were a normal creature. There was a considerable gathering and we tried to avoid him as much as possible by keeping to its edges, but he insisted upon following us about and pressing his simian attentions on us. Meanwhile, Cabell spoke to him and of him as if there were nothing wrong with him—a truly appalling manifestation of family pride. A Cabell of Virginia, it appeared, simply could not admit that he had an idiot son.

The boy's mother, Priscilla Bradley Shepherd, was a widow when Cabell married her and had had three perfectly normal daughters by her first marriage. These very charming girls, by this time grown, were forced by their stepfather, as their mother was forced, to take no notice of their half-brother's infirmity, and all the *noblesse* of Richmond had been similarly schooled. But to Patterson and me it was exactly like going into an animal cage, and we left the party as soon as we decently could, and returned to our hotel for some restorative drinks.

When Ballard reached puberty he became dangerous to women, and had to be put away. He was incarcerated in an asylum near Doylestown, Pennsylvania, not far from the home of Hergesheimer, and once or twice, when visiting him, his father dropped in on Joe. So far as I know, he is still there (1948).

Cabell seldom visited anyone else, and I have never known him to be in New York since the 30's. In Richmond it was whispered that, as a youth, he had killed a man, said to have been the lover of his mother, then a widow. This man's body was found on the porch of the mother's house in a Richmond suburb, with his head bashed in, and beside him lay a heavy walking-stick belonging to Cabell. He was never publicly accused of the crime, though every Virginian who ever mentioned it to me believed that he had committed it. However, Joe Hergesheimer told me on May 22, 1948, that Hugh Walpole (with whom Cabell was intimate) had once told him that Cabell had assured him (Walpole) that he was innocent. In any case, a Cabell, in Virginia, can do no wrong. Nor can he be, in its higher social circles, a Mongolian idiot.

IT WAS IN MARCH, 1921, that I became a contributing editor to the *Nation*—a purely honorary post held for eleven years, to the astonishment of the journalistic nobility and gentry, and my own great amusement. Oswald Garrison Villard had taken it over two years before, and was trying to get together a competent staff and convert it into something better than an outhouse to the New York *Evening Post*, which it had been for a long while before he sold his interest in the *Post* and put the *Nation* on its own. Its managing editor was Ernest Gruening, its literary editor was Carl Van Doren, and its associate editors were William MacDonald, Freda Kirchwey, Arthur Warner, Lewis S. Gannett and Ludwig Lewisohn. Villard, like most other American Liberals, had been lured by Wilson's lascivious prose into supporting the first war to end war, but by 1920 he was in the throes of a bitter disillusionment, and in consequence the *Nation* showed a relatively enlightened spirit on the political side—certainly one much more enlightened than that of any of the newspapers.

But on the literary side it was still a bit conventional and even old-fashioned, for Van Doren was an ex-pedagogue only recently delivered from the rattan, and believed that such academic quacks as Paul Elmer More and Stuart P. Sherman were honest, competent and even profound. In my *Smart Set* book article, for July, 1920, entitled "Observations Upon the National Letters," I had described the *Nation* as "far to the left in its politics, but hugging the right desperately in letters," and this was picked up in *Prejudices: Second Series*, published in October of the same year. Van Doren must have got hold of an advance copy of the book, for on September 4 he printed an article entitled "The Ivory Tower," in which it was argued foolishly that I was trying to kill all the literary classics and substitute my current stalking-horses, notably Dreiser. This article, which was by Lewisohn, was quite good-humored, and on a sudden impulse I wrote a letter to the editor protesting against its errors in the same spirit.

Van Doren replied at once, asking for permission to print the letter, but I had to refuse, for it might have been mistaken for an effort to defend myself, and I was very eager to avoid any appearance of defending myself. It was already my settled policy then, as it has remained ever since, to make no public protest against anything printed about me, however false and even libellous: as I have before noted, that plan bore defiant fruit in *Menckeniana: A Schimpflexikon*, published in 1928. There ensued a pleasant correspondence with Van Doren, and he was presently asking me to do some reviews for the *Nation*. I was both amused and astonished when Van Doren proposed to me, on February 28, 1921, that I become one of the "honorary figures" that were being added to the staff "with the title of Contributing Editor." Obviously, I hardly fitted into the *Nation* scheme of things, for I was not only not a liberal, but a libertarian, which is something almost exactly opposite, for liberals are always advocates of more and more laws. But it was also plain that the connection proposed might serve to confuse and mystify my rapidly growing battalion of enemies, so I decided to accept.

Van Doren now proposed that he and I engage in a sort of debate in the *Nation* on the theme, "How I Feel About Democracy," but with memories of Robert Rives La Monte and *Men vs. the Man* in mind, the idea seemed to me to be a bad one, and nothing came of it. It must have been about this time that I first set eyes on Van Doren, probably in New York. He turned out to be a tall, well-set-up, expansive, talkative and amusing fellow with prematurely gray hair, closely clipped, and I took a liking to him at once. It was plain from the start that he did not share all the political notions of Villard—he had too keen a sense of humor for that—but they apparently got on very well, for Van Doren was a diligent and competent literary editor, and soon outgrew his academic delusions.

We were Van Doren and Mencken to each other—until 1929, when we slipped into Carl and Henry. The appearance of my name on the flagstaff of the *Nation* naturally produced some comment, but it is my recollection that no one assumed or suggested that I had become a liberal: all the surmises ran the other way. On May 5, 1921, Van Doren asked me to come to a dinner planned "pretty largely to raise funds during the present hard season," and proposed that I "speak for about ten minutes on 'Why I Became a Contributing Editor,' in such fashion as to show that a good man need not agree with the *Nation*'s politics and economics at all points to approve of its general course." I refused, for I believed that Villard was well able to meet its deficits, but agreed to send in a letter to be read at the dinner. This letter, if I remember correctly, was the primordial zygote of the chapter on the *Nation* in my *Prejudices: Fifth Series*, published in 1926, though it appeared in more mature form in the Baltimore *Evening Sun* for July 6, 1925, and in that form was circulated by Villard as a promotional handbill.

In 1934, more than a year after my name had disappeared from the *Nation*'s flagstaff, my former connection with it was recalled by the once celebrated Mrs. Elizabeth Dilling, and she listed me in *The Red Network*, her "who's who and handbook of radicalism for patriots." This imbecility delighted me, especially since La Dilling also included Newton D. Baker, William E. Borah, Marc Connelly, Glenn Frank, Mrs. J. Borden Harriman, Henry Hazlitt, Sergei Koussevitzky, George W. Norris, Raymond Pearl, Roscoe Pound, Louis Untermeyer and Van Doren in her roster of dangerous Reds. Her counts against me were that I was a member of the National Mooney-Billings Committee and the National Committee on Freedom from Censorship (both offshoots of the American Civil Liberties Union) and had been a member of the John Reed Club and a contributing editor of the *Nation* until 1932. As a matter of fact, I had never been a member of the two committees named, though I occasionally sent a small donation to the one on Freedom from Censorship, and I certainly never belonged to the John Reed Club, a frankly Communist organization. I was dropped from the *Nation* at the end of 1932, not at my own suggestion but because Villard was retiring as editor to become contributing editor himself, and desired a monopoly upon the title.

I had pretty well forgotten, by this time, that I was a contributing editor to the *Nation*, and so had those who speculated and surmised when the fact was announced in 1921, so there was no moaning of farewell. "As for dropping my name from the flagstaff," I wrote to Villard on December 23, "please give it no thought. I have often marvelled that you kept it there so long." As incredible as it may seem, I have never been told, either by Villard himself or by any of his associates, why it had been put there in the first place, and it was not until March 13, 1942, that I learned.

This happened at a dinner to Villard in New York on his seventieth birthday. I was one of the speakers and Van Doren was another. He laid in a few drinks in preparation for his ordeal and when his time came he broke the flow of unctuous eulogy by offering some realistic reminiscences of life on the *Nation* in his time. They were all very amusing, but nothing was more amusing to me than his statement that I had been a sort of war-club in a battle between Villard and the staff. A Puritan from head to heels, and full of the chronic moral indignation of his Abolitionist grandfather, William Lloyd Garrison, Villard was all for supporting Prohibition; worse, he had a tender feeling for the Comstocks, then in violent eruption in New York. Van

Doren, Lewisohn and MacDonald were hot against these follies, and so were the younger members of the staff, and the result was a long and gory struggle, at the end of which Villard was more or less convinced.

But it was conviction against his natural instincts, and they feared that he would presently resume the role of wowser, so they resolved to nail him down by flaunting the name of one notoriously and uncompromisingly against moral endeavor in all its horrible forms. He knew very little about me at the time, and it was thus possible to hoodwink him. Once I was signed up, they dangled before him the fear that if the *Nation* ever showed any leaning toward either Prohibition or comstockery I would resign with indignation and denounce the magazine in a public and violent manner.

Van Doren, his tongue loosed by ethyl alcohol, told most of this at the dinner, somewhat to Villard's embarrassment but to the apparent delight of the assembled celebrants, and certainly to my own. I followed as an added starter with another kidding speech, and the dinner, which had begun as a solemn and even lugubrious affair, ended cheerfully and a shade merrily, though Villard's own speech of thanks was pretty deadly. After the orgies were over Van Doren and S. K. Ratcliffe and I went to the Ritz bar, and there Van Doren told me all the details of the story and we drank beer for a couple of hours.

I had a hidden and perhaps somewhat nefarious hand in Villard's book *Newspapers and Newspaper Men*, published in 1923, in which the Baltimore *Sunpapers* were treated with great politeness, and in fact hailed as glories to American journalism. Nobody knew better than I did that this was a hope rather than a fact, but I was still optimistic about making something of them, and when Villard came to me for information about them—I was the only member of the staff he knew—I saw that he was properly oriented. Then I turned him over to J. Haslup Adams, Paul Patterson, Stanley M. Reynolds, John W. Owens and J. Edwin Murphy, and they gave him a lunch party (I was not present myself) and finished the business. The result was a chapter that gave an enormous lift to the *Sunpapers'* professional reputation and credit, and had an excellent effect in the office, where it provided all ambitious men with something to be proud of, and a mark to shoot at. Even such implacable enemies of my scheme of reform as Adams and Owens were affected more or less, and during the four or five years following there was some evidence that the papers might eventually become almost as good as Villard had been led to believe they were already.

In 1942 Villard undertook a revision of the book, and again applied to me for help. He came to Baltimore on October 19 and I had him to dinner at the Maryland Club. His dubieties about the *Sunpapers* embarrassed me, for if I told him the truth and he printed it in the new edition of his book it would be devastating indeed, and everyone in the office would guess that his information had come from me. I got rid of the difficulty by arguing that his encomiums of 1923 had been largely forecasts, that the progress of time had necessarily worked some changes in the *Sunpapers'* program, that an adequate account of their present situation would involve a complete rewriting and much labor, and that it would be easier to drop the chapter altogether, and give its space to other papers. As he was already inclined this way himself—I think he was largely moved by the growing indolence of his advancing years—it was thus not hard to persuade him. When his revision came out in 1944, under the new title of *The Disappearing Daily*, his omission of the *Sun* chapter was naturally marked in the office, but by that time no one there was interested in the grand projects of 1921, and the matter was quickly forgotten.

Villard had had enough disappointments of his own to make him appreciate my situation with respect to the *Sunpapers*. When he dined with me on October 19, 1942, his talk was mainly of the decay of his two lost children, the New York *Evening Post* and the *Nation*. The former, after vicissitudes which included its purchase in 1933 by the Philadelphia fake, J. David Stern, was now in the hands of Dorothy Backer, and had become a frantic advocate of the second war to end war. The latter, turned over to Freda Kirchwey as editor in 1932 and as publisher in 1937, had become even worse: indeed, it was hardly more than a cruel burlesque on the *Nation* of Villard's day.

He told me on May 3, 1944, that Freda had sworn to him, when he yielded control to her, that she would resist to the last ditch American participation in a second World War, but when the Communist party line shifted she went over to blood and thunder in the grand manner, exactly like Bruce Bliven of the *New Republic*. Villard complained that she had surrounded herself with a gang of prehensile Jews, and was completely in their hands: he showed a considerable anti-Semitism in his tale of this treason. I suggested that perhaps some of these Jews had gained access to her heart and person, but he said not: she was faithful, he believed, to her husband, Evans Clark, a third-rate professional radical who had gone to work for the Russians so early as 1919 and had since wrung a living out of the Twentieth Century Fund, the Public Affairs Committee, the Council for Democracy and other such Communist outworks, with occasional divagations into journalism. The *Nation* had shown more circulation under Freda than it had ever shown under Villard, and maybe this fact had something to do with his dudgeon, but she had failed to make it pay its way. On March 3, 1943, she wrote to me that "within the next two months we must raise $25,000" and solicited a contribution.

Simultaneously she organized a bogus verein called the *Nation* Associates, with dues of $25, $50 and $100 a year for contributing, sustaining and foundation members, respectively, but it seems to have been a failure, for on March 23, 1944, she was passing the hat again. When Villard left the *Nation* in 1935 his title was transferred to a Jew who promised to endow it in perpetuity, but this Jew failed to make good, and after 1937 La Kirchwey found the whole burden of raising money on her hands. Villard told me on December 14, 1941, that one of the Warburgs was supposed to be her current backer, but Warburg apparently failed her too. She followed her 1944 request for help with several dunning letters, but I did not reply to them.

Soon afterward the newspapers reported that the *Nation* Associates had held a dinner in New York, and subscribed $25,000 to carry on the weekly for another year: most of them, I gathered from the names listed, were Jews. During the summer of 1945 another dinner was announced, this time ostensibly in honor of Thomas Mann, the German émigré novelist, who was seventy on June 6. I received an invitation, but did not reply to it, for I had always considered Mann, in his political character, a jackass. Alfred Knopf, his American publisher, also refused to go, for he discovered that Mann was only a cover for a scheme to pass the hat for the *Nation* at the table. In brief, Freda had begun to be more than a little disingenuous. Knopf, formerly one of her followers, went about New York denouncing her, and there was sharp criticism of her from others.

CHAPTER XXV

BEGINNING WITH the issues for February, 1921, Nathan and I tried to get rid of the candy-box-top covers that had marked the *Smart Set* for years past, and to substitute designs more in keeping with the pretensions of the magazine. But it was not easy to find artists capable of designing anything really clever, and by March we were back to the reliable but somewhat stodgy Archie Gunn. We did not, however, abandon the quest, and eight of the twelve covers for the year were at least unconventional and showed some trace of humor. The best artist we unearthed was one who signed himself A.G.L., but who he was I forget.

As I have recorded I let Nathan have a pretty free hand in this department, for buying covers meant a great many palavers with artists, and he was at the office every day and endured seeing visitors much better than I. Now and then, when he bought an especially bad one, I protested politely, but it was not often and we seldom had any real disagreement. The *Smart Set*, physically, seemed doomed to disgrace its contents to the end of the chapter, what with the sleazy paper that Crowe's goon sent us and the indifferent printing, and I gave myself as little concern about the matter as possible.

We turned up relatively little stuff in 1921 that really lifted us. I can recall only "Miss Thompson," a novelette by W. Somerset Maugham; *The Jewel Merchants*, a play by James Branch Cabell; "Hang It All," a grotesque short story by Charles G. MacArthur and Lloyd D. Lewis, two Chicago reporters; "Unlighted Lamps," by Sherwood Anderson; "The Merry-go-Round," the first of a series of stories by Julia Peterkin; and "A Homecoming," the story with which Ruth Suckow made her debut.

Maugham was already well known in New York for *Of Human Bondage*, published in 1915, and *The Moon and Sixpence*, which followed in 1919, but "Miss Thompson" was meat too strong for the popular magazines which were the chief American markets, and so his agent, the American Play Company, was unable to sell it. As a last resort it was sent to Nathan by the hand of Charles Hanson Towne, then working for the company, and we published it in the issue for April, 1921. The Comstocks made no bother over it, and it went almost unnoticed, but soon afterward a woman named Clemence Randolph, one of the girls of the then famous Sheriff Bob Chandler, painter and voluptuary, decided that it would make an effective play and set to work dramatizing it. Maugham himself, who was an experienced playwright, did not believe that there were any stage possibilities in it. John D. Williams, a friend of Nathan's and mine and one of Sheriff Bob's booze companions, heard through him of La Randolph's project, and after taking a look at her MS. called in a Broadway jobber named John Colton to give her help. Also, he got Maugham's permission to proceed.

The result was *Rain*, produced by Williams and Sam Harris at the Garrick Theatre, Philadelphia, on October 9, 1922, with a young and unknown actress named Jeanne Eagels in the star part of Sadie Thompson. The Philadelphia critics roasted the play, and Williams became so dubious of its success in New York that he offered to sell a quarter interest in it for $2500. But when it opened at the Maxine Elliott Theatre on November 7 it made an enormous hit, and Eagels became a Broadway celebrity overnight. It ran for six hundred forty-eight performances in New York and then had a prosperous road tour. Williams's share of the profits came to $253,000. What we paid for "Miss Thompson" I do not recall precisely, but I think it was about $150. Maugham's usual price for a story, of course, was very much more, but, as I have said, his agent could not sell this one anywhere else.

I met Maugham at some time after the great success of *Rain*, but saw him very seldom, and had but infrequent communication with him, though he was always very polite to me. Born in 1874, he got his early education at King's School, Canterbury, and then studied medicine, but after getting his degree found that practice was distasteful to him, and so took to writing. He came of a good English family and his elder brother, Frederic Herbert, rose to high places at the English bar and on the bench, and was made a life baron. Maugham was married to Syrie, a daughter of the celebrated Dr. Thomas J. Barnardo, founder of a chain of homes for English slum children, and they themselves had a daughter, but that daughter and her mother had vanished by the time I met their father and husband.

He was reputed in New York to be a homosexual of the school of Hugh Walpole, and I was thus somewhat shy of his society. He wrote to me from Washington on February 21, 1939, saying that he would be at the Belvedere Hotel, Baltimore, two days later and asking me to have lunch with him there. I refused the lunch, but dropped in on him during the afternoon, and found that he was travelling with a suspicious-looking young man. Despite this, we had a pleasant palaver of an hour or two, with the young man hovering discreetly in the background.

Maugham reprinted "Miss Thompson," with the title changing to "Rain," in a collection of short stories entitled *The Trembling of a Leaf*, published in 1921, and I noticed it briefly in the *Smart Set* for January, 1922. Very few of his books save *Of Human Bondage* and *The Moon and Sixpence* were worth reading, and when I reviewed them at all I usually sniffed at them.

I HAVE OFTEN been credited with having discovered both Miss Suckow and Mrs. Peterkin, but the former was actually turned up by John T. Frederick, then editor of the *Midland*, a small but excellent *Tendenz* magazine launched by him at the University of Iowa in 1915. He printed Miss Suckow's first story, "Uprooted," in the *Midland* for February, 1921; her second, "Retired," two months later; and her third, "The Resurrection," in June. It must have been during the spring of this year that she sent me several of her manuscripts, probably at his suggestion. I did not take them, but they interested me very much, and I urged her to send me more. Toward the end of July she forwarded three, and they were held for my reading at the *Smart Set* office.

I well recall picking them up one hot, lazy afternoon as Nathan and I sat in our room, he struggling with proofs and I trying to make some headway against a mountain of accumulated manuscripts. They were written single-space on a bad typewriter, and reading them was not easy, but I had not got beyond page two of the first before I was fascinated. The stuff had but little movement and it dealt with country people of a sort beyond my ordinary range of interest, but the dialogue, the management of the narrative, and the little touches of color were all superb. "Here," I said, throwing the manuscripts to Nathan, "are three masterpieces. I vote for all of them." He objected on the ground that buying three stories from one author at one time was against our thrifty policy of living from hand to mouth, but I waved him away. "I'd be willing," I said, "to print all three in one issue, and with her name signed to every one." Then, while I resumed my struggles with the mountain, he went through them, and in a little while we agreed. We printed one of the three, "A Homecoming," in November, giving it the place of honor for short stories, and the other two, "The Top of the Ladder" and "Mame," in December. Meanwhile, I wrote for more, and was presently rewarded with two of the best stories printed in the *Smart Set* in my time. They were "Just Him and Her" and "A Pilgrim and a Stranger." We printed both of them in January, 1922, and thereafter we had a Suckow story in the magazine every time we could get one.

I was naturally curious about their author, and soon pumped her story out of her, with the assistance of Jay G. Sigmund, an insurance man and literary amateur of Cedar Rapids, with whom I had been in communication for some time. She was born at Hawarden, a country town in western Iowa, forty miles above Sioux City, on August 6, 1892, and was the daughter of the Rev. W. J. Suckow, a small-time Congregationalist clergyman. Pastor Suckow seems to have held appointments only briefly, for during Ruth's childhood the family was almost constantly on the move, and lived at different times in villages stretching from end to end of the state. Her paternal grandfather was a German shoemaker from Mecklenburg, later turned Iowa farmer, and her maternal grandfather was a West German, Kluckhohn by name, who had come out, along with his father and several brothers, to preach Methodism to the Indians in the Michigan woods.

She got her early schooling in a long series of Iowa villages, and proceeded to Grinnell College in 1910. After three years there she was sent to the Boston School of Expression to study elocution, which still ranked as a fine art, and indeed as the queen of the fine arts, among the Iowa rustics of the era, but she apparently developed no talent for it, for in 1916 she transferred to the University of Denver, and there took her A.B. in 1917. Apparently her going to Denver was suggested by the fact that a married sister, Ema S. Hunting, was living there.

She began to write verse while she was still in college, but apparently did not attempt prose until 1921. Simultaneously, or maybe a little before this, she took over a bee-farm at Earlville, Iowa, and until 1926 this was her chief means of support. Her first stories in the *Smart Set* were quickly noticed in New York, and she received invitations to contribute to various other magazines, including *Harper's* and the *Century*. She was also recognized and hailed by a number of more mature authors, notably Sinclair Lewis. But in her native Iowa only Frederick, Sigmund and a few others showed any appreciation of her. To the rest of the state's illuminati her realistic (though always kindly and understanding) pictures of the life of its country people seemed harsh and even treasonable. This hostile faction was led by a dunderheaded pedagogue named Lewis Worthington Smith, professor of English at Drake University, a cow college at Des Moines, and a frequent writer of bad books.

But La Suckow was too sincere an artist to be intimidated by such imbeciles, and through the years from 1921 to 1926 she worked very hard, devoting her summers to her bee-farm and her winters to writing. She told me, when I first heard from her, that she had a novel under way, and by 1923 she had finished it. It was *Country People*. On August 9, 1921, I advised Knopf to take a look at it, and though it was shorter than the normal novel and promised to have only a small sale, he published it in 1924, hoping to get something more profitable from her later on. *The Odyssey of a Nice Girl*, which followed in 1925, was largely Suckow's own early story—that is, the story of an Iowa country girl who makes an attempt upon fame in the character of an elocutionist. It was longer than *Country People* and better organized and I gave it a good notice in the *American Mercury* for April, 1926. Before the end of that year Knopf brought out a volume of Suckow's short stories, by title *Iowa Interiors*, and I reviewed it in November along with various other new works of fiction. In May, 1928, I reviewed her *The Bonney Family*, which lifted me a great deal less than its predecessors, and in January, 1929, her *Cora*, which also seemed to me to fall below her highest mark. She had, by this time, ceased to write short stories; indeed, she told me so early as 1926 that she had lost interest in the form.

When I first met her I don't recall, but it must have been in late 1924. She came to New York and called at the *American Mercury* office, where I had a somewhat strained palaver with her, for she turned out to be drab and homely, besides being very shy and having no conversation. An advance copy of *The Odyssey of a Nice Girl* was on my desk, and as she prepared to leave I asked her to autograph it. She hesitated a moment, as if embarrassed by the request, and then wrote her simple name on the fly-leaf. After she gave up her bee-farm in 1926 she took to wandering, and was in New York not infrequently.

In 1929 she went to Southern California, the Paradise of all Middle Western country people, and I gave her letters of introduction to various movie folk, including Aileen Pringle. She was vastly impressed by the vivacious and very talkative Pringle, and Pringle was apparently considerably amused by her. It would be impossible to imagine two women more unlike. From San Diego, on March 6, 1929, she sent me the surprising news that she was about to marry Ferner Nuhn, a young pedagogue and critical aspirant from her native wildwood. She was then thirty-seven years old, and Nuhn was hardly more than twenty-five. But this marriage apparently turned out well—at least *qua* marriage. On the artistic side its effects seem to have been less happy, for Suckow wrote nothing after 1929 that was up to the promise of her earlier days, and Nuhn's talents, if he ever had any, have borne no noticeable fruit.

Some time late in 1930 or early 1931, on reaching New York on one of my frequent trips, I was shown a newspaper clipping by Alfred Knopf that was vastly astonishing to me, as it had been to him. It said that the Cosmopolitan Book Corporation, a new Hearst organization, was about to print a book by Suckow. This, of course, was after the historic collapse of the stock market, but the effects of that collapse had not yet revealed themselves in the publishing business, and Hearst was still full of money and eager to extend his enterprises.

The Cosmopolitan Book Corporation was organized on a characteristically grandiose scale. Its aim seemed to be to round up all the writers of fiction who could be pried loose from their old publishers, by whatever device and on whatever terms. New York was full of reports of fabulous offers to this or that one—a $50,000 advance on a novel still unwritten, guarantees of $25,000 a year to authors who had never made $10,000, and so on and so one. Attempts had been made on a number of Knopf authors, and one or two had succumbed, but all of them were good riddance.

But Suckow was something else, for both Knopf and I believed that she would develop, soon or late, into a valuable property, and he had invested a lot of money in her early books, which paid their way but hardly more, in the hope that she would write a big success when she got her growth. But here she was selling out to Hearst—and without so much as notifying Knopf. Worse, she was doing so in the face of a contract—for *The Kramer Girls*—which gave him an option on her next two books. He asked me what he should do, and I advised him at once to send her a sharp letter calling her attention to this contract, and informing her that he would hold her to it. I also advised him to send a copy to the Cosmopolitan Book Corporation, for the consideration of its lawyers.

All this was done, and presently she replied with a highly apologetic but also evasive letter, pleading that she did not know her contract bound her and arguing fatuously that she was also unaware that she should have notified Knopf of her proposed desertion. This was too irritating to be borne, and I advised him again to hold her rigidly to her contract. He did so, and her next book, *Children and Older People*, appeared under his imprint in 1931. He naturally made no effort to promote it, and it was a failure. He thereupon notified her that she could do what she pleased with its successor, but before it was finished the Cosmopolitan Book Corporation had blown up, and she had to turn to Farrar and Rinehart. This book was *The Folks*, which came out in 1934. It was a failure likewise, and so was *Carry-Over*, which followed two years later. After that she published nothing until 1941, when Farrar and Rinehart brought out *New Hope*. It got only indifferent notices, and poor Suckow was apparently done for.

I suspect that her husband, Nuhn, was the nigger in this woodpile. Like any other pedagogue, he was very cocksure, and after the serialization of *The Kramer Girls*, which appeared in one of the popular magazines, he no doubt had dreams of fortune. Whatever the fact, the whole transaction was very damaging to her, and in fact virtually finished her.

She was not the only female writer, alas and alack, who let me in for such a mess. Another, and even worse, was Julia Peterkin. This strange woman was the wife of a country banker in South Carolina, and her home was at Lang Syne Plantation on the swampy banks of the Congaree river, forty miles from Columbia. When I first heard from her I don't recall precisely, but it must have been early in 1921. She sent me, then, a number of short sketches of life among the Gullah Negroes of the South Carolina lowlands, and I was much taken with them, though their dialect was sometimes hard to understand. Nathan, who had a prejudice against all dialect stories, was in doubt about them, but in the course of time I persuaded him to try some of the less recondite, and we did the first one, "The Merry-go-Round" in December, 1921. Others followed later, but we printed much less than a fourth of those she sent in.

There was something extraordinarily grim and impressive about some of these pieces, and I was always glad to get one that was printable. They dealt realistically, and yet in fine sympathy, with the life of blackamoors who were barely two removes from savagery, and they made something of a sensation in the South, and especially in South Carolina. It was impossible, under the local mores, for anyone to denounce the author for them, for she was a lady by Southern standards, and hence could do no wrong. But her editor was a damned Yankee and vulnerable, so I had to serve as a sort of whipping-boy for her, and every time I printed one of her pieces some of the state newspapers belabored me with great ferocity, though always without mentioning the reason. The leader in this onslaught was a poor fish named William Watts Ball, then the editor of the Columbia *State*.

Mrs. Peterkin was certainly a most unusual woman to be living in that desert of the intellect. The daughter of a country doctor and the sister of another, she was educated at Converse College, a small female seminary at Spartanburg, which passed her A.B. in 1896. The year following she made her A.M., and in 1927, after her *Black April* had become a best-seller, D.Litt. She was a good amateur actress and an even better pianist, and once she confessed to me that she was very fond of cock-fighting. In 1922 she wrote to me: "My brother, my father, my husband, my son, my four natural protectors, are annoyed by the few sketches I've printed. . . . Somehow there seems to be in me a lack of the modesty and reticence women normally have. I have been making an effort to record simple, pitiful facts of life as I see them here."

Soon after we got into communication she began inviting me to come to Fort Motte for a visit, for life there must have been dismal indeed to a woman of her mental restlessness. I declined on the advice of counsel, but various other literati seem to have made the trip, for example, Carl Sandburg, Harriet Monroe and Joel E. Spingarn.

Whenever the chance offered she escaped for a trip northward—to see Cabell and Emily Clark in Richmond, to visit a sister in New York, and so on. I met her in New York toward the end of 1921, and saw her there more than once afterward. She was a tall, somewhat slim woman with a curiously exotic air. Her speech was clearly Southern, and she showed a good deal of the traditional Southern blarney in her dealing with men, but otherwise she was as far from the Southern norm as if she had been an Eskimo. She was forty-one years old in 1921—just my age—and she looked it, but there was something unmistakably *séduisante* about her. If I had to describe her in a word I should say that she was distinguished.

When I first heard of her she was meditating a book of her Gullah sketches. Some time later Sandburg and Spingarn got wind of it, and urged her to submit it to Harcourt, who was the publisher of both, and in whose firm Spingarn was a stockholder. I advised her, however, to give Knopf a chance at it, and she eventually took my advice. Knopf was not too eager for it, mainly because he believed that readers would be flabbergasted by the Gullah dialect, but I advocated doing it on the same ground that I advocated doing Suckow's first book, to wit, because I believed that there were excellent possibilities in the author, and that the chances were good that she would do a more likely book later on.

Knopf finally yielded, and *Green Thursday* was duly published in 1924. It got good notices, but it sold badly, and Knopf had to take consolation in his hopes for her next. In 1925 she wrote to me that the next was under way, but when she finished it it turned out to be badly organized and badly written, and soon afterward she abandoned it and went to Europe. The next year she did *Black April*—and the first thing either Knopf or I heard of it was that it was in the hands of the Bobbs-Merrill Company.

I had learned too much about lady authors by this time to waste any argument on her. *Black April* was a big success—in fact, a best-seller—so I had to listen to Knopf's groans throughout 1927. I did not review it, nor did I print any more of her pieces in the *American Mercury*. In 1928 she followed with another success, *Scarlet Sister Mary*, which was awarded the Pulitzer Prize for the year, and later on she did three other books, all published by Bobbs-Merrill. In 1932 she was in New York and proposed that I meet her, but I declined politely. She then invited Sara and me to visit her at Lang Syne

Plantation, with the same result. After that I heard from her only once or twice, and never after 1932.

THE ONLY OTHER *Smart Set* debutantes of 1921 who interested me were Charles MacArthur and Lloyd Lewis. Their excellent comic story, "Hang It All," was printed in the issue for December. Two years later, in November, 1923, MacArthur alone followed it with what I have always thought of as the best hanging story of all time, to wit, "Rope." He was a Pennsylvanian by birth, and the son of a Scotch-Irish preacher father and an apparently Pennsylvania German mother—the same combination that made Joseph Hergesheimer, though no two writers could be more unlike. There was nothing of Hergesheimer's delight in elegance about MacArthur: he was a rough product of Chicago journalism in the days of the epic battle between Hearst and the Chicago *Tribune*. But he knew how to put a story together, and he had a rich and gorgeous humor. He always wrote best in collaboration, and when he took to the theatre his chief successes were *Lulu Belle*, 1926, done with Edward Sheldon; *Salvation*, 1927, with Sidney Howard; and *The Front Page*, 1928, *Twentieth Century*, 1933, and *Ladies and Gentlemen*, 1939, all with Ben Hecht. After 1929 he devoted most of his time to the movies. A year before he had married Helen Hayes.

One day early in 1943 I encountered him on a Washington–New York train in the uniform of a colonel in the Army, and in response to my state of inquiry he told me that he was on the staff of Major General William N. Porter, chief of the Chemical Warfare Service of the Army, in the capacity of press-agent. A little while later Porter came to Baltimore to deliver a patriotic harangue, and MacArthur, who trailed with him, invited me to meet him. But the military, at that time, were not on my calling list, and I declined. I used to see MacArthur frequently in No. 21 and other such night spots in New York. He was a considerable boozer, but a very pleasant fellow. I never met his wife.

Lewis hailed from Indiana, was educated at Swarthmore, and rose to be managing editor of the Chicago *Daily News*. He had a hand for unearthing curious facts from the catacombs of history, and wrote many articles in that field and several amusing and valuable books, for example, *Myths After Lincoln* and *Sherman, Fighting Prophet*. Not many more diverting and instructive volumes of history have ever been printed in These States, or indeed in any other country. Lewis wrote a novel in collaboration with Sinclair Lewis in 1935, by title *Jayhawker*, but I did not read it. Before becoming managing editor of the Chicago *Daily News* he was its dramatic critic, and also lectured on history at the University of Chicago. He was a very charming fellow.

Despite my feeling that 1921 was largely a wasted year, my extra-curricular activities while it lasted covered an ever-increasing range. I read manuscripts for Knopf (always as an unpaid volunteer), I lent a hand to young authors who needed help of one sort or another, I was beset by invitations to write articles for other magazines, some of them hard to refuse, and I began to stagger under a correspondence that grew constantly—part of it from readers well worth knowing, but the rest coming from nuisances who ranged from simple bores to outright maniacs.

Knopf and his wife Blanche (who was already showing signs of that alarming lack of tact which was later to distinguish her) often asked me to read a manuscript or advise them about an author at a moment when I was up to my ears in work, and sometimes I probably answered testily. There was one such clash in the autumn of 1921, and on October 26 I wrote to Blanche: "I am working sixteen hours a day on the indices of *The American Language*—15,000 entries." On November 3 Knopf wrote to me proposing that I read the galley-proofs of Thomas Beer's *The Fair Rewards* and write a blurb for it. What I replied to this I do not know, for all of my letters to Knopf at this time have not been preserved, but it must have been somewhat tart, for on November 4 I was writing to Fielding H. Garrison that a row was in the making. I was eager, through 1921, to get on with *Notes on Democracy*, for in it I hoped to put my judgment upon the hypocritical fustian of World War I, but though I managed to produce a great many fragments, and some of them were printed in "Repetition Generale" or in my book reviews, I found it difficult to get the time and leisure needed to organize the volume, and it kept on riding me until 1926.

Meanwhile, it was some consolation to encourage other critics of the bogus idealism of Woodrow and company, and I did so at every chance. The first of these dissentients that I heard from was a Socialist named John Kenneth Turner. He wrote to me late in 1919, asking me to read a manuscript that he had concocted on the American share in the war, and I did so soon afterward. It turned out to be badly planned and worse executed, but there was a great deal of excellent stuff in it, with precise documentation. Unhappily, it was obvious that it could not be printed at that time, for Woodrow was still on his throne, the United States had not yet made peace with Germany, and the Espionage Act was still running. I accordingly advised Turner that he would have to wait, and suggested that he turn the delay to profit by carefully revising his book.

Meanwhile, I informed Knopf of it, and suggested to him that it should be possible to bring it out on March 5, 1921, the day after the inauguration of Wilson's successor. Knopf read it but was in doubt, and his doubts continued after March 5, for the peace treaty with Germany was still hung up in Congress. When it was signed at last, on July 2, 1921, Turner sent in the MS. for another reading, but again Knopf refused it. During the delays Turner had fallen into the hands of the Socialist shyster E. Haldeman-Julius, then publisher of the *Appeal to Reason* at Girard, Kansas, and Julius was trying to get his permission to run the book serially. This would have ruined it, so I suggested to Turner that he try another publisher, B. W. Huebsch. This, alas, was bad advice, for though Huebsch did not object to the thesis of the work he had had five books suppressed during the war, and was thus very wary. He accordingly declined it without reading it, but when the coast was clear at last I asked him to consider it again, and he agreed to do so.

The negotiations that followed ran on into October, 1921, and put me to a great deal of trouble. Huebsch, who was an indolent fellow, dipped into the MS. and was favorably impressed, but it seemed impossible to induce him to read it in full. Finally, I went to see him in New York and he promised faithfully to do so the next day which was a public holiday. I called him up the day after the holiday and asked him what his verdict was—and he confessed that he had still not read it. "I took it home," he said, "fully determined to give the whole afternoon to it, but we had a heavy lunch and I felt somewhat drowsy afterward. I got out my fiddle to wake myself up, but got so interested that I kept on fiddling all afternoon, and in the evening my wife and I had dinner guests. But I am going to print it anyhow. I take it on your recommendation."

Thus it was sent to the printer at last, and some time in the spring of 1922 it came out. I printed a preliminary notice of it in the *Smart*

Set for August, 1922, and then reviewed it at length the month following. I had to admit that there were some defects in it, but on the whole I whooped it up loudly, for it gave me a fine chance to unload my opinion of the ignominious role played by the United States in the war. "The whole course of the country between 1914 and 1917," I said, "was that of a pick-pocket, a stool-pigeon and a scoundrel." The title of the book was the banal one of *Shall It Be Again?*. The only alternative suggested by Turner was *The Greatest American Swindle*, which seemed to me to be even worse.

My effort, successful at last, to sell it to Huebsch, and my interminable correspondence with Turner, consumed a lot of valuable time, and I learned once more, as I had learned in the case of "Robert Steele," recounted as "Portrait of an Immortal Soul" in *Prejudices: First Series*, that it was dangerous to try to help a bad author. "Steele," whose actual name was R. A. Lindsey, wrote to me at least once a day for a period of several years—first, while I was trying to show him how to write his book, and then while I was trying to sell it to Mitchell Kennerley. Kennerley, like Huebsch, was a man who found it hard to make up his mind, and Lindsey was impatient almost beyond compare. Finally, as in the Turner case, I had to go to see the publisher and apply the heat to him, and at long last the book came out. It got very small notice, but it at least gave me a text for a long article in the *Smart Set* for June, 1915, reworked four years later for *Prejudices*.

Lindsey, having tasted blood, proceeded at once to another book, but so far as I know it never came to anything. He was, when I first heard from him, a drummer making a very good income, but the Depression apparently threw him on his uppers, for early in 1935 he wrote to me (after a long and refreshing silence) from Lake Geneva, Wisconsin, saying that his wife and children (he had generated nine of them by that time) were starving, and asking me for a loan. Whether or not I sent him any money I do not recall, but probably not, for by that time I had learned that needy literati, whether amateur or professional, never repaid what they borrowed.

CHAPTER XXVI

THREE EVENTS MARKED the somewhat depressing history of the *Smart Set* in 1922—the advent of "Americana," an experiment with illustrations, and an effort by Warner and his idiot advertising manager, Irving T. Myers, to scare up more advertising for the magazine. "Americana" was not my invention, though I gave it its title. The first installment of it came in unsolicited from an occasional contributor named Milnes Levick, of whom I know nothing save that he existed. It consisted, in this first form, of quotations from various sources—speeches, advertisements, news dispatches, overheard remarks, and even books—and they were sorted out according to theme—Music, Diet, Citizenship, Religion, etc. The thing was not very well done, and Nathan had some doubts about it, but we printed it in November. After that I began playing with the idea that it embodied, for I saw that it could be greatly improved.

The result was the launching of the regular department in May, 1923, with Major Owen Hatteras, D.S.O., as its ostensible editor. It was mine altogether, for Nathan never read anything printed outside New York, and could not help me. But after the first installment of less than a page and a half had been printed I began to receive contributions from readers, and by the issue for December, 1923, the last of the *Smart Set* that we edited, it ran to four and a half pages, and a great deal of unstable stuff had to be left out. I changed the arrangement to a classification by states, and this was continued when I took the department into the *American Mercury* with its first number, for January, 1924. It had attracted but little notice from other editors while it ran in the *Smart Set*, but when it was transferred to the *American Mercury* it was imitated widely and at once, and by the end of 1924 at least a dozen departments of the same general sort were flourishing in the United States and England.

Early in 1925 the English publishers, Martin Hopkinson & Company, proposed that I make an annual book of it for them, for the English at that time were full of dudgeon against Uncle Shylock and eager for evidence that he and his lieges were imbeciles. I complied willingly, and wrote a buffoonish gloss for the first volume describing the characters of the different States. This book, *Americana, 1925,* was republished in New York by Knopf, and in 1926 the *American Mercury* brought out a special edition of it. *Americana, 1926* followed, also republished by Knopf, but after that there were no more, for No. 2 brought Hopkinson the threat of libel suit.

It was not our plan to illustrate the stories in the *Smart Set,* but simply to print an occasional portfolio of satirical drawings. The first artist we invited to submit one was William Gropper, a young East Side Jew—he was then twenty-five years old—who was beginning to attract attention. After training at the National Academy of Design, he went to work for the New York *Tribune* in 1919, but soon afterward succumbed to the Marxian revelation and became the cartoonist for various Communist papers. But Nathan and I did not care what his politics were, for we would determine what he should draw for the *Smart Set.* His first contribution was a series of four "Portraits of American Ecclesiastics," printed in the issue for July, 1922. I planned them and wrote the captions for them, and Gropper did an excellent job. We asked for more, and for the August issue he drew a series of four entitled "Americanization: A Movie"—a satire on the 100% Americanism then displaying itself in the Ku Klux Klan. It was less effective than the first series, and we began a search for other artists, but the only one we unearthed who really fitted into our scheme was Hans Stengel, and he was far too eccentric and unreliable to be a comfortable collaborator. Nathan was in favor of taking this scheme into the *American Mercury,* but I vetoed it, for I had had a great deal of experience with artists on newspapers, and had very little confidence in them.

Nathan and I had been ding-donging at Warner for a long while about the advertising in the *Smart Set.* It was meagre in quality and mainly unsavory. About the only even half decent advertisement we printed regularly was a quarter page of Bromo-Seltzer, and that was an inheritance from the days of Colonel William D. Mann, acquired

by blackmail. The head of the Bromo-Seltzer Company was a Baltimore druggist named Isaac E. Emerson, who, when immense profits
began to roll in on him, took to social pushing in the grand manner.
In this capacity he attracted the attention of the colonel's weekly,
Town Topics, and was given some rough handling. In order to escape
from it he made an agreement to advertise his headache cure in both
Town Topics and the *Smart Set*, and this agreement he kept after the
Smart Set had been sold to John Adams Thayer, for he apparently
suspected that the colonel still had some interest in it. At all events,
his quarter-page kept on coming in, and we usually printed it on the
inside back-cover, for as a rule we had no other advertising pages.
Our remaining steady ads bore such captions as "Diamond-Watches—
Cash or Credit," "Reduce Your Fat," and "Your Face is Your Fortune." Now and then Warner and Myers collared a better one, but
it was usually on some trade arrangement that brought us no cash.

The advertising agents of those days, as of these, did business according to formulae that were mainly idiotic, and one of the most
absurd of these formulae was to the effect that a magazine made up
wholly of fiction could not be a good advertising medium. This was
not true, and in later years its falsity was proved in a massive manner, but in the early 1920's it was piously believed. Applied to the
Smart Set, it was doubly ridiculous, for the magazine contained a
great deal of matter that was not fiction, and it was precisely this
matter that gave it its character. But Warner and Myers, who believed in and venerated advertising agents, were unable to shake
them, so we got no advertising save a little rubbish. I tried to convince them that there should be good pickings for us among the
smaller specialty advertisers, but it took years to convince them.

Finally, early in 1922, they made an attempt in that direction, and
in the May issue they had eight small ads on the inside front cover
under the heading of "The Shops of the Smart Set," and two more
on the back inside cover. The advertisers were modistes, jewelers,
hair-dressers, and the like. In June there were three pages of such
ads, in July three again, and in August and thereafter four. This
success bestirred Warner and Myers to new and feverish activity, but
it did not improve their intelligence, for they presently took the *Smart
Set* into a combination seeking advertising jointly, under the name
of the Newsstand Group.

Inasmuch as all the other members of this group were such dubious pulps as *Snappy Stories*, *Breezy Stories* and *Young's Magazine*, Nathan and I were perturbed more than gratified, and our doubts were not allayed when we saw the advertisements that began to come in. They included everything in the shabby line save lost manhood and bust developer ads, and we had to take a pretty severe kidding from readers and friends. But under our agreement with Warner he had full control of advertising, and we could do nothing save protest. The issue for December, 1922, contained twenty-three pages of advertising—the largest amount the *Smart Set* had printed since 1914. Some of the captions on it were "Get This Wonderful Ring," "How to Paint Signs and Sho' Cards," "Learn How to Restore Gray Hair," "Bathe Your Way to Slenderness," "Bunions," "How to Make Love," "Be an Artist," "How to Get the Most Out of Marriage," "Don't Wear a Truss," "Write the Words for a Song," and "Sex." There were several ads headed "Send No Money" and half a dozen or more announcing ways to make fortunes by spare-time work at home.

Editorially, 1922 was an average year. Of our twelve novelettes, four were by such hacks as L. M. Hussey, Richmond Brooks Barrett and Eleanor Ramos, but two others were by Thyra Winslow, and we had one each by James Hopper, F. Scott Fitzgerald, Ruth Suckow and Harold H. Armstrong. The Fitzgerald was "The Diamond as Big as the Ritz," reprinted in *Tales of the Jazz Age* in 1922. We also printed novelettes by two newcomers, Marian Spitzer and Whit Burnett. La Spitzer was a young and handsome Jew who, in those days, showed a lot of promise, but soon afterward she married a well-heeled Christian, settled down to connubial bliss, and disappeared from the grove of Athene.

Burnett, who appeared again as a novelette writer in February, 1923, was a newspaper reporter hailing from Salt Lake City and in 1922 was working in New York. He had literary ambitions and in 1926 joined the American *emigrés* in Paris, where he presently became city editor of the Paris edition of the New York *Herald*. In 1929 he moved on to Vienna as a correspondent of the New York *Sun* and the Consolidated Press, and there I encountered him early in 1930. On the Paris *Herald* he had found a women reporter from Boston named Martha Foley, and they were married in June of the same year. Both wrote short stories and both got a good many rejection slips from magazines, so they decided to set up a magazine of their own. They were too poor to employ a printer, but a mimeograph machine sufficed for them, and soon they were circulating five hundred or six hundred copies a month. Burnett lost his job in 1931, and they moved themselves and their magazine, which was called *Story*, to Majorca. In 1933 they came to New York, found a backer and brought out *Story* in orthodox form.

Its success was only moderate, but it attracted the attention of Edward J. O'Brien, the racketeer who had made a good thing from 1915 to 1940 by issuing an annual volume of *The Best Short Stories of* —, and in his 1931 volume he reprinted three stories from it. In 1932 he reprinted eight, and called it "the most distinguished short-story magazine in the world."

Burnett, in his Paris and Vienna days, wore a Latin Quarter beard, but after his return to New York he chopped it off. His own writings never made much impression, but his editorship of *Story* got him many invitations to lecture and he also took to bringing out anthologies. In one of these, *This Is My Best*, published in 1942, he included "The Days of the Giants" from my *Newspaper Days*.

La Foley also resorted to the lecture and anthology rackets, and when O'Brien died in 1941 succeeded him as editor of *The Best Short Stories of* —. In 1942 Burnett turned her out in favor of a woman working in his office, Hallie Southgate Abbett by name. Another of his editorial aides was Edith Lustgarten Kean, who had been editorial secretary on the *American Mercury* in my time. I tried her out on various minor editorial jobs, but found her incompetent for any of them; on *Story*, however, she seems to have been the chief reader of MSS. La Foley appeared in the *American Mercury* in August, 1933, as the author of an article entitled "Blessed Event in Vienna," describing her experiences when she had a baby there in 1932. Neither she nor her husband had much talent, and their writing never rose much above the Left Bank level.

Meanwhile, "The Higher Learning in America" dragged its weary length along, with articles by Gilbert Seldes (Harvard), John Gunther (Chicago), Hendrik Willem Van Loon (Cornell) and others now forgotten. Gunther, in those days, was a young reporter on the Chicago *Daily News*. Once, visiting New York, he came to the office and told Nathan and me his plans to become a foreign correspondent. He made a poor impression on us, but, once he got abroad, he began to be heard from, and, beginning with his *Inside Europe* in 1936, his books were great successes.

Another debutante who was destined to become a best-seller was Dorothea Brande, who contributed short stories to the issues for May and November, 1922. When the *American Mercury* was started she turned up as its circulation manager, and served in that capacity for three years. In 1936 she published an inspirational book called *Wake Up and Live* and it had an enormous sale. On leaving the *American Mercury* in 1927 she joined the editorial staff on the *Bookman*, the mortal remains of which had just been acquired by a rich young man named Seward Collins. When it vanished at last in 1933 she followed him to the *American Review*, and in 1936 she married him. Collins, who was reputed to be consumptive, had a vast yearning to shine as a publicist, but no apparent gift for the art. The *American Review*, which was strongly Fascist in tendency, went down with all hands in 1937. La Brande carried more weight than the beauty doctors advise, but she was a pleasant woman, and in her days on the *American Mercury* she made a good circulation manager.

I contributed nothing to the *Smart Set* in 1922 beyond my monthly book article and my share of "Repetition Generale," but in the latter, in March, I printed a "Threnody" which was presently taken into *Prejudices: Third Series* 1922, with the title changed to "Memorial Service." Toward the end of 1921, chafing under the misunderstandings bred by the absurd title and shabby format of the magazine, I wrote an editorial statement which was printed in the issue for February, 1922, facing the opening page. It was as follows:

A Note from the Editors

A curious misconception of the *Smart Set* seems to persist in certain quarters. Not a few persons appear to be under the impression that the magazine is still much as it was in its early days—that is, a publication given over in considerable part to the fluffy and inconsequential in literature, comment and criticism. This impression, of course, is that of readers who have not actually looked into it during the last half dozen years.

Take a glance at the magazine as it exists today. In the matter of literature, its editors have introduced to the American public in the period named the majority of the younger native writers who have subsequently with their novels attracted the widest and most sober attention. In a number of instances, their novels have appeared in part in the magazine. Among these new writers are

F. Scott Fitzgerald, author of *This Side of Paradise;* Harvey Fergusson, author of *The Blood of the Conquerors;* Ben Hecht, author of *Erik Dorn;* Sherwood Anderson, author of *The Triumph of the Egg;* Elisabeth Sanxay Holding, author of *Invincible Minnie;* Floyd Dell, author of *Moon-Calf,* and others.

The two young American poets at present most widely discussed, to wit, John McClure, author of *Airs and Ballads,* and John V. A. Weaver, author of *In American,* were first brought out by the *Smart Set.*

The foremost of the young American dramatists, Eugene G. O'Neill, was introduced to the public through these pages. The *Smart Set* also published the early work of Zoë Akins and Rita Wellman.

Among the English writers who have come into their own in the last few years, the *Smart Set* was instrumental in introducing Lord Dunsany, W. S. Maugham, W. L. George, James Joyce, Aldous Huxley, Stacy Aumonier, Harold Brighouse, John Cournos, Phyllis Bottome, and others.

The magazine is currently presenting the work of three young American writers whose celebrity is a matter of only a few years, to wit, Ruth Suckow, one of the most extraordinary short story writers that America has produced; Thyra Samter Winslow, the originator of the *Main Street* type of American fiction; and Stephen Ta Van, a writer of the utmost promise.

The *Smart Set* brought out part of *Jurgen,* the masterpiece of James Branch Cabell, who received his first hearing in these pages. It has brought out Theodore Dreiser as a dramatist, and first printed the finest piece of writing in Willa Sibert Cather's *Youth and the Bright Medusa.*

The Boston *Transcript*'s annual survey of American magazines for last year placed the *Smart Set* at the top of the list in the number of distinguished stories published.

This, of course, was somewhat boastful, but there was enough truth in it to make it plausible. It failed of its aim, for the *Smart Set* languished below the salt to the end of the chapter.

During 1922 I put in some hard licks upon *Notes on Democracy* and the third edition of *The American Language.* The latter was finished before the end of the year and Knopf published it in February 1923, but the former hung fire, and it was not until 1926 that it finally came out. My only publication in 1922 was *Prejudices: Third Series*, which was completed in the spring. It was set up by the first week of June, and by the end of July 1 had passed the page proofs. The first copy reached me on October 29. It had to be reprinted during November, and I seized the chance to correct a number of errors in the text, mainly due to my far from perfect proof-reading. I had an errata sheet printed for friends to whom I had sent the first printing, and it was also inserted in twenty-five copies signed for Blanche Knopf.

Prejudices: Third Series got mainly hostile reviews, but most of their fury was directed, not to anything in the book itself, but to the general position of the author, for I had become by 1922 the symbol and to some extent the leader, however undesigned and unwilling, of the revolt of post-war youth against the Old American certainties. Some of the reviewers continued to flog me on the ground, by now familiar, that I was no more than a sedulous ape to the abhorred Nietzsche, turned loose upon a Christian people by the machinations of the late Kaiser and his gang of malefactors. Others, more subtle, tried to dispose of me by arguing that I was only a transient hob-goblin, and would soon be laid. Yet others, even subtler, tried to make it appear that the success of my alleged propaganda was my ruin, and that in a little while I would find myself running out of opponents.

As I have recorded, this popularity among the young was not of my seeking and not to my taste, but it continued until the mounting woes and insoluble problems of the Depression threw the college boys and gals into the arms of Roosevelt II. I was relieved to get rid of them, but not surprised by their defection, for it had always been my theory, constantly expressed, that the average American, whether young or old, simply lacks the mental stamina to face the concept of the irremediable. In 1922 I found consolation for their often embarrassing partisanship in the growth of my reputation abroad, and in this there was also an effective answer to the older reviewers who tried to dispose of me at home.

Continental approbation did not reach most of the American reviewers, but when they began to see me getting attention in England they were considerably wobbled, for American opinion has always been extremely docile to English precept and example. This notice also had an effect on book buyers and book collectors, and after 1921 each of my successive books appeared in the best-seller lists, and my earlier works began to be collected. In June, 1922, the *Publishers' Weekly* published a list of "the forty American authors most favored by the booksellers as judged by a ballot." I was No. 24 on that list, with a number of third-raters, including Owen Wister, Henry Van Dyke, Irving Bacheller and Christopher Morley ahead of me, but soon afterward I began to move up, and the prices asked for my first editions rose. Early in 1922 the Centaur Bookshop in Philadelphia offered first editions of *A Book of Burlesques*, *A Book of Prefaces* and the first two *Prejudices* books at $5 each, and before the end of the year Meredith Janvier of Baltimore was asking $12.50 for *Heliogabalus* and $15 for the first edition of *The American Language*. In January *Biblio* reported that my first editions were in such demand that only the books of Herman Melville stood ahead of them.

Meanwhile, I got more and more notice in the newspapers and magazines, whether favorable or unfavorable. Poets tackled me with pasquinades and other poets replied in my defense, and I was the theme of frequent magazine articles. My manner of writing was burlesqued; I was interviewed on all sorts of subjects; psychoanalysts, graphologists and astrologers printed studies of my aberrations; sages in great variety (including Eugene Debs) were asked what they thought of me, and I began to be discussed in books as well as in articles, both at home and abroad. I was heavily beset by requests for magazine articles, but yielded to them only infrequently, for the *Smart Set* and *Evening Sun* gave me opportunity to say pretty well all I wanted to say.

CHAPTER XXVII

MY RELATIONS with Dreiser in 1921 and 1923 continued to be outwardly cordial, and I lent him a hand in many of his numerous difficulties, but I was increasingly perturbed and disgusted by some of his quirks of character, and the way was laid for the break which came in 1925. At the beginning of 1922 he went to California and there took refuge behind the mysterious address of P.O. Box 181, Los Angeles. I never learned where he actually lived and it was some time before I found out what he was doing. In the very citadel of the quackery for which he always had a weakness he inevitably fell for the master quack of them all, Dr. Albert Abrams of San Francisco. I had met this Abrams in 1920 through George Sterling, who believed in him innocently and was one of his loudest advocates, along with Upton Sinclair. How and through whom Dreiser encountered him I don't know, but my letter-file shows that on November 14, 1922, after his return to New York and St. Luke's Place, he wrote to me suggesting that I seek the help of the Abrams machine in the cure of a gastritis that was then bothering me.

It was never possible to argue with Dreiser about the quacks he was constantly discovering—and believing in. I learnt at an early stage of our acquaintance that this appetite for marvels always submerged his common sense, and as our intimacy developed I saw frequent evidence of the fact that the hand of heredity was heavy upon him. He had two minds, and they operated before and behind a sort of curtain. The one in front was acute enough, but the one in back was dark and barbarous, and its habitual provender was supplied by the evil powers of the air. My frequent glimpses through holes in that curtain were always shocking, and sometimes downright horrifying.

He believed in all the worst frauds who flourished in his time, from Charles Fort, the inventor of super-science, to the current psychotherapists, swamis, spiritualists, numerologists, faith healers, Ouija board operators, etc.

What that "ailment of 25 years" was that he mentioned he did not say and I did not ask. It sounded suspiciously like syphilis, but I never saw any reason to believe that he had it. Abrams, I believe, told *all* his patients that they had it, and usually threw in cancer for good measure. This, at any rate, was his fearsome diagnosis in the case of Sterling. Sterling was naturally much alarmed—and very grateful when Abrams announced that the mysterious machine had cured him. That machine, changed somewhat, was later borrowed by the chiropractors, and they are still using it to gouge money out of the gullible.

Late in 1921 I became involved once more in *The "Genius"* case, which had been lagging for three or four years. The American branch of the John Lane Company had gone bankrupt in the interval and its assets, such as they were, had been acquired by Dodd, Mead & Company, a highly respectable and even somewhat prissy American house. *The "Genius"* was among them, and its status remained dubious, for Dreiser's suit against Lane had got hung on a dead center and the Comstocks were unrelenting, so the book was still, at least in theory, suppressed. Dreiser did not like being sold down the river to Dodd; in fact, he had been negotiating with Horace Liveright to take over all his books, and this complicated the situation considerably.

Meanwhile, he had been turned out of his Tenth Street house by a new owner, and had gone to California, where his only address, so far as I knew, was P.O. Box 181, Los Angeles. This mystification was characteristic of him, and it nettled me to have to communicate with him in so absurd a way. He had various other hopes and worries at the time, and afflicted me at long distance with all of them. For one thing, he was hoping to sell an abbreviated version of *The "Genius"* to some magazine. For another, he was negotiating, against my urgent advice, for a stage presentation of *The Hand of the Potter*. For a third, he had finished his *Newspaper Days* and was eager to place it as a magazine serial, or, at all events, parts of it. For a fourth he was promoting a monument to his brother Paul at Terre Haute, on the Wabash.

In September, not having heard from him for two months, I sent a letter to his postoffice box, addressed to "The Executors of the Estate of the Late Theodore Herman Dreiser, Deceased," and inquiring what his last words had been. Under date of September 26 he replied in the same sportive vein, but vouchsafed no precise information about his doings and desires, though I was representing him in some of the aforesaid negotiations.

In December, 1921, I received a letter from a lawyer named Arthur Carter Hume, at 1 East 45th Street, saying that he had a plan to rescue *The "Genius"* from the Comstocks, and asking me to see him. I called up Hume the next time I was in New York and arranged to wait on him. Dreiser himself meanwhile asked me to do so and to find out what was in Hume's mind. It turned out that the lawyer was a friend to Edward H. Dodd, and was eager to dispose of the old row between Dreiser and the John Lane Company. Lane had a counter-claim against Dreiser for royalties advanced but unearned, and Dodd was willing to use his good offices to have it scaled down. He was willing, too, to reissue *The "Genius"* with a few cuts, to be approved by Dreiser, and he was eager to get his hands on *The Bulwark*, which seemed to be headed for Liveright. On March 2, 1922, I wrote to Dreiser: "It seems to me that the important thing is to release *The 'Genius'*, and get it into print again. If necessary, I advise making a few discreet cuts, but I don't think it will be necessary. I doubt that it will be possible to get any substantial damages out of John Lane. His American house was apparently bankrupt when he sold out."

Sumner agreed to these changes, and I so wrote to Dreiser on June 16. "It is highly important," I reminded him, "that when the resetting is done every cut agreed upon be observed strictly." He replied on June 24: "Grateful, grateful, grateful. Herewith my Gastonian compliments and an Alphonsian bow. . . . I have written Hume & Dodd." On May 1 he had written to me: "Of course I am willing that you should purify *The 'Genius'* and grateful to you for being ready to perform the service." On May 16 he had followed this with "I am perfectly willing to have Dodd-Mead publish an expurgated edition." And on June 8 he had written to Estelle Kubitz, Dreiser's secretary: "Mencken went to the mat with Sumner the other day anent *The 'Genius'* and got him to rescind a few [sic] of his objections. Still, to bring it out with his consent quite few cuts must be made. Just the same it was nice of von Ludendorff to go to all this trouble. It may be brought out in that form." After that I heard nothing more from Dreiser, and early in August I sailed for Europe, thankful that a somewhat vexatious job was off my hands.

Alas, I was too trustful, and had something to learn about his way with gentlemen's agreements. When I got back in October the first thing I heard of him was that he had abandoned Hollywood and was moving into 16 St. Luke's Place, and the second was that he was negotiating with Liveright for the publication of an *unexpurgated* edition of The *"Genius"*.

This last naturally upset me greatly, for I had given my word to Sumner, based on Dreiser's categorical authorization, that our agreement would be respected. I accordingly wrote to Dreiser on October 28 protesting that this reported deal with Liveright, if carried out, would put me in a very embarrassing position. Sumner, I said, "acted very decently, and I don't want him to think that I was stringing him." His reply, dated November 5, was to announce coolly that "Dodd, Briggs, Liveright and others" had convinced him that an expurgated version of The *"Genius"* would not sell, and that Liveright was having "certain lawyers and other vultures of the local District Attorney's staff look into the possibility of defeating Sumner in a fight which is to begin with the publication of the book as it is." There followed an innocent exposition of his idea of decency, as follows: "I did not ask him [Liveright] to do this. He asked me if I would not prefer to have the book reissued as it stands. Of course. Then he asked permission to look into the chances of winning via a process of fixation. I believe I have given that permission." There was no possible reply to this, so I made none. When, early in 1923, I heard that the Liveright "process of fixation" had been completed, and that the book was to be published without the cuts that Dreiser had agreed to, I could only write to Sumner telling him of that fact, and offering him my apologies for wasting his time.

Meanwhile, Dreiser had made a characteristic effort to conciliate me in a way almost as loutish. As I have recorded, he had given me the manuscript of *Sister Carrie* in 1914, and it was now in storage in Baltimore. On October 29, 1922, he wrote to me saying that I would shortly receive an inquiry regarding the manuscript from a gentleman who would "want to know your selling price" and asking me to demand not less than $2,000. He went on:

Unless you do you will be underselling me and some others—cutting the price. "Free" brought $300, "The Blue Sphere" $300, "Laughing Gas" $300. "The Girl in the Coffin" is now held at $800 by the owner. I have received a record price for the original of "Jennie Gerhardt," and it will be no hardship to you to receive $2,000 in case you decide to sell.

My reply is not preserved, and I am not sure that I sent one in writing. More probably I delivered it the next time Dreiser and I met. However it was conveyed, it was to the effect that the manuscript was not for sale—that I simply could not imagine selling a present from him. This, unhappily, did not daunt him, and he was apparently quite unable to see the point of it. On November 5 he wrote to me again:

I do not ask you to sell the book. As a matter of fact, if approached again, even with an offer of $2,000, I wish you would rest until you hear from me. Certain things have developed which make a high-priced sale entirely possible. If I should arrange a deal such as you personally could not effect and it meant a good sum & you wanted to take over some ready cash would you split the return? Your share should be over $2,000. Same to me & same to a third mysterious grafter.

This put me in a difficult position, for I assumed that he was short of money, and disliked to deprive him of $2,000. I therefore told him that I stood ready to return the manuscript to him, but that under no circumstances would I take any part of the proceeds of its sale. I had to say this four or five times more before I finally threw him off. In the course of these unpleasant parleys he told me that he actually hoped to get $10,000 for the manuscript, and that the prospective purchaser was Belle DaCosta Greene, librarian of the J. Pierpont Morgan Library. Who the "third mysterious grafter" was he never told me. Nor could I ever make out whether he proposed to stand pat on $2,000 as my share or give me a larger cut of the probably imaginary $10,000.

The "Genius" affair bobbed up again in 1923, when Dreiser got into a row with the Authors' League. This began when a committee of the league headed by Rex Beach, and including Clayton Hamilton, Irvin S. Cobb and Ellis Parker Butler, invited him to take part in "a

proposed international two days' congress" in New York on June 7
and 8 to frame a plan "to advance the artistic and cultural standards
of moving pictures." A little while before this the legislature at Albany had come close to passing a so-called Clean Books Bill backed
by the Catholic church, the Y.M.C.A. and the Comstock Society,
and the Authors' League had been rather backward in opposing
it. It was only killed, indeed, by the heroic efforts of Jimmie Walker,
then a state senator from New York City and majority leader in the
Senate. Dreiser, who had been naturally much interested in this battle, let go with the following blast at Beach:

> My mature opinion is that the Authors' League of America
> might be much more appropriately concerning itself at this time
> with calling conferences of such forces as it can muster to make
> safe the cultural and artistic privileges and necessities of serious
> letters, than which there is nothing more important at this time.
> To be sure the arbitrary and inquisitorial Clean Books League
> Bill has been temporarily scotched in the state senate at Albany,
> but how long will it be before it will be before that body in
> another form, or before some one of the other forty-eight state
> legislatures. This issue is pressing,—a genuine menace;—whereas
> the other is not. Motion pictures, buttressed by full financial bun-
> kers and encircled by well paid lawyers and such literary assis-
> tance as their intelligence will permit them to employ, can wait.

The Authors' League told off Gelett Burgess to answer this denunciation, and he gave his reply to the newspapers. In it he spoke of
Dreiser's "dubious sex fiction." This brought forth another tirade from
Dreiser, addressed to Burgess, in which the recreancy of the league
was rehearsed at length, and with not a little rhetorical exaggeration.
Dreiser sent me copies of all these documents, and I read them with
great interest. In particular, I was interested in this passage: "I fought
The 'Genius' issue single handed for five years. And I am still fighting
it—single handed."

The news that he had fought the Comstocks in The "Genius" case
"single handed" was news indeed, but my first shock was quickly
followed by a sort of wry amusement. In him I saw revealed unpleasantly what I had before noticed in others: that a man whose ideas
are animated by moral indignation is seldom if ever sensitive to points
of honor. Moreover, I could see constantly augmenting evidence that

his unhappy heredity and his even more unhappy early environment were gaining upon him as he grew older.

He was essentially a German peasant, oafish, dour and distrustful of all mankind, and he remained one to the end of the chapter. It was always unsafe to assume that he would react to a given situation in the manner of what is called a gentleman. He might do it on occasion, but he was much more likely not to do it. His customary attitude to the world was that of any other yahoo, say an Allegheny hill-billy or a low-caste Jew. He trusted nobody, and was always suspicious of good will—save only when it was pretended by palpable frauds. He saw himself surrounded by threats and menaces. Some of them, alas, were real enough, but most were only figments of his lush but always rather childish imagination. He had a vast confidence in ghosts, banshees and hobgoblins, and there were whole areas in which his thinking was hard to distinguish from hallucination.

I had a considerable fondness for him, mainly, I suppose, because of my awareness of his intense unhappiness, and I certainly greatly admired him as an artist, at least when he was at his best, but by 1922 I had begun to believe that close personal association with him, save on the ground of idle raillery, was not likely to be long-enduring.

CHAPTER XXVIII

MY PRINCIPAL ASSOCIATES in New York in the 1920–23 era were George Nathan, Philip Goodman, Tom Smith, Ernest Boyd, and, until his death in 1921, James Huneker. I also saw something of Harold Stearns, Hendrik Van Loon and Carl Van Vechten in those years, and after the publication of *Main Street* late in 1920 was more or less intimate with Sinclair Lewis. Beginning in 1921 Goodman and I undertook beer-hunts every time I was in town, and after we discovered good *Wirtschäfte* on the Jersey shore we often took Boyd, Nathan and Lewis with us, and not infrequently others, including Dreiser.

Dreiser, by this time, had abandoned his former virtual teetotalism, and had progressed from the multichrome liqueurs of Greenwich Village to the beverages of honest Christians. He had even developed a liking for beer. Unhappily, he lacked capacity for it, and a few *Seidel* set him to guffawing and slapping his knees. But like most men, he was better company alight than cold sober, and Goodman and I enjoyed our sessions with him. When *Prejudices III* came out in October, 1922, I sent him an early copy, inscribed, but he did not acknowledge it until December 6, and then only in response to a reminder. It was still hard for him to think of me save as a mere disciple, and more time would have to pass before he would realize that I now had my own fish to fry.

Stearns, when I first got to know him in 1920, was already deep in plans for his book, *Civilization in the United States*, which finally came out in 1922. My recollection (somewhat vague) is that I met him through Grace Johnson Livingston, the divorced wife of Dr. Burton E. Livingston, professor of plant pathology at the Johns Hopkins.

On their divorce in 1918 she moved to New York and took a flat in the Washington Square section, and there I saw her off and on in the 1918–20 period. *Civilization in the United States* made a tremendous pother in its day, and Carl Van Doren, then literary editor of the *Nation*, considered it so important that he gave over his entire book section to it, but my royalty records show that it sold but 4,931 copies down to April 25, 1924, including the English and Canadian sales, and that I got only $81.38 from it for my chapter on politics.

Stearns inhabited squalid quarters at 31 Jones Street in Greenwich Village, and dressed so badly that he always looked dirty, but he somehow managed to keep himself supplied with the nauseous bootleg sherry that was his favorite tipple. When he called a conference of contributors at his place there was always a bottle of it on the table and he got down frequent long stoups. I tried it only once; after that I pretended to have stomach ulcers. Stearns had been married early in life but his wife had died in childbirth, leaving him a son, and he was now cohabiting with a girl named Frances, of whom I never learned anything save her name. In August, 1937, he married a well-heeled widow named Elizabeth Chalifoux Chapin, and went to live with her at her place, "Frost Pond," at Locust Valley, Long Island. He wrote to me on September 24, 1937: "I am happy, busy, and this address, for the first time since I have ever written to you, is typed from what I have the right to call, and the fact attests it, my home." But by this time he was a hopeless drunkard, and I never heard from him afterward. Eventually he developed cancer and died in great pain on August 13, 1943—the thirteenth and a Friday.

I saw him often while *Civilization in the United States* was under way, and had some hand in the selection of contributors thereof. It was I, I believe, who suggested Elsie Clews Parsons for the chapter on sex, and she was the first to turn in her chapter. Stearns asked me to try to interest Dr. Lewellys F. Barker, Sir William Osler's successor at the Johns Hopkins Medical School, in the chapter on medicine, but if I actually made the attempt it failed, and the chapter was finally written by Paul de Kruif, whom I nominated. Stearns wanted George Santayana, who was one of his idols, or James Harvey Robinson to do religion, but both declined, and he then turned, at my suggestion, to Woodbridge Riley, whose excellent chapter on popular Bibles in the *Cambridge History of American Literature* had been expunged by the craven Putnams at the behest of the Christian Scientists. Others whom I had some hand in roping were Robert H. Lowie, who wrote on science, and Katharine Anthony, who wrote on the family. I advised against including various papers that seemed to me to be inferior, including one by a man named McMahon on advertising and one by Burton Rascoe on the movies, and they were left out.

The book, when it was put together at last, was very uneven in texture. Some of the chapters were excellent, but others were only so-so, especially mine on politics, which was written under the heavy pressure of other work. But, as I have said, the book made a considerable sensation, if only because of its sharply realistic point of view, and Stearns got some stature as a pundit. I came to know him pretty well while it was under way, and acquired some appreciation for his parts, though his alcoholism impeded his exercise of them. He must have saved some money from the fund put up by his angel, for he sailed for England July 4, 1921. He had promised, some time before this, to do an article on Harvard for the *Smart Set*'s college series, but he never produced it, and in the end I had to get Gilbert Seldes to do it.

Stearns remained in Europe for three years or so, existing I don't know how. When he returned at the end of 1924 it was by way of Cuba and California. He showed up in Baltimore in January, 1925, and asked me to introduce him to the editors of the Baltimore *Sun*. I did so, and he proposed to go back to Europe, and send them some correspondence from Paris. They accepted, but he never sent anything worth printing. Instead he became a leading figure in the world of American expatriates then collected on the Left Bank, and I soon heard that he was making a meagre living serving as race-track tipster for one of the American papers in Paris. He went downhill steadily, and was soon the champion drunk of the American colony. I heard nothing from him until 1933, when he bobbed up again in Greenwich Village and proposed to do some articles for the *American Mercury*. I told him to go ahead, but nothing, of course, came of it.

During the next few years he published a book or two on the theme of *Civilization in the United States* but they fell dead, and so did *The Street I Know*, an autobiography. After his marriage in 1937 he pulled himself together and projected a companion volume to *Civilization in the United States*, to be done cooperatively on the same plan, and it was finished at the end of the year. He put me down for the chapter on religion, but I refused, and then he tried to induce me to do one on the American language. I finally wrote to him on October 1, 1937: "I am sorry to be drawing out, but I simply can't go along with some of your collaborators. It would be much more reasonable and graceful for me to remain cut." I heard no more from him after that, and never saw the completed book, which seems to have come out in 1937 as *America: A Reappraisal*.

MY FIRST CONTACT with Hendrik Willem Van Loon was toward the end of 1920, when he wrote to the *Smart Set* objecting to an item in "Repetition Generale" for November—four paragraphs upon the biological effects of war. In the same letter he mentioned his book, *The Fall of the Dutch Republic* (1913), and soon afterward I read it. I was greatly impressed by it and so wrote to him, and before the end of the year we met in New York.

I was a good deal less impressed by Van Loon himself. He was a huge and burly fellow and somewhat blatant and noisy, and I was not surprised when he told me that he had Jewish blood. Born in Rotterdam in 1882, he came to America at twenty-one equipped with English good enough to get him through Cornell at twenty-three. During the next year he was a student at Harvard and in 1911 he got a Ph.D. from Munich. He was a man of considerable information and decided intelligence, but there was nevertheless something cheap about him, and by 1920 he was already tiring of the serious history with which he had begun and turning to popular stuff. The first fruit was *The Story of Mankind*, which came out in 1921. I gave it a brief but friendly notice in the *Smart Set* for February, 1922, calling it "the best book ever heard of to give a boy" and promising to review it at greater length later.

But this longer review was never written, for the book became an instant and enormous success, not among boys but among the adult yearners for predigested knowledge who had devoured H. G. Wells's *Outline of History* and were to gulp Will Durant's *The Story of Philosophy* in 1926. On November 5, 1920, Van Loon had written to me: "I have given up writing ponderous books. The freshman generation of our land is beyond salvation anyway. I am trying to get at the kids." This enterprise he pursued until the end of his life, but he never had another success to match *The Story of Mankind*. It was catnip to the women's clubs all through 1922, and seemed such a masterpiece to J. Edwin Murphy, then managing editor of the Baltimore *Evening Sun*, that he offered the author a job as columnist on that paper. He was also offered and took briefly the chair of history at Antioch College, Yellow Springs, Ohio, but he seems to have spent little time harassing its sophomores, for he was often roving the country, and especially the Middle West, on lecture tours. What between royalties and lecture fees he had a considerable income in 1922, but very little of it went into his privy purse, for he and his second wife, a third-rate actress named Helen Criswell, were divorced during the year, and she collared most of his assets.

His matrimonial affairs were rather curious. Early in life, when he was a young historian looking for a job and existing precariously on occasional newspaper commissions, he was fed by one Eliza Bowditch, always called Jimmie, who kept a tearoom in Greenwich Village, and in 1906 he married her. She was a mere wisp of a woman, and beside his huge bulk looked tiny. She supported him through his lean years, but in 1919 he met La Criswell and was so inflamed by her pulchritude and learning (she was a Bryn Mawr A.B.) that he dragooned poor Jimmie into getting a divorce and at once married the new charmer. They were at loggerheads in little or no time, and in 1922 there was another divorce. Not long afterward he remarried Jimmie, and she was still his wife, I believe, when he died in 1944. I met her not infrequently during the early 20's. She was the most self-effacing little woman ever heard of, and like everyone else who knew the two of them I sympathized with her in her troubles.

Between his marriages Van Loon stopped at the Algonquin Hotel and I saw him often—in fact, much too often, for he had a habit of barging into my room without notice, sometimes to my embarrassment. He alleged in *Who's Who in America* that he had been a correspondent in Europe from May, 1915, to February, 1918, but it was commonly believed in New York that he had been working for the English press-bureau. This I believed myself, and it thus amused and delighted me when, in 1922, the English refused him a visa to visit England—and gave *me* one with every show of cordiality.

As I have recorded, the *Smart Set* printed an article by him, on Cornell, in its college series, in May, 1922. I got it from him. Nathan, who was a loyal Cornell alumnus, disliked it and I was not enamored of it myself, but the hullabaloo over *The Story of Mankind* was then raging, and we printed it because of its possible sales value. To the

American Mercury for July, 1924, he contributed a short and indifferent piece called "The Wages of Peace," and to the issue for January, 1926, an even shorter and feebler one called "Bread." After that I printed him no more. His writing always seemed to me to be a bit strained and stilted, and I have some doubt that he ever really became at home in the English language.

He attained to greater ease in English as he grew older, but he never quite mastered it, and he was certainly always incapable of such writing as Conrad did in *Youth*. We kept up an intermittent correspondence so long as he lived, but I seldom saw him after the early 30's. When World War II broke out he resumed the howling against the Germans that he had done in World War I. The invasion of Holland, of course, gave him plenty of excuse, but I nevertheless held aloof from him.

AMONG THE OTHER literary characters I came to know pretty well in the early 20's were Robert H. Davis, John Farrar, Carl Van Doren, Carl Van Vechten, Albert Jay Nock, Paul de Kruif, Vachel Lindsay, Carl Sandburg, Benjamin De Casseres, Fred Lewis Pattee, Harry Elmer Barnes, Isaac Goldberg, Edgar Lee Masters, Frank Harris, Sinclair Lewis, James Branch Cabell, Upton Sinclair and James M. Cain.

Davis (1869-1942), whom I met back in 1913, was then the chief editor of all the Munsey magazines and had an office in the Flatiron Building. In that office, which was very roomy, there was a bookcase covering one whole wall and in the bookcase were copies of all the bad novels that Bob had inspired. He was immensely fertile in devising complicated and melodramatic plots and retailed them to Munsey authors on a fifty-fifty basis. He also took a cut of the movie rights, which were just then beginning to have market value, and between the two schemes he made plenty of money. The pulp authors in the Munsey stable did not object to the arrangement, for they could turn out a novel, once they had a plot, in not more than thirty days, and they knew that if they used a Davis plot it stood a very good chance of being accepted for *Munsey's*, *All-Story*, the *Ocean*, the *Cavalier*, the *Live Wire* or some other of the Munsey magazines that came and went.

I liked Bob very much and though I of course had no business with him I saw him often. He had been born and brought up in Nevada, and was full of tall tales of its wild and woolly days. His father had been a clergyman but his own youth was anything but sedate. One of his best stories recounted how, as a boy, he had robbed a blind gambler—by climbing to the rafters above the gambling hall, and picking up money with a billiard cue tipped with shoemaker's wax as the gambler counted up his takings (all in coin) after hours.

Bob was a great gourmet and loved to give gaudy stag dinners at his house. His wife, Madge, after seeing that all was in order for the feast, would go to the theatre, and Bob would fall upon the victuals with his guests. There were immense roasts and high piles of vegetables, along with plenty of prime bootleg wine, and dinner would go until Madge returned home. Nathan and I were frequent guests, and another was a handsome priest from St. Patrick's Cathedral. No one ever got tight, but I recall that I seldom had any appetite for twenty-four hours afterward.

When Munsey died in 1925 and his string of magazines blew up, Bob transferred to the New York *Sun*, which was the last of Munsey's numerous newspapers, and the only solvent one. The *Sun* was controlled after September 30, 1926, by William T. Dewart, another Munsey lieutenant, and Bob had stock in it and sat on its executive board. He also served it as a roving correspondent until his death, and had what was, to his taste, a swell time. His hobby was photography, and he produced some remarkable portraits with a small German box-camera. But it was almost impossible to beg, borrow or steal a print, and he forbade their reproduction. In 1932, however, he brought out a handsome leather-bound folio volume under the title of *Man Makes His Own Mask* and gave me a copy. There was a foreword by Benjamin De Casseres—in which I was described as "the roughneck idealist"—and opposite each portrait was a note on the sitter by Bob himself.

Bob was an intimate of Irvin S. Cobb (1876-1944), and sweated painfully under my ferocious assaults upon Cobb in the *Smart Set*. I began in February, 1913, with a very unfavorable notice of his *Anatomy*, dismissed his *Roughing It De Luxe* with a few lines in October, 1914, and after a short review of *Speaking of Operations*—in February, 1916, gave him and it the works in March of the same year. This last denunciation I took into *Prejudices I* in 1919. Some of Cobb's short stories seemed to me to have more or less merit, and I said so in February, 1913, and September, 1917, but his efforts at what may be called pure humor set my teeth on edge. He had an eager follow-ing of customers and they hailed him grandiloquently as "the heir of Mark Twain," but to me he appeared to be rather the heir of Ayers' Almanac.

After 1915 my choler against him was increased by his singularly dishonest conduct in World War I. He had been in Belgium during the German invasion, and joined the other American correspondents there in certifying that the "atrocities" reported by the British press bureau were imaginary, but as the United States moved toward en-tering the war he had a patriotic change of heart and began to howl against the Germans. This howling culminated in *Speaking of Prus-sians*—in 1917, in which he made full use of all the lies he had hitherto denounced. This *volte face* filled me with something almost akin to moral indignation, and in the amplified form of my review of *Speaking of Operations*—, in *Prejudices I*, I had at him in a truly brutal manner.

The result was that Bob Davis invited me to meet him at lunch, in the hope that personal contact might abate my dudgeon. We duly met in 1921, but Cobb did not impress me. He was a very fat fellow and far from amusing in his talk, though it should be added that his uneasiness in my presence no doubt cramped his customary style. We exchanged a few polite but hollow letters afterward, but so far as I can recall never met more than casually and then only a few times. I never noticed any of his books after 1917: none of them seemed to me to be worth the space. His chief outlet in the 20's was the *Satur-day Evening Post*, and it was reputed to pay him as much as $5,000 for a short story. But he eventually quarrelled with George Horace Lorimer (1868-1937) and transferred his flag to some other maga-zine—I think it was Hearst's *Cosmopolitan*. After that, like many another deserter from the *Saturday Evening Post*, he went downhill. By 1930 he was going on lecture tours and crooning for the radio, and then he took to the movies, even appearing as an actor. When he died in 1944 he was living at Santa Monica, one of the faubourgs of Hollywood, and had been pretty well forgotten. The notice of his death in *Variety*, the movie organ, ran to but eighteen lines.

JOHN FARRAR was one of the really fabulous characters of the early 20's. A blond, girlish and blushing young fellow with nothing to his credit save a few sheaves of banal verse, he got more attention and adulation than any of his granddads of the literary trade. It was seldom, indeed, that a bookish gossip column came out without some mention of him, and his occasional forays into literary society caused as much buzzing as the appearance of such contemporary dignitaries as Gertrude Atherton, Alexander Woollcott and Heywood Broun. He was commonly spoken of as the leader of the Younger Generation of American authors, though who constituted this generation and what it was doing were never clear.

A native of Vermont, he was delivered from both Yale and the Army in 1919 and went to work as a cub reporter on the New York *World*, then just beginning its brief career as a literary newspaper. He made no impression there, but suddenly, in 1921, George H. Doran made him editor of the moribund *Bookman*, which had been steadily disintegrating since the resignation of the salty and highly competent Harry Thurston Peck (1856–1914) in 1907. Farrar was as hopeless in the job as a ship's cook set to command a battleship, for his knowledge of books was no wider than that of any other young Yale man and his ideas of editing were wholly puerile, but he nevertheless leaped into eminence instanter and began to be bathed in the notice I have mentioned.

In part, I suppose, this strange phenomenon was to be blamed on the fact that all the bad authors of the time, realizing his inexperience and incapacity, saw a chance to grab space in his magazine, but in part it must have been due simply to his unusual physique. He was slim and graceful and had the peaches-and-cream complexion of a young girl not yet condemned to night work. As a result, he became at once the darling of all the fat women who like to rub noses with authors, and in a little while he was touring the country haranguing the women's clubs and driving the old girls crazy. Of that dismal trade there was never any more successful practitioner, at least in my time. He drew houses as big as those of Woollcott, and the next day the spinsters who wrote literary news for the local papers swooned over him.

Johnnie took all this quite seriously, and frequently pontificated on literary themes. He was always very polite to me, and pressed me to contribute to the *Bookman*, but I seldom did so, for I could never see him save as a comic character. Unhappily, the magazine did not make any money for Doran, and he gradually took a somewhat bilious view of his editor. When, in 1926, Johnnie married a young woman named Margaret Petherbridge, a concoctor of crossword puzzles, and proceeded to beget children, there was a marked letdown among his fans, and the next year his employer dispensed with his services and shut down the *Bookman*.

He had meanwhile got a job as literary advisor to Doubleday, Page & Company, but this also petered out, and in 1929 he went into business on his own with Stanley M. Rinehart, Jr., the very smart son of Mary Roberts Rinehart, under the trade name of Farrar & Rinehart, Inc. Mainly because of the skill and enterprise of young Rinehart, this firm did very well, but in the course of time it began to be whispered that Johnnie was to be thrown out. This, however, did not actually happen until 1944. Johnnie, who had been a first lieutenant in the Air Service in World War I, served gallantly in the Office of War Information in World War II. When he returned from the Mediterranean theatre in the autumn of 1944, where he had been engaged in what was called Psychological Warfare, Rinehart got rid of him, and went on alone under the style of Rinehart & Company. Johnnie, for a while, had no publishing connection, but in 1945 or 1946 he snared a backer in the person of a rich young Jew named Straus, and by 1947 he was functioning again as Farrar, Straus & Company. Whether or not this new venture is a success I do not know.

Ben De Casseres stood at the opposite pole from Farrar, physically and mentally. He was a lean and sardonic Jew, hawked of nose and almost bald of head. Few men that I knew in those days had more original ideas, or maintained them with a greater pungency, but unhappily a great many of them were extravagant and indeed nonsensical, and he was late in learning to set them forth in a connected and coherent manner. His contributions to the *Smart Set*, which stretched from December, 1914—the second issue under Nathan's and my editorship—to October, 1922, were all short and some of them ran to only a few lines.

Ben came to a family of Sephardic Jews settled in Philadelphia, and claimed to be a collateral descendant of Spinoza, whom he sometimes imitated rather heavily. He was allusive, sententious and mystical, and often concocted a thumping epigram that remained of dark and even unfathomable meaning. This was a quality that naturally appealed to Dreiser, who regarded him as a very profound writer, and denounced me violently in 1915 for not printing more of him. I admired him myself, and printed first and last a great deal of his stuff, and there was a lot more that neither I nor any other editor ever printed. His books were mainly only pamphlets and most of them were brought out at his own expense. Between 1936 and 1938 he published no less than twenty-three of them under the general title of *The De Casseres Books*, with such individual titles as *I Dance With Nietzsche*, *The Last Supper* and *Spinoza Against Rabbis*. In the days when I first knew him, *c.* 1914, his writing was only a sort of side-line; he got his chief income, to wit, $40 a week, working as a proof-reader for the New York *Herald* and before that he had done the same work on the Philadelphia *Press* and the New York *Sun*. Simultaneously he did book reviews for these papers and for others, and in the course of time he made his way into the magazines.

I saw him often during the middle and later years of the *American Mercury*, on which he was one of my stand-bys, for he could do precisely the gay, ribald sort of thing that so few other writers produced. He began with his usual groups of short pieces and now and then he went back to them, but I gradually induced him to tackle more sustained articles, and he turned out many very good ones. Perhaps his best was "Lüchow's," one of a series on the drinking-places and companions that he knew and esteemed. He also did some studies of American personages who happened to interest him and many miscellaneous pieces embodying his agnostic and subversive philosophy. He produced a great deal more stuff than I could use, and one of the things I had to reject was excellent but unprintable. Not a few of those I printed needed rewriting. I made numerous efforts to induce Knopf and other publishers to do his books, but always in vain, for they saw no sales in them, and they were probably right. He was one of those authors who acquire violent fans, but not enough of them.

Nevertheless, one of those fans made his fortune for him. This was some functionary in the Hearst organization, to me unknown. One day late in 1934 he induced the higher authorities to take Ben on the New York *Mirror* to do a daily column, and in a little while he was turning out editorials, book reviews and other stuff for all the Hearst papers and getting a salary that made him comfortable and even opulent for the rest of his life. His style, to be sure, was somewhat cribbed, cabined and confined by Hearst prejudices and pruderies, but when he undertook a theme on which the former ran with his own, which was not unseldom, he was free to lay about in a coruscating and berserker manner. What he was paid I don't know, but it was a great deal more than he had ever earned before. He moved from East 19th Street, where he had been living for some years, to a fine apartment at 593 Riverside Drive, and there he eased himself in his Zion. His work was light, his editors were amiable, and he liked the sense of power and importance that went with his job. "The Hearst people," he wrote to me on May 17, 1935, "are simply great to work for. Never once in five months have I written a line that was contrary to my convictions—although, naturally many eds. are trivial and ephemeral."

Ben married a woman named Bio Terrill in 1919. She was supposed to have Indian blood. I never met her, but I gathered from his talk and letters that they got on splendidly. Bio, it appeared, was convinced that Ben was the greatest genius then extant on earth, and Ben whooped up Bio as the perfect wife. As money rolled in on them, they began to enjoy the luxuries of life, including travel. They went to Miami Beach in 1940 and stayed at the St. Moritz Hotel on the ocean, paid $12 for a room and meals for the two of them, and met Ben Hecht. Another time they made a journey to Jamaica, where Ben tried to find his and my colored relatives, for some of his people, like mine, had been settled there before they came to the United States, and the bachelors among them left a numerous progeny.

Isaac Goldberg, like De Casseres, was a Jew, and like De Casseres again, one of the better sort. He lacked altogether De Casseres's bawdy and ribald charm, but he was a man of very considerable learning, and what is more, of fundamental decency. I first heard from him in 1918, when, in the July *Smart Set*, I denounced the villainous translation of one of the *Nine Humorous Tales* by Anton Chekhov, brought out by him and Henry T. Schnittkind. I had hitherto praised his competent version of *Six Players of the Yiddish Theatre*, and it thus surprised me to find him mauling Chekhov's *Vengeance*. He wrote to me on June 16, 1918, to say that he had had nothing to do with the translation of the story, and had in fact objected to it on the very grounds that I had adduced. The actual translator, I gathered, was Schnittkind.

Goldberg was born in the West End of Boston, and educated at the English High School and Harvard. He took his A.B. in 1910, his

Am.M. in 1911, and his Ph.D. in 1912. Early in life he had become interested in languages, and by the time he left college he had a firm grasp of Spanish, Portuguese, French, Italian, German and Yiddish. It was this possession which chiefly supported him afterward. He was in demand for translations, he wrote a great deal of critical stuff about the Latin-Americans, and at Harvard, where he was never a member of the faculty but only a special lecturer, he aroused an interest in Latin-American literature.

When I first knew him his English was somewhat gnarled and bookish, but by the late 20's he had achieved a style that was fluent and graceful. His point of view scarcely fitted into the scheme of the *Smart Set*, but when the *American Mercury* was under way I naturally turned to him, and he was a frequent and useful contributor. His first contribution was a review of a Brazilian book, *Patria Nova*, by Mario Pinto Serva, in our very first number, January, 1924. In those early days I was toying with the idea of farming out the book reviews, for after doing them for fifteen years in the *Smart Set* I was growing tired of them, but it soon appeared that the scheme was unworkable and so I took them over again and did them alone until I left the *American Mercury* at the end of 1933. Goldberg's second contribution was an article entitled "As Latin America Sees Us," in the issue for December, 1924.

Thereafter he wrote on various Latin Americans, on music (chiefly of the most popular sort) and on miscellaneous subjects, including his own early memories. He played at composing, and once sent me a hymn that he had written in 1914, to words by Schnittkind; an "English High School March and Two Step," 1915, and a vocal setting of "Tell me where is fancy bred" from Shakespeare's *Merchant of Venice* (1917). There were five of these Shakespearean songs, but only one was ever published. It is stated in *Twentieth Century Authors*, by Stanley J. Kunitz and Howard Haycraft, that Isaac was music critic of the *American Mercury* for two years beginning with 1930, but this is something of an exaggeration. I employed him to do an occasional leading article for the department of music that was set up in March of that year, and he wrote most of the reviews of sheet music, scores and phonograph records, but I was myself the editor thereof, and many other critics and musicologists contributed.

He was an odd fish, and full of strange inhibitions. He used neither alcohol nor tobacco, and also avoided meat, coffee, and tea. Once I went out to his house at 65 Crawford Street, Roxbury, for lunch with him and his wife, and they gave me a meal lacking all of these things. When he came to New York and Nathan and I essayed to entertain him we were stumped, for all the other guests we ever saw were boozers and we had what amounted to conscientious scruples against offering anyone buttermilk, Coca-Cola or chocolate, his favorite tipple. These sessions with poor Isaac were commonly held in Nathan's apartment in the Royalton, 44 West 44th Street, and though we both liked him they tended to be somewhat strained affairs.

From 1919 onward I saw him rather often, and in the intervals of his visits to New York he wrote to me at length about his various enterprises. Throughout the 20's and early 30's his steadiest patron was E. Haldeman-Julius, the racketeer who published five-cent books at Girard, Kansas. How many of these he did for Julius I do not know, nor how much he was paid for them—probably very little. In 1924 he added one on me—a pamphlet of sixty-four pages, $3\frac{1}{8} \times 5$ inches in size. In a letter dated February 7 he described it as "the result of some seven or eight years' gradual accumulation of attitude." It was done with painstaking and his work upon it naturally suggested that he expand it into a full-length book. He thereupon proposed such a book to M. Lincoln Schuster, of Simon & Schuster, and on February 14 he reported that Schuster was "very enthusiastic about the possibilities." They soon came to terms and by February 25 Goldberg was hard at work upon the book. Unhappily, it quickly turned out that he really knew next to nothing about me, and so I had to dictate long memoranda for his use. I also lent him clippings, letters and illustrations, allowed him to quote from my early writings, including *Ventures into Verse*, and tried to keep him straight on names and dates.

The book came out toward the end of October, 1925, and seems to have had a very fair sale, for there was a second printing in November. It sold at $4, which was high for that time. It was, of course, very friendly, and I doubt that it could be called penetrating. Goldberg, though we agreed about almost everything else, inclined toward Socialism, and this made it quite impossible for him to understand my political and economic ideas. However, he made a gallant attempt, and the book got me a great deal of useful notice—chiefly, to be sure, abusive, but nevertheless useful. Inasmuch as Ernest Boyd's little book[1] on me appeared almost simultaneously, it began to be admitted that I had to be attended to, and though the attention I got was very far from flattering it was valuable to the *American Mercury* and probably also to my own fortunes.

I kept in more or less contact with Goldberg until his death in 1938, though after I left the *American Mercury* I had little business with him. He suffered a good deal of ill health, but whether his impossible diet was the cause or the effect thereof I do not know. The advent of Hitler in 1933 naturally upset him, as it upset all Jews, but he kept his head better than most. When, in 1933, Ludwig Lewisohn, hitherto a militant agnostic, returned to orthodox Judaism and began to pray for Israel and howl for the Zionists, Goldberg flayed him in a letter to the *Nation*.

In April, 1935, poor Isaac had a coronary attack and was put to bed. By July he was sufficiently recovered to be planning a history of the *American Mercury* under my editorship, but I discouraged it, for the time for it was obviously not yet. He then turned to a biography of Mordecai Manuel Noah, a Jew very active as journalist and politician in the early years of the Nineteenth Century, and this was published in 1937. One more book followed, *The Wonder of Words* (1939), but it was still in galley-proof at the time of his death. He died on July 14, 1938.

Goldberg's devotion to his wife I well knew. They were an extremely happy, if somewhat subdued and gloomy couple. I saw her several times after his death, and was in correspondence with her. She died in Brookline, Massachusetts, in September, 1943, of the same coronary diseases that took off her husband. They had no children. Goldberg was a learned, diligent and honest man, and he did a great deal of useful work, but he never developed a body of ideas that attracted attention and as a result he is now pretty well forgotten.

(*This is as far as H. L. Mencken had completed in* My Life As Author and Editor, *just before his illness in November, 1948.*)

1. *H. L. Mencken* (New York: McBride, 1925).

APPENDIX I

A NOTE TO AUTHORS

THE AIM OF THE *Smart Set*, in general, is to interest and amuse the more civilized and sophisticated sort of reader—the man or woman who has lived in large cities, and read good books, and seen good plays, and heard good music, and is tired of politicians, reformers and the newspapers. It is not what is known as a popular magazine; it hasn't a circulation of 1,000,000 a month, and it never will have. This fact frees it from any necessity to take a hand in the uplift, or to pretend that it is made sad by the sorrows of the world. It assumes that its typical reader, having a quarter in his pocket to spend for a magazine without either gaudy pictures in it or "inspirational" rubbish, is quite satisfied with both the world and himself, and that even if he isn't, there are times when he doesn't want to worry over schemes of improvement. It offers him, on a small scale, the kind of intelligent entertainment that such a play as Shaw's *Caesar and Cleopatra* offers him on a large scale, or Strauss's *Der Rosenkavalier* on a still larger scale.

That is, as we have said, it *tries* to do so. The fact that it often falls a good deal short is one to which we are already painfully privy. We do the best we can with the means at hand. If Joseph Conrad's *Youth* were yet unpublished, and if Conrad offered it to us tomorrow, we'd mortgage our salaries to buy it, and stop the presses to get it into the next number. For Anatole France's *The Revolt of the Angels* we'd do the same. Or for anything by Arthur Schnitzler as good as *Anatol*. Or for a play by Lord Dunsany comparable to *The Gods of the Mountain*. Or (supposing it new) for Millington Synge's *Riders from the Sea*. Or for one of John Masefield's sea songs. Or for a ballad by Otto Julius Bierbaum. Or for an essay by Walter Pater. Or for a single epigram by Oscar Wilde. . . . Failing such masterpieces, we take the next best that offers, and whether that next best be by so well-known a man as Dunsany or Dreiser, or by some clever youth just out of college, it is all one to us. We read personally every piece of printable manuscript that comes into this office, and we are unfeignedly delighted every time a newcomer sends in something that is good.

With this programme, it must be plain that we do *not* want the conventional sentimentality of the cheap magazines, the rubber-stamp stuff that presents old ideas, old situations, old points of view. For example, we don't want war stories; they were all written when Zola wrote *The Attack on the Mill*, and the best of them that are now getting into type are feeble and empty. Again, we don't want newspaper stories, or stories of the Canadian Northwest, or stories about prostitutes, or political stories, or stories of the occult, or stories of A.D. 2,000, or stories of the cow country, or stories about artists or authors: we believe that all of these have been overdone, and that civilized readers are tired of them. Yet again, we don't want plays in which, as the curtain rises, the heroine is explaining the plot into a telephone, or in which either burglars or married women come to the apartments of rich New York bachelors, or in which husbands come home unexpectedly to find their wives kissing their best friends; we believe that these, too, have been done to death. Yet again, we don't want anything "delightfully optimistic," whether in play form, in story form, or in any other form: we believe that the persons who enjoy such mush know where to get it, and that they do not look for it in the *Smart Set*.

True enough, some of the things in our *index expurgatorius* occasionally edge into the magazine, but that is only saying that we are weak mortals, and not as good editors as we ought to be. We take, as we say, the best that offers, and authors would help us a lot if they offered less commonplace and stupid stuff, and more novel, original and lively stuff. Anything that is thoroughly new is doubly welcome; we always try to give originality the right of way. Every other article in our code is subordinate to this one. If you have an idea that is genuinely new, the *Smart Set* is the place for it. But please don't try to fool us with old ones in false faces!

Some authors seem to have a notion that the *Smart Set* wants only society stories. Nothing could be more ridiculous. The magazine addresses itself, not merely to what are called (by the newspapers) society people, but to all persons who are well-fed, educated, worldly-wise, and of good taste. Naturally enough, these persons are more interested in their own class than they are in the struggles and aspirations of garment workers, pick-pockets, Pullman porters, pothouse politicians and missionaries to the heathen, and so the people of our stories are usually well-fed and worldly-wise, too, but we like to think that our readers put human interest and artistic value above mere milieu and point of view, and we'd print a new Mulvaney story, if we could get it, as gladly as we'd print a new Henry James story.

Our present chief need is for novelettes of from 15,000 to 25,000 words. A novelette, remember, is not a short novel but a long short story; its internal structure must be that of the short story; it must get under way, like a short story, in the very first paragraph. We desire a rapid dramatic action in our novelettes, and after that, dialogue with wit in it. We are very hospitable in this department; we have printed detective stories, domestic comedies, stories of international society, stories of the super-*vin-rouge* Bohemia; we have even printed a novelette with an undertaker for its hero. But spare us the Eternal Triangle! It begins to crinkle and lose its shape. It has done service in too many bad novelettes. . . .

As for short stories, we have indicated some of our likes and dislikes, and a glance at the magazine will tell the rest of the tale. We desire, above all things, good workmanship. We send back many stories that, with interesting ideas in them, are crudely written. We believe that our readers have a sense of style, that they see the difference between a short story by Lord Dunsany or Lilith Benda and an ordinary short story. . . . We use essays, too, and never have enough of them. But they must be essays that avoid the usual labored whimsicality and triteness of thought, and plough up some new ground. Here style is two-thirds of the battle. We'd make room any month for an essay that showed truly distinguished writing, no matter how much its doctrines outraged our private notions of the true, the good and the beautiful.

Poetry? We print twenty to thirty poems every month, and a good many of them get into the anthologies. But don't send us sentimental things of the Poet's Corner variety; we are tired of odes to the meadow thrush, and war-songs arguing that the death of a soldier is a grief to his mother, and clumsy attempts at *vers libre*, and lyrics of amour in which "heart" rhymes with "part" . . .

Our short prose pieces, no doubt, you know; a dozen other magazines are imitating them. We want novelty, cleverness, good writing: a little prose poem, a piece of wit, a felicitous turn of phrase—above all, what we have never had before. And so with epigrams. Please don't send us puns, or platitudes, or cribs from Oscar Wilde. We have never had half enough good epigrams.

In conclusion, there are two things for authors to remember. First, we employ no readers, and all manuscripts not downright impossible are read by one of the two of us. Secondly, we try to make every decision within a week, and every accepted manuscript is paid for immediately without any regard to the date of publication.

George Jean Nathan
H. L. Mencken

To Your Interest and for Our Convenience

1. Put your full name and address in the upper left-hand corner of the first page of your manuscript.
2. Enclose a fully stamped and self-addressed envelope.
3. See that your typist has ink on her ribbon. Faint manuscripts are very hard to read.
4. Don't write us unnecessary letters. Let your work speak for itself.
5. Send your manuscript by mail; *don't bring it!*
6. If you send in a novelette, attach a brief summary of the plot, say in 250 words.
7. Don't ask for letters of criticism. We are too busy to write them.
8. Don't try to sell us anything until you have read two or three issues of the magazine from cover to cover, and so know something of our requirements.

A PERSONAL WORD BY
H. L. MENCKEN

GEORGE JEAN NATHAN and I took over the editorial direction of the *Smart Set* in the summer of 1914, just after the outbreak of the late war. I had been doing my monthly book article since November, 1908, and Nathan had been doing his article about the theatres since a month or two later. It never occurred to me, in those years, that I should ever assume a larger share of editorial responsibility for the magazine. John Adams Thayer, then the publisher and majority stockholder, had offered me the editorship several times, but I had always refused it for a single and simple reason: I didn't want to live in New York, which seemed to me then and seems to me now a most uncomfortable city. My home was and is in Baltimore, which I like much better.

But in the summer of 1914, that impediment was suddenly removed. Thayer disposed of the magazine to Eltinge F. Warner, publisher of *Warner Publications*, and his associates. Some time before this, by one of the trivial accidents of life, Warner had met Nathan on a ship bound home from England; the two happened to be wearing overcoats of the same kind, and stopped to gabble idly, as fellow passengers will, on deck one morning. They had a few drinks together, parted at the dock, and never thought to meet again. But when Warner looked into the magazine that he was to manage, he found the name of Nathan on the list of regular contributors, and, recalling their brief meeting, sought him out and asked him to take the editorship. Nathan said that he would do it if I agreed to help him. There ensued negotiations, and the upshot was an arrangement that is still in force.

Our authority as editors is exactly equal; nevertheless, we are never in conflict. I read all the manuscripts that are sent to us, and send

Nathan those I think are fit to print. If he agrees, they go into type at once; if he dissents, they are rejected forthwith. This veto is absolute, and works both ways. It saves us a great many useless and possibly acrimonious discussions. It takes two yeses to get a poem or essay or story into the magazine, but one no is sufficient to keep it out. In practice, we do not disagree sharply more than once in a hundred times, and even then, as I say, the debate is over as soon as it begins. I doubt that this scheme has ever lost us a manuscript genuinely worth printing. It admits prejudices into the matter, but they are at least the prejudices of the responsible editors, and not those of subordinate manuscript readers. We employ no readers, and take no advice. Every piece of manuscript that comes into the office passes through my hands, or those of Nathan, and usually through the hands of both of us. I live in Baltimore, but come to New York every other week.

So much for editorial management. Our financial organization is equally simple. Warner made over some of the capital stock of the magazine to Nathan and me, and we three continue in joint control today. Warner's problem, when we took charge, was to pay off the somewhat heavy floating debt of the property, and put it on a sound basis. This he accomplished before the end of 1915. From the moment he came into the office the *Smart Set* has paid all authors immediately on the acceptance of their manuscripts, paid all printers' and paper bills promptly—and absorbed not a cent of new capital. Warner operates all of his enterprises in that manner. We trust his judgment in all business matters, as he trusts ours in editorial matters. The usual conflict between the editorial room and the business office is never heard of here.

II

AN IMPRESSION seems to be abroad that the *Smart Set*, selling at 35 cents, makes an enormous profit, and that Warner, Nathan and I have got rich running it. This is not true. Warner is a man of many enterprises and has made a great deal of money, and Nathan and I are both able to exist comfortably without looking to the magazine. Had we been inclined, we might have turned it into a very productive money-maker. This is not merely tall-talk; we actually did the thing with three other magazines.

But from the start we viewed the *Smart Set* as, in some sense, a luxury rather than a means of profit, and this view of it has always conditioned our management of it. We have never made any effort to attract readers in large numbers; we have always sought to print, not the most popular stuff we could find, but the best stuff. And we have never made any effort to load the magazine with advertising: it prints less than any other magazine of its class.

This desire to be free—to run the thing to suit ourselves without regard to either popular taste or the prejudices of advertisers—has cost us much revenue, and the fact has not only deprived us of good profits, but also made it impossible for us to compete with the more popular magazines in bidding for manuscripts. But we have never regretted our policy. The authors who expect and demand enormous prices for their wares—the Carusos and Babe Ruths of letters—are but seldom the sort of authors we are interested in. It has been our endeavor, not to startle the booboisie with such gaudy stars, but to maintain a hospitable welcome for the talented newcomer—to give him his first chance in good company, and to pay him, if not the wages of a moving picture actor, then at least enough to reward him decently for his labor.

We believe that this scheme has cost us very few manuscripts worth printing. We have not only brought out by it more novices of first-rate ability than any other American magazine; we have also had the pleasure of printing some of the best work of contemporary American authors of assured position, including Dreiser, Cabell, Sherwood Anderson and Miss Cather. Such authors, we believe, regard the atmosphere of the *Smart Set* as different from that of the commercial magazines.

But our purpose, of course, has not been altruistic. We are surely not uplifters, either as critics or as editors. We have run our magazine as we have written our books—primarily to please ourselves, and secondarily to entertain those Americans who happen, in general, to be of our minds. We differ radically in many ways. For example, Nathan is greatly amused by the theatre, even when it is bad, whereas I regard it as a bore, even when it is good. Contrariwise, I am much interested in politics, whereas Nathan scarcely knows who is vice-president of the United States.

But on certain fundamentals we are thoroughly agreed, and it is on the plane of these fundamentals that we conduct the *Smart Set*, and try to interest a small minority of Americans. Both of us are against the sentimental, the obvious, the trite, the maudlin. Both of us are opposed to all such ideas as come from the mob, and are polluted by its stupidity: Puritanism, Prohibition, comstockery, evangelical Christianity, tin-pot patriotism, the whole sham of democracy. Both of us, though against socialism and in favor of capitalism, believe that capitalism in the United States is ignorant, disreputable and degraded, and that its heroes are bounders. Both of us believe in the dignity of the fine arts, and regard Beethoven and Brahms as far greater men than Wilson and Harding. Both of us stand aloof from the childish nationalism that now afflicts the world, and regard all of its chief spokesmen, in all countries, as scoundrels.

We believe that there are enough other Americans of our general trend of mind to give a reasonable support to a magazine voicing such notions. We believe that such men and women have the tolerance that is never encountered in the nether majority—that they like a certain amount of free experimentation in the arts. We thus try to assemble for them the novelties that seem to us to be genuinely worth while—not the tawdry monkey-shines of Greenwich Village, but the new work of the writers who actually know how to write. Thus we printed the plays of Eugene O'Neill when he was still an unknown newcomer, and the strange, sardonic short stories of Ben Hecht before ever he started to write *Erik Dorn,* and the sketches of Lord Dunsany before his vogue began.

As I say, we do not pursue neologism for its own sake: the *Smart Set* avoided all the extravagances of the free verse movement, as it is now avoiding the extravagances of such foreign crazes as Expressionismus and Dadaism. We try to entertain the reader who can distinguish between genuine ideas and mere blather. It is for this reason, perhaps, that our poetry, to some readers—and especially to many of the new poets—seems excessively conservative. But here conservatism, we believe, has served a good purpose, for we have certainly printed as much sound poetry, during the past seven or eight years, as any of the magazines devoted to *vers libre,* and a great deal more than most. Practically all the genuine poets of the country have been in the magazine during that time, and most of them have been in it very often.

III

NEEDLESS TO SAY, what we print does not always correspond exactly with what we'd like to print. We buy the best stuff that we can find, and that is within our means—and sometimes the supply of such stuff is distressingly short. There have been months when we felt that only a small portion of the contents of the magazine was really fit to set before the readers we have in mind—when the larger part of those contents, read in manuscript and proof, filled us with depression. In particular, we have often found it difficult to obtain suitable novelettes. The ordinary novelettes of commerce are fearful things, indeed; once or twice, failing to discover anything better, we have had to print one. Invariably there came protests from many readers—a thing that pleased us, despite our distress, for it showed clearly that we were reaching a public that was not content with the average magazine fare. But in the face of this chronic scarcity we have printed many novelettes of quite extraordinary merit, including W. Somerset Maugham's "Miss Thompson," Miss Willa Cather's "Coming, Eden Bower!", Thyra Samter Winslow's "Cycle of Manhattan," and several capital pieces by other writers.

Essays have also given us much concern. Practically all of the essayists who flourish in the United States devote themselves to whimsical fluff in imitation of Charles Lamb—stuff that is poor in ideas and conventional in execution. We have tried hard to find and encourage writers with more to say, but so far without much success. However, even in this bleak field we have unearthed an occasional piece of sound quality—for example Stephen Ta Van's "Tante Manhattan" and Thomas Beer's "The Rural Soul" and "The Mauve Decade"—and we have hopes of doing much better hereafter.

In the field of the short story we believe that we have presented a great deal of genuinely first-rate work. The stories we print are not reprinted in the annual anthologies issued by admirers of the late O. Henry, but in a good many cases the authors of them—for example, Mr. Hecht, Sherwood Anderson and F. Scott Fitzgerald—have later shown their quality by brilliant successes in the larger form of the novel.

Our own contributions to the magazine I need not discuss: opinion about them seems to be very divided. But I have reason to believe that they are read rather widely, both when they are serious and when they are not serious, and I know that, when reprinted in books, they have sold far better than such books usually sell, and got a great deal more notice, both at home and abroad. Of my own books since 1914, all those save *The American Language* have consisted in large part of matter reworked from articles first printed in the *Smart Set*. So with all of Nathan's books.

I have mentioned the difficulty of filling the magazine each month with stuff that is wholly up to the mark we try to set; we print what we can get, but we can't print it until it is written. Various other handicaps have beset us, and still beset us. One lies in the fact that we are determined to make the magazine pay its own way—that we are convinced that a subsidized magazine, conducted at a loss, is unsound in principle, and very apt to be led astray by all the current aesthetic crazes, to the dismay of the sort of readers we try to reach.

This policy, during the days of the war-time and post-bellum paper famine, reduced us to printing on a paper that was frankly atrocious. It was too thick and rough, it would not take the ink cleanly, and its stiffness made the magazine hard to open. Hundreds of readers denounced us for using it, and with justice. We abandoned it as soon as possible, and have since improved the quality of our paper steadily, as the market price has fallen. I am also inclined to think that for a while we neglected our covers, and that many readers found them out of harmony with the general contents of the magazine. If so, the matter has been remedied, and will be further remedied hereafter.

But the worst of all our handicaps lies in the name of the magazine. A great many persons, unfamiliar with its contents, assume that it is a society paper, or that it is chiefly devoted to tales of high life. Unluckily, changing the name is not a simple matter. We inherited a bond issue with the property, and by the terms of the mortgage no change may be made without the consent of the bondholders—and inasmuch as they are scattered and view all such radical innovations with distrust, that consent is not easy to obtain.

The matter is further complicated by the fact that there is an English Smart Set Company, reprinting most of the contents of the magazine under the same name in England. Our contract with that company is of such character that a change in the name of the magazine would cause serious difficulties, and perhaps subject us to great loss. So we have to continue the *Smart Set* on the flagstaff, though both Nathan and I believe that the name loses us many readers who might otherwise buy the magazine. At some time or other in the future we may solve the problem.

Finally, there is the fact that, in the days before we acquired editorial control, the *Smart Set* passed through the hands of many editors, some of them sharply at odds with the others on questions of general policy, and that the resultant aberrations alienated a good many readers. There was a time when the magazine ran to "daring" stuff, often of a highly sexual and sophomoric character. That was before our day, and the experiment was soon abandoned, but there are many old readers, scared off then, who still believe that the magazine is full of *risqué* stories. This, of course, is not true. We do not aim to astonish sucklings; the readers we address are assumed to be of adult growth, and hence capable of bearing occasional plain-speaking without damage. But neither do we devote ourselves to providing diversion for the dirty old men of the vice societies.

One more misunderstanding remains. The *Smart Set* is often spoken of as a fiction magazine, and there are persons who seem to think that it prints nothing else. This was true years ago, but it is certainly not true now. In our average number fully half of the contents is not fiction. Very soon we hope to make that proportion even larger.

IV

Now for the lesson of the day. Most of our circulation, at the moment, is what is called news-stand circulation. That is to say, it tends to be irregular. A reader buys the magazine for three or four months running at some news-stand he passes now and then, and perhaps likes it enough to look forward to each new ·number. But soon or later he finds that his dealer has sold out—or he looks for it at some stand that doesn't keep it. Then, for a few months, he drops out. Meanwhile, the dealer of whom he has inquired for it has ordered some extra copies, or begun to stock it.

The result is easily seen. There are 60,000 news-stands in the United States. Some of them, of course, carry only the cheap magazines, but perhaps 20,000 of them have a sufficiently civilized clientele to stock such publications as the *Smart Set*. To cover all of them on this hit-or-miss plan subjects us to inevitable losses—for we must take back copies that are unsold. In consequence, our printing and paper costs are a good deal larger than they ought to be, and we have that much less to spend upon the contents of the magazine.

The conversion of a substantial part of our news-stand circulation into subscriptions would lead us into easier waters, and enable us to improve the magazine. Not only would our readers get a better magazine, but they would get it regularly and surely, with no need to look for it at the corner stand, and no chance of not finding it. Finally, they would save something every year—not much, but something. I thus make the suggestion that you who read this send in your subscription on the blank herewith. I assume that you already know the magazine—that you have read at least a few numbers, and found them not altogether stupid. If you like my own writings you will find them regularly in the *Smart Set*—and seldom anywhere else.

So far as I know, there is no other American magazine that is trying to do precisely what we are trying to do. We offer every year, at a total cost of $4, 1,728 pages of the best stuff we can write or find. This is the cost of two ordinary novels. We believe that you will go far before you find two novels that are more amusing.

H. L. Mencken

APPENDIX III

SUGGESTIONS TO OUR VISITORS

1. The editorial chambers are open daily, except Saturdays, Sundays and Bank Holidays, from 10.30 a.m. to 11.15 a.m.

2. Carriage calls at 11.15 a.m. precisely.

3. The Editors sincerely trust that guests will abstain from offering fees or gratuities to their servants.

4. Visitors expecting telephone calls while in audience will kindly notify the Portier before passing into the consulting rooms.

5. Dogs accompanying visitors must be left at the *garde-robe* in charge of the Portier.

6. Visitors are kindly requested to refrain from expectorating out of the windows.

7. The Editors regret that it will be impossible for them, under any circumstances, to engage in conversations by telephone.

8. The Editors assume no responsibility for hats, overcoats, walking sticks or hand luggage not checked with the Portier.

9. Solicitors for illicit wine merchants are received only on Thursdays, from 12 o'clock until 4.30 p.m.

10. Interpreters speaking all modern European languages are in daily attendance, and at the disposal of visitors, without fee.

11. Officers of the military and naval forces of the United States, in full uniform, will be received without presenting the usual letters of introduction.

12. The House Surgeon is forbidden to accept fees for the treatment of injuries received on the premises.

13. Smoking is permitted.

14. Visitors whose boots are not equipped with rubber heels are requested to avoid stepping from the rugs to the parquetry.

15. A woman Secretary is in attendance at all interviews between the Editors, or either of them, and lady authors. Hence it will be

unnecessary for such visitors to provide themselves with either duennas or police whistles.

16. Choose your emergency exit when you come in; don't wait until the firemen arrive.

17. Visiting English authors are always welcome, but in view of the severe demands upon the time of the Editors, they are compelled to limit the number received to 50 head a week.

18. The objects of art on display in the editorial galleries are not for sale.

19. The Editors regret that they will be unable to receive visitors who present themselves in a visibly inebriated condition.

20. Cuspidors are provided for the convenience of our Southern and Western friends.

21. The Editors beg to make it known that they find it impossible to accept invitations to public dinners, memorial services or other functions at which speeches are made, or at which persons are present who ever make speeches elsewhere.

22. The Editors assume that visitors who have had the honor of interviewing with them in the editorial chambers will not subsequently embarrass them in public places by pointing them out with walking sticks.

23. Photographs of the Editors are on sale at the Portier's desk.

24. Members of the hierarchy and other rev. clergy are received only on Thursdays, from 12 o'clock noon to 4.30 p.m.

25. The Editors cannot undertake to acknowledge the receipt of flowers, cigars, autographed books, picture postcards, signed photographs, loving cups or other gratuities. All such objects are sent at once to the free wards of the public hospitals.

26. Positively no cheques cashed.

INDEX

C

INDEX

INDEX

PERMISSIONS ACKNOWLEDGMENTS

Grateful acknowledgment is made to the following for permission to print previously unpublished material:

The Lord Alfred Douglas Literary Estate: Excerpt of letter from Lord Alfred Douglas to H. L. Mencken. Reprinted by permission of The Lord Alfred Douglas Literary Estate.

George Jean Nathan Literary Estate and Julie Haydon: Excerpt from telegram from George Jean Nathan to H. L. Mencken. Reprinted by permission of Julie Haydon (Mrs. George Jean Nathan) and Patricia Angelin, Literary Executrix of the George Jean Nathan Literary Estate.

Harold Ober Associates Inc.: Excerpts from letters of F. Scott Fitzgerald to H. L. Mencken. Reprinted by permission of Harold Ober Associates Inc. as agents for the Estate of F. Scott Fitzgerald.

Saturday Evening Post: Excerpt from Sept. 12, 1916, letter from Churchill Williams to H. L. Mencken. Copyright 1916 by *The Saturday Evening Post*. Reprinted by permission.

The Society of Authors: Excerpt from March 23, 1915, letter from James Joyce to H. L. Mencken. Reprinted by permission of The Society of Authors, London, as the Literary Representative of the Estate of James Joyce.

Van Pelt Library, University of Pennsylvania: Excerpts of letters from Theodore Dreiser to H. L. Mencken. Copyright of unpublished writings of Theodore Dreiser held by the Trustees of the University of Pennsylvania. Reprinted by permission of Van Pelt Library, University of Pennsylvania, Special Collections.

ABOUT THE AUTHOR

Henry Louis Mencken was born in Baltimore, Maryland, in 1880 and died there in 1956. A son of August and Anna (Abhau) Mencken, he was educated privately and at Baltimore Polytechnic. In 1930 he married Sara Powell Haardt, who died in 1935.

Mencken began his long career as journalist, critic, and philologist as a reporter for the Baltimore *Morning Herald* in 1899. In 1906 he joined the staff of the Baltimore *Sun*, thus initiating an association with the *Sunpapers* that would last until a few years before his death. He was coeditor of the *Smart Set* with George Jean Nathan from 1914 to 1923, and with Nathan he founded the *American Mercury*, of which he was sole editor from 1925 to 1933.

Jonathan Yardley is a book critic and columnist for the Washington *Post*. Previously, he worked as book editor for the Washington *Star*, the Miami *Herald*, and the Greensboro *Daily News*. He won the Pulitzer Prize for criticism in 1981. He is the author of *Ring: A Biography of Ring Lardner*; *Our Kind of People: The Story of an American Family*; and *Out of Step: Notes from a Purple Decade*. He has recently completed a new book about the Middle Atlantic States.